D0927497

EASTERN AFRICAN STUDIES

ing Prophets
d by DAVID M. ANDERSON
)UGLAS H. JOHNSON

African Expressions
ristianity
d by THOMAS SPEAR
ARIA N. KIMAMBO

Poor Are Not Us
d by DAVID M. ANDERSON
GDIS BROCH-DUE

Brews
IN WILLIS

li Origins
S DE VERE ALLEN

Maasai
d by THOMAS SPEAR
CHARD WALLER

Kali Kenya
NETH KING

l & Crisis in Colonial Kenya
CE BERMAN

ppy Valley
One: State & Class
Two: Violence
hnicity
CE BERMAN
HN LONSDALE

Mau from Below
ET KERSHAW

Mau Mau War
rspective
IK FUREDI

ters & the Roots
au Mau 1905–63
THA KANOGO

omic & Social Origins
au Mau 1945–53
ID W. THROUP

-Party Politics in Kenya
ID W. THROUP
HARLES HORNSBY

re State-Building
NNA LEWIS

onization & Independence
nya 1940–93
ed by B.A. OGOT
ILLIAM R. OCHIENG'

ing the Commons
ID ANDERSON

ration & Protest in Tanzania
IA N. KIMAMBO

dians of the Land
ed by GREGORY MADDOX, JAMES
BLIN & ISARIA N. KIMAMBO

Education in the Development
of Tanzania 1919–1990
LENE BUCHERT

The Second Economy in Tanzania
T.L. MALIYAMKONO
& M.S.D. BAGACHWA

Ecology Control & Economic Development
in East African History
HELGE KJEKSHUS

Siaya
DAVID WILLIAM COHEN
& E.S. ATIENO ODHIAMBO

Uganda Now • Changing Uganda
Developing Uganda • From Chaos to Order
Religion & Politics in East Africa
Edited by HOLGER BERNT HANSEN
& MICHAEL TWADDLE

Kakungulu & the Creation
of Uganda 1868–1928
MICHAEL TWADDLE

Controlling Anger
SUZETTE HEALD

Kampala Women Getting By
SANDRA WALLMAN

Political Power in Pre-Colonial Buganda
RICHARD J. REID

Alice Lakwena & the Holy Spirits
HEIKE BEHREND

Slaves, Spices & Ivory in Zanzibar
ABDUL SHERIFF

Zanzibar Under Colonial Rule
Edited by ABDUL SHERIFF &
ED FERGUSON

The History & Conservation of Zanzibar
Stone Town
Edited by ABDUL SHERIFF

Pastimes & Politics
LAURA FAIR

Ethnicity & Conflict in
the Horn of Africa
Edited by KATSUYOSHI FUKUI
& JOHN MARKAKIS

Conflict, Age & Power in
North East Africa
Edited by EISEI KURIMOTO
& SIMON SIMONSE

Property Rights & Political
Development in Ethiopia & Eritrea
SANDRA FULLERTON JOIREMAN

Revolution & Religion in Ethiopia
ØYVIND M. EIDE

Brothers at War
TEKESTE NEGASH &
KJETIL TRONVOLL

From Guerrillas to Government
DAVID POOL

Mau Mau & Nationhood
Edited by E.S. ATIENO ODHIAMBO
& JOHN LONSDALE

A History of Modern Ethiopia,
1855–1991
(2nd edn) BAHRU ZEWDE

Pioneers of Change in Ethiopia
BAHRU ZEWDE

Remapping Ethiopia
Edited by W. JAMES, D. DONHAM,
E. KURIMOTO & A. TRIULZI

Southern Marches of Imperial Ethiopia
Edited by DONALD L. DONHAM
& WENDY JAMES

A Modern History of the Somali
(4th edn)
I.M. LEWIS

Islands of Intensive Agriculture in
East Africa
Edited by MATS WIDGREN
& JOHN E.G. SUTTON

Leaf of Allah
EZEKIEL GEBISSA

Dhows & the Colonial Economy
of Zanzibar 1860–1970
ERIK GILBERT

African Womanhood in Colonial Kenya
TABITHA KANOGO

African Underclass
ANDREW BURTON

In Search of a Nation
Edited by GREGORY H. MADDOX
& JAMES L. GIBLIN

A History of the Excluded
JAMES L. GIBLIN

Black Poachers, White Hunters
EDWARD I. STEINHART

Ethnic Federalism
DAVID TURTON

Crisis & Decline in Bunyoro
SHANE DOYLE

Emancipation without Abolition in
German East Africa
JAN-GEORG DEUTSCH

Women, Work & Domestic
Virtue in Uganda 1900–2003*
GRACE BANTEBYA KYOMUHENDO &
MARJORIE KENISTON McINTOSH

Cultivating Success in Uganda*
GRACE CARSWELL
* forthcoming

Mafia-Insel Bueni/ Mafia Island, Bueni (n.d.)
The majority of people in this picture were probably slaves.

Note: A copy of this photo was kindly made available to me
by the late Reinhold Siebentritt, Gunzenhausen/ Germany.
The photographer is unknown.

Emancipation without Abolition in German East Africa
c. 1884–1914

JAN-GEORG DEUTSCH
Lecturer in Commonwealth History
University of Oxford

James Currey
OXFORD

Mkuki na Nyota
DAR ES SALAAM

Ohio University Press
ATHENS

James Currey Ltd
73 Botley Road
Oxford
OX2 0BS

Mkuki na Nyota
PO Box 4246
Dar es Salaam

Ohio University Press
19 Circle Drive, The Ridges
Athens, Ohio 45701, USA

1 2 3 4 5 10 09 08 07 06

British Library Cataloguing in Publication Data
Deutsch, Jan-Georg
    Emancipation without abolition in German East Africa, c.
    1884-1914. - (Estern African studies)
    1. Slavery - Africa, East - History - 19th century 2. Slavery
    - Government policy - Germany - History - 19th century
    3. Slaves - Emancipation - Africa, East - History - 19th
    century 4. Germany - Colonies - Africa
    I. Title
    306.3'62'09676'09034

    ISBN 10: 0-85255-986-0 (James Currey Cloth)
    ISBN 13: 978-085255-986-4 (James Currey Cloth)
    ISBN 10: 0-85255-985-2 (James Currey Paper)
    ISBN 13: 979-085255-985-7 (James Currey Paper)

Library of Congress Cataloging-in-Publication Data
Deutsch, Jan-Georg
    Emancipation without abolition in German East Africa, c.1844-1914/Jan-George Deutsch.
    p. cm. -- (Eastern African studies)
    Includes bibliographical references and index.
    ISBN 0-8214-1719-3 (alk. paper) -- ISBN 0-8214-1720-7 (alk. paper)
    1. Slavery--German East Africa. 2. Germany--Colonies--Africa--History. I. Title. II.
    Series.
    HT1401.D48 2006
    306.3'6209676--dc22   2006045320

    ISBN 10: 0-8214-1719-3 (Ohio University Press Cloth)
    ISBN 13: 978-08214-1719-5 (Ohio University Press Cloth)
    ISBN 10: 0-8214-1720-7 (Ohio University Press Paper)
    ISBN 13: 978-08214-1720-1 (Ohio University Press Paper)

66463776

Typeset in 9/10½ pt Baskerville
by Long House Publishing Services, Cumbria, UK
Printed and bound in Britain by Woolnough, Irthlingborough

Contents

Contents

List of Maps & Tables

A Note on Currencies

According to Sheriff (1987: xix) 1 Maria Theresa Dollar (MT$) was valued between 2.10 to 2.23 Indian Rupee (Rs) in the first half of the nineteenth century. In the early 1890s MT$1 was exchanged for Rs2.12 or Reichsmark (RM)2.92 (Stuhlmann 1894: 63). As £1 Sterling roughly equalled MT$4.75, the currency conversion rate between the Indian Rupee and Sterling was thus about Rs10 to £1. When in 1920 the renamed East African Rupee was withdrawn from circulation by the British authorities, it was replaced by the East African Shilling (Shs) at the rate of Rs10 to Shs20 (or £1). Roughly calculated, Rs1 in 1900 would be worth about £6 in today's money (http://www.eh.net). Note that currency rates fluctuated widely in the latter half of the nineteenth century.

Acknowledgements

This study would not have seen the light of the day without the support I received from Professor T. O. Ranger from the University of Oxford, Professor W. J. Mommsen of the University of Düsseldorf and Professor A. Wirz from Humboldt University, Berlin. I did most of the research and writing while employed by the Centre of Modern Oriental Studies in Berlin and I am grateful to its directors for being patient with the slow progress of my work, particularly Professor P. Heine, Professor U. Haarmann and Professor I. Baldauf. While doing research in Tanzania, I was advised by Professor A. Sheriff, who taught me more about writing African history than he is probably prepared to accept. I am also keenly aware of the intellectual debts I owe to the works of H. Bley, F. Cooper, J. Glassman, S. Feierman, L. Harding, J. Iliffe, M. Klein, J. Lonsdale, F. Morton, S. Miers and M. Wright. I had numerous discussions with several friends and colleagues about slavery in East Africa. They are too many to list them all, but I would like to thank R. Ahuja, B. Barth, W. Bissel, K. Bromber, C. Cornelißen, L. Fair, U. van der Heyden, A. Harneit-Sievers, J. Glassman, T. Nisula, A. von Oppen, P. Pels, S. Rockel, J. Willis, K. Zirkel and T. Zitelmann for their good advice. Parts of the manuscript have been read by R. Abrahams, L. Harding, J. Iliffe, F. Morton, H. Sippel, J. Willis and an anonymous reader. I cannot claim that I have always followed their guidance, which I probably should have done, but I am extremely grateful to them nevertheless. All remaining mistakes in this study are of course entirely my own responsibility. In the preparation of the manuscript I was greatly helped by S. Greve, V. Ovaert, D. Pohl and L. Taylor. The research for this study was generously funded by the Deutsche Forschungsgemeinschaft which I would like to acknowledge with gratitude. The greatest thanks, however, I owe to H. Schmidt.

One

Introduction
A 'Silent Revolution'
in German East Africa?

When the League of Nations asked the British government in 1923 whether slavery existed in Tanganyika Territory, the answer was an emphatic 'No'.[1] It was argued that the Involuntary Service Ordinance of 1922 had legally abolished the institution of slavery and that in any case what remained of the erstwhile relationship between slave owners and slaves could now hardly be called slavery. Yet, only some 25 years earlier, the German colonial authorities had estimated that over 400,000 slaves were resident in German East Africa.[2] In the two decades before the First World War a 'social revolution'[3] had taken place under German colonial rule, which irrevocably changed not only the lives of owners and slaves, but also the social, political and economic structures of societies in which slavery had previously flourished. However, if it was a 'revolution', then it was evidently a quiet one. One of the central aims of the present study is to reconstruct this 'silent revolution', its nature and extent and, above all, its social and economic dynamics.

Many, if not most societies in Africa have been affected in one way or another by slavery and the slave trade. On the eve of the colonial conquest it was the most widespread form of labour recruitment, generating the surplus on which many pre-colonial empires and their rulers, religious leaders and merchants had thrived, albeit at terrible cost to human life. Thus, the study of slavery and emancipation in Africa has attracted considerable scholarly interest, not least from African historians based in the United States where, especially after the Second World War in the context of the Civil Rights Movement, the question of slavery and its aftermath had always generated particular interest.[4] A number of studies that have appeared in recent years recount the end of slavery in great detail; for instance Martin Klein's and Richard Robert's work on French West Africa, Paul Lovejoy's and Jan Hogendorn's study of Northern Nigeria or the groundbreaking volume edited by Suzanne Miers and Richard Roberts. As far as East Africa is concerned there are a number of excellent studies on various aspects of slavery and its transformation in the nineteenth and twentieth centuries, notably by Ned Alpers, Frederick

Cooper, Fred Morton, Marcia Wright, Richard Allen, Jonathan Glassman, Ahmad Sikainga and Allen and Barbara Isaacman.[5] The 1999 special issue of *Slavery and Abolition* that was entirely devoted to the relationship between 'Slavery and Colonial Rule in Africa', the second edition of Paul Lovejoy's survey *Transformations in Slavery* and the recent volumes edited by Temperley, Campbell and Alpers as well as Suzanne Miers's book on international efforts to suppress slavery and the slave trade in the twentieth century could be added to this list.[6] The broad outline of the history of the end of slavery in Africa is thus well known.[7] This begs the question of whether there is really any need for yet another study on this topic.

The end of slavery in German East Africa presents a special case. First of all, all the studies concerning slavery in East Africa and its end in the colonial period almost exclusively focus on the towns on the northern Kenyan coast and the adjacent islands. Places like Malindi, Mombasa and Zanzibar have received considerable scholarly attention but slavery in the southern coastal region, in the coastal hinterland or in the vast interior of East Africa is often only mentioned in passing.[8] This study attempts to address this imbalance.[9]

Second, few writers on the subject seem aware that, in contrast to the policy pursued by other colonial powers in Africa, the German authorities did not legally abolish slavery in their colonial territories.[10] Thus, in East Africa slavery was abolished in 1897 in Zanzibar, in 1900 in Uganda, in 1907 in coastal Kenya and in 1910 in Mozambique, for instance, but only in 1922 in Tanganyika – *after* the former German East Africa had become a Mandate of the League of Nations under British administration.[11] Colonial officials elsewhere in Africa were probably as reluctant as the German administrators to actively emancipate slaves. In many African colonies, local administrative officers ignored the practices they were supposed to suppress, circumvented them, or neglected to inform slaves of their legal rights.[12] In Northern Nigeria and the Anglo-Egyptian Sudan, for instance, the British colonial authorities did everything in their power to delay the effective end of slavery, especially for women, while in the Belgian Congo Free State the terms and conditions of legal emancipation in 1910 seemed more like a continuation of slavery by other means.[13] The basic reason for this policy was that early colonial authorities – not only in Northern Nigeria, the Sudan and the Congo, but all over Africa – were far too weak to enforce abolition in areas in which a high percentage of the population were slaves. They relied on the cooperation of slave-holding elites to mobilise labour for export production and the development of the infrastructure of the colonial state. But, on the whole, they did not officially recognise slavery to be a lawfully existing institution within their respective spheres of power.[14] In practical terms, this meant that German colonial officials in East Africa handled the purchase and sale of thousands, if not tens of thousands of slaves.[15] In the early 1900s the debate in British, French and Portuguese colonial circles largely centred on the best method to effect the end of slavery, but the necessity for legal abolition was largely undisputed.[16] The German government apparently chose a different approach, which is somewhat surprising given that the German authorities – like other colonial powers – had initially invoked the abolition of slavery and the slave trade as a moral justification for colonial conquest and expansion in Africa. This study tries to illuminate the reasons for this peculiar policy.[17]

Third, it appears that despite the remarkable protection and support slave owners enjoyed from the German colonial state, slavery itself declined sharply in the years following the establishment of colonial rule in 1890, a fact that cannot be explained by the suppression of the regional slave trade alone. This suggests that in German East Africa the end of slavery was a social process driven by forces other than colonial intervention and legislation. In fact, self-emancipation seems to have preceded legal abolition to a considerable degree. Thus, beyond adding another case study to the already very impressive existent body of secondary literature on the abolition of slavery in Africa and its aftermath, this study seeks to emphasise the pre-abolition, 'home-grown', locally made character of the process.[18] If it succeeds in convincing the reader that the end of slavery, at least in German East Africa, depended only to a minor extent on government policy and the activities of 'enlightened' colonial officials, and to a far greater extent on the persistent attempts of slaves to gain more meaningful control over their lives and day-to-day affairs, then a small contribution to one of the central themes in African history will have been achieved.

The sources for this study include, first, the various administrative reports that local district officers were required to produce for the German colonial authorities in Berlin. These sources have not been examined to any great extent before. Second, some use was made of British administrative records, especially district and provincial books, since they often refer to the German colonial period in the history section. Third, both British and German missionary records were employed to counterbalance the bias of the German and British administrative records. Mission records are of particular significance, since they contain biographies and life stories of ex-slaves that allow rare insights into aspects of their everyday life.[19]

This study is not the first full-length academic investigation into the subject of slavery in German East Africa. In 1915 a book entitled *Die Haussklaverei in Deutsch Ostafrika* was published by the Reichskolonialamt (German Colonial Office), in which Fritz Weidner, a former colonial administrator, presented an analysis of the problem from the administrative point of view.[20] He based his study on secondary material, mainly published reports by colonial Governors to the German Parliament, especially its colonial advisory committee, the Kolonialrat. Weidner had no access to internal government files, and certainly not to original district records. His study is now rather dated. While it does contain a certain amount of information on the administrative history of slavery in German East Africa, social and political aspects have been largely neglected. It was written explicitly as a defence of government policy and, within that framework, probably served its purpose well.[21] Weidner's book is par-ticularly relevant as a historical source, since it reflects the official attitude towards slavery in German East Africa at the time.[22]

The examination of slavery and abolition, not only in Africa, poses certain historiographical and methodological problems.[23] This applies in particular to the unit of study. Most historians would agree that slavery or slave status is defined by two essential criteria. First, it is a property relation-ship, the ownership of one person by another, which permits the latter to sell or exchange that person – actually or potentially – for personal gain.[24] Second, it is a labour regime, since the main, but not always the foremost, purpose of becoming the owner of slaves is to obtain cheap labour, which otherwise would not be available, at least not at that price. These defini-tions make it possible to distinguish slavery from other forms of dependent labour, such as pawnship or indentured labour. However, since they say little about the specific historical conditions that determined the lives of slaves, they are not sufficient to describe slavery as a social phenomenon.[25] Drawing from his work on Greek and Roman society, M. I. Finley has pointed out that slavery varies according to the social structure of the society in which it is embedded.[26] As these structures are highly variable, so, too, are the many social forms of slavery, denoting particular configurations of social and economic domination. Thus, 'to analyse a slave system … entails understanding the place of slavery in the economy *and* in society' [emphasis added].[27]

Furthermore, Finley argued that, as a social relationship between individuals, slavery was only partially determined by economic or judicial considerations. In all known slave societies, owners were unable to permanently reduce the personhood of a slave to mere commodity status, not least because if owners wanted to obtain the labour power of the slaves they had to recognise their humanity.[28] Although enslavement by force or by birth was an act of utter depersonalisation, it was rarely a permanent state. From the moment of purchase or capture, slaves strove persistently to improve their social condition and reduce their marginal position in society. As Frederick Cooper put it, 'the factors of production had wills of their own'.[29] Moreover, Miers and Roberts have argued that particularly in Africa the power of owners was limited by a lack of coercive means, such as a well-developed state with an effective police force to prevent slaves from running away. Thus, not least in order to prevent their flight, the owners themselves, whatever their background or personal persuasion, had an interest in forging social ties with their slaves. As a result, rather than being merely a system of outright exploitation and coercion, slavery in Africa was characterised – as elsewhere – by contestation, negotiation and accommodation.[30]

The conflicts between slaves and their owners centred essentially around the nature of the mutual rights and obligations among each other and within society, which often resulted in a subtle but always fragile 'equi-librium' between slaves and their owners. The alternative was flight.[31] The rights and obligations of slaves and their owners were highly variable even within a given society, and, among a host of other criteria, depended on the age and gender of the slave, his or her skills and upbringing, the profession of the owner, and the local political set-up. Finally, more recent literature has emphasised that the individual status of slaves often changed during their lifetime. Over time, many slaves, especially women, became acknowledged 'free' members of the owners' kinship group, although their rights were strictly limited.[32] Moreover, in many societies, the adult children of slaves, although born into slavery, often had rights and obligations similar to other members of the owners' household, including the owners' own offspring. Such lifecycle 'intergenerational mobility' was of particular importance in East Africa, especially for kinship groups in matrilineal societies who measured their strength and well-being primarily by the number of their members.[33] These processes have been called the 'slavery to kinship continuum' and describe the establishment of (fictive) kinship relationships as the most common way for slaves and their descendants to be gradually absorbed into kinship and community structures.[34] As has been observed in many African societies, kinless 'outsiders' who had been brought by force into their owner's society to occupy its very margins, forged social ties over time and acquired protective rights of various descriptions, sometimes even a measure of honour and respect. As they gradually became 'insiders', their social marginality was slowly reduced to a manageable proportion.[35] One of the differentiating marks between the various slave-owning societies was, therefore, the degree to which social boundaries between insiders and outsiders were open or closed to transgression, and these were, as Glassman has argued, largely determined by 'struggle and conflict'.[36] In fact, the borderline between the 'slaves' and the 'free' was often blurred; while in some societies absorptive integration into local societies was achieved in a comparatively short period of time, in others the marginality of slaves was rigidly maintained, in some historical instances even increased when people who had regarded themselves as 'free' realised that their owners saw them as personal property, which could be put to any use, even sold at their 'master's' will. Thus, far from being fixed and well defined, the closer the observer looks at the unit of study, the more its fluid, variable and locally made and contested nature becomes apparent. This has prompted one eminent scholar of East African nineteenth-century history to conclude almost in despair that 'the word slavery is *dangerous* (my emphasis) to use, because it means such different things at different times and places'.[37]

Based on the works by Frederick Cooper,[38] the more recent scholarship has thus regarded slavery in Africa not so much as a fixed institution within a social structure but rather as an embedded social process, the reality and meaning of which was constantly reworked over time in the local context of the changing of society at large.[39] In so far as significant cultural, political and economic aspects of society changed, so, too, did the institution of slavery and vice versa.[40] Following this line of argument, the term 'slavery' employed in this study does not merely denote a set of property rights enshrined in a specific social institution. 'Slavery' is seen rather as an everyday conflict between slave owners and slaves competing for wealth, honour and power in the historical setting of a particular locality.[41] The outcome of this conflict was uncertain[42] and depended largely on the economic and social resources available to the individual or collective contestants at a given moment in time in that particular locality. The distribution of such resources among slaves varied greatly, depending on their individual gender, age and descent status within a particular society.[43] From this perspective, the end of slavery is seen as a social and political process through which the precarious balance of power between owners and slaves changed fundamentally and irrevocably in favour of the latter.

There is, however, considerable historical debate about the direction of that change. Some authors have argued that slaves aimed at obtaining greater personal autonomy by primarily seeking to readjust existing social relationships, thereby becoming clients, retainers, or dependants of their former owners in the process. Others have argued that, whenever possible, slaves sought to sever ties with their owners through flight, in order to determine the course of their own lives more fully, escape punishment from their owners, enjoy the fruits of their labour and control their family relationships.[44] These different views sparked off the related debate as to whether the end of slavery should be regarded as a 'non-event', a 'quiet social revolution', or a 'dramatic moment'.[45] Beyond the question of terminology, this issue has probably attracted more attention than it really deserves. Apart from enslavement, emancipation in its various forms was probably one of the most significant events in the lives of most slaves. Yet, the same cannot be said with equal validity for the societies in which they lived, since this depended on the relative importance of slavery in each individual society. Moreover, both 'dramatic' and 'silent' conflicts occurred simultaneously even in the same locality, at least in German East Africa, as exemplified by sudden flight movements and the subtle readjustment of existing social relationships. Similarly, while the end of slavery reorganised the forms of 'production, social reproduction and dependence' dramatically in some areas, others remained unaffected.[46] Who then can say that this was a 'non-event' or, on the contrary, a 'revolution' when it was often both, depending on whose life perspective was at stake?

Defining the end of slavery as a locally made social process is a helpful way of overcoming the historical sterility of simplistic universal, legal or economic definitions. Yet, at the same time, this approach raises a series of new questions, particularly concerning the spatial boundaries of the social arena in which these processes are supposed to have taken place.[47] Clearly, the end of slavery in a particular locality was strongly influenced by factors that originated elsewhere, often operating on a much wider scale, such as at the territorial colonial level and even at the level of the world economy. To exclude these levels from the analysis would seem to do injustice to the complexity of the social developments at hand.

The aim of this study is to examine and compare differences in the local histories of slavery in the colonial period. This perspective undoubtedly privileges 'supra-ethnic' political and economic factors over 'sub-ethnic' local social and cultural factors and, thus, some of the latter's subtleties will inevitably receive less attention than they deserve.[48] Nevertheless, this approach permits a varied and multifaceted analysis that is also relevant for the historical study of the end of slavery elsewhere in Africa. The present study takes the boundaries of German East Africa (Tanganyika/ mainland Tanzania) as its analytical-territorial framework. The *Residenturen* of Ruanda (Rwanda), Urundi (Burundi) and Bukoba will be exempted because of their different administrative set-up.[49]

The question of the temporal framework of the end of slavery in East Africa is even more difficult to answer. It was not a single event but a pro-tracted, long-drawn-out process, lasting probably longer than one generation. This study will show that the main features of this process did not emerge in the colonial period, but rather had much earlier origins. If, as will be argued in Chapter 3, earning relative personal freedom was an in-built feature of the various forms of pre-colonial slavery, then German colonial rule and capitalism by and large brought about a shift in the distribution of resources between owners and slaves, thereby hastening social mobility and increasing the rate of social change. In this process, the status and actual living conditions of slaves and free-born individuals gradually converged, as both became colonial subjects with strictly limited rights.[50] Apart from politically motivated manumission, the German administration did not invent new social patterns of emancipation, nor did it basically alter the direction of the latter. Most of the forms through which slaves became free in the German period had been there before the establishment of colonial rule: manumission by the owner, flight, slave (self-)ransoming and the integration of slaves into their owners' kinship group or patronage network. The present study recounts the history of slavery and emancipation in German East Africa up to the outbreak of war in 1914.[51]

It should be mentioned that studying the history of slavery in the period of its decline poses serious methodological problems as far as the inter-pretation of European sources is concerned. While archival records held in Tanzania and in Germany are relatively rich on the actions and thoughts of local administrative officers and imperial bureaucrats, the activities, let alone the voices, of slaves and ex-slaves have not been recorded on a similar scale. This makes a comparative analysis of 'slave consciousness' in late-nineteenth-century and early-twentieth-century East Africa an extremely difficult undertaking.[52] Moreover, European observers, especially administrative officers, almost invariably used fixed legal categories to describe the social differences between free-born individuals and slaves. Thus, the extremely fluid character of slavery – as locally made and unmade social relations between the slaves and their owners – tends to be constantly underplayed, and the manifold social nuances between free and unfree are often overlooked. Given the absence of historical documen-tation on how slave owners, slaves or ex-slaves viewed the changes they experienced in the period concerned, the available archival material must be interpreted with special care.[53] In this connection it might also be noted that administrative officers were often reluctant to put into writing matters that could compromise them and endanger their professional careers. In political terms, slavery was a sensitive topic and thus the archival record is full of omissions and distortions. Above all, most administrative officers tended to portray slavery as a benign and equitable institution, because that justified their actions, whereas in fact, this was not the case. As long as slave owners have the right to take their slaves – men, women and children – and sell them in the market whenever they like, the notion of the slave owner's benevolence has to be regarded as largely fictional.

Finally, there is the problem that a large proportion of the local colonial records was destroyed by the German authorities in East Africa in the First World War, unfortunately precisely those documents that dealt with subjects like 'slavery' or 'labour' in German East Africa and most of the district records.[54] The exploration of the remaining documents during six months of research in the Tanzanian National Archives in Dar es Salaam yielded only a somewhat incomplete picture, even though these documents are highly important in themselves. The records held at the Bundesarchiv in Berlin can only partly fill in this gap.

The reader will notice that the source material used for the first two chapters consists largely of contemporary accounts as well as retrospective descriptions from the early colonial period. With few notable exceptions,[55] these were written by European travellers, missionaries and colonial administrative officers. A central aspect of these accounts is their often synchronic and essentialist perspective on social phenomena such as slavery, gender relations or chiefship. For this reason, they are almost unyielding to the historian's endeavour to use them for the reconstruction of social change in central and coastal Tanzania, particularly in the early half of the nineteenth century. The authors of these accounts take for granted that certain core traditions and customs are historically inert and, moreover, that these can be firmly attributed to a specific group of people living in a clearly defined geographic area. This assumes both a high degree of homogeneity of social practices within such culture areas and a strong measure of social difference from neighbouring areas. Thus dates or specific place names are only rarely given. For historical reasons, not least nineteenth-century commercial expansion and the forced migration of large numbers of people, each of these assumptions is highly problematic, at least as far as the coast or Unyamwezi is concerned. Moreover, it should be noted that although a good deal of documentary evidence is available about slavery in Unyamwezi and on the coast before the colonial conquest, much of it is fragmentary and uneven in quality. Thus reconstructing nineteenth-century social change poses a particular challenge to the historian. There is no straightforward solution to this historiographical problem, except to take heart from Marcia Wright's dictum that imaginative 'inference is a legitimate historical method' as long as it is explicitly noted in the text.[56]

In this study it will be argued that while the government did not compel owners to free their slaves in German East Africa, the establishment of colonial rule and the development of the colonial economy facilitated the forces that eventually led to the end of slavery. As will be shown in Chapter 7, the end of slavery in German East Africa was set in motion by two developments in particular. First, there was the gradual but forceful suppression of slaving and of the regional slave trade following the colonial conquest. This offered fugitive slaves greater security to permanently escape servitude. Previously, these slaves had always had to reckon with the distinct and dreaded possibility of being violently re-enslaved. On the other hand, the suppression of slaving and the regional slave trade separated slave owners from established sources of supply for new captives. This provided a powerful impetus to renegotiate their relationship with their slaves, since the local commercial stock of slaves was dwindling away through flight, natural death and social assimilation. The other development that contributed fundamentally to the abolition of slavery in German East Africa was the emergence of a territorial wage labour market. Neither European plantation companies nor the large private construction firms that built the railway system – to name the largest employers – were particularly interested in the social status of their African employees. Their concerns were primarily dictated by their insatiable appetite for cheap labour. Over time, this strong and ever-increasing demand created a territorial wage labour market that enabled slaves, especially males, to gain economic independence from their owners.

Both the suppression of enslavement and the emergence of a territorial wage labour market greatly aided the slaves who wished to leave their owners. It removed some of the obstacles that had previously prevented them from running away and ensured owners a measure of control over their slaves without the use of force. But these developments also helped the slaves who wished to remain with their owners for whatever reason, for instance, as members of their owners' household or as dependants or clients in the vicinity of their owners' residence. These slaves were enabled to renegotiate the terms of their 'service' or 'employment', since, with the emergence of a viable alternative in the form of flight, slavery itself became a socially untenable relationship.

This study endeavours to provide a novel perspective on social change in the early colonial period in the broadest sense. It illuminates both a significant aspect of colonialism and an important facet of the social history of Africa. Chapter 2 of the study outlines the development of slavery and the slave trade in nineteenth-century Tanganyika. Its basic purpose is to provide the framework and background for the analysis of slavery under colonial rule in the subsequent chapters. Chapter 3 introduces the societies and economies most heavily involved in slavery in the nineteenth century, namely Unyamwezi in central Tanganyika and the areas bordering the Indian Ocean in the east. It asks how people became slaves, what kind of work they did and how at least some of them became 'free' – that is, obtained a social status that gave them a measure of protection against being sold.

The second part of the study examines the policy of the German colonial authorities, especially the decision to recognise the legal status of slaves. Compared with anti-slavery policies pursued by other colonial powers in East Africa at the time, this was a unique approach. Various groups were involved in framing this policy. Principal among them were the colonial authorities in Berlin, the political parties in the Reichstag, the local colonial administration and, last but not least, extra-parliamentary pressure groups such as the Catholic and Protestant Churches. The political debate in the Reichstag will be discussed in Chapter 4. Special attention, however, has to be paid to the position of the 'men on the spot', especially the governors and administrative officers of German East Africa, as their voice was the single most important influence in the long debate. Their arguments, analysed in detail in Chapter 5, very clearly reflect the more general anxieties and constraints of German colonial rule in East Africa.

The third part of the book reviews the main factors that account for the decline of slavery in German East Africa in the colonial period. Chapter 6 analyses the impact of colonial rule, especially the suppression of the long-distance slave trade and wholesale violent enslavement. It also examines the issue by the colonial administration of official certificates of emancipation (*Freibriefe*) to about 60,000 (ex-)slaves. A considerable number of these slaves bought their own freedom from their owners. But they first had to obtain the means to do so. Chapter 7, therefore, will explore the widely scattered and often rather tentative evidence regarding the active role of predominantly male slaves in the gradual transformation of local slave labour regimes to contractual labour arrangements. This happened all over German East Africa, but particularly in the areas most strongly affected by the growth of the colonial economy. Yet not all slaves attempted to get away from their owners. Many, the majority of them women, remained in their places of work or continued to live in the vicinity of the owners' household. These slaves also became 'free' in the sense that they could no longer be sold freely by their owners, primarily for social reasons. These (ex-)slaves often had an inferior social status compared with the 'free'-born in a particular locality or household, and remained dependent on their previous owners in various ways. But, compared with their parents, their prospects had improved considerably. These minute renegotiations 'from below' of dependency and social marginality will also be investigated in this chapter.

In the conclusion, the main arguments of the study will be drawn together. First, it will be suggested that the incorporation of a large part of East Africa into the world economy in the nineteenth century changed local economies, politics and societies. Slavery became much more widespread during this period, so that at the time of the conquest German colonial administrators found slaves in almost every area under their authority. Second, it will be shown that the political weakness of German colonial rule dictated its peculiar approach to the problem of slavery in East Africa. The decision to recognise officially the legal status of slaves largely rested on the apprehension that by abolishing slavery the administration would undermine the political power, material wealth and social prestige of its main local African allies. Third, it will be demonstrated that the growth of the colonial economy, especially the emergence of a territorial wage labour market, greatly hastened the demise of slavery as a regime of work and a form of social life. More specifically, it will be argued that becoming free took a variety of age- and gender-specific forms, which comprised both the sudden severance of social ties between slaves and their owners as well as the more gradual reconfiguration of slavery into less oppressive forms of dependency.

This study does not claim to be 'history from below'.[57] If it is anything, it is a detached attempt to reconstruct the social history of slavery in the later nineteenth century and its end in Tanzania in the early colonial period. Given its methodology, its scope, and the nature of its sources, this study cannot be anything else. Incremental social change – the subtle transformation of unequal relationships between members of a society – is, after all, only rarely consciously and collectively perceived and expressed at the time by those who are making it.[58] It is up to the historian to 'reveal what contemporaries could not recognise'.[59] It is only in the wider perspective and the larger temporal framework that what might appear to be inconsequential, even to the historical actors, acquires greater historical significance. For better or worse, these have to be provided by the latter-day observer, which is both the strength and the weakness of all historical writing.

Notes

1 Tanzania National Archives (in the following, TNA) 11193, League of Nations, Doc. A 25 (a), Letter from the British government, 20 May 1924.

2 Bundesarchiv Abteilungen Berlin (in the following, BAB) Reichskolonialamt (in the following, RKolA) 7382/27: 42–93. Berichte der einzelnen Verwaltungsstellen in Deutsch Ostafrika über die Sklaverei, n.d. [1897–1901]. More detailed documentation regarding the magnitude and geographic distribution of slavery in Tanzania at the end of the nineteenth century will be provided in Chapter 5.

3 For this phrase, see Roberts and Miers 1988: 30.

4 For an extensive review of the literature, see Deutsch 1997. See also Cooper 1979, Wrigley 1971.

5 Roberts 1987, Klein 1998, Lovejoy and Hogendorn 1993, Miers and Roberts 1988. For East Africa, see Alpers 1975a, Cooper 1977, Cooper 1980, Morton 1990, Wright 1993, Glassman 1995, Sikainga 1996, Allen 1999, Isaacman and Isaacman 2004.

6 Miers and Klein 1999, Lovejoy 2000, Temperley 2000, Miers 2003, Campbell 2004, 2005, Alpers 2005. Note that this list is by no means comprehensive.

7 The most comprehensive review can still be found in Roberts and Miers 1988: 3–68. For the most recent survey on the literature, see Miers 2000: 237–64, but see also Miers and Klein 1999: 1–13 and Miers 2003: 29–46. For an older survey, see Lovejoy 1983: 254–68, reprinted in Lovejoy 2000: 252–75.

8 The notable exception is Morton's research on coastal Kenya and its hinterland. See Morton 1990.

9 It should be noted that a comparative study of the history of slavery in late nineteenth-century Tanzania does not exist, despite the fact that many observers regard slavery as crucial to the understanding of both colonial and contemporary society. See, for instance, Lienhardt 1968: 12f., Middleton 1992: 24. For reason of brevity and manage-ability, this study explores the decline of slavery in just two regions in Tanzania, Unyamwezi and the coast. However – as will be shown below – slavery existed in one form or another in almost all societies in Tanzania at the end of the nineteenth century.

This study hopes to encourage further, especially oral historical research on this topic.

10 See, for instance, the recent surveys by Ewald 1998: 41–6 and Roberts 1998: 40–2. However, the non-abolition policy is noted by Maier 1987: 73–92, Sunseri 1993(a): 79–131, Harding 1995: 280–308, Eckert 1998: 133–48.

11 Note that the legal status of certain female slaves – or 'concubines' – was not abolished in Zanzibar until 1909.

12 See, for instance, with regard to Kenya, the detailed discussion by Morton (1990: 119–44) on the anti-abolitionist policies of the Imperial British East Africa Company (1888–95) and subsequent inaction by the British colonial administration until 1907. See also Roberts and Miers 1988: 12ff., Klein 1998: 126–40, Miers 1999: 21 and Miers 2000: 249–53.

13 For Northern Nigeria, see Lovejoy and Hogendorn 1993. For the Sudan, see Sikainga 1995: 1–24 and Sikainga 1996. The authors show that a 'state akin to slavery' persisted right up to the mid-1930s. For the 'end' of slavery in the Eastern Belgian Congo, see Northrup 1988a: 462–82 and Northrup 1988b.

14 According to Klein (1998: 214) and Miers (2003: 37) the legal status of slavery was not abolished in Sierra Leone and in the Sudan until after the First World War. For a discussion of the 'legality' of slavery in the German colonies, see Chapter 4.

The fact that the German authorities recognised slavery was apparently widely known at the time, at least to the British public, but perhaps – in its consequences – not fully appreciated. Thus, for instance, the *Encyclopædia Britannica* (1910: 773) somewhat tersely states that in German East Africa 'The slave trade has been abolished ... though domestic slavery is allowed....'

15 For more detail, see Chapter 6.

16 Miers 2003: xiii.

17 A comparison between the German approach and the policies pursued by other colonial powers in Africa, notably Britain (in Nigeria, the Sudan and Zanzibar), France (in Senegal and Mali), Portugal (in Mozambique) and Belgium (in the Congo) lies outside the scope of this study, but the author hopes to return to this subject in a future publication.

18 This study thus follows the path set by Klein (1998) in his recent seminal study on slavery and colonial rule in French West Africa.

19 Wright 1993: 23ff.

20 Weidner 1915. The book is the published version of Weidner's doctoral dissertation, which was submitted to the Faculty of Law at the University of Jena in 1914. The dissertation was supervised by Professor G. K. Anton.

21 BAB RKolA 1007/16. Anton to Kolonialrat, 8 February 1914.

22 Deutsch 1996.

23 This and the following paragraphs have greatly profited from Cooper 1977: 1–20, Lovejoy 2000: 1–8 and Miers 2004: 1–16.

24 See, for instance, Meillassoux 1991 [1986]: 11. This is a long established tradition. In 1924, for instance, the League of Nations defined slavery as 'the status of a person over whom any or all of the powers of ownership' were exercised. For this quote, see Miers 2004: 11.

25 Glassman 1991: 289 n. 32.

26 Finley 1968: 307, citing Niboer 1910 [1900]. See also Finley 1980 [reprinted 1998] and Miers 2004: 11.

27 Cooper 1977: 15, 253.

28 Finley 1968: 308. See also Klein 1998: 14 and Iliffe 2005: 137.

29 Cooper 1977: 212.

30 Roberts and Miers 1988: 3. See also Willis and Miers 1997: 479–95. For an earlier version of this argument, see Cooper 1977: 153–70, 179, 200–10.

31 For the term 'equilibrium', see Cooper 1977: 155, 208 and Morton 1990: 1–19. See also Christie 1871: 42f., cited in Cooper 1977: 169.

32 Wright 1993: 25. The radical commodification of the human body through the slave trade and the 'social death' that it entails is arguably only a specific moment in the life of a slave as new social ties such as fictive family and kinship connections are forged over time to replace the lost ones. This theme has been discussed at great length by Patterson 1982. See also Kopytoff and Miers 1977: 3–81 and Meillassoux 1991 [1986]. 'Free' is, of course, a highly value-loaded term. In this study it is merely used to refer to

perceived 'non-slave' status of a person, the degree of equality with the 'free' in economic, political, economic and religious affairs that offered a measure of protection against the sale of that person. For a discussion of the ambivalence of slavery and freedom, see Kopytoff 1998: 676–83, Miers 2000: 257–9, Miers 2004: 1–16 and Iliffe 2005: 120.

33 For this phrase, see Kopytoff and Miers 1977: 20.

34 For a short summary of the debate about the slavery to kinship paradigm, see Glassman 1991: 279, 283.

35 Kopytoff and Miers 1977: 3–81.

36 Glassman 1991: 284, 289, 297 and 1995: 22ff., 116.

37 Feierman 1995: 368. For this reason, Miers has argued that the term 'slavery' – and its antithesis 'freedom' – should be always defined in local terms. See Miers 2004: 2, 11.

38 Cooper 1977, Cooper 1980.

39 Lovejoy 1983, Wirz 1984, Klein 1993, Wright 1993, Glassman 1995, Palmié 1995, Klein 1998, Kopytoff 1998.

40 I am largely following Cooper's (1977: 15, 153–6) and Glassman's arguments here (1991: 283ff.).

41 On the theme of the honour of slaves, see Iliffe 2005: 119–39. The term locality is used here solely as a descriptive category. For a more analytical definition, see Appadurai 1995: 205–25.

42 Glassman 1991: 281.

43 Robertson and Klein 1983.

44 Roberts and Miers 1988: 29. See also Morton 1990: 5–7 and Kopytoff and Miers 1977: 73–5.

45 Roberts and Miers 1988: 27–33.

46 Roberts and Miers 1988: 32.

47 On this issue, see Feierman 1990: 13–17. See also Binsbergen 1981–2: 51–81.

48 This is particularly true for the social memory of slavery as expressed, for instance, in the stigma that was (and still is) attached to people of slave origin. Slavery has lived on both in public and private discourse. Their in-depth examination, however, exceeds the scope of the current study. Research on this topic would have required a different research methodology, involving the collection of oral testimonies. Slavery is a highly sensitive topic and many people in Tanzania, particularly members of families of slave origin, are reluctant to talk about this issue. Gathering such oral testimonies would have meant staying for prolonged periods of time in particular localities. Due to the limitations set by the funding institution this was not feasible at the time. However, some oral testimonies were collected (see Deutsch 2000a), but because of their incomplete and highly fragmented nature they have not been used for this study. The author hopes to return to this subject in a future publication. For the oral history of slavery and its aftermath on the Kenya coast, see el-Zein 1972, Ylvisaker 1979, Strobel 1979, Romero Curtin 1983, Romero 1986, Herlehy and Morton 1988 and Romero 1997. For West Africa, see Haenger 1997 and Klein 1998: 237–51.

49 See Hubatsch 1984: 385, 409, 419.

50 Mamdani 1997; see also Comaroff 2001.

51 The cut-off date of 1914 has been chosen because of the exceedingly difficult archival situation with regard to evidence of the effects of the First World War. The question as to whether these were significant or not thus lies outside the scope of this study.

52 For an analysis of slave consciousness in late-nineteenth-century Tanganyika, see Glassman 1995: 1–29.

53 Yet, for life stories of slaves, see Wright 1993.

54 For more detail, see National Archives of Tanzania 1973. This is markedly different from the situation with regard to coastal Kenya, where detailed local administrative records are available. In this connection it might be also noted that a substantial part of the records held in Berlin was destroyed during the Second World War – those files, for instance, which dealt with 'forced labour' and 'railway construction'.

55 Tippu Tip 1902, Velten 1898, 1903. Glassman (1995: 117) suggests that the compilation *Sitten und Gebräuche der Suaheli* was actually written by Mtoro bin Mwenyi Bakari. However, according to the introduction to the book (Velten 1903: IV) this was not the case. Moreover, a comparison with the previously published *Sitten und Gebräuche der Suaheli* (Velten 1898), on which the later volume was based, reveals that Mtoro bin

Bakari's actual input was comparatively small. In this connection it should be noted that Velten himself never claimed authorship of the 1898 text, but diligently noted the names of his informants, Baraka bin Shomari, his brother Mwenyi Hija bin Shomari and Muhamedi bin Madigani.

56 Wright 1993: ix. See also Collingwood 1993 [1946]: 252–4.
57 This phrase refers to Fabian 1990: 1.
58 On the relationship between 'class position', historical change and political conscious-ness, see Glassman 1995: 16.
59 Miller 2000: 3.

Part I

═══

Slavery & the Slave Trade
in Nineteenth-Century
Tanganyika

The social history of slavery and the slave trade in East Africa in the nineteenth century evolved around the interaction, tensions and contradictions of the social relations that defined personhood within a community (as *insiders*), and the commercial transactions that actually or potentially reduced people to mere objects of exchange and exploitation (as *outsiders*).[1] It was within these social extremes, which seem to represent opposing configurations of social relations, that slaves had to make their living. Yet historically they overlapped: whether a person was regarded as tradable currency or as an upright member of a household, extended family or local community was often defined situationally and thus subject to sudden change, particularly in periods of social dislocation such as internal strife, war or famine. This 'radical uncertainty' was probably the most critical feature in the everyday life of a slave.[2]

Configurations of social relations are politically, culturally and economically circumscribed and, of course, subject to historical change. They also vary greatly between different societies and locations. Moreover, developments in one sphere necessarily influence others, not least because social actions in Africa, as elsewhere, are not perceived to be exclusively economic, political or cultural in nature. As far as the procurement and use of slaves on the East African mainland are concerned, perhaps the single most important development in the nineteenth century was the quantitative expansion and qualitative change of the caravan trade centred in Zanzibar, transforming not only local patterns of commodity production, distribution and consumption, but – as will be shown in Chapter 3 – also those of political authority, public morality and social interaction.[3] In the late eighteenth and early nineteenth century, when the long-distance slave trade and commercial slavery gradually spread along the trade routes, 'attitudes to life and freedom were brutalised' all over East Africa.[4] This transformation has been aptly described with regard to the late nineteenth century as the *commodification of social relations*, that is, as an incomplete and historically 'uneven process by which an increasing amount of social interaction [is] mediated through market relations'.[5] This process took place in localities showing a high degree of social, cultural and political diversity. It is to this diversity that the following chapter will pay particular attention.

Two

The Geography of Slavery & the Slave Trade

Much has been written about the development of the external East African slave trade and the extent of slaving by 'foreigners' on the mainland in the eighteenth and nineteenth centuries.[6] Yet, except for the coastal region, comparatively little is known about slavery in the interior or the internal slave trade before the second half of the nineteenth century. From early colonial records and travellers' accounts it appears that by about mid-century two large slave populations resided in the area that later became Tanganyika, one around present-day Tabora in central Tanganyika and the other along the coast, roughly between Tanga and Lindi.[7] This does not mean, however, that slavery or the slave trade did not exist elsewhere. In fact, by the mid-1850s slavery and the slave trade had probably permeated most Tanganyikan societies, and there were precious few whose leaders or members refused to take part in either of them.[8]

As far as archival sources are concerned, the volume and historical depth of the documents relating to the coast vastly exceed the documents relevant to the history of slavery and the slave trade in the interior. Although this feature produces a certain unevenness in the narrative presentation, it is unavoidable if details are not to be sacrificed. Even for areas where some documentation is available, however, the general lack of source material makes it impossible to establish with any degree of certainty whether East African slave trading developed from within or was initiated solely by outsiders, for instance from the Arabian peninsula. It is more than likely that rudimentary intermittent local slave trading had already existed within East Africa even before the emergence of external markets. It had probably developed from older forms of social dependency, involving the contractual transfer of people between different descent groups.[9] But this kind of slave trading was locally circumscribed and only became fully commercial after having been integrated into transregional trade networks. Whatever the case may be, the internal East African and external overseas slave trades in the eighteenth and nineteenth century were closely connected, and the interaction between the two reinforced and expanded both.[10]

Central Tanganyika

In the early nineteenth century the area around Tabora acquired the name Unyamwezi and its inhabitants came to be called Nyamwezi.[11] This was an assigned name; at the time Nyamwezi preferred to identify themselves by the chiefdom in which they were born. The label Nyamwezi was coined from outside and indicated that the Wanyamwezi lived somewhere in the far west; one possible meaning of the word Nyamwezi is 'people of the new moon', a term coastal people associated with that particular direction.[12] For them, the label carried the derogatory connotation of being 'uncivilised' or 'rural'.[13] In the European literature the name Nyamwezi or a recognisable variant appears in various nineteenth-century exploration accounts of East Africa, but it is often uncertain precisely what area was being referred to.[14] Sometimes Unyamwezi merely denoted the immediate environs of Tabora, sometimes the powerful chiefdoms of Unyanyembe or Urambo, but equally often the entire area between Lake Tanganyika and Lake Victoria.[15] In this study the descriptive term Unyamwezi relates to a geographical area that was considered to be the heartland of Unyamwezi settlements by most contemporary observers. In German colonial times the area was called Tabora district.[16]

The local language was first recorded by missionaries in the second half of the nineteenth century.[17] As elsewhere, this process accentuated the linguistic differences from the languages spoken by neighbouring peoples, for instance by the Sukuma and Sumbwa in the north or the Kimbu in the south. Yet, cultural differences between these groups were not as pronounced as their ethnic or linguistic labels suggest. Owing to intermarriage and large-scale migration movements in the eighteenth century, neighbouring peoples in this region were usually able to understand each other, especially in the border areas. However, they faced communication problems when longer distances were involved, as people living in Ufipa on the south-eastern shores of Lake Tanganyika did with people living in Uzinza on the southern shores of Lake Victoria.[18] The Nyamwezi were ruled by separate but historically often closely related headmen and chiefs of very different local making, involving various kinds of religious beliefs and local political traditions that included different forms of dynastic rules of succession. Thus, in terms of cultural identity, language and political organisation Unyamwezi was neither a homogeneous ethnic unit nor a clearly defined territorial entity, although many nineteenth-century observers believed that this was the case.[19]

In the mid-nineteenth century Unyamwezi was one of the most densely populated areas in what later became Tanganyika. This was due to its agricultural potential. The traveller Richard Burton, who visited Unyamwezi in the late 1850s, called it the 'Garden of Central Africa'.[20] In addition to tobacco (hemp), millet and sorghum, people produced large quantities of maize, rice and sweet potatoes: foreign crops, which had been introduced into the area earlier in the century, probably in the 1830s or 1840s. Large herds of cattle were found especially in the northern parts of Unyamwezi, which were less infested by tsetse fly than the southern forest areas.[21] The size of these cattle herds increased considerably in the first half of the century. They were evidently not looked after by Nyamwezi pastoralists but by an ever-increasing number of immigrants, mainly 'Tutsis', as they are called in archival sources, who came from the north and north-west, that is from present-day Bukoba region, Rwanda and Burundi.[22] Agriculture was augmented by the craft industry, particularly extensive iron working and the making of cotton cloth, which only declined when the consumption of imported goods acquired social prestige in the second half of the century.[23]

Another important source of wealth was trade. In the eighteenth century, probably even much earlier, Nyamwezi traders appear to have engaged in regional commercial transactions involving the exchange of salt, iron hoes, pottery and foodstuffs, including honey, dried fish and grain.[24] Around the turn of the century Nyamwezi traders then seem to have discovered the rewards of long-distance trade.[25] Using the wealth and experience generated in regional trade, they ventured further afield, exploring various routes to the coast and exchanging locally produced commodities including iron hoes, salt, cattle and, increasingly, ivory for imported goods such as beads, cotton cloth (in ki-Swahili, *kaniki* or *merikani*, according to their Indian or American origin), guns and metal and brass and copper wire.[26] Moreover, Nyamwezi traders extended their regular commercial contacts towards the north-west (Bunyoro, Buganda), the south-west (Ufipa, Katanga), the north (Lake Victoria), and to Ujiji, a settlement on the eastern shores of Lake Tanganyika.

During the first half of the nineteenth century Unyamwezi developed into an ivory trading centre where professional hunters (in ki-Nyamwezi, *badandu*) from the region brought their elephant tusks and hippopotamus teeth. Previously, ivory had had little commercial value in Unyamwezi. As elsewhere in Central Africa, it was probably used for decorative and ceremonial purposes only – indeed, elephants were largely hunted for their meat.[27] But with rising Indian and later European and American demand, East African ivory prices steadily improved. Having already been in commercial contact with the coast, it is likely that the prospects of obtaining foreign goods, especially cotton cloth, induced some Nyamwezi traders to explore ways and means of exporting ivory from their home region on a more regular basis. Very early on they also seem to have been accompanied by slaves.[28] The caravans went to coastal settlements such as Pangani, Saadani and Mbwamaji, towns and villages situated opposite the islands of Pemba and Unguja, whose capital Zanzibar was the largest East African staple place for ivory at the time.[29]

For security reasons, early-nineteenth-century Nyamwezi caravans consisted of large numbers of porters (in ki-Swahili, *wapagazi*, sing. *pagazi*), at times several hundred, even thousands, as one mid-nineteenth-century observer reported.[30] These caravans elected their own leaders who were called *viongozi* (sing. *kiongozi*) in ki-Swahili.[31] Many porters made the arduous and dangerous 350-mile journey to the coast on their own or their families' account.[32] At this period, the caravans were usually accompanied by local headmen and probably consisted of young men seeking to escape control of the elders by earning enough independently and, above all, rapidly to pay the often immense bridewealth expenses due (either in goods, such as cattle, or personal services) should they wish to marry the elders' daughters.[33] Porterage also meant that young men could acquire the capital to start trading on their own rather than their families' account. In the first half of the century, trading and porterage seem to have developed at great speed into more than just a means of gaining (bride-)wealth. It became an accepted way of life and a source of male prestige.[34] 'Youth worth the name … could not afford to remain at home', as one writer puts it.[35] Nyamwezi men, it was said, were not allowed to marry until they had been to the coast and brought back a piece of cloth, beads or some metal wire.[36]

Participating in the caravan trade was not exclusively a male occupation.[37] Nyamwezi women also joined the caravans to make the long journey to the coast either independently or with their often temporary husbands. A number of these women even worked as porters alongside the men, carrying smaller parcels of merchandise or foodstuffs. Neither was porterage the occupation of 'free' Nyamwezi alone, since some local notables employed trusted slaves as carriers, or even agents. However, such cases were the exception. It was more common for enterprising slaves to leave their owners and join the caravans as 'free' porters, never to return to Unyamwezi again.[38]

Those who came back from the coast brought hitherto unknown commodities with them, novel experiences and new ideas, particularly religious ones. This was one of the main avenues by which variants of Islamic beliefs and coastal manners of dress, speaking and behaviour found their way into the interior.[39] Conversely, however, Nyamwezi religion and culture, and in particular ki-Nyamwezi, acquired currency along the trade routes. By mid-century the language had not only developed into an important regional lingua franca, but was set to become one of the three most widespread languages in the whole of Tanganyika, its number of speakers probably even surpassing those who used ki-Swahili or ki-Yao as their main medium of communication in the nineteenth century.[40] The rapid expansion of Nyamwezi culture was further underpinned by the founding of semi-permanent Nyamwezi settlements not just on the coast, but also in the west near the copperbelt area of Katanga in what later became the Belgian Congo, in the south-west around the southern end of Lake Tanganyika, especially Ufipa, and to the east in Ugogo, Irangi and Usandawe.[41] The most important settlement in the west was that of Msiri in Katanga. He had moved there in the 1850s with a large group of Unyamwezi henchmen and, in the possession of guns, ousted the local ruler and established himself as an independent chief. His principal trade was in slaves, ivory and copper.[42]

The establishment of long-distance trade routes necessarily also affected regional and local economies through which the caravans passed. On their

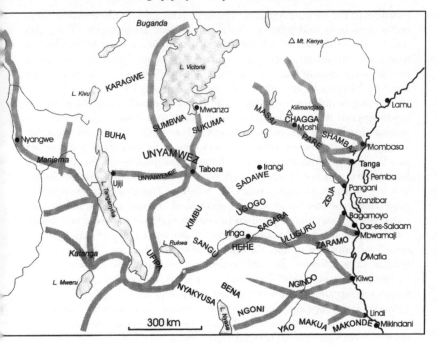

Map 1: Major Caravan Routes in the Later Nineteenth Century

Note: Adapted from A. Sheriff, *Slaves, Spices and Ivory in Zanzibar*, London 1987, p. 191 and
'Karte der Zollämter und Karawanenstraßen', *Deutsches Kolonialblatt* (3) 1892, annex.

journeys to the coast, Nyamwezi porters exchanged goods, including salt, cattle, iron hoes and tobacco, for foodstuffs and trade goods. They also had to pay road tolls. Supplying the caravan stimulated the production of food and commercial crops, particularly in areas previously less important to translocal commercial transactions, such as Ugogo, Usangu and the Uluguru Mountains in central and eastern Tanganyika.

Developments took a different turn from about mid-century onwards as the independent Nyamwezi ivory trade began to decline.[43] Caravans from the interior had probably outnumbered those originating from the coast up to the 1850s,[44] when coastal traders appear to have gained the upper hand. This was due, first, to the changing tax regime on the coast that heavily favoured local traders, particularly those based in Zanzibar. In the first half of the nineteenth century the Sultan of Zanzibar had succeeded in establishing customs houses on the coast, and 'foreign' traders had to pay much higher taxes than Zanzibari or coastal traders if they wanted to have their ivory shipped to Zanzibar. Some Nyamwezi traders managed to sell their ivory directly in the Zanzibar market. They even had their own quarter in the town.[45] But the majority of the Nyamwezi traders were induced, not least by the Zanzibari tax regime, to sell their ivory to local merchants, apparently at a very heavy discount.[46]

Second, it appears that the ivory frontier was rapidly advancing towards the west, moving out of the ambit of local Nyamwezi hunters and traders.[47] Between the 1850s and 1870s the number of elephant herds in Unyamwezi and the adjoining areas declined sharply and local elephant hunters found it exceedingly difficult to track down their prey. Some Nyamwezi hunters and traders followed the ivory frontier, but owing to lack of capital and military power their success was limited, especially in the later period when they were faced with strong competition.

Third, and perhaps most decisively, in the early 1830s traders from the coast and from Zanzibar had already begun to settle in the interior along the caravan routes, founding resting places such as Ujiji on the eastern shores of Lake Tanganyika (see Map 1). Having resided at different places in the area, notably Kwihara, for some time, in the early 1850s coastal and Zanzibari traders established the more permanent settlement of Kazeh, near present-day Tabora, in the heart of Unyamwezi.[48] Thereafter, coastal presence in the East African interior expanded rapidly.[49] By 1870 Tabora 'town' consisted of about 50 scattered homesteads (in ki-Swahili, *tembe*). These were large square dwellings, accommodating in some cases several hundred people, with an inner courtyard, adjacent garden plots, store-rooms, servant quarters and outhouses for slaves.[50] Tabora was surrounded by dense clusters of Nyamwezi villages, from which porters and soldiers were drawn for the caravans. According to one source, Tabora market was filled with petty traders, food sellers, ivory hawkers and labour seekers.[51] At the time, the settlement was governed by an appointed representative of the Sultan of Zanzibar. Superseding the older Nyamwezi trade networks, Tabora developed into the junction of the 'coastal' trade routes, one radiating northwards to Mwanza on the southern shores of Lake Victoria, a second one passing through Karagwe to the Kingdom of Buganda in the north-west, a third running west towards Ujiji on the eastern shores of Lake Tanganyika, and a fourth extending to Ufipa in the south-west.[52]

Thus, in the period between 1850 and 1870, coastal and Zanzibari traders, some of whom were financially or personally well-connected to Indian and Omani merchants in Zanzibar, were able to get the better of their Nyamwezi competitors, especially in long-distance, wholesale trade.[53] They had better access to long-term credit provided by Zanzibar moneylenders and could offer the commodities used for the exchange of ivory and slaves more cheaply. These entailed imported goods such as cotton cloth and arms as well as regional commodities like salt and copper wire. After exhausting Unyamwezi ivory supplies, they had the financial and, above all, the military means – in contrast to their local Nyamwezi competitors – to extend the ivory frontier beyond Katanga and Kazembe on the south-western side of Lake Tanganyika towards the north into Manyema Region, an area that today belongs to eastern Congo (Zaire). In the 1870s, the most prominent of these ivory and slave traders, such as Rumaliza and Tippu Tip, were able to build up commercial empires where ivory trading by local competitors was – to say the least – strictly limited.[54]

The retreat of the ivory frontier and the relative decline of the independent, Unyamwezi-based ivory trade forced younger men to look for other sources of income. Some seem to have followed the westward movement of the ivory frontier,[55] while others engaged in commercial food production. However, the great majority appear to have sought employment in the growing long-distance caravan trade between Unyamwezi and the coast. Wage labour employment was by no means unknown. In the early 1830s some Nyamwezi men had already been hired as carriers by Tabora and Ujiji merchants to carry goods to and from the coast or to accompany them on their trading journeys into the east for an agreed wage. Earlier on, merchants had used coastal slaves for this task, but since so many of them tried to flee as soon as an opportunity arose, their employment costs were found to be too high. Consequently, the merchants turned more and more to local sources of labour when they became available.[56]

Porterage had become a significant source of income for many young Nyamwezi men by the 1850s and gained further importance as the century progressed. This transition was very likely helped if not caused by the substantial increases in wages porters received, which – according to one source – doubled between the 1860s and the 1870s.[57] In any case, in the early 1880s tens of thousands of Nyamwezi porters – according to another source half of the male able-bodied population[58] – arrived annually at the coast, particularly in Bagamoyo, where consequently there emerged small semi-permanent Nyamwezi settlements of those who preferred to work on the coast for a while, finding employment as labourers in the growing coastal economy or tending small garden plots of vegetables and cassava.[59] Those who stayed on the coast often became indebted to coastal traders, particularly those of Indian origin who had also come to settle there in the second half of the nineteenth century. Indebtedness was probably chiefly responsible for the impoverishment of the Nyamwezi porters who were sold as slaves to work on the Pemba clove plantations in the 1870s.[60] After having stayed on the coast for some time, other Nyamwezi porters appear to have completely severed their family ties. They abandoned their non-coastal, 'non-Islamic' identity and tried to present themselves as Waswahili.[61]

By the 1890s up to a third of the adult male population in Unyamwezi were engaged as porters in the caravan trade each year.[62] Taking Tanganyika as a whole, Nyamwezi porters and traders were probably the single most important means of long-distance transport in the nineteenth century and also the key medium of cultural (ex)change. It was only in the early twentieth century that their numbers actually began to decline, primarily owing to the construction of the central railway, which ran almost parallel to the old caravan route.

In the nineteenth century, the increase in the number and size of the caravans passing through and resting in Unyamwezi, at times for several weeks, especially in Tabora, was accompanied by the expansion of commercial food production.[63] In the early part of the century, Nyamwezi participation in the caravan trade was largely a seasonal activity, pursued mainly in the months between May and November when the demand arising from agricultural pursuits was comparatively low.[64] Many Nyamwezi porters sought to return to their villages at the beginning of the rainy season, which usually starts around December. Food crops would then be harvested in the dry season, starting around May, before the majority of caravans left for the coast.[65] Initially, therefore, the expansion of the caravan trade had a comparatively low impact on agricultural food production. Yet Nyamwezi men increasingly regarded long-distance trading and porterage as their full-time rather than seasonal occupation. Their absence necessarily affected local food production. Moreover, with some notable exceptions, the growing coastal communities in Ujiji and Tabora, which were thought to number several thousand people in the late 1870s,[66] did not engage in agricultural market production; nor did their slaves, although the latter produced foodstuffs for their own and their owners' consumption. In the 1870s, Tabora and Ujiji were probably still primarily trading stations, although by that time they had already become permanent settlements, particularly for traders who did not wish to return to the coast or to Zanzibar for medical, economic or political reasons.

In any case, the inhabitants of 'coastal' settlements like Tabora were unable to produce enough food crops to sustain the growing number of long-distance caravans passing through or resting in the area. Instead, these caravans purchased their provisions from Nyamwezi foodstuff traders, particularly in the regional markets of Tabora and Ujiji, and consequently local food prices started to rise.[67] Large quantities of grain, rice and sweet potatoes as well as meat, (dried) fish, beans, tomatoes and bananas changed hands regularly. Given that by mid-century a sizeable proportion of Nyamwezi men were already engaged in porterage all year round, the task of producing these foodstuffs fell increasingly on immigrants from Buha and Burundi, Nyamwezi women and, probably of equal significance, on agricultural slaves (in ki-Nyamwezi, *basese*, sing. *msese*) who worked the farms in the absence of their owners.[68]

Nineteenth-century commercial expansion was, therefore, marked by a contradictory development. While more and more young Nyamwezi men engaged in various forms of wage labour elsewhere – a process one historian has described as 'proletarianisation'[69] – the use of slaves became more widespread at home because the demands of the local economy could not entirely be met by family or immigrant labour.[70] By the late 1830s a few Nyamwezi notables are said to have already owned several hundred slaves, and slave holding increased throughout the century, especially in the southern, commercially more developed parts of Unyamwezi, where even ordinary Nyamwezi seemed to have acquired slaves.[71] Most of these slaves lived with their owners' families, so that for the outside observer it was almost impossible to distinguish those regarded as 'free' from those who could be sold to a passing caravan or a neighbour when the need arose.[72]

Commercial expansion in Unyamwezi was aided unintentionally by the partial blockade of the ocean-going slave trade carried out by the British naval squadron from mid-century onwards. In the first half of the nineteenth century Zanzibar had developed into one of the main slave ports of East Africa, satisfying not only the local clove plantation owners' demand for cheap labour but also supplying slaves to more distant coastal markets in the north. The blockade aimed at containing the clandestine overseas maritime slave trade to India, Arabia and the Americas. Subsequent to the conclusion of the 1873 anti-slave-trade treaty between Britain and Zanzibar, suppression of the illegal importation of slaves to the islands of Unguja and Pemba became the squadron's main task. Initially, the long-distance supply of slaves continued unabated, but as shipment to Zanzibar became more difficult, slave prices dropped, probably first on the coast and subsequently in the interior. Slave traders were thus encouraged to look for new customers. They not only found them on the coast, but also in areas adjacent to the long-distance caravan routes, principally in southern Unyamwezi. The centre of this activity appears to have been Unyanyembe, the most prosperous area of the region.[73] Due to long and intense involvement in the caravan trade, there was a particular demand for labour in this area and many of its inhabitants had the means to buy slaves, especially female slaves. As slave prices dropped, local residents felt encouraged to employ more and more slaves. Thus, when German colonial forces occupied Unyamwezi in the 1890s, they found a large number of slaves, probably the highest number that had lived in that area at any one time. According to a report written in the late 1890s by Hauptmann Puder, one of the first permanent German officials in the area, more than a quarter of a million slaves lived in Tabora district alone.[74] These were largely owned by the local Nyamwezi elite – local chiefs, elders and village headmen – who had invested some of their trading profits in slaves.

Another group of large-scale slave owners consisted of the coastal inhabitants of Tabora and Ujiji.

Unyamwezi was a region that imported rather than exported slaves.[75] As far as slaves of Nyamwezi origin were concerned, export slave trading took place only on a minor scale, as Tabora-based coastal slave traders did not consider Unyamwezi to be a slave-hunting ground. The reason for this is unclear, but these traders probably felt that local slave raiding in Unyamwezi would seriously disturb their precarious political relations with the local chiefs.[76] Moreover, the most pressing problem – finding enough labour for the caravans – was already solved by young Unyamwezi men willing to undertake that work. In any case, with the notable exception of Mirambo and Nyungu ya Mawe, local chiefs also appear to have largely abstained from local slave raiding for export.[77] They largely retained their slaves once they had been settled down.[78] Yet, Nyamwezi transit slave trading was extensive. The first slave caravans from Unyamwezi probably reached the coast in the early 1810s.[79] The trade seems to have grown from then on, especially in the second half of the century when both Nyamwezi traders and coastal merchants brought growing numbers of captives to Tabora and Ujiji from neighbouring regions such as Sukuma in the north, Manyema in eastern Congo, present-day Burundi, and the area around the southern end of Lake Tanganyika. According to one estimate, in the 1870s at least 1,000 slaves left Unyamwezi for the coast every year.[80] Their broad social composition was the same as everywhere else in East Africa: those who were kidnapped, bought or judicially enslaved were the most vulnerable in local society – predominantly women and children unprotected by their families, victims of famine and local wars, and the unfortunate who fell prey to their autocratic chiefs.[81]

In addition to selling slaves directly to the coast, Nyamwezi slave traders supplied large numbers of slaves internally, especially to Zanzibari slave traders and local notables who were their main customers.[82] More importantly, they used imported slaves as a medium of exchange to obtain the ivory they subsequently carried to the coast. This was particularly the case in areas, such as Ugogo, that were rich in ivory and where the inhabitants had little demand for foreign goods.[83]

Apart from bridewealth payments and imported commodities, the proceeds from the slave and ivory trade seem to have been of great help to some chiefs and Nyamwezi men in acquiring guns and ammunition from about mid-century onwards. The weapons were primarily used for defence purposes, but also to expand hunting activities, including elephants, and as a means of kidnapping more slaves. The slave, arms and ivory trades fed on each other in rapidly widening cycles of violence, as Nolan noted: 'The introduction of firearms and the appreciating value of prisoners of war in the slave trade, seem to have changed the nature of war, people replacing cattle as a prime object of plunder.'[84] Whereas Burton found few firearms in the hands of Nyamwezi notables or chiefs in the late 1850s,[85] by the late 1870s even 'ordinary' Nyamwezi porters sometimes received their wages in firearms.[86] Probably overstating the extent of their use, missionaries working in the area claimed that by the 1890s every adult man in Unyam-wezi was carrying a gun, even if it was only an old musket.[87]

The 'militarisation' of Nyamwezi society was also reflected in changing settlement patterns.[88] In the early part of the nineteenth century, Unyam-wezi was cluttered with small settlements and hamlets (in ki-Nyamwezi, *makaya*, sing. *kaya*) of about 20–100 people who were ruled by a headman, usually the founder of the village (in ki-Nyamwezi, *muzenga kaya*).[89] In the third quarter of the century, these settlements appear to have given way to a much smaller number of stockaded villages (in ki-Nyamwezi, *limbuda*) when the use of firearms became more widespread in the region. Armed men were in a far better position to defend stockaded villages against raiders, especially against groups such as the dreaded Ngoni who, from the 1850s on, regularly invaded Unyamwezi from the south and south-west looking for cattle and women.[90] Thus, in the second half of the nineteenth century, some observers compared Unyamwezi to a sea, in which isolated villages provided a safe harbour for the intrepid traveller passing through the area.[91]

Along with social and economic transformation, Unyamwezi also underwent considerable political change in the nineteenth century. While central political authority had never been particularly strong in this part of Tanganyika, especially in northern Unyamwezi, the second half of the nineteenth century saw the rise of powerful chiefs.[92] Some *batemi* (sing. *butemi* or *mtemi*), as they were called in ki-Nyamwezi, such as Fundikira in the 1840s and 1850s or Mirambo, Nyungu ya Mawe and Isike in the 1870s and 1880s, had large numbers of personal followers. This strength in numbers enabled them to challenge militarily not only their immediate neighbours, whom they raided for cattle, ivory stores and, increasingly, slaves, but also the coastal merchants of Tabora whom they constantly pressed for tribute when they were not actually at war or in partial alliance with them.[93] The third quarter of the nineteenth century brought particularly troubled times, when local wars forced people to move away from their predatory neighbours or relocate to the stockaded defence villages of strong headmen and chiefs.[94] Even at that time, however, local chiefs were not always strong enough to prevent subjects from occasionally relocating their residence from one stockaded village to another if they were dissatisfied with the local headmen or chief.[95]

The centralisation of power in the hands of a few chiefs was accompanied by a change in the nature of their political authority. Their main instruments to attain wider territorial recognition in the early part of the century were translocal marriages and the installing of family members in outlying, newly conquered sub-chiefdoms. Religious authority, in particular rainmaking magic, was still one of the main pillars of the chiefs' political power. Authority was only rarely absolute but was based, at least to some extent, on the consent of other local notables such as competing members of the ruling family. The caravan trade changed that balance.[96] Local hunters were required to hand over part of the ivory they had collected –

one tusk out of two, as a rule – to the local chief. This rule was probably not observed regularly in remote areas where chiefs were of little consequence, but in the more centrally organised chiefdoms it was rigidly enforced.[97] The growing ivory trade enabled some chiefs to amass considerable wealth. In addition, these chiefs levied passing caravans with a sometimes very heavy toll tax (in ki-Swahili, *mahongo*, sing. *hongo*), the payment of which allowed members of the caravans to purchase foodstuffs from the chiefs' subjects.[98]

As nineteenth-century trade increased, so, too, did the revenue Nyamwezi chiefs derived from these sources. This provided ambitious chiefs with an extra income to create networks that bound people, especially headmen, by rewarding their personal loyalty with a share in the spoils of trade. It also provided the means for building standing armies, often comprised of unruly and brutal bands of young, unmarried men (in ki-Swahili, *ruga-ruga*).[99] These bands consisted largely of slaves, many of whom regarded themselves as personal followers of the chief, having been bought as children from passing caravans in exchange for ivory. These young men were rewarded for their services by the chiefs with part of the loot they had collected on their raids, especially with slaves. The latter were sold to local or coastal traders by the chiefs, if and when the need arose.[100] These bands were mostly led by members of the ruling chiefly family, but also by elevated slaves who had shown military aptitude. Thus, chiefs became less and less reliant on their subjects as they could now use slaves to expand the numbers of their followers.[101] Consequently, at the end of the nineteenth century prestige was no longer measured in terms of charismatic virtues, but rather in the possession of material wealth – cattle, women and slaves – and in commercial success.[102]

The most important and best known of these new chiefs was Mirambo, who lived north-west of Tabora in the 1860s and 1870s.[103] He came from a Nyamwezi noble family and was a well-known rainmaker; but, above all, he was a much-feared warlord who successfully subdued smaller, less powerful neighbouring chiefdoms. His *ruga-ruga* bands raided deep into Sukuma in the north, returning with cattle and slaves, particularly female slaves. His persistent attempts to gain control over the caravan routes running to Lake Tanganyika and Lake Victoria brought him into constant conflict with the coastal merchants of Tabora, an issue that was only settled after his death in 1884.[104] He was known for his involvement in the slave trade, exporting war captives to the coast.[105]

Yet, while commercial expansion created opportunities for chiefs, ultimately they were unable to monopolise long-distance trade. Some of their local subjects, particularly headmen living far from the chiefs' main residence, gained the means to become more independent of them.[106] In the early part of the century some of these headmen had already become free-trading, long-distance merchants (in ki-Nyamwezi, *wandewa* or *vbandevba*) who led their own caravans to the coast.[107] Contrary to the wishes of the chiefs, they often traded on their own account, exchanging slaves, ivory and arms, and forging their own political alliances – with like-minded coastal merchants in Tabora, for instance. Thus, while commercial expansion had strengthened some chiefs, enabling them to build up sizeable empires that only the German occupation force was finally able to destroy – as in the case of Isike, for instance – it also strengthened their local rivals, the ambitious and commercially minded headmen.[108] Much of the political history of nineteenth-century Unyamwezi, therefore, centred around the competition, conflicts and alliances between local power holders, chiefs and headmen whose authority and personal fortune came increasingly to rest on their successful participation in trade and their possession of arms and, above all, slaves.

Slavery and the slave trade thus played an important, if not crucial role in nineteenth-century Nyamwezi. Both commercial expansion and the development of militarised chiefdoms depended on the importation and social control of slaves. Like the imposition of colonial rule, commercial expansion had different effects on different groups of people. It enabled some people, especially those who had already enjoyed privileged access to local resources, like chiefs and merchant headmen, to advance their interests further, while it dispossessed others, especially those who were already vulnerable and living on the margins of their society. In short, the growth of slavery and the slave trade in the nineteenth century exaggerated already existing social and political divisions within local societies. Furthermore, and perhaps more decisively, it changed the social and political relationship between social groups. Young men – and at times even slaves – could at least partially escape the control, for example, of male elders, village heads and chiefs. A somewhat similar development occurred under very different social and political circumstances on the East African coast, as will be shown in the next part of this chapter.

The Coast

Today, the majority of the people living on the East African littoral and on the islands of Pemba, Unguja and Mafia are called the *Waswahili* (sing. *Mswahili*) on the basis that they seem to have shared the same habitat and history, speak the same language (that is, one of the local dialects of ki-Swahili), adhere to the same religion – Islam – and live predominantly in towns.[109] There are, however, a number of historical features that complicate this simple description.

First, the *Waswahili* have been strongly influenced by migrants who came from southern Arabia, India and Persia and interacted with the resident population economically, socially and culturally for probably more than a thousand years. Thus, for instance, when ki-Swahili word lists were recorded for the first time in the mid-nineteenth century, about 30 per cent of the words they contained were loans from Arabic, although the grammatical structure of the language retained its African 'Bantu' origins.[110] The overseas immigrants had come to East Africa at different times, intermarrying and settling down mostly in different commercial centres and towns such as Lamu and Mombasa in the north or Zanzibar, Lindi and Kilwa Kisiwani in the south, which was already an important trading area by the twelfth century.[111] They interacted with socially and linguistically different resident societies, and this is probably the reason why even today the spoken ki-Swahili and 'Swahili society' as a whole show such a great deal of local diversity on the coast.[112]

Second, it appears that the majority of the Swahili-speaking people only first came to live in towns in the twentieth century.[113] In the nineteenth century most coastal inhabitants who spoke ki-Swahili lived in the countryside. Moreover, living in a town did not necessarily mean living in a multi-storied, flat-roofed stone house. Although archaeological research has shown that stone houses made with coral lime mortar already existed on the coast in the eleventh century, this was by no means the common form of residence. Only a tiny elite could afford to live in buildings of this kind – the vast majority of town dwellers resided in single-storied *makuti* huts, which took their ki-Swahili name from the peaked palm-thatched roofs. These houses were no different from the larger square mud huts found in surrounding hamlets and villages. In fact, many townspeople possessed strong ties to the rural areas, not least because they owned farms (in ki-Swahili, *mashamba*, sing. *shamba*), which they worked in the wet season.

It should also be mentioned that politically even the larger towns interacted closely with the surrounding countryside.[114] In the second half of the nineteenth century, for instance, a place like Lindi in the south was as much a Yao as a Swahili town, while in the north the politics of places like Bagamoyo, Pangani or Dar es Salaam were strongly influenced, if not occasionally determined, by local Zigua and Zaramo chiefs rather than by Omani merchants residing in distant Zanzibar town.[115]

Furthermore, to portray coastal society as uniformly Islamic without further differentiation is certainly to oversimplify. Both in rural areas and in the coastal hinterland as well as in coastal towns many ki-Swahili people, but not necessarily the local elite, adhered to a variety of different religious beliefs.[116] Islamic traders – and in their wake, scholars – probably arrived on the coast before the millennium, but conversion first seems to have taken place on a noticeable scale only in the twelfth and thirteenth centuries.[117] Although many coastal people became avowed Muslims, they often retained local beliefs and religious ideas. Moreover, with migration, people from other parts of Tanganyika and beyond came to settle on the coast, bringing cultural ideas with them that were different from those of the established Islamised populations. Today, this is apparent in the great variety of religious beliefs on the coast, many of which have non-Islamic roots. Beyond the observance of the major tenets of Islam, such as fasting in the hours of daylight in the month of Ramadan, coastal people engaged in religious practices, ranging from spirit possession to ancestor worship, according to locality; Muslims in other parts of the world would regard these with abhorrence as idolatry or as highly blasphemous.[118] A similar pluralism existed in the dispensation of law. As far as the close observance of Islamic law and doctrines – the Shari'a – are concerned, on the whole these were followed by only a tiny minority of those few members of the coastal elite who could read Arabic script. The majority of coastal people adhered to the orally transmitted, local version of customary Islamic beliefs and legal doctrines. Whether these were always in strict accordance with the letter of the *Qu'ran* or the interpretations of the various law schools was a matter of frequent dispute.[119] In any case, Islamic law was only applied, for instance in civil cases, if both parties agreed. Where Islamic law and its solutions for particular problems were perceived to be insufficient, its stipulations were ignored and local 'customary' law prevailed.[120] This seems to suggest that Islamic beliefs and legal doctrines often only provided a loose normative framework that needed to be interpreted by the parties involved in order to be socially meaningful in a particular local context. Thus, for instance, Islamic beliefs certainly shaped the relationship between slaves and their owners on the coast, providing them with a structure in which they could negotiate their mutual rights and responsibilities. Islamic beliefs therefore significantly contributed to the 'ideological hegemony' of owners over their slaves, but, as Frederick Cooper has argued,[121] that hegemony was never complete and, as the flight movements of the late nineteenth century and early twentieth century show, under certain conditions rather easily broken.

Finally, the ethnonym Waswahili, labelling the coastal population, first gained wider currency only in the early nineteenth century. It was then primarily used by foreign observers. Previously, and indeed thereafter, people on the coast used other names more often in self-reference. For instance, in the early and mid-nineteenth century part of the local elite and their followers defined themselves as Shirazi to indicate that they had initially migrated from Shiraz in Persia. [122] This probably fictive claim of origin was maintained and elaborated in order to accentuate social and cultural differences both in relation to people living elsewhere on the mainland and to overseas newcomers, especially from Southern Arabia, who arrived in increasing numbers to settle among them. In contrast, in the late nineteenth and early twentieth centuries, the coastal people who actually called themselves Mswahili were primarily those who wanted to shed their up-country origins and could not lay a convincing claim to any other ethnic or social identity. A sizeable section of them were probably of slave origin.[123]

These features have given rise to a long debate in the secondary literature as to who should rightly be called the Waswahili.[124] Contemporary observers were similarly puzzled. The missionary Charles New, who had spent some ten years on the East African coast, noted in 1873:

> It would be hard to say what they really are. The modern Msuahili is a medley of almost everything.... If any mortal could claim relationship with half the world, and a little more, that man is a Msuahili.[125]

This study is not centrally concerned with this debate. It is probably sufficient to use the term here as a working definition for the majority of the people who lived in the coastal region between Tanga in the north and Lindi in the south opposite the island of Zanzibar in the nineteenth and early twentieth century. They encompassed different social and political groups who shared only one or two of the elements mentioned above – such as a common language, history, habitat, culture or religion – though not necessarily at the same time in equal strength in all localities of the area in question. It should also be noted that the meaning and usage of the word *Swahili* changed over time.

Despite the influx of considerable numbers of people from the interior and southern Arabia to the area, the cultural heterogeneity of the coastal people decreased as the nineteenth century progressed and more distinct elements of a common Swahili identity emerged.[126] This process was accompanied and reinforced by the emergence of Zanzibar as the dominant power in the region.[127] In the eighteenth century, the town of Zanzibar had already developed into an important outpost of the Omani Empire, and then became its core under the rule of Said b. Sultan who reigned between 1806 and 1856. Said b. Sultan had first visited East Africa in 1828; in 1840 he finally moved his court from Oman to Zanzibar. Other immigrants arrived around the time of the Omanis, especially from India and the Hadhramaut, and resided in Zanzibar under special protection of the Sultan. Some of them were merchants who had brought capital and wide-ranging commercial contacts with them.[128]

In the first half of the nineteenth century most urban settlements and principal staple places on the East African coast came under the rule of Zanzibar governors (in ki-Swahili, *maliwali*, sing. *liwali*), while Zanzibar customs houses and smaller military posts dotted the coast.[129] Zanzibar appointees also came to rule over the coastal enclaves in the interior such as Tabora, Mwanza and Ujiji. Yet even on the East African coast Zanzibar's authority was never complete or locally undisputed as, for instance, was shown by the prolonged confrontation with the Mazrui leaders of Mombasa in the 1830s.[130] Nevertheless, during the course of the nineteenth century the court of the Sultan of Zanzibar became the centre of a political patronage network that corresponded neatly with Zanzibar's development as an economic power and its commercial interests, particularly in the ivory trade. Zanzibar's prime concern was the encouragement and control of commerce, which largely determined the form and extent of its political involvement on the mainland. This is why Zanzibar's presence was so strongly felt on the coast across from the island, whereas on the periphery, at the most northern tip on the Benadir coast or the most southern around Cap Delgado, the political and commercial impact of Zanzibar's rule was comparatively weak.

Perhaps the most important economic measure the Sultan undertook was the creation of Zanzibar's commercial monopoly in the overseas ivory trade.[131] From the early years of the century onwards, overseas merchants, mainly British, German, French and American, were prevented either by agreement or by treaty from buying directly from coastal merchants. If they wanted to purchase ivory, they had to go to Zanzibar instead. Since both the volume of the trade and the export prices on the international markets rose during the nineteenth century, the Sultanate of Zanzibar enjoyed increasing customs revenues, most of which were generated by taxing ivory imports coming into Zanzibar from the coast and the interior.[132] Moreover, the Sultan himself was heavily engaged in trade. The monopoly of the overseas ivory trade was the main pillar on which Zanzibar's wealth rested in the nineteenth century.

The second pillar of Zanzibar's prosperity was the expansion of commercial agriculture on the island, based on the importation of slave labour.[133] In the early years of the nineteenth century various export crops such as cloves, nutmeg, sugar cane and coffee were tried. Clove plantations proved to be the most profitable. Seedlings are said to have been brought to Zanzibar by an Arab merchant who had visited Réunion and Mauritius (then called the Mascarene Islands). Originally from the Moluccas in eastern Indonesia, cloves had probably already thrived there in the islands since the 1770s. From about 1810 onwards, large tracts of land in Zanzibar, previously used for growing food crops, were converted into commercial clove plantations, especially in the 1830s when a 'clove mania' seemed to have gripped the island. The clove plantations brought great wealth and power to Zanzibar's rulers and their followers, at least in the first half of the nineteenth century. However, by 1840 the great clove boom had already come to an end as prices on the international markets began to decline. Despite rising production costs and higher taxation, exports continued to increase between 1840 and 1870, at least partially offsetting the loss sustained by falling world market prices. Eventually, the profitability of the industry declined somewhat towards the end of the nineteenth century. Moreover, in the early 1870s the industry suffered from the combined effects of suppression of the seaborne slave trade and a devastating hurricane, which put many marginal plantations out of production.[134]

The import of large numbers of slaves to the island provided a great stimulus for the East African slave trade. But it should be noted that Zanzibari merchants and plantation owners did not introduce commercial slave trading or slavery into the region. After all, its origins probably date back to long before East Africa became part of the Indian Ocean trade network in the fourteenth century.[135] Slave exports from the coast were comparatively small until the eighteenth century when they dramatically increased. At that time, trade largely centred on the port of Kilwa in the south. Probably pioneered by Yao traders from northern Mozambique, Kilwa developed into the terminus of slave caravans from the densely populated areas around Lake Malawi (Lake Nyasa), the first long-distance trade route to be established in East Africa by which slaves from the interior reached the Tanganyikan coast.[136]

In the earlier part of the eighteenth century, slave exports were primarily directed towards the north, that is Southern Arabia, the Persian Gulf and western Indian markets.[137] But this trade was insignificant compared with the slave exports to the Mascarene Islands, where the French had established slave plantations that started to produce sizeable quantities of sugar and coffee on the Caribbean model in the second half of the eighteenth century.[138] French slave traders were most active in the 1770s and 1780s. They bought several thousand slaves each year, most of them directly from the coast, mainly from Kilwa.[139] But in the last decade of the eighteenth century the French slave trade from Kilwa had already declined and was brought to an end in 1810 when Mauritius fell to the British towards the end of the Napoleonic wars. Yet, slave exports from southern ports, notably from Kilwa to Madagascar, continued, though now under the firm control of merchants based in Zanzibar, since Kilwa had lost its commercial independence following the imposition of Zanzibari authority in the major trading towns on the coast.[140]

In the early years of the slave trade based in Zanzibar, the majority of slaves were imported from the coast and then re-exported to northern destinations, but when clove plantations were expanded in the early part of the nineteenth century, internal demand for slave labour rapidly increased. Thus it is estimated that by the 1810s Zanzibar imported about 8,000 slaves annually, most of them from Kilwa. Their numbers increased in the late 1830s and early 1840s to about 13,000, peaking in the later half of the 1860s and early 1870s, when perhaps between 15,000 to 20,000 slaves landed on the islands each year.[141] The majority of these slaves came to work on Zanzibar plantations, but a substantial number of them were still being re-exported to the north. In 1866/7, for instance, the town of Lamu, on what later became the Kenyan coast, was a major customer, obtaining more than 5,000 slaves from Zanzibar.[142]

According to Burton, by the mid-1850s the slave trade based in Zanzibar had already reached far beyond the confines of the coast.[143] An indication of this development is the different prices paid for slaves in different places. Slaves could be bought comparatively cheaply in Ujiji and the areas bordering Lake Tanganyika and Lake Victoria, where Zanzibari presence was relatively insignificant.[144] They were more costly in Tabora, while they were at their most expensive on the coast, particularly in Zanzibar. Burton also reports that at that time the prices for female slaves were generally higher than those for male slaves of the same age, although there were great variations within the respective age and gender groups. Younger slaves, for instance, generally obtained higher prices than older slaves. The highest prices were paid for male slaves with particular skills (in ki-Swahili, *mafundi*, sing. *fundi*) and younger female slaves.[145]

From 1873 onwards, however, the slave trade based in Zanzibar began to decline. Sultan Barghash b. Said was forced by the British consul in Zanzibar to agree to a treaty outlawing slave shipments from the Sultan's possessions and areas of influence on the mainland to Zanzibar. Shipments between the islands which constititute the Zanzibar archipelago, Pemba and Unguja, were also banned. The treaty also gave the British naval squadron sweeping powers to search and, if necessary, impound any ship believed to be carrying slaves or which could be used for that purpose. For some time, a sizeable clandestine trade seems to have continued to supply Zanzibar, especially the Pemba plantations, where they fetched particularly high prices, with an unknown number of slaves.[146] They came from nearby coastal ports such as Pangani and Bagamoyo, where slaves were brought overland in their thousands from southern coastal locations or from the interior. [147] The overseas slave trade only finally came to an end in the 1890s when the German colonial administration established its presence on the coast, controlling towns, villages and smaller riverside outlets which had previously functioned as departure points for slave shipments to Zanzibar.

The development in the ivory trade took quite a different turn.[148] In the eighteenth and early nineteenth centuries, trade was largely directed towards India, a pattern that had been established much earlier. In the eighteenth century the trade was conducted from Mozambique and the southern coast and was rather limited in scope. In the late eighteenth century, however, internal strife in Mozambique in the wake of excessive slave raiding for the French as well as increased taxation by the Portuguese gradually drove Yao traders northwards, in particular to the town of Kilwa. This enabled both Zanzibari and coastal traders to take advantage of the worldwide expansion of the ivory trade and the accompanying increase in ivory prices due to a dramatic rise in the demand from Europe and elsewhere.[149] In the fifty years between 1823 and 1873 the price of ivory increased from MT$ (Maria Theresa Dollar) 23 a *frasila* to MT$ 89 a *frasila* (about 35 lb or 16 kg).[150] Initially, overseas buyers obtained East African ivory in Bombay, but in the 1830s and 1840s American, British, French and German as well as Indian and Arab merchants arrived in Zanzibar in growing numbers to obtain ivory more cheaply. Subsequently, supplying ivory to Zanzibar proved an enormous incentive to both short-distance coastal as well as long-distance caravan trade.

Initially, the demand for ivory, slaves and other export commodities impacted strongest on coastal towns and their immediate hinterland, creating economic opportunities for coastal traders, although on a much smaller scale than in Zanzibar itself, since they were not directly linked with international markets.[151] Coastal traders were not wealthy enough to participate fully in the expansion of trade on their own. They had to rely on the credit supplied mostly by Indian merchants based in Zanzibar, for which they often paid a heavy price in the form of excessive interest rates.

In the latter half of the eighteenth and the early nineteenth centuries, trade was carried out through some kind of relay system.[152] Small quantities of merchandise, including slaves, were sold through many hands and markets until they reached their final destination. Most of the coastal export commodities – especially ivory, slaves, gum copal and sesame, but also more commonplace commodities such as tobacco, millet, maize and dried fish – were either purchased directly on the coast or brought down from nearby markets, for instance Vuga in the Usambara Mountains in the north or the Makonde plateau in the south.[153] They were exchanged on the coast for locally made goods but also increasingly for small quantities of imported commodities which were sought after in the interior, such as cotton cloth, arms and various luxury items. As the nineteenth century progressed, imported commodities, particularly American cotton cloth, became available to a growing number of potential consumers, at first only on the coast but later extending to the hinterland along the trading routes. Consumers were not just chiefs and town notables but also lower social groups, such as traders, artisans, farmers and porters, and even slaves.[154]

In the early half of the nineteenth century, slave and ivory traders, as well as traders in other commodities, began a large-scale expansion of their operational field into the interior.[155] Financed by merchants of mostly Indian origin based in Zanzibar who provided imported commodities on a long-term credit basis, they began to organise trading expeditions. In the second half of the nineteenth century these consisted of hundreds, occasionally even thousands of traders, porters and soldiers who travelled along the entire length of the caravan routes between the Indian Ocean and the Great Lakes (Nyasa, Tanganyika and Victoria), and sometimes even beyond.[156] These expeditions could sometimes take several years. Thus, though the small-scale relay trade continued and may even have increased, nineteenth-century expansion was at least partly due to the introduction of novel forms of wholesale commerce which, while reacting to the westward movement of the ivory frontier, took advantage of the lucrative opportunities arising from the long-distance caravan trade.

Yet it should not be forgotten that, at least up to about mid-century, caravan routes on the mainland were not dominated by traders from the coast or from Zanzibar. In the early part of the century, Yao, Makonde and Nyamwezi traders from the interior controlled the supply of ivory and slaves to the coast and to Zanzibar. At that time, 'Arab' or 'Swahili' traders were at best tolerated in the interior, and it was only through their access to commercial long-term credit and the expansion of Zanzibar's political power on the coast that they were finally able to gain the upper hand over their 'African' competitors in the long-distance wholesale trade in the second half of the nineteenth century.[157] Moreover, there were limits to coastal political and commercial expansion. Even at the height of caravan trade, the political might of the Sultan of Zanzibar was strictly limited and fragmented in the interior. Coastal traders had to compromise their commercial advantages once they were confronted with powerful, large-scale political units. More importantly, rapid commercial expansion had rested on the over-exploitation and depletion of limited animal resources. By the late 1870s most of Tanganyika's ivory had been hunted down, and competition from the north (Sudan) and the west (Angola) limited Zanzibar's westward expansion.[158]

In the course of the nineteenth century, the importance of coastal towns as the termini of long-distance caravan routes grew enormously. At the same time, the number of ships calling at the ports multiplied. Coastal maritime trade boomed particularly in the second half of the nineteenth century. During this period the towns became more closely linked not only to each other but also to ports located further away, such as Aden, Sur and Muscat on the Arabian Peninsula, and Bombay in India.[159] The most important staple places on the south coast were Lindi, Mikindani and Kilwa, the latter having somewhat recovered from losses sustained by the termination of the French slave trade. In 1840 almost a third of all ivory imports to Zanzibar came from Kilwa.[160] On the north coast, Tanga and Pangani served the northern caravan route which ran in a north-westerly direction along the Pangani river valley towards the Kilimanjaro region and beyond, while Saadani, Bagamoyo and Mbwamaji near Dar es Salaam were the termini for the great central caravan route, the single most important avenue towards central Tanganyika in the second half of the nineteenth century.[161] An indication of their importance can be seen in the fact that in 1870 about half of Zanzibar's imports from the mainland originated from these three towns. The caravans leaving the coast first converged on the Uluguru Mountains, only to branch off in a north-westerly direction leading to Tabora, and a south-westerly direction heading towards the southern tip of Lake Tanganyika.[162]

In this connection it should be mentioned that coastal people derived considerable profits from servicing the caravan trade, supplying food and shelter for porters and caravan leaders, as well as providing storage and maritime transport facilities for the goods they carried. In the nineteenth century, the principal towns on the coast were not just staple places but also the sites where traders and merchants met to conduct their commercial transactions, where caravan leaders employed porters and bought provisions, and where on the return from a successful journey, traders, merchants and porters alike celebrated their good fortune with elaborate feasts.[163] This was a considerable business. According to one observer, the population of Bagamoyo increased during the trading season from between 10,000 to 15,000, to as much as from 20,000 to 25,000. These people had to be fed and housed, but – perhaps even more importantly – they bought and consumed goods produced on the coast.[164]

Thus, in the first half of the nineteenth century commerce spread deep into the interior. Enterprising chiefs and smaller farmers quickly learnt to exploit the commercial opportunities provided by caravans passing through their areas of residence.[165] By levying taxes for the provision of foodstuffs and protection, by petty trading or taking up short-term wage employment as porters, many people who lived along the trade routes were drawn into the coastal commercial economy. Consequently, consumption of imported goods such as cloth increased rapidly in the interior, though geographically at a highly uneven pace. However, people living near the trade routes also began to fear the caravans. Some caravans used extortion and violence to obtain provisions, and anxiety over family members being kidnapped by passing caravans was probably never far from the surface.[166] This is perhaps one of the main reasons why certain villages situated along the caravan routes were fortified in the second half of the nineteenth century, while other villages were abandoned by their inhabitants, who moved to more secure areas such as the higher reaches of the Uluguru mountain range.[167] In the same period, political and social relations, particularly those between chiefs and their subjects, also changed.

In the coastal hinterland villages were increasingly ruled by warlords who did business with coastal traders and merchants, exchanging ivory, slaves and the agricultural surplus they had taken as 'tribute' from their subjects and neighbours. In return, they obtained imported prestige goods and arms, which they distributed among their personal followers.[168] Strongmen like Kingo in Uluguru, Semboja in Shambaa or Mandara of Moshi undermined older verities and traditions of political legitimacy as commercial relations with the coast gave them access to alternative sources of wealth, power and prestige.[169]

In addition to commerce, the character of coastal agriculture changed during the course of the nineteenth century. With the establishment of clove plantations, Zanzibar and Pemba were less and less able to produce sufficient foodstuffs for their growing population, especially for the Zanzibar 'aristocracy'. This created a large and ready market for food crops grown on the mainland and the coast, especially in the hinterland of towns like Mombasa, Takaungu, Malindi, Pangani, Kilwa and Lindi. From about 1840 onwards, a number of coastal merchants as well as some wealthy immigrants from Zanzibar and other parts began to invest their capital in agriculture. They acquired substantial landholdings which they worked with agricultural slaves in order to supply Zanzibar's and – to a lesser extent – South Arabian markets with fruit, beans and grain, especially maize, sesame and millet.[170] They also established extensive coconut, rice and sugar plantations, the latter especially on the northern Tanzanian coast.[171] In the 1870s and 1880s the commercialisation of plantation agriculture on the coast advanced considerably. This was partly due to a fall in international clove prices, prompting Zanzibari financiers and merchants to seek more profitable outlets for their capital on the mainland. It was also due, however, to the abundance of slave labour in coastal towns such as Pangani (sugar plantations), Dar es Salaam (coconut plantations) and Kilwa (food crop plantations and farms) that served as entrepôts for the then largely illegal overseas slave trade. In any case, these new plantations and farms were not just producing food crops for Zanzibar markets, but also agricultural products of increasingly high quality. Sugar, for example, was exchanged in the interior for ivory, other foodstuffs and even slaves, while sesame was exported to Zanzibar for re-export to Europe.[172] In terms of size and working conditions for slaves, some of these plantations represented an innovation in the organisation of coastal agriculture. Like their counterparts elsewhere in the Indian Ocean, plantation owners in East Africa attempted to practise a particularly regimented form of slavery.[173] Slaves on these plantations were almost reduced to chattels, to an expendable factor of production that could easily be replaced by acquiring fresh labour on the markets created by the overseas slave trade.

Agricultural expansion on the coast was greatly aided by falling slave prices.[174] The successive anti-slave-trade treaties between Britain and Zanzibar (1822, 1839, 1845, 1873) as well as the gradually more effective policing of trade routes increasingly curtailed the scope, volume and profits of the overseas slave trade.[175] Moreover, the demand for slaves in Zanzibar stagnated from about mid-century onwards. Consequently, slave prices dropped along the caravan routes and on the coast as massive supplies still came forward from the interior.[176] During this period, coastal areas such as the Pangani rice and sugar estates, for example, absorbed the greater part of the slaves arriving on the coast and only the remainder was exported to Zanzibar and Pemba.[177] It is estimated that slave prices fell by half on the coast between the 1780s and 1820s, dropping another 25 per cent after the treaty of 1847. A further decline probably occurred in the 1870s.[178] As the demand for agricultural produce increased and production costs in the form of slave prices steadily decreased, commercial agriculture based on slave labour thrived on the coast for much of the second half of the nineteenth century and probably reached its height just before the colonial conquest.[179]

Coastal plantation owners, traders and merchants were, however, not the only group who profited from agricultural expansion. In the second half of the nineteenth century, leading Makonde and Ngindo families in the hinterland of Lindi and Mikindani, and Zaramo and Zigua chiefs living in the southern environs of Bagamoyo joined the move towards commercial agriculture. They greatly extended their farms in the hinterland adjacent to the coast, bought increasing numbers of slaves from the interior and sold their products on Zanzibar markets.[180] Finally, and perhaps of equal importance, a growing participation of small peasants was evident at the food crop markets located in the coastal towns.[181] In the first third of the nineteenth century, the majority of coastal rural cultivators were primarily engaged in self-sufficient food crop production. The economic boom on the coast drew more and more people to urban markets, selling their surplus, so that by the last third of the century coastal agriculture had become closely intertwined with the commercial economy.[182]

Economic, social and cultural factors also contributed to the emergence of food and export crop plantations on the coast. When some of the coastal merchants became landowners in the 1840s, they followed a path that had been set earlier by members of the Zanzibar elite. The caravan trade was a notoriously high-risk and arduous business. Investing in land and possessing slaves allowed coastal traders and merchants a lifestyle more commensurate with what they believed was expected of a landed 'Arab aristocracy'. This particular lifestyle became the model for the coast (see below).[183]

It should also be mentioned that the increase in trade and agricultural production on the coast supported the development of a highly diversified craft industry, comprising artisans (*mafundi*) of various professions, including shipbuilders, blacksmiths, net and basket makers, carvers, bricklayers, tailors, shoemakers and, already in the 1860s, watch menders.[184] The craft industry had been in existence for a long time, probably since the original formation of coastal society around the first millennium. In the nineteenth century, however, it grew enormously as products were sold not only locally but also all over the mainland and in Zanzibar. These *mafundi* were not necessarily free-born 'citizens', but often slaves (see Chapter 3); the vast majority of them were men, as women tended to be excluded from such professions.[185]

Up to about the mid-nineteenth century, coastal towns were ruled by a small number of elite families whose social prestige depended on their Islamic education, their wealth, a certain lifestyle and their putative Shirazi descent (that is, the probably fictive antiquity of their arrival on the coast).[186] Through marriage alliances with other ruling families, their power went far beyond the confines of their individual towns. Towns-people who owned sizeable plantations in the rural areas had particularly strong social ties to the countryside, as these were farmed by their personal dependants, debtors and slaves. The social prestige of these families was measured by the number of clients they had and the largesse they could display in public. Apart from Islamic erudition, wealth was the principal male avenue to rank and authority in the towns, especially if it had been generated in the caravan trade; women, on the other hand, were basically considered to be of inferior status, even though some of them were of elite origin and had inherited substantial plantations, urban property and numerous slaves.[187]

At the other end of the social scale were those who had arrived on the coast just recently, whose descent status or 'Muslim' credentials were questionable and, above all, who possessed no discernible wealth. As clients, they were more or less dependent for their livelihoods on their patrons, mostly members of the land-owning elite and the urban rich. Many slaves belonged to this social stratum since they could only trace their ancestry back to distant parts of the interior, if at all. They had no economic resources of their own and little knowledge of coastal social values, language or modes of behaviour.

The middling strata were made up of artisans, small farmers, retail traders, self-employed fishermen and sea captains who possessed their own boats. Significantly, during the second half of the nineteenth century, these middling strata also began to own slaves in increasing and probably greater numbers than those who worked on the plantations of the elite[188] – although an outside observer could hardly discern any difference in the living conditions of slaves and their owners, as they shared the same single-storied, palm-thatched house and dressed in the same manner, particularly on working days.[189]

Members of elite families regarded themselves as 'civilised', not least because of their corporate Shirazi identity, which, they thought, set them apart from other African people, especially 'non-believers' in the interior. In self-reference they often used the ki-Swahili term *waungwana* (sing. *mwungwana*) or 'coastal gentlemen' in order to accentuate their honour (in ki-Swahili, *heshima*) and highlight their difference from those at the other end of the social scale, whom they despised as dishonourable *washenzi* (sing. *shenzi*) or 'barbarians'.[190] Many elite *waungwana* regarded themselves as members of the leisured classes. As the missionary New noted somewhat critically in 1873, 'The male *munguana* ... is altogether above work. Work is the badge of the slave, and it is, therefore, in his estimation disgraceful.'[191]

As Pouwels has pointed out, a *mwungwana* was believed to be 'a person who dressed in a certain way, ate certain foods, earned his livelihood in certain ways, attended his prayers assiduously, lived in certain types of houses, behaved in certain ways in public, and above all, spoke the vernacular Swahili well'.[192] In contrast, a *mshenzi* was a person who usually did not even wear a *kanzu* (ankle-length white gown), who did manual work in the fields, probably lived in the countryside in a thatched hut, professed non-Muslim beliefs and spoke ki-Swahili with great difficulty. From the point of view of the coastal elite, the word *washenzi* was basically a disparaging expression for people living in the interior as well as a derogatory term for the urban and rural poor on the coast, the majority of whom were slaves.[193]

In the middle of the nineteenth century, Swahili society was thus stratified between the rich and the poor, between those who possessed land and had it worked by others and those who cultivated land they could not call their own, between various newcomers and 'ancient' − supposedly Shiraz − families, between patrons and clients, and, last but not least, between slave owners and slaves.[194] However, despite these seemingly clear-cut social divisions, in principle it was possible to advance within coastal social hierarchies and become a respected member of urban society, because social status depended largely on the possession of personal wealth, and because, in spite of the many overseas cultural influences, mainland and coastal cultures shared many common features.[195] Access to coastal secular and religious knowledge was to a certain extent open to all new-comers, even to slaves.[196] As Pouwels phrased it: 'within the towns there was a "sphere of public knowledge" which was accessible to all who lived in the community, the essentials of which had to be mastered by all who hoped to be accepted as *waungwana*'.[197] This enabled some of those who came from the interior to the coast, especially if they had gained wealth, clients and political influence, to improve their former lowly status dramatically. Significantly, many coastal people called themselves *waungwana* while travelling in the interior, whether they were of slave origin or free-born.[198] Being *waungwana* was thus not a clearly defined status but often just a claim, which was more or less disputed by other members of the coastal urban community.[199] They were not fundamental social opposites, akin to class divisions in industrial societies, but rather vague and often ambiguous assertions of honour and pretensions of wealth.[200] Within two or three generations, imagined genealogies and the acquisition of a measure of wealth and coastal manners, such as proper speech and dress, obscured the more humble origins of many coastal 'gentlemen' and, indeed, 'gentle-women'. For this reason, many of the social conflicts in coastal towns arose from claims and counter-claims to status and prestige.[201] The fluidity of these social attributes is shown by the fact that slaves from the coast travelling as traders or porters in the interior often seem to have claimed *waungwana* status.[202]

However, the ascendance of Zanzibar in the nineteenth century changed local perception of social status. Three factors seem to have been responsible for this development. First, whereas 'Arabness' (in ki-Swahili, *ustaarabu*) was probably not regarded as a foundational principle for social status up to about mid-century, the apparent wealth and ensuing social prestige of the Omani elite in Zanzibar convinced members of the coastal elite to 'Arabise' their life style. This was expressed in dress, manners, embroidered genealogies and elaborate religious rituals and practices – but above all in the change from *uungwana* to *ustaarabu* as the common way to describe the desired state of 'being civilised'.[203]

Second, during the course of the second half of the nineteenth century, the older leading Shirazi families of the coastal towns gradually lost out to newcomers from Zanzibar. Initially only appointed as temporary town governors (*maliwali*), over the years a number of elite Zanzibari families acquired substantial holdings of urban property and *mashamba* (sing. *shamba*) estates from the *waungwana* families, slowly undermining the political power of local office holders, the *wajumbe* (sing. *jumbe*). These offices had been the prerogative of older *waungwana* families and the *wajumbe* did not welcome the intrusion into their political domain, especially as they had derived increasing personal wealth from this position throughout the nineteenth century.[204] Still, some Omani families from Zanzibar had gained an important say in town affairs by the 1870s. Moreover, older coastal traders and merchants were increasingly deprived of participation in the ivory trade because they could not compete with the newcomers in the long-distance trade. Zanzibar merchants had comparatively easy access to commodities and long-term credit, something the coastal traders did not have. Losing one of their main sources of income, the older Shirazi families ran into debt, especially to Indian merchants and financiers who had come to settle on the coast. Although the lifestyle of the coastal Indians was modest, their wealth easily rivalled that of members of the old elite, especially after lending the latter large amounts of money at often exorbitantly high interest rates.[205]

Finally, in the course of the nineteenth century, the size and composition of the urban and rural low-income strata underwent a transformation. In the early part of the century, manual labour in towns and on farms was performed mainly by poor people who came from the interior (the *washenzi* mentioned above) and from areas adjacent to the coast (the *wanyika*, sing. *nyika*) and most probably also by some slaves. Towards the end of the century, not least because of the expansion of commercial agriculture, imported and locally born slaves came to dominate this stratum. Moreover, as the coastal plantation economy grew and work practices changed, their number greatly increased. By the end of the nineteenth century, a stage was reached in which agricultural slaves accounted for over half the local population in some of the coastal districts.[206]

It is, therefore, hardly surprising that in the second half of the nineteenth century the above-mentioned self-appellation 'Shirazi' gained much wider currency among the coastal elite. Threatened from above by wealthy Zanzibari newcomers taking over important political offices and needled from below by slaves and other low-status groups striving for participation in urban commercial and communal life, the coastal elite accentuated their difference by highlighting their descent from Shiraz – that is, their putative intimate association with a region of great Islamic learning and commercial prosperity.[207] Thus, in the second half of the nineteenth century, coastal society became more exclusive. As social and cultural divisions deepened, social mobility between the various status groups declined.[208] One important outward indicator of this development was that social conflict centring on the legitimate participation of low-status groups in town and community life increased.[209]

At this point, some tentative conclusions can be drawn regarding the similarities and differences between the experiences in Unyamwezi and on the coast. The ruling elites of both Unyamwezi and the coast eagerly exploited commercial opportunities offered by the rise of Zanzibar, the commercial expansion of the caravan trade and of agriculture production. Both in Unyamwezi and on the coast commercial expansion rested to a considerable extent on the import and use of large numbers of slaves. But there were also differences. Political divisions within the coastal strip were not as pronounced as in Unyamwezi, as they were overlaid by the incorporation of the coast into the political structures of the Zanzibar Empire. Therefore, the militarisation of political relations, which deeply marked Unyamwezi in the second half of the century, did not occur on the coast, though its immediate hinterland was probably as severely ruptured by the rise of the trading warlords. On the other hand, the establishment of plantations on the coast engendered social conflicts that differed from those occasioned by the emergence of commercial agriculture in Unyamwezi. Internal social divisions became much more pronounced on the coast, especially in the latter half of the nineteenth century when older working practices and social hierarchies rapidly changed and status conflicts emerged as a consequence. As will be shown in the following chapter, these conflicts were embedded and expressed in the structure and language of patron–client relationships on the coast. In Unyamwezi, however, the importance of family and kinship relations, and the role of slaves therein, appears to have remained paramount, despite the fact that 'social interaction was increasingly mediated through market relations'.

Notes

1   For a brief discussion of the 'insider/outsider' problem, see Glassman 1991: 279, 283ff., 289, 298.
2   The phrase 'radical uncertainty' was first used by D. B. Davis in an article in the *New York Review of Books* about the transatlantic slave trade (17 October 1996: 51). It is cited in Finley 1998: 13.
3   For a brief introduction to the history of slavery and the slave trade in East Africa in the nineteenth century, see Feierman 1995: 352–76. See also Iliffe 1979: 40–88.
4   Iliffe 1979: 50.
5   Glassman 1995: 36.
6   For an overview, see Iliffe 1979: 40–87, Alpers 1975a, and Sheriff 1987: 33–76. For a detailed estimate of the export slave trade in the nineteenth century, see Martin and Ryan 1977: 71–91. For somewhat different figures, see Austen 1989: 21–44. For a very

detailed contemporary account, see University of Birmingham Library, Church Missionary Society (CMS) Archives, CA 5016/179, 'Memoir on the East African Slave Trade etc' by J. L. Krapf, Rabai Mpia [Mombasa], 1853.

7   See, for instance, Krapf 1858, Burton 1860, Speke 1863, Livingstone 1874, Elton 1879, Wissmann 1889, Hore 1892, and Kandt 1914. For administrative reports, see, for instance, BAB RKolA 7382, Material über die Sklavenfrage, 1891–1901.

8   Iliffe 1979: 73. It appears, for instance, that the ki-Nyakyusa speaking peoples in the south-east abstained from involvement in slavery or the slave trade. For evidence on the widespread incidence of slavery in nineteenth-century Tanzania, see BAB RKolA 4997/1-503, 'Beantwortung des Fragebogens über die Rechte der Eingeborenen in den deutschen Kolonien', various dates [1909–1913]. See also Dundas 1921: 263–6. For the history of the 'Fragebogen', see Redmayne 1982: 22–8 and Sippel 1997: 714–38.

9   For examples, see Rhodes House Oxford (in the following RHO) Micr Afr 472 R.19/MF 42, Tabora Regional Book, 'Extracts from Nyamwezi Law and Custom by H. Cory', 1952: 6, Reichard 1890: 277, Tawney 1944: 6–9, Hartwig 1977: 261–85 and Feierman 1974: 174–6, 1995: 368.

10 Alpers 1975a. For a discussion of this issue, see Sheriff 1987: 155ff.

11 Roberts 1970: 49. This and the following paragraphs have greatly profited from Abrahams 1967a, Roberts 1968: 117–50, Roberts 1970: 39–74, Unomah 1972: 75–125, Sheriff 1987: 155–200, Rockel 2000a: 173–95.

12 Iliffe 1979: 80.

13 Nolan 1977: 21.

14 For the first contemporary discussion of the problem, see Burton 1860: 280–4. He asserts that the term Unyamwezi was already in use in the seventeenth century, probably even in the sixteenth century. For subsequent attempts to define 'Unyamwezi', see Reichard 1890: 228ff., Bösch 1930: 3–21, Blohm 1931 vol. I: 6–10, RHO Micr Afr 472 R.19/MF 42, Tabora Regional Book, 'Notes on Banyamwezi', 6 May 1932. For the history of the nineteenth-century 'exploration' of Unyamwezi, see Blohm 1931 vol. I: 1–6.

15 Abrahams 1967a: 24, Nolan 1977: 23ff. See also Rockel 2000a: 175.

16 In early colonial times the great majority of the inhabitants of Tabora district were believed to be ki-Nyamwezi speakers, but it should be noted that other language groups lived among them. See RHO Micr Afr 472 R.19/MF 42, Tabora Regional Book, 'Notes on Banyamwezi', 6 May 1932. For the geographical extension of Tabora district in the German colonial period, see Map 2 in Chapter 3.

17 The first Nyamwezi word list was probably compiled by Bishop Edward Steere. See Steere 1871.

18 Burton 1860: 284. See also Roberts 1968: 120.

19 See, for instance, Speke 1863.

20 Burton 1860: 285.

21 For more details on cattle in Unyamwezi, see Kjekshus 1996: 44, 62–4.

22 RHO Micr Afr 472 R.21/MF 46, Kigoma District Book, 'Native Administration: The Wajiji', 13 July 1931. See also Grant 1864: 51 and Blohm 1931 vol. II: 36 [extract from interview, n.d. (pre-1914)].

23 Pieces of cloth bearing a trade mark such as 'Massachusetts Sheeting' were particularly sought after. According to Grant (1864: 87), 'the man who got the stamped portion was thought a considerable swell'. For the local cotton-weaving industry, see Reichard 1890: 276.

24 Sutton and Roberts 1968: 45–86. See also Iliffe 1979: 19.

25 For a recent summary (and an extensive bibliography), see Rockel 2000a: 175–9.

26 For an extensive contemporary description of mid-nineteenth century commercial practices, see Burton 1860: 527–44, especially 538–40 (ivory trade). For the later period, see also Velten 1903: 284–301.

27 Tippu Tip 1902: 268. Tippu Tip's autobiography , *Maisha ya Hamed bin Muhammed el Murjebi Yaani Tippu Tip* (ed. and tr. W. H. Whiteley), Nairobi 1966, was first published by H. Brode as 'Autobiographie des Arabers Schech Hamed bin Muhammed el Murjebi, genannt Tippu Tip', *Mitteilungen des Seminars für orientalische Sprachen*, 1902: 175–277, 1903: 1–55. The same text has also been translated into French by Bontinck (1974) with comprehensive notes and an extensive bibliography.

28 Krapf 1858 vol. II: 181, 279. See also Roberts 1970: 50.

29 This chapter has profited greatly from Stephen Rockel's 1997 PhD thesis (as yet unpublished) on caravan porters in nineteenth-century Tanzania. Some of the material can be found in articles and conference papers. See Rockel 1995a, 1995b, 1998, 2000a and 2000b.

30 For a contemporary depiction of these porters, see Sheriff 1987: 178, plate 27. They are also described in great detail by Burton 1860: 153, 169, 186, 237ff. See also Krapf 1858 vol. II: 182, Cameron 1877 vol. I: 78 and Tippu Tip 1902: 198. See also Beidelman 1982: 602 and Rockel 2000a: 182.

31 Burton reports that in Unyamwezi caravan leaders or guides were also called *kirangozi* in ki-Swahili. See Burton 1860: 240. For more details on caravan organisation, see Beidelman 1982: 617–21 and Rockel 2000a: 180–5.

32 Roberts 1970: 66. On the dangers of the caravan trade, see Tippu Tip 1902: 208.

33 Roberts 1968: 128. For an extensive discussion on the payment of bridewealth in Unyamwezi, see Bösch 1930: 348–99, Blohm 1931 vol. II: 90–9. See also RHO Micr Afr 472 R.19/MF 42, Tabora Regional Book, 'Extracts from Nyamwezi Law and Custom by H. Cory', 1952: 6. According to Blohm (1931 vol. II: 90) bridewealth payments consisted of cattle, guns, slaves, cloth and iron hoes. See also Löbner 1910, cited in Gottberg 1971: 149ff. For the increase in bridewealth following commercial expansion in the hinterland of Mombasa in the nineteenth century, see Willis 1993a: 69ff.

34 Burton 1860: 235.

35 Unomah 1972: 100.

36 Roberts 1970: 66.

37 Reichard 1892: 485 and Kandt 1914: 45, 139ff. According to colonial records, in the year 1900/1 exactly 35,665 adult porters left Tabora for the coast, of which 2,858 were said to be women. See 'Jahresbericht der Station Tabora 1900/1901, Bezirkschef Gansser 20. Juni 1991', cited in Dauber 1991: 255. For female traders and caravan porters in nineteenth-century Tanzania, see Rockel 2000b, 748–78, especially 757ff.

38 See Grant: 1864: 43 and Reichard 1892: 465, 485. See also Wright 1993: 182 and Rockel 1998: 17.

39 By the mid-century, consumption patterns in Unyamwezi had begun to change. The local cotton cloth industry is a good example of this process. It apparently suffered severely from competition with imports manufactured either in India, the US or Europe. People attached special social prestige to the consumption of imported cloth, and as more and more people were able to afford it, local cloth industries declined. See Grant 1864: 87. See also Kjekshus 1996: 105–9.

40 Roberts 1970: 66.

41 Roberts 1970: 68.

42 Cameron 1877 vol. II: 117ff., 168. See also Roberts 1971: 9ff., Birmingham and Martin 1983: 131–3 and Wright 1993: 156–60.

43 Sheriff 1987: 182. For a different view, see Rockel 2000a: 186.

44 Burton 1860: 238.

45 Burton 1860: 46. See also Toeppen 1885–6: 225.

46 See Burton 1860: 538–40, Reichard 1892: 435–44.

47 This movement is already noted by Burton, who visited Unyamwezi in 1857. See Burton 1860: 318. See also Grant 1864: 48.

48 When Burton visited Kazeh in 1857, its 'Arab' population probably did not exceed a dozen households. He counted some six *tembe* although there were others in a village nearby. See Burton 1860: 228. See also Tippu Tip 1902: 180. It should be noted that the population of Kazeh fluctuated heavily during the trading seasons. Thus it is very difficult to estimate with any degree of accuracy the size of the 'Arab' population in the interior in the second half of the nineteenth century. The best description of Ujiji in the late 1870s can be found in Hore 1971 [1877–88]: 66–151. For a description of Tabora in the early 1870s, see Livingstone 1874: 182 (3 May 1871); for the early 1880s, see Reichard 1890: 66ff., Reichard 1892: 344ff. and, for the early 1890s, Stuhlmann 1894: 58–94 and Baumann 1894: 105ff. For a detailed drawing of a *tembe*, see Cameron 1877 vol. I: 131 and Stuhlmann 1894: 65. Note that in the early 1890s the commercial situation in Tabora significantly changed for the worse. Owing largely to the discontinuation of the ivory trade with the Belgium Congo, the population declined, although by the early 1900s it had started to grow again. See Baumann 1894: 105, 245

and Becher 1997: 58.

49   Sheriff 1987: 179. See also Brown 1971: 617–29 and Unomah 1972: 82ff., 117. It should be noted that, as Unomah writes, in Tabora not all coastal migrants were or became rich merchants. By the 1870s a number of decidedly poorer 'Arabs' had followed the coastal traders and merchants, earning their living in Tabora as artisans (tailors, rope makers) or as small-scale rice farmers.

50   RHO Micr Afr 472 R.20/MF 44, Tabora District Book, 'Notes on an Interview with Jaba bin Zaid by Assistant District Officer N. Burt', 24 May 1927.

51   Unomah 1972: 81.

52   Sheriff 1987: 191, Map 5.1: The Hinterland of Zanzibar, *c.* 1873 and Kwamena-Poh 1992: 39. See also Burton 1860: 227 and Holmes 1971: 477–503.

53   Tippu Tip 1902: 183, 201–3. Even after Nyamwezi traders had lost their predominant position in the wholesale trade, independent small-scale trade with the coast continued for some time, although at a reduced scale. It came to an end in the early colonial period when Indian retail traders arrived in Tabora and drove Nyamwezi traders out of the local market. See Blohm 1931 vol. I: 171. See also Rockel 2000a: 186–9. On the role of Indian financiers in the caravan trade, see Tominaga 1996: 295–317. For a contemporary report, see Elton 1874: 227–52 and Reichard 1888: 378. For the persistence and organisation of the Nyamwezi trade in early colonial times, see the informative note by Schweinitz 1894a: 18–20.

54   Cameron 1877 vol. II: 20–32. For more details, see Tippu Tip 1902: 248ff., 258. See also Bennett 1971, Bennett 1986: 112–18, Renault 1987 and Hahner–Herzog 1990.

55   Cameron 1877 vol. I: 307.

56   Rockel 1997: 57.

57   Unomah 1972: 97.

58   Beidelman 1982: 614.

59   Roberts 1970: 68. See also Velten 1903: 225.

60   Glassman 1995: 60.

61   Burton 1860: 236. For a different view, see Glassman 1995: 64.

62   This figure is, of course, at best a rough estimate, as more precise data are not available for this period. For contemporary estimates, see Stuhlmann 1894: 89 and Coulbois 1901: 41. See also Raum 1965: 170 and Sheriff 1987: 182.

63   Burton 1860: 257.

64   Reichard 1890: 241.

65   Burton 1860: 236.

66   Bennett 1986: 36.

67   For a detailed description, see Livingstone 1874: 124ff. (18 May 1871). Livingstone notes that the market was attended by about three thousand (!) female traders. See also Baumann 1894: 227–37, Unomah 1972: 105 and Unomah and Webster 1976: 296–7.

68   Abrahams 1967a: 68. See also Bösch 1930: 440ff. and Blohm 1931 vol. I: 166.

69   Sheriff 1987: 182.

70   According to the missionary Burgess, slavery was already common in Unyamwezi by the late 1830s. Therefore it cannot be argued that slavery developed in this particular area exclusively in response to the increasing demand for slaves in other parts of the world economy. See 'Letter from Mr Burgess, dated 11 Sept. 1839', reprinted in Gottberg 1971: 95–7.

71   Baumann 1894: 234. See also Roberts 1970: 59, Unomah and Webster 1976: 284–5 and Sheriff 1987: 181. In this context it should be noted that slave holding was an alternative to holding cattle as a means of storing wealth. Rockel notes that in the first half of the nineteenth century cattle were extensively used for that purpose. After the mid-century, slaves seem to have become a more commonly sought alternative. See Rockel 1997: 110.

72   Reichard 1892: 468. See also Dundas 1921: 265.

73   Nolan 1977: 49, 141ff.

74   See BAB RKolA 7382/27: 89, Berichte der einzelnen Verwaltungsstellen in Deutsch-Ostafrika über die Sklaverei, Station Tabora, Berichterstatter: Hauptmann Puder, n.d. [1900]. These figures are discussed in greater detail in Chapter 3.

75   Burton 1860: 299. See also Unomah 1972: 108.

76   Swann 1969 [1910]: 62, Nolan 1977: 142. In Unyamwezi the title 'chief' covered a great variety of different office holders. On the difficulties of defining chiefship in

Unyamwezi, see the lengthy discussion in RHO Micr Afr 472 R.19/MF 42, Tabora Regional Book, 'Notes on Banyamwezi', 6 May 1932. For a rather different account, see Bösch 1930: 493–504.

77 Roberts 1970: 59 and Nolan 1977: 49. On local slave trading by Mirambo, see Tippu Tip 1903: 2, 4. For further detail on Mirambo, see Bennett 1971, Chretien 1977 and, more recently, the article by Reid 1998. According to Unomah, the 1860s and 1870s saw a fair degree of local, small-scale slave raiding and kidnapping. The groups involved were called in ki-Nyamwezi *vbungi-vbungi* and consisted of powerful individuals and their followers or small gangs of slave raiders. Sometimes, the captives were not sold but returned to their families after payment of a ransom. See Unomah 1972: 108ff.

78 *Ibid.*

79 Roberts 1970: 50.

80 Unomah 1972: 11.

81 Nolan 1977: 142.

82 For a description of a slave auction in Tabora in 1874, see Cameron 1877 vol. I: 144.

83 Burton 1860: 182, 212, 214ff., 539. For more detail on slavery in Ugogo see Hermann 1892: 191–203 and Claus 1911: 58, 60.

84 Nolan 1977: 161. See also Wissmann 1888: 352. For a similar argument concerning the Shambaa kingdom, see Feierman 1974: 168–84. See also Iliffe 1979: 49ff.

85 Burton 1860: 295, 321, 479. The nineteenth-century arms trade with East Africa has not yet been fully explored; German archival sources, in particular, have not been used for this purpose. For an example of German arms export to East Africa in the 1850s, see Burton 1860: 479.

86 Cameron 1877 vol. I: 175. See also Reichard 1892: 325, 374, 480. For an overview, see Beachey 1962: 451–67. In this connection it should be noted that, according to an official estimate, annual imports of firearms in East Africa in the late 1880s amounted to 80,000 to 100,000 (!) single items, most of which were light guns. For this estimate, see Euan Smith to Salisbury, 28 June 1888, in Great Britain, *Parliamentary Papers. Further Correspondence respecting Germany and Zanzibar*, C. 5603, London 1888: 26, cited in *Traite des esclaves* 1889: 153. Children in Unyamwezi were already playing with toy guns by the 1860s. For this observation, see Grant 1864: 99. For a similar observation in 1872, see Livingstone 1874: 227, cited in Roberts 1971: 9.

87 Baumann 1894: 101ff. See also Roberts 1970: 71.

88 For the term 'militarisation', see Wright 1993: 6. See also Iliffe 1979: 50.

89 Löbner 1910, cited in Gottberg 1971: 172. According to Löbner, sub-chiefdom (in ki-Nyamwezi, *gunguli*, pl. *magunguli*) was made up of distinct sets of villages or *makayas*. These sub-chiefs were called *vanachalo* in ki-Nyamwezi.

90 Shorter 1968: 135–59. See also Tippu Tip 1902: 210, Grant 1864: 57 and Cameron 1877 vol. I: 175, Reichard (1890: 263ff.). Reichard also noted that the construction of houses had changed. They were bigger and thus easier to defend against slave raiders. For a description of defensive 'housing' in north-eastern Tanzania, see Fosbrooke 1954: 50–7.

91 Burton 1860: 176. See also Cameron 1877 vol. I: 190.

92 Nolan 1977: 50. See also Bösch 1930: 493.

93 Nolan 1977: 90ff.

94 Nolan 1977: 39. For a detailed description of such villages, see Grant 1864: 65, Reichard 1892: 168ff., Stuhlmann 1894: 74ff.

95 Nolan 1977: 51. This is an important point since the mobility of the local population greatly increased in early colonial times.

96 Abrahams 1967a: 26, 38ff. For further detail on this aspect, see Sheriff 1987: 181, 194 and Unomah 1972: 89–96.

97 Roberts 1970: 71.

98 Tippu Tip 1902: 214.

99 A social history of the *ruga-ruga* troops remains to be written. They were used as a main standing fighting force not only by African chiefs and coastal merchants but also by the German *Schutztruppe*. As unofficial auxiliary troops they did most of the actual fighting in the conquest period, during the Maji Maji War and the First World War. Some material on pre-colonial *ruga-ruga* troops can be found in Shorter 1968: 235–59, Page 1974a: 69–84, Mann 2002: 170 and Morton: 1990: 40–9. For a detailed contemporary description of the *ruga-ruga*, see Storms (1889), cited in *Traite des esclaves* 1889: 110. In

this connection, it is interesting to note that the ki-Nyamwezi grammar produced in the early 1890s by the Moravian missionary R. Stern was based on a local dialect he called *kirugaruga*.

100 Reichard 1892: 479. According to Reichard this was the mechanism by which the most successful chief attracted the most ferocious 'warriors'. See also Unomah 1972: 113.

101 Wright 1993: 6.

102 Blohm 1931 vol. II: 36 [extract from interview, n.d. (pre-1914)], 37. See also Unomah 1972: 115–25.

103 Another notable Nyamwezi warlord was Fundikira, whom Burton met in 1857. See Burton 1860: 300.

104 For more detail on the relations between Nyamwezi chiefs and Tabora merchants, see Bennett 1978.

105 On Mirambo, see Becker 1887: II: 174, Spellig 1927–8: 205–9, Bennett 1971 and Chretien 1977.

106 Burton 1860: 284.

107 Sheriff 1987: 180. See also Unomah 1972: 93.

108 Roberts 1968: 134.

109 This definition of the word *Swahili* can be found in Pouwels 1987: 1. It is derived from the Arabic word *Sahil* (pl. *Sawahili*) meaning coast. According to Tolmacheva, the word was already in use as a *geographical* term in the ninth century. See Tolmacheva 1976: 29.

110 Pouwels 1987: 1ff.

111 Kilwa's regional importance declined after it was looted and destroyed by the Portuguese in the early sixteenth century.

112 Prins 1961: 24–7, 78–87. For more detail, especially the history of the language, see Nurse and Spear 1985.

113 For Bagamoyo, see Brown 1970: 69–83; for Dar es Salaam, see Sutton 1970: 1–20; for Kilwa, see Aas 1989. The history of Pangani is covered by Glassman 1995.

114 Prins 1967: xi.

115 Sheriff 1987: 173. See also Brown 1971: 107–44, particularly 141ff. For more detail, see Middleton 1992: 54–82.

116 See Trimingham 1964: 31–125. This and the following paragraphs have also greatly profited from Cooper 1981: 271–307 and Morton 1990: 8ff. For the normative Islamic framework with regard to slavery, see Brunschvig 1960: 24–40. See also Fisher and Fisher 1970 and Fisher 2001.

117 Pouwels 1987: 22. Fore more detail, see Trimingham 1964: 39–78.

118 Becker 1911: 2ff. See also Giles 1987: 234–57 and Giles 1999: 142–64.

119 This arguments was first advanced by Niese 1902: 13.

120 Pouwels 1987: 65. See also Middleton 1992: 161 and Spear 1984: 292. For the frequently pronounced difference between formal laws and the reality of people's lives, see Mann and Roberts 1991: 3–58.

121 Cooper 1981: 271–307.

122 The literature on the Shirazi problem in East is vast and cannot be reviewed here in any detail, but, for further detail, see Prins 1961: 13, Trimingham 1964: 34, Pouwels 1984: 237–67, Spear 1984: 291–305, Pouwels 1987: 36, 72ff., Glassman 1995: 4 and Spear 2000a: 260, 289.

123 Beech 1916: 146, note 2 and Lienhardt 1968: 11ff. See also Glassman 1995: 25, 66.

124 See, for instance, Reusch 1953, Prins 1961, Eastman 1971, Arens 1975, Tolmacheva 1976, Salim 1985, Maw and Parkin 1985, Pouwels 1987, Middleton 1992, Allen 1993 and Mazrui 1994. For a summary of the debate, see Glassman 1995: 29–54 and Spear 2000a: 257–90.

125 New 1873: 56. About 90 years later, Prins made the same argument, writing that 'a man is never a Swahili and nothing else'. See Prins 1961: 11.

126 On the process of 'Swahilicisation', see Maw and Parkin 1985: 1–13.

127 This and the following paragraphs are based on Cooper 1977: 23–46, Iliffe 1979: 35–52, Sheriff 1987: 8–32, Pouwels 1987: 97–124 and Glassman 1995: 29–54. This chapter has also profited from Nicholls 1971: 324–75 and Biermann 1993: 117–204.

128 For some further details, see Nicholls 1971: 246–77.

129 For a diplomatic history of the consolidation of Omani rule on the coast, see Nicholls 1971: 295–323.

130 Pouwels 1987: 100–5. For more detail, see Berg 1971: 129–35.

131 Sheriff 1987: 94. For a detailed description and precise figures on the Zanzibar import and export trade in the years 1857–9, see Burton 1872: 405–25. For similar figures and a detailed description for the year 1897, see Baumann 1898. In addition to ivory, the Sultan of Zanzibar monopolised the wild gum copal trade. Gum copal was collected by small groups of men, often slaves, on the northern part of the coast, most of it in the hinterland of Bagamoyo, Saadani and Dar es Salaam. It is a kind of resin that was then used in the production of high class varnish for coaches and pianos. See Burton 1860: 535–8.

132 For more details on the ivory trade, see Sheriff 1987: 77–115. See also Beachey 1967. For the Zanzibar tax system, see Sheriff 1987: 116–27.

133 This and the following paragraphs have greatly profited from Cooper 1977: 23–79, Sheriff 1987: 48–76 and Morton 1998: 265–7.

134 For more detailed information, see Cooper 1977: 38–46 and Sheriff 1987: 51, 61–73.

135 For a concise summary of the east African slave trade, see Alpers 1967: 4–13. See also Nicholls 1971: 197–217, Beachey 1976: 181–218, 260–2, Sheriff 1987: 8–32 and Clarence-Smith 1989: 1–20, 21–45, 131–45.

136 For more detail, see Alpers 1967 and Alpers 1975a: 172–243. For this reason, *Wanyasa* (sing. *Mnyasa*) became a widely used term in Zanzibar and probably also elsewhere for slaves or persons of servile origin, whatever their ethnic or linguistic background. See Cooper 1977: 120.

137 Sheriff 1987: 35–41. On the history of the involvement of Indian merchants in the expansion of Indian Ocean trade, see Sakarai 1980: 292–338 and 1981: 2–30. For a recent study of Zanzibar's ocean-going dhow trade to Southern Arabia and western India in the nineteenth and early twentieth centuries, see Gilbert 2004: 21–83.

138 On the history of slavery in Mauritius, see Nwulia 1981 and Allen 1999.

139 Sheriff 1987: 41–8. See also Allen 2004: 33–40. For the Mozambique slave trade further south, see Machado 2004: 17–32.

140 Despite the demise of the French slave trade in Kilwa, European involvement in the East African slave trade did not come to an end. In fact, Portuguese slave traders exported large numbers of slaves from Mozambique to Brazil, reaching an all-time high in the 1830s and 1840s. This only ceased in 1847, when overseas slave exports from East Africa to India, the Americas and the Arabian peninsula were prohibited. On the Mozambique slave trade, see Campbell 1989a and 1989b.

141 Sheriff 1987: 226. For a detailed description of the East African slave trade by a contemporary resident observer in the mid-nineteenth century, see University of Birmingham Library, Church Missionary Society, CA 50 16/179, 'Memoir on the East African Slave Trade', by J. L. Krapf, Rabai 1853.

142 For these figures, see Martin and Ryan 1977: 71–91 and Sheriff 1987: 226, 231. For a somewhat different set of figures, see Cooper 1977: 116 and Austen 1989: 21–44.

143 Burton 1860: 520.

144 Burton 1860: 520. Reichard (1892: 471), who travelled through East Africa/Unyamwezi in the 1880s, provides a similar description. See also Blohm 1931 vol. II: 37 [extract from interview, n.d. (pre-1914)] and Toeppen 1885–6: 235.

145 Burton 1860: 520. See also Storms 1889, cited in *Traite des esclaves* 1889: 110.

146 Sheriff 1987: 223ff. See also Cooper 1977: 130.

147 The administrative measures undertaken in 1876 by the Sultan of Zanzibar to suppress slave trading by land seem to have been largely ineffectual. See Cooper 1977: 124.

148 Sheriff 1987: 77–115. For more detail, see Alpers 1975a.

149 In Europe and North America ivory was mainly used for such utilitarian purposes as the manufacture of piano keys, billiard balls and combs, while in India ivory was mainly valued as an article of adornment.

150 Feierman 1995: 356. There were two kinds of ivory, known as *gendi* and *pembe* in ki-Swahili. The latter was more valuable since it was softer and less brittle than the former. According to Sheriff, in the period between 1828 and 1860 the Zanzibar price for ivory rose from about MT$ 22 a *frasila* (35 lb) to about MT$ 48 a *frasila*. For more detail, see Sheriff 1987: 254ff.

151 Sheriff 1987: 159ff.

152 Sheriff 1987: 159.

153 For a description of the Pangani and Tanga ('Wamasai') hinterland trade, see Burton 1872: 116ff., 145ff.; for the Kilwa hinterland trade, see Eberstein 1896: 175–7.

154 Glassman 1995: 46.
155 A detailed description of the actual bartering process between ivory sellers and buyers can be found in Reichard 1892: 438–46. For a general description, see Velten 1903: 284–301.
156 Reichard reports that in the early 1880s he travelled with a caravan of about 2,500 people from the coast to Tabora. See Reichard 1892: 329ff. For the financial arrangements and the practical organisation of a coastal caravan, see Tippu Tip 1902: 201–6, Velten 1898: 370ff., 387 and Toeppen 1885–6: 222–35.
157 For a different view, see Rockel 2000a: 190.
158 Sheriff 1987: 191.
159 For the boom of the coastal trade in the second half of the nineteenth century, see Toeppen 1885–6: 225–8 (northern coast). See also Thompson 1882: 1 (southern coast).
160 Sheriff 1987: 160.
161 For a detailed contemporary geographical description of the Pangani trade routes, see Farler 1882, 730–42. For further details on the Pangani and Bagamoyo trade, see Toeppen 1885–6: 227ff.
162 Sheriff 1987: 191ff. Sheriff makes the point that caravan routes changed constantly according to natural and political circumstances. Therefore, these routes should be envisaged as corridors through which traders and porters walked to the coast.
163 For a description of late-nineteenth-century Pangani street life, see Glassman 1995: 4. For the commercial competition between coastal towns for caravans and their wealth, see Burton 1860: 30ff., 82. See also Reichard 1892: 438. For the feasts, see Velten 1903: 208, 292 and Lamden 1963: 161.
164 Toeppen 1885–6: 228.
165 Glassman 1995: 46.
166 For an example, see Wright 1993: 184. See also Storms 1889, cited in *Traite des esclaves* 1889: 110.
167 Burton 1860: 76, 129.
168 Krapf 1858 vol. I: 184., Burton 1860: 99.
169 See, for instance, the account regarding Semboja in Feierman 1974: 182ff. See also Glassman 1995: 47ff. For a detailed description of a village raided by a coastal 'commando', see Burton 1860: 139. For contemporary reports about the effects of slaving in the coastal hinterland of Lindi, Kilwa, Tanga, Pangani and Dar es Salaam, see Kirk to Granville 22 December 1884, Kirk to Granville 14 February 1885, Kirk to Granville 13 April 1885, in Great Britain, *Parliamentary Papers. Correspondence Relating to Zanzibar*, C. 4776, London 1886: 93, 105ff., 119, cited in Traite 1890: 115–17. See also Chapter 3.
170 For the development of food crop plantations around Malindi and Mombasa in what later became the British East African Protectorate (Kenya), see Cooper 1977: 81–110 and Morton 1990: 1–51.
171 Pouwels 1987: 181, Sheriff 1987: 159–64, Glassman 1995: 4, Willis 1998: 731. For a description of coastal sugar plantations near Pangani, see Meinecke 1895b.
172 Glassman 1995: 101ff. For a different view, see Meinecke 1894: 154, who states that in the late 1880s and early 1890s most of the sugar produced in Pangani was exported to Zanzibar, Southern Arabia and even Bombay in India. According to official trade statistics, Pangani exported almost 1,200 tons of sugar and sugar syrup in 1893, which were valued at about Rs90,000 at the time. For these figures, see Meinecke 1895a: 154.
173 Cooper 1977: 170–82, Morton 1990: 1–18, Glassman 1995: 96–106. For more detail, see Chapter 3.
174 Sheriff 1987: 36. A similar development took place in West Africa. See Hopkins 1973: 143.
175 For the various treaties and their history, see Nicholls 1971: 218–45.
176 Smith 1887. 101ff. See also Sheriff 1987: 68.
177 See Kirk to Granville, 13 April 1885, in Great Britain, *Parliamentary Papers. Correspondence Relating to Zanzibar*, C. 4776, London 1886: 119, cited in *Traite des esclaves* 1889: 115–7. See also von Wissmann 29 August 1889, in Deutsches Reich, *Sammlung von Aktenstücken Ostafrika betreffend*, Berlin 1889, cited in *Traite des esclaves* 1889: 263ff.
178 Glassman 1995: 105. For a different view, see Brown 1971: 212. For a list of the export numbers and prices of slaves supplied to the northern mainland towns from Zanzibar in 1874, see Cooper 1977: 123. For a list of Zanzibar slave prices 'in the closing days of

the slave trade', see Cooper 1977: 196. According to that list, in Zanzibar an agricultural slave was sold for £5 to £8, a 'self-employed' slave for £6 to £10, a skilled slave for £8 to £12, a domestic servant for £12 to £25 and a 'concubine' for £15 to £50.

179 Sheriff 1987: 70, 166. For more detail on the number of slaves living on the coast at the time of conquest, see Chapter 4.

180 See Sheriff 1987: 164. For the Kenya coast, see Morton 1990: 1–18 and Willis 1993a: 21–46. For an example, see Burton 1860: 92.

181 Glassman 1995: 52.

182 Iliffe 1979: 71. See also Glassman 1995: 44–6, 52.

183 Cooper 1977: 38ff., Pouwels 1987: 4.

184 New 1873: 62ff. See also Glassman 1995: 42–5.

185 Pouwels 1987: 115, Glassman 1995: 43. It should be noted, however, that in some coastal towns women were traditionally allowed to earn money through beer brewing, mat making and shoreline fishing. For a detailed discussion of the gendered character of slavery, see Chapter 3.

186 Pouwels 1987: 77–9.

187 For comparative purposes, see Strobel 1979, Mirza and Strobel 1989, Caplan 1989.

188 For more details on slave ownership, see Chapter 3.

189 See, for instance, Leue 1900–1c.

190 Pouwels 1987: 72. For an interesting use of the term in ki-Swahili, see Tippu Tip 1902: 246, where he called non-coastal slave owners *waungwana*. See also the discussion of these term in Glassman 2004: 33.

191 New 1873: 64.

192 Pouwels 1987: 73, Glassman 1995: 78. For the older coastal families, participation in the long-distance caravan trade was the most prestigious way of earning one's livelihood.

193 Ohly 1975: 29–35.

194 New 1873: 46. See also Pouwels 1987: 36ff. On the concept of slave ownership and stratification, see Iliffe 1979: 43, 129 and Glassman 1995: 39, 42. On the issue of stratification of Swahili society, see also the informative review by Constantin 1989: 145–59.

195 Pouwels 1987: 85.

196 Pouwels 1987: 85.

197 Pouwels 1987: 85.

198 Schweinitz 1894a: 18.

199 Glassman 1995: 62, 76.

200 Glassman 1995: 94–6. For the problems of applying the concept of class divisions to non-industrial societies, see Lloyd 1966: 49–62. In this study, the more descriptive and pragmatic Weberian typology of status groups was used in order to highlight the cultural and political aspects of social divisions in nineteenth-century Tanganyika. The power of high-status groups was, of course, ultimately based on the possession of wealth and the degree to which such groups were able to exploit the labour of others. For the classical definition of status groups, see Weber 1948 [1921]: 180–95.

201 Glassman 1995: 76.

202 See Burton 1860: 515, Speke 1863: 10, Reichard 1892: 472, Schweinitz 1894a: 19.

203 Pouwels 1987: 73, 128–30. See also Ohly 1976: 77–9 and Morton 1977: 638–41. However, as Cooper (1977: 79) suggests, despite these changes, older social values and structures 'remained a vital part' of Zanzibari and coastal society.

204 Velten 1903: 274, 278f. For a different view, see Glassman 1995: 7.

205 The gradual replacement of the Maria Theresa Dollar (MT$) by the Indian silver Rupee (Re, pl. Rs) as the main unit of exchange on the coast can be seen as a measure of the Indian merchants' success. This probably occurred in the 1850s and 1860s. See Pouwels 1987: 113. For more detail, see Brown 1971: 145–85 and Glassman 1995: 57ff. According to Glassman, the spread of Shirazi marginalisation was geographically highly uneven. For instance, in Saadani neither Omani merchants nor Indian financiers were able to push the Shirazi families aside, while in Bagamoyo the older Shirazi families seem to have completely lost out to newcomers.

206 See, for instance, BAB RKolA 7382/27: 68, Berichte der einzelnen Verwaltungsstellen in Deutsch-Ostafrika über die Sklaverei, Bezirksamt Lindi, Berichterstatter: Bezirksamt-

mann Zache n.d. [1900].

207 Glassman 1995: 25, 33. Embroidering their imagined origins coastal people often took an Arabic descent name such as *al-Mafazii*.

208 Glassman 1995: 23.

209 Glassman 1995: 23. Writing on Pangani, Glassman points out that 'ongoing conflict ensued as slaves, plebeians and rural people, both Swahili-speaking villagers from the coast and non-Swahili speakers from the further hinterland, sought full membership in the urban community, and as Shirazi patricians just as persistently fought to exclude the newcomers or relegate them to distinctly inferior roles'. See also Glassman 1995: 78, 117–74. The 'Arabisation' of the coast would probably not have mattered so much, had it not been for the urban elite's self-presentation as true Arabs to the European explorers and colonial administrators who arrived on the coast in the second half of the nineteenth century. Subsequently, much of colonial policy was based on the colonial perception of an essential historical difference between the coast and the interior, whereas, in fact, not least because of large-scale forced migration, the links between the two grew stronger as the century progressed.

Three

The Social Life
of Slaves

This chapter explores the life chances of slaves in Unyamwezi and on the coast in the second half of the nineteenth century. In the previous chapter, the commercialisation of social relations following the expansion of the caravan trade was examined more generally. Here, the accompanying transformation of the life of slaves, particularly of servile women, will be investigated in detail, and it will be shown how this particular change took place.

A review of the various ways in which people became slaves in Unyamwezi and on the coast is followed by detailed, descriptive accounts of slaves' work practices and the kind of life chances they possessed in the societies concerned.[1] The third part introduces some tentative, more analytical suggestions as to how the social life of slaves changed historically during the second half of the nineteenth century.[2]

Focusing on the occupational life of slaves is justified in that working patterns significantly influenced how the majority of slaves were absorbed over time into the societies concerned, although this often meant living at the very margins. Slaves' work practices varied between and within these societies, according to the prevailing cultural norms and ideas governing the division of labour between age, gender and status groups. This draws attention to the argument that slavery was socially embedded and that an analysis of its intimate association with other forms of social and economic relations, such as kinship, clientelism and community, is crucial to an understanding of its historical dynamic. Local age, gender and status differences of slaves will thus receive particular consideration in this chapter because they shaped, if they did not determine, the social perspectives and life chances of slaves, and the degree of social mobility that some but not all could hope to achieve during their lifetime.

The Making of Slaves

In the second half of the nineteenth century there were four major modes of enslavement: the application of brute force and coercion, judicial processes, the power of adverse circumstances such as famine and indebtedness, and birth.[3] As will be shown further on in this chapter, all these modes occurred in principle both in Unyamwezi and on the coast, although not to the same degree. At this point they are reviewed together, as the similarities between these areas are greater than their differences. Moreover, with the notable exception of those who were born into slavery, the making of slaves occurred outside the societies in which they were subsequently forced to spend their lives.

The majority of people were enslaved through acts of physical violence.[4] Large-scale organised slave-raiding operations as well as more opportunistic small-scale kidnapping activities took place both in the neighbouring areas of Unyamwezi and in the coastal hinterland. From the sources available it is impossible to determine whether small-scale kidnapping occurred more frequently than large-scale raiding, but from circumstantial evidence, such as biographical accounts and descriptive sources, it appears that on the whole small-scale kidnapping was probably more prevalent.[5]

Violence was used primarily during the initial capturing of slaves. Apart from the indiscriminate killings that frequently occurred during slave raids, captives who resisted were often beaten into compliance.[6] After being captured, adults were usually bound individually or chained together in groups of ten or more people, at least for the first few days.[7] The dreaded slave stick (in ki-Swahili *kongwa*, pl. *makongwa*) was sometimes applied to particularly disobedient captives.[8] Children, however, were usually left unconstrained, since they had little choice but to accompany their enslaved relatives after the devastation of their home villages.

The violence of enslavement was also experienced in the aftermath of local wars and civil strife in the neighbouring areas of the coast and Unyamwezi. Members of the defeated side were rounded up and sold to slave traders. Sometimes the traders themselves actively participated in these wars, since they were rewarded with captives for the military services they and their followers had rendered to the victorious side. The involvement of slave traders in local wars very likely increased as the possession of firearms became more and more important in these conflicts. Slave traders had more access to imported arms and ammunition than local chiefs and headmen, so that their support was often crucial in local conflicts and, consequently, much sought after. In turn, they hired out the services of their followers, often slaves, to anyone who offered the right kind of inducement, usually the prospect of acquiring large amounts of ivory or of slaves.[9]

During local wars and slave raids, women, and children were captured, while men were frequently killed.[10] It was thought that, if left alive, these men would seek retribution. It was also believed that they would show resistance or attempt flight, especially in the first few days after their capture, while still in the vicinity of their home areas. This does not mean that women were acquiescent to their fate.[11] Importantly, though, there was a strong belief both on the coast as well as in Unyamwezi that adult men do not make 'good', that is docile, slaves.[12]

According to one observer, Paul Reichard, who visited East Africa in the mid-1880s, the violence of enslavement came to an end after capture. Having forcefully broken their resistance, commercial slave raiders and traders had little interest in wilfully maltreating slaves, as this would only diminish their exchange value.[13] Reichard states that according to his own observation 'only' very few, perhaps less than 5 per cent of the captives were killed in the days following a raid. However, he apparently did not reflect upon the possible effect of his presence on the behaviour of the slave traders he observed, nor was he too concerned about those who were killed. His account contradicts one of the most enduring stereotypes in missionary and early colonial descriptions of the East African slave trade, according to which the brutality of slave raiders and traders was the reason why the majority of those captured never reached the first point of sale.[14] Moreover, according to Reichard's observations, between a quarter and half of those captured usually escaped in the first few days after the raid, and most of the actual deaths on the march can be attributed to illness and disease.[15]

Both in Unyamwezi and on the coast in the latter half of the nineteenth century, a second way in which people became slaves was by a judicial process involving punishment for such crimes as adultery and 'witchcraft'.[16] Furthermore, supposedly 'free' persons[17] were transferred between families[18] as compensation for criminal offences perpetrated by a member of one family against another. Typical offences included theft, grievous bodily harm and homicide. Those handed over as compensation were regarded as slaves and could be sold freely.[19] Finally, local chiefs and headmen in Unyamwezi enslaved an unknown number of 'free' people, most of them women, in order to exchange them for goodwill from distrustful traders or hostile neighbours.[20]

Thirdly, debt settlements could lead to enslavement, especially when a member of the family had already been given away as security for a loan. These pawns were frequently younger women. Although they could not be sold immediately, the creditor could enjoy the fruits of their labour until the debt was paid. Yet, in the event that the debtor or his family eventually failed to honour the debt, the creditor had the right to recoup the loan by enslavement and subsequent sale of the pawn.[21] It is likely that enslavement as a result of debt settlements was more widespread on the coast than in Unyamwezi, since the process of monetisation of commercial transactions had begun much earlier on the coast.

Furthermore, people were pawned into slavery by their relatives, often the male head of the household, in periods of ecological crisis such as famines caused by drought, plant disease or animal pest epidemics.[22] These famines were often distinctly local affairs, one acute observer noted, pointing out that 'until the smallness of the resources of the people and the difficulties of transport have been considered, the sharpness of the boundary between want and plenty is amazing'.[23] Pawning a family member was done with the greatest reluctance in the majority of cases, and only if such a measure appeared to assure the physical survival of the family.[24] Pawning was presumably accompanied by a promise that his or her relatives would eventually ransom the person in question, but since only a minority of the enslaved actually remained within reach of their home areas, such promises were more likely to be broken than honoured.[25] In effect, pawning was often a means of disguising the outright sale of a person by his or her family, since it was regarded as an exceedingly dishonourable act.[26] Local chiefs and headmen in Unyamwezi acquired these slaves in order to swell the number of their followers and dependants. On the coast, usually only the wealthy and well-connected – that is, members of the urban elite – obtained slaves through pawnship, as the transfer of such persons involved a measure of trust between the parties.

Finally, there was a group of people who were treated as slaves because their parents, or, in the case of the coast, their grandparents or even great-grandparents had been enslaved and they had inherited that status.

Slaves were traded regularly at slave auctions held in local markets both on the coast and in Unyamwezi.[27] At these auctions slaves were publicly displayed and their bodies closely investigated.[28] The traveller Cameron described an auction he had observed in Tabora in the early 1870s. He noted:

> In two large rooms were assembled nearly a hundred and fifty traders – Arabs, Wasuahili and Wamerima – and three auctioneers. The first part of the sale consisted of household utensils ... the second was devoted to the sale of slaves. They were led around, made to show their teeth, to cough, run, and lift weights, and in some instances to exhibit their dexterity in handling a musket. All the slaves were semi-domestics and fetched high prices; one woman who was reputed to be a good cook going for 200 dollars, and many of the men reached eighty dollars....[29]

Slaves intermittently changed hands, often several times, in private transactions between individual buyers and sellers before reaching their final place of residence.[30] They were also offered to passing caravans, either near the coast or up-country in the hinterland.[31] How slave transactions were actually conducted is largely unknown – whether, for instance, the buying and selling of slaves always involved lengthy negotiations about the price of the 'commodity' in question, as was the case with the purchase of ivory. There is, however, one description of such a sale by Wilhelm Blohm, a Moravian missionary. He cites an extract from an interview with a Nyamwezi convert conducted before the outbreak of the First World War. The convert in question is reported to have said:

> If a man wants to buy a boy, he will stay there over night. When the principals [*Herren*] have come to an agreement about the purchase, then the one who owns the boy will say: 'I want thirty pieces of cloth'. But the one who has the cloth will say: 'I will give you twenty'. If the slave owner agrees [on that price], the purchase [contract] is sealed. Then, the owner of the cloth gives [the slave owner] something, perhaps one or two lengths of cloth or a hoe. This piece is called *tja lufupi* or *tja luywili* 'the thing which has to be spit on' (with sacrificial porridge). When the *tja lufupi* has been handed over, the slave owner takes some flour and water and prepares the sacrificial porridge. He then spits on the slave boy whom he had just sold and says: 'Go and have many children and acquire wealth for your master'. When he has done that, the one who had the cloth [the buyer] takes the boy he has bought....

When he [the new owner] comes back to his village, his wife will take some sacrificial porridge and spit on the person he [her husband] had bought. After that she returns to the house. She cooks some food for her husband and for the slave. When the meal is prepared, they do not eat with the slave; only if he [the slave] is well known, will they eat together.[32] [Translation and additions in brackets by the author.]

This quotation brings out the entanglement of social, religious and commercial aspects that arose during the transfer of slaves from one owner (and his family) to the other. In the case above, a ritual was performed in order to tie the slave symbolically to his new 'family'. The ceremony represents a 'rite of passage',[33] a symbolic change from one social status to another, but the sources are silent as to when, where and, above all, to what extent the ritual described above was actually performed. Without further information, however, it is difficult to come to more general conclusions.

When the link to kin and community was cut at the point of enslavement, the person in question was stripped of his or her social value, indeed dying a 'social death'[34], sometimes even a physical one, since he or she was 'heartbroken' as Livingstone phrased it. In one of the most moving passages in his journal, Livingstone described the capture of a group of young men, noting that:

they had endured the chains until they saw the broad river Lualaba roll between them and their free homes; they then lost heart. Twenty-one were unchained as being now safe; however all ran away at once, but eight, with many others still in chains, died in three days after the crossing. They ascribed their only pain to the heart, and placed the hand correctly on the spot.... Some slavers expressed surprise to me that they should die, seeing that they had plenty to eat and no work ... it seems really heart-brokenness of which they died.[35]

Yet such cases were the exception, and more often than not the newly enslaved stayed with their new owners for a considerable period of time, in many cases their whole lives. Others were traded several times over long distances until they were given a more permanent residence. In any case, the moment slaves remained in a particular locality, they sought and acquired new social ties, which they hoped would ensure greater security. As will be shown in the next section of this chapter, the various ways in which these new social ties developed over time determined the life chances of slaves in a new social environment.

Working Patterns and Life Perspectives of Slaves in Unyamwezi

In the period immediately after their arrival in Unyamwezi, most of the slaves were said to be regarded as 'strangers' or 'foreigners'.[36] The great majority of them had not been captured or purchased in Unyamwezi itself but in neighbouring areas, especially when these were suffering from famine or civil war. According to Burton, the 'Wanyamwezi rarely sell one another',[37] but they

> will sell their criminals and captives; when want drives, they part with their wives, their children and even their parents. For economy, they import their serviles from Ujiji and the adjoining regions; from the people living towards the south-east angle of the Tanganyika Lake, as the Wafipa, the Wapoka, and the Wagara; and from the Nyanza races and the northern kingdoms of Karakwah [Karagwe], Uganda, and Unyoro.[38]

Some, however, came from much further afield, especially from Katanga and the southern Manyema region in the eastern Congo, where Nyamwezi slave traders and raiders had been particularly active from the 1860s.[39] According to a later observer, these raiding expeditions were carried out with traders from Zanzibar and the coast. They 'consisted of the leaders – rich men who provided muzzle loaders and gunpowder – and the *ruga-ruga* who carried and used the firearms and a number of porters'.[40]

There are no figures available on the number of slaves living in Unyamwezi in the period before the arrival of German military officers in the area in 1890. Based on his visits to the town of Tabora in the mid-1880s, the traveller Reichard noted that between 70 and 75 per cent of the population in Unyamwezi were slaves.[41] The first who actually estimated their numbers was Hauptmann Puder, one of the earliest administrative officers in Tabora district. Without giving an indication of which inhabitants he considered to be slaves or how he arrived at this particular estimate, he reported that in 1890 about two-thirds of the total population of around 350,000 were slaves.[42] Both Reichard's and Puder's figures are probably on the high side.[43] First of all, estimates of population figures are notoriously unreliable for this period. Some of them proved to be wide of the mark.[44] Moreover, according to oral historical research carried out in the 1970s, the slave population was most densely concentrated in the chiefdoms of Unyanyembe, the most prosperous and populous areas of Unyamwezi.[45] They are situated relatively close to the town of Tabora, where both Reichard and Puder resided during their stay in Unyamwezi, and this could be one of the reasons why they overestimated the numbers of slaves in other parts of Unyamwezi. In any case, even allowing for a wide margin of error, the numbers are still impressive.[46]

Some of the enslaved were ransomed by their relatives during the first few months after their capture or purchase. The vast majority, however, remained slaves. The generic term for slave in ki-Nyamwezi was *msese* (pl. *basese*). The slave owners were known as *ise bugonzo*. These were mostly chiefs, elders and village headmen who, as head of the 'extended' household, sometimes comprising several hundred people, exercised a large measure of control over human and material resources, especially labour.[47] During the initial period of ownership, the masters perceived their slaves primarily as a commodity, as a convenient means of storing wealth or as a medium of exchange, since no social ties existed between the two.[48] This was the period when slaves were most eager to escape, so that they were frequently tied up or chained to prevent their flight.[49] The power of the owners over their newly acquired slaves was apparently unlimited since in Unyamwezi, as elsewhere in East Africa, a slave had 'no creature he can appeal to' as one contemporary observer noted.[50] Yet over time their relationship changed, not least because the slaves and their owners worked together in the fields, shared the same house and ate from the same bowl.[51] They also wore the same attire and, more often than not, there were no visible marks that distinguished the two groups. At any rate, to the outside observer, there was usually no discernible difference between the lifestyle of owners and slaves, at least as far as 'ordinary' slave owners were concerned. [52] It is likely, though, that 'insiders' had a much clearer view as to what constituted social difference.

The majority of the slaves in Unyamwezi were women,[53] believed to be more 'docile' than men. Burton reports, for instance, that in the south-easterly regions of Unyamwezi, from whence huge numbers of slaves were imported, adult men were rarely sold because they were thought to have 'obstinate and untameable characters' since 'many of them would rather die under the stick than level themselves with women by using a hoe'.[54] It was also argued that female slaves were less likely to flee since it was more difficult for them to improve their circumstances with this option.[55] If they were within reach of the area they were born in, male adult captives were evidently more likely to run away than female slaves; thus they were often sold 'abroad', in the case of Unyamwezi to slave traders going to the coast.[56] In this context it should be mentioned that most contemporary accounts agree that female slaves in Unyamwezi were considerably higher priced than male slaves of the same age.[57] Female slaves, it seems, were easier to control and were valued as agricultural labourers, sexual partners and potential mothers whose children belonged to the owners' household. This applied especially to young women of childbearing age, although the sources do not state explicitly that female slaves were generally more expensive because they could be absorbed more expediently than male slaves into kinship groups.[58]

After capture, the transformation of the relationship between owners and slaves proceeded along distinct gender and age lines within the owner's household. Adult male slaves usually lived in their own quarters, especially in households with large numbers of slaves.[59] A few even gained their own homesteads, in particular those who had lived for some time with their owner, had acquired some wealth or managed to marry a free-born woman. According to a later observer, however, this did not happen frequently.[60] In such cases, the relationship between slave and owner was reduced to acknowledgement of the master's higher social standing, and assistance during harvest time.[61] In a few instances, male slaves in this situation were formally manumitted, albeit rarely and, more significantly, only in Usoke which was quite close to the coastal town of Tabora where the influence of coastal manners and religious practices was particularly strong.[62] Thus, on the whole, it was possible for male slaves to advance considerably in Nyamwezi society, especially when they worked as porters or trade agents for their owners or were employed by a chief in the administration of the territory under his (in some cases her) control.[63] In this way, some male slaves even managed to accumulate a measure of wealth, including slaves, in their own right.[64]

Yet, the fortunes of these few obscure the fact that a larger proportion of male slaves remained within the ambit of the owner's household. They were treated as distant non-kin members in everyday life, especially if their owners had allowed them to marry a female slave. Despite their intimate entanglement with the owner's household, they, and more importantly their children, were regarded as slaves and not as members of the immediate family.[65] They worked primarily on their owners' farms. Male slaves could own property, but as long as they belonged to the owner's household they themselves were not allowed to buy slaves. Not their own children but their owners inherited their material possessions after they died.[66]

The situation for female slaves was remarkably different. In contrast to male slaves, women frequently became part of their owner's family. They were usually addressed as 'children' or 'relatives', a term that more than likely covered several meanings.[67] The work of female slaves and slave girls was no different from the work performed routinely by other female members of the household, such as working in the fields, grinding corn, cooking, cleaning the house, looking after the children, fetching water and collecting firewood.[68] Younger female slaves are said to have usually worked in the house, whereas older female slaves were more frequently seen toiling on their owners' farms.[69] Some owners formally married their own slaves, and the rise of bridewealth payments for free women in the second half of the nineteenth century probably induced an increasing number of less affluent Wanyamwezi men to do so. But since no bride-wealth was paid for female slaves, their social status within the household was lower than that claimed by free wives.[70] Women did not own slaves, as they were excluded from holding property except for what they had brought with them into their marriages. Still, such 'customary' stipulations were occasionally disregarded in practice.[71] This contrasts with the coast, as will be shown further on in this chapter.

If a Nyamwezi man married a slave woman, he was not required to pay bridewealth to the owner. The children of these marriages belonged to the slave owner's household.[72] If, however, an unmarried female slave had children by her owner, she and her children were 'free' in the sense that 'under normal circumstances' they would not be sold and were thus equal to the other female members of the household.[73] In exceptional circum-stances, such women even lived separate lives from their owners.[74] Yet, in periods of famine or in cases of judicial compensation, debt and inheritance settlements, slave wives were still the first in the household who had to face the threat of sale or re-enslavement.[75] As Marcia Wright has argued, 'the kinship idiom cuts both ways. It could give comfort to the woman who knew her vulnerability as a slave ... or it could obscure the peril of one who regarded herself as at home.'[76] The grandchildren of female slaves, however, were regarded as free from any obligation arising out of their grandparents' status.[77]

Slave boys faced different perspectives.[78] When they were young, they performed the same kind of work as other boys living in the household, helping in the construction of houses, fetching firewood and working in the fields. Yet, on growing older, a number of them would be relieved of agricultural and household work and sent by their owners on trading expeditions as agents or porters. Apparently, these owners greatly 'trusted' their slaves, which is arguably explained by the fact that male slaves who had grown up in the household had no 'relatives' other than their owner's family whom they could turn to in periods of crisis; this necessarily deepened their personal dependency.

Male court slaves played a special role in Wanyamwezi society. They belonged to the chief or had lived for longer periods of time in his, sometimes her, settlement. People owned by the chiefs were known as *vanikulu* (*banyikulu*) in ki-Nyamwezi.[79] They worked as tax collectors, messengers and soldiers (widely referred to as *ruga-ruga*). They usually shared the spoils of their employment and could thus acquire considerable wealth and prestige.[80] The most trusted ones were sometimes even installed as advisers to the chief (in ki-Nyamwezi, *mgawe*) or even as sub-chiefs (in ki-Nyamwezi, *vanachalo*).[81] Yet, it would be misleading to portray slavery in Unyamwezi as a 'compassionate relationship', as a number of German colonial officials have argued.[82] Slaves were despised for their lack of knowledge of local 'customs' and manners of speech, for example.[83] Both female and male slaves were constantly faced with the threat of sale. Owners could use slaves as debt and bridewealth settlements, in commercial exchanges, as well as for compensation purposes.[84] Moreover, owners could punish their slaves. Disobedient slaves, especially those who had attempted to flee, were either severely beaten or put into chains or the slave stick, sometimes for lengthy periods of time.[85] In certain circumstances, owners were even allowed to kill their slaves with impunity.[86]

Yet, despite the potential or actual social marginalisation of slaves, there was a precarious balance between the kinds of demand owners could impose on slaves and the probability that slaves would seek to escape.[87] The owners' power over their slaves was limited, perhaps more in practice than in 'legal' terms – which were virtually comprehensive. Slaves had few means of internally disputing the 'customary rights' that kinship ideas attributed to the household head. However, if slaves felt they had been treated badly enough by their owners – subjected to physical abuse, for instance, or refused even minimal access to household resources – they could resolve to escape, or at least attempt to do so.[88] This argument is supported by some tentative evidence regarding the existence of substantial fugitive slave communities in areas adjoining Unyamwezi.[89] The incidence of flight, however, not only depended on the desire of individual slaves to escape their harsh treatment but also to a considerable extent on local circumstances beyond the control of both the slaves and their owners. In general, slaves were reluctant to free themselves by flight if they felt that their personal safety was likely to be threatened by their immediate re-enslavement.[90] Running away meant taking great risks[91] because, from as

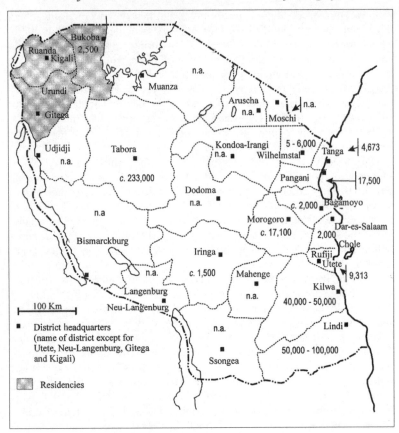

Map 2: Slave Populations Resident in German East Africa, c. 1900

Sources: BAB RKolA 7382/27: 42–93, 'Berichte der einzelnen Verwaltungsstellen
in Deutsch-Ostafrika über die Sklaverei', n.d. [*c.* 1900].
Note: The archival spelling of place and district names has been retained in this map.

early as the mid-nineteenth century, Unyamwezi was an area in which 'slaves and muskets were the stranger's sole protection', as Burton phrased it.[92] Though there is little evidence on this point, it is likely that there was a divergence in the 'exit options' for male and female slaves. For the latter, running away often meant having to find a new male protector or (temporary) husband.[93] For male slaves it was comparatively easier to join runaway communities independently or to find employment in Tabora and Ujiji, where traders from Zanzibar and the coast were always looking for soldiers and male porters.[94] In any case, slaves usually only attempted to escape when their security and economic survival were somewhat assured.[95] Thus, for instance, areas with economies deeply involved in translocal commerce provided slaves with an opportunity to offer their services as porters, servants and, in the case of female slaves, temporary wives to passing caravans without the consent of their owners. According to the traveller Reichard, who visited Unyamwezi in the early 1880s, slave owners were usually glad to see such slaves returning from 'trading journeys' and often abstained from punishing them, even if they had left without their owner's consent.[96]

Thus it appears from available sources that in Unyamwezi, as in various other parts of East Africa in the latter half of the nineteenth century, servility was primarily understood and expressed in terms of kinship relations (even if these were largely fictive for the great majority of female and male slaves).[97] Kinship facilitated the absorption of large numbers of 'outsiders' into Wanyamwezi society.[98] Though this did not work particularly well for male slaves, whose aspirations could not be controlled easily and who were thus kept at a distance, female slaves became part of their owner's family, which involved having the same set of rights and obligations as the natal members of that family.[99] The intersection between the position of women and female slaves within households becomes apparent in the sources that describe how slaves and free women responded to particularly bad treatment from the household head.[100] According to these accounts, female slaves and free women could seek the protection of the chief by touching or damaging certain insignia such as the royal drum. Both would instantly become court slaves, the former free women joining the ranks of the chief's slave wives.[101] Only after payment of a heavy fine were such slaves or women returned to the household head. Orphaned children also sometimes became court slaves.[102]

Moreover, it appears that according to almost all accounts in Unyamwezi, especially in the more prosperous parts of Unyanyembe,[103] household heads were equally reluctant to sell servile and natal members of the larger family in periods of crisis such as famine. Selling children, whether slaves or free, was regarded as shameful and dishonourable.[104] Finally, there is tentative evidence to suggests that women who had greatly misbehaved, according to perceived local standards, were treated as slaves. In records of a meeting to discuss the position of women in Unyamwezi customary law, a participant is quoted as saying in 1930 that 'in former times a woman leaving her husband without "just" cause was sold into slavery if the dowry could not be returned to her husband by either herself, her father or her relatives'.[105] This again underscores the argument that in Unyamwezi there was no clearly defined social boundary between those who were regarded as family members in the natal sense and slaves who had acquired fictive kinship rights. Kinship provided a mode through which people moved in and out of servility.[106] Hence, as far as Unyamwezi in the nineteenth century is concerned, kinship and slavery should be seen as social frontiers that shifted historically according to the particular political and economic circumstances governing everyday life.

Working Patterns and Life Perspectives of Slaves on the Coast

For the purpose of highlighting local differences on the coast it is useful to divide the area into a northern and a southern sphere, comprising clusters of towns and their adjacent hinterlands.[107] Tanga, Pangani, Bagamoyo and Dar es Salaam in the north emerged in the second half of the nineteenth century in response to the commercial expansion of the Zanzibar Empire. The southern towns of Lindi, Mikindani and Kilwa were much older.[108] As was pointed out in the previous chapter, these towns were served by different trade routes in the latter half of the nineteenth century. In the north, Tanga and Pangani received traders coming primarily from the Kilimanjaro area and beyond, while Bagamoyo and Dar es Salaam were the termini of caravan routes running towards Tabora in central Tanzania. Kilwa, Lindi and Mikindani were also linked to central Tanzania, but their main trading activities were directed to the south and the south-west, particularly to the areas surrounding Lake Nyasa (Lake Malawi).[109] The coastal towns, particularly those in the south, exported large numbers of slaves from mid-century on, primarily to Zanzibar and Pemba.[110]

As the slave trade was intimately linked to the ivory and arms trades, the origins of coastal slave populations closely reflected general patterns of commercial expansion in the nineteenth century.[111] This is also apparent in the registers which German colonial officers were required to keep for statistical purposes on the issue of official certificates of emancipation (in German these were called *Freibriefe*, sing. *Freibrief*) to 'liberated' slaves.[112] They indicate that in the northern coastal area, some freed slaves received their *Freibriefe* in the towns of their birth (Tanga, Bagamoyo, Pangani), in nearby villages (such as Kaole) or in neighbouring areas according to place or 'ethnic' names recorded in the registers (for instance 'Zaramo', 'Usambara', 'Massai', 'Bonde', 'Schambaa'). But the great majority of freed slaves came from areas adjacent to the great nineteenth-century northern and central trade routes.[113] Some of these 'imported' slaves were born in Tabora and Ujiji or nearby, but the vast majority were said to have come from Manyema country in what is today eastern Zaire, as well as from the western and southern shores of Lake Tanganyika.[114] Similarly, in the southern towns, some slaves who were freed in Lindi, Kilwa and Mikindani were either born locally or in the vicinity (in the case of Lindi, for instance, on the Makonde Plateau or in the Rovuma Valley). The majority of the freed slaves in the south, however, were said to have come either from the regions bordering Lake Nyasa (Lake Malawi), areas which today constitute part of north-western Mozambique, central Malawi and southern Tanzania, or from 'Yao country' in what is today northern Mozambique. In the late 1880s and early 1890s slavery increased significantly on the southern part of the coast. Yao traders are reported to have brought large numbers of slaves to the coast in that period, particularly to Mikindani and Lindi, only a minority of whom were subsequently exported overseas.[115] In any case, the records on the issue of *Freibriefe* show that there was little cross-over between northern and southern towns as far as the slave populations were concerned. Only a few 'Manyema' lived in the south while hardly any 'Nyassa' resided in the northern towns, despite the fact that, at least in the 1870s, vast numbers of slaves were brought from Lake Nyasa to Kilwa where they were marched overland to Pangani, the point of shipment to the islands of Zanzibar and Pemba.[116]

As in the case of Unyamwezi, the number of slaves resident on the coast was first estimated by European observers in the early colonial period. Again, it is not known how the German district officers arrived at these figures, but, according to their reports, the coastal districts harboured around 125,000 to 200,000 slaves, of which Tanga district was said to have 4,673 slaves, Pangani district 17,500 slaves, Bagamoyo and Dar es Salaam districts about 2,000 slaves each, Rufiyi district 9,313 slaves, Kilwa district between 40,000 and 50,000 slaves, and Lindi district between 50,000 and 100,000 slaves[117] (see Map 2). The records also state that most of these slaves lived in or close to coastal towns, while the coastal hinterland was reported to accommodate only comparatively small resident slave populations.[118] In the south, the majority of slaves, probably as many as two-thirds, were women, whereas the gender proportion in the north was more equal.[119] As in the case of Unyamwezi, there are no means to establish the degree of accuracy of these figures. Nevertheless, even allowing for mistakes, they indicate that a large number of slaves lived on the coast in the late 1880s, accounting in certain places, such as the town of Lindi or Mafia Island, for more than half the local population.[120]

The generic term for slave in ki-Swahili is *mtumwa* (pl. *watumwa*), meaning 'one who is sent or used'.[121] From the owners' perspective, the slaves were more or less regarded as dispensable personal clients, relative to the nature of the personal ties to their owner. The number of these dependants corresponded closely to the honour and respect slave owners could command in their respective communities.[122] Yet, the term *mtumwa* covered a whole range of different social realities and conditions. The lives of slaves on the coast not only varied – as one would expect – in different places and periods but also, significantly, according to the gender, age, religion, personal reputation, profession and descent status of the individual slave. These qualifying markers reflected the general hierarchical divisions of Swahili urban society that were reproduced in its slave segment.[123] As far as everyday life was concerned, these divisions denoted different degrees of personal autonomy and were probably as vital to the slaves as the division between owners and slaves.[124]

In the late nineteenth century the majority of the slaves were owned by men who were born on the coast, though it was also said that some of the largest individual slave owners had recently arrived from Zanzibar or had come from the southern Arabian Peninsula.[125] As far as the treatment of slaves was concerned, there was no principal difference as such between immigrant slave owners and those who were born locally. The social relationship between slaves and owners rather depended on how many slaves the latter owned. Most slave owners probably had no more than five slaves, though quite a few owned several hundred.[126] The latter were often substantial landowners and, more tellingly, carried important local political titles, such as *liwali* (pl. *maliwali*) or *jumbe* (pl. *majumbe*).[127]

Thus the owners of vast numbers of slaves tended to belong to the local elite, who often claimed to practise a form of Islam more closely related to the doctrines and stipulations laid down in the *Qur'an* and the *Shari'a* (Islamic law).[128] It is difficult to ascertain whether this claim is true, but according to one knowledgeable contemporary observer, the elite's more devotional religious orientation greatly influenced the way they treated their slaves in everyday life.[129] In this connection it should be noted that since Islamic law and legal practice on the coast allowed free women to both own and inherit property,[130] including slaves, the legal owners of slaves were sometimes women. They usually belonged to the upper echelons of Swahili society and their number was comparatively small.[131]

In addition to the gender division of labour between male and female slaves, the principal factor differentiating their experiences was the location of enslavement. Those who were enslaved in the interior usually fetched far lower prices on the coast than those who were enslaved locally or born into slavery.[132] They were purchased by traders in exchange for goods such as cotton and beads at markets located in towns like Ujiji and Tabora or from chiefs in the interior, while others were awarded slaves for their participation in local conflicts. A smaller number of slaves were kidnapped by traders in the hinterland and areas adjacent to the caravan routes. Finally, there were slaves who were sold because they or their families could not pay their debts or had been convicted by chiefs for offences such as adultery or witchcraft. This was a common occurrence in the northern hinterland of the coast.[133] In short, a number of sources provided a steady supply of slaves from the interior to the coast, which at times greatly increased, especially in periods marked by local conflicts or ecological crises such as the collapse of the Ushambaa kingdom in the late 1860s.[134]

Slaves who had only recently arrived on the coast were called *mateka* (sing. and pl., 'booty' or 'captive'), *washambala* (sing. *mshambala*, 'rural person' or 'country bumpkin'), *washenzi* (sing. *mshenzi*, 'barbarian'), or *wajinga* (sing. *mjinga*, 'fool, ignorant or stupid person') in ki-Swahili.[135] According to one source, after their arrival the adult *wajinga* slaves 'who do not know how to do the washing or to cook'[136] – pointing to the fact that these slaves were predominantly women – were given a few pieces of cloth and a hoe and brought to the plantation or garden plot. They also received a new ki-Swahili name. According to Krenzler, an employee of the German East Africa Company, who was evidently describing a wealthy household, slaves were frequently given that new name the day after their arrival on the coast. The next morning the overseer, usually an older slave, showed the *mateka* where they were assigned to work in the fields for the owner and the garden plot they could use to grow their own food. After that they were left very much to themselves.[137] Owners sometimes took younger *wajinga* slaves, especially girls, into the house where they were taught by older female slaves to do household work. According to Burton, *wajinga* slave boys were sometimes given an Islamic education and professional training.[138] In later life these boys would usually work as 'self-employed' artisans and craftsmen (in ki-Swahili *fundi*, pl. *mafundi*).

On the other hand, there were slaves who were born on the coast. They were called *wazalia* (sing. *mzalia*), which usually implied that their mother or both parents had been slaves.[139] Contrary to the stipulations of Islamic law, which prohibit the enslavement of fellow Muslims, a few of these slaves had been free coastal citizens. Particularly in periods of famine in the rural areas, according to one source, children on the coast were sold into slavery in order to ensure their survival, but this did not happen often; most of those who were enslaved on the coast were immediately sold 'abroad' – to the islands of Zanzibar and Pemba, for instance.[140] In general, the social status of *wazalia* was higher than that of slaves who had only recently arrived on the coast, not least because they spoke ki-Swahili, had some knowledge of the teachings of Islam, and frequently had respectable urban professions in the service sector, such as skilled artisans. Because of the prevailing gender division of labour, most of these skilled slaves were men. The economic relationship with their owners was often reduced to a monthly or annual payment of a previously fixed amount of money or a specified portion of their earnings. These payments varied a great deal between the northern and southern coast. It was reported that in the 1890s in Lindi, for example, slaves kept half their earnings, whereas in Pangani in the same period the amount was reduced to probably less than a third.[141]

Both *wajinga* and *wazalia* slaves were expected to show deference and respect to their owners. They were supposed to walk behind them and, if they met them in the street, they were to remove their caps immediately. 'The slaves could not use their master's wells, nor might they look up when they passed their master's house, nor swing their arms,' states one source.[142] They also had to address the owner in a certain manner. The usual slave greeting in ki-Swahili was *shikamo*, which means 'I clasp your feet' and metaphorically acknowledged the slave's subordination to the owner in public.[143] In some areas, slaves were not allowed to cover their heads at all, a stipulation requiring female slaves to walk around the town unveiled. In the eyes of the more pious Muslims this marked them as 'bad' women with whom social contact should be avoided at all costs.[144] According to one source, male slaves were specifically forbidden to cover their feet, wear sandals, put on a turban (in ki-Swahili, *kilemba*) or carry arms.[145] It was also stated that in the wealthier households male slaves and their owners, although sharing the same food, did not usually eat together. Neither did they sleep under the same roof, as a rule. When slaves accompanied their owners to public ceremonies, rituals and festivities, they were supposed to sit apart from their owners, again publicly highlighting the social difference between the two.[146] Moreover, slaves were to be excluded from performing certain religious rituals and from holding public offices.[147] Yet, it is not clear whether these elaborate rules were always binding on the coast. As fields of contestation many of these customs were probably more often honoured in their breach than their observation.[148]

The social life of slaves differed according to the division between imported and locally born slaves, as well as between slaves who worked in the fields and those whose duty was to conduct household work. The majority of the latter were young women born into slavery on the coast.[149] In the market, they not only fetched higher prices than unskilled male slaves of the same age group, but also outpriced older women. In ki-Swahili they were known as *vijakazi* (sing. *kijakazi*).[150] In the more well-to-do households they carried out ordinary household tasks, such as running errands, fetching water, cooking, cleaning, doing the washing and looking after the children – basically, relieving the owner's wife or wives of the usual female chores.[151] In less affluent households, the owner's wife or wives and female slaves shared these duties. Moreover, female slaves could venture outside the house when 'free' women were prevented from doing so by the more pious Muslim household heads, who insisted on the strict observance of Islamic doctrines and beliefs regarding the proper behaviour of women in public. According to these rules, women were not supposed to leave the house, at least not during the day. Thus, in a limited sense, the actual freedom of movement of these female slaves was greater than the nominal freedom of movement of their mistresses. However, this stipulation was probably observed only in wealthier households.[152] In any case, female slaves delivered messages, purchased mundane supplies in the markets and ran errands for their mistresses.[153] Finally, female slaves sold in the streets the food and other commodities, such as bread, cakes, fried fish and mats, that had been produced in the house by the free women. The earnings were usually shared between the female free members of the household and the female slaves.[154] Thus, although female household slaves were owned as a rule by the male household head, it was his wife or wives who directed their work in daily life. Female slaves also accompanied their mistresses to marriage ceremonies and other festivities. In the case of elite families, the *kijakazi* was expected to carry an umbrella to protect her mistress from both the sun and male curiosity.[155] Some of these female slaves rose to a position of trust. Similar to some of the male slaves (see below), they were manumitted by their male or female owners, especially if the latter belonged to the more wealthy strata of Swahili society.[156] In general, these female slaves received food, housing and clothing but no wages, except for the occasional gift of small amounts of money. According to one report, they earned some extra money by selling foodstuffs and vegetables, which they grew in small garden plots.[157]

The slave owner's concubine, known as the *suria* (pl. *masuria*), occupied a special position in the house. *Masuria* were the most expensive slaves and therefore found only in the more affluent households. According to Islamic law and practice on the coast, Muslims were allowed to marry up to four wives, but possess as many concubines as they liked – and could afford.[158] *Masuria* had to provide sexual services to the male household head, even against their will.[159] Female household slaves – the *vijakazi* – were probably in a similar position. If they refused to cohabit with their owners they were put to work in the fields as a form of punishment. According to Velten there was a popular ki-Swahili saying on the coast at the time which ran: *kijakazi kina meno, chauma / Sikitaki tenna, kipileke shamba / kikalime.* Roughly translated it meant: The slave girl has teeth, she bites/I do not want her any longer, send her to the *shamba/* to do agricultural work![160]

In comparison to other female slaves, the *masuria* had a more elevated position, as they had their own rooms in the house, sometimes even their own outhouse. It was customary for them to receive better food and superior clothing.[161] Some *masuria* accompanied their owners on trading expeditions. If their owner was particularly poor, they sometimes carried the owner's cooking and other household utensils.[162] A few of them were even formally married after their owners had manumitted them.[163] Whether they were widely respected, as some sources seem to suggest, is a matter of argument.[164]

If an owner acknowledged parentage of his *suria*'s children, both she and the children were 'free' in the sense that they could no longer be sold.[165] This practice also applied to other female household slaves. Thus it appears that, even when not specifically bought for this purpose, female household slaves attained *masuria* status through the birth of the owner's children. Both female household slaves and *masuria* usually received their freedom on the death of their owners. Their children had the same formal rights to his or her inheritance as the non-slave children of the household; according to one source, however, such rights were frequently disputed.[166]

Male slaves also worked in the household, especially in the more affluent ones.[167] They were employed as watchmen, messengers and servants, and occasionally as cooks. They were known as *vitwana* (sing. *kitwana*) in ki-Swahili when they were young, while older slaves were referred to as *watwana* (sing. *mtwana*). In contrast to most female household slaves, the majority of male slaves probably did not share the house with their owner. This depended to a large extent on their owner's occupation. Male slaves living outside their owner's house were given food, clothing and, since they were required to have their own accommodation, some kind of housing allowance. They received no fixed wages apart from an occasional small amount of pocket money.[168] These slaves worked at least five days per week for their owners and, in addition, tried to earn some money independently as casual workers or small traders. Preparing and selling firewood was a typical way of acquiring an income in their spare time.[169] Over time, however, male household slaves could rise to a position of trust in some elite families and acted as advisers (*watumwa wa shauri*) or trading agents for their owner, whom they also accompanied on trading expeditions.[170] In times of war, they were often armed to support their owners in the fighting.[171] Furthermore, they were the only group of slaves in the houses of the local elite who ate with the household head and who sometimes even dressed like him. They were normally manumitted on the death of their owners.[172]

Those who worked in the fields did so either on the plantations or on plots of land they had been given to farm on their own. Older slaves were trusted by the owner to organise the slave labour force on their plantations and to enforce discipline. This entailed the strict supervision of the other slaves. They also had greater autonomy and were often left to cultivate their plots entirely on their own, supplying surrounding markets with vegetables, grain and small livestock such as goats and chickens. The position of these older slaves was akin to servile sharecroppers. They had their own families since their owners 'had neither the desire nor the cohesiveness to repress their autonomous reproduction' as Glassman has phrased it.[173] Like the professional urban *wazalia*, they had agreements with their owners, paying a specified sum of money at regular intervals – Rs10 per year in the case of men and Rs6 per year in the case of women, according to one source – or to hand over part of what they had produced.[174] The amount received by the owner was known in ki-Swahili in some areas as *ijara*, in other areas as *taja*, irrespective of whether such dues were paid in kind or in money.[175] As far as the 1880s and 1890s are concerned, such *taja* arrangements were found more often in the south than in the north.[176]

Slaves working on plantations did not usually earn 'wages' but received food, housing and clothing from their owners instead. Clothing for women consisted of a gift of two *kanga* (pieces of patterned cloth) twice a year; at the same time male slaves received a *kanzu* (long-sleeved, straight cotton gown), a *kofia* (a white embroidered cap), and perhaps a few pieces of cotton cloth.[177] The *kanga* and the *kanzu* were only worn on special occasions. The normal slave garment was the loincloth or some tattered pieces of cloth.[178] The typical work of a coastal agricultural slave consisted of cleaning and planting coconut plantations, cutting nuts and preparing copra. The length of the working day on the plantations varied greatly, even within one particular locality.[179] The majority of plantation slaves were new arrivals, most of whom were women.[180] They were allowed to work their own garden plots for an agreed period during the week, usually two or three days that always included Friday, the day of Islamic prayer.[181] Frequently they lived dispersed on the plantation in their own houses, but in some instances, especially when fertile land was particularly scarce as in the Pangani valley, these slaves were grouped together in slave villages further away, under the tutelage of an older slave who was appointed by the plantation owner.[182] Like the slaves who were left to work their own fields, plantation slaves sold part of the produce from their garden plots at urban markets.[183] According to colonial records, working arrangements in the south generally left slaves with more time for their own activities than was the case in the north.[184]

Finally, there were a vast number of slaves who worked on their own account.[185] The great majority of them were men. As mentioned above, they shared their earnings with their owner or had to hand over a fixed sum of money each month.[186] There were two groups. First, there were those engaged in petty trade as hawkers or in unskilled menial jobs as day labourers, messengers, porters, stevedores, mangrove cutters, builders and – in the case of women – cleaners, water carriers and sex workers.[187] In the coastal rural areas they worked mainly as casual labourers. They also did the most unrewarding and tiresome 'self-employed' work, such as preparing copra or digging up and cleaning gum copal. It is hardly surprising that many of them, dissatisfied with rural life and its meagre income opportunities, were drawn to the coastal towns in search of more lucrative employment, as one observer noted.[188] There they 'could be found lurking at the waterfront' as Glassman phrased it, looking for daily paid work.[189] In ki-Swahili this type of slave was called *kibarua* (pl. *vibarua*) and formed a significant part of the local slave populations almost everywhere on the coast.[190] The *vibarua* were often owned by less affluent owners. For the 'investor' short of other means, such slaves represented a convenient savings device that would bear interest in the form of labour.[191]

Some of these self-employed slaves were made to work for the creditors of their owners when the latter failed to honour their debts. In the 1870s and 1880s they constituted the primary source of casual labour for Indian merchants and plantation owners who had lent large amounts of money to members of the urban elite. Indian merchants and plantation owners, who as British subjects were not allowed to own slaves, were in constant need of 'hired' labour.[192] In addition, Indian merchants and traders awarded credit to those who wished to marry but had insufficient funds to pay the brideprice to the bride's family. In exchange, these people pawned themselves to their creditor. Some of them were subsequently sold as slaves.[193] In this connection it should be noted that in the 1880s and 1890s Indian merchants and contractors, like the famous Sewa Haji, supplied European travellers with guides and porters.[194] It is very likely that the latter were slaves. Their European employers paid them a daily living allowance, known as *posho* in ki-Swahili, but no wages. On the contrary, their remuneration was paid to the labour contractor.[195]

The second group of slaves working on their own account were those who worked as self-employed artisans or skilled workers, some of whom had previously worked as day labourers but had learnt a more lucrative trade. They worked as sea captains, fishermen, hunters, sailors, boatmen, rope makers, halva makers, tailors, shoemakers, potters, mat makers, wood carvers, weavers, palm wine tappers, carpenters, boat builders, metalworkers, bricklayers, lime burners, stone masons and even as silversmiths.[196] Others joined caravans as porters, petty traders, and itinerant artisans, some even as caravan leaders and guides.[197] Finally, there were those who worked as professional mercenary soldiers.[198] Women were generally excluded from these professions, but some female slaves managed to become small foodstuff sellers, buying cheap meat or fish in the market, for instance, putting it on small wooden sticks, grilling it and then selling the sticks in the streets and local markets. A number of female slaves also engaged in beer brewing, evidently a profitable undertaking.[199]

These self-employed slaves were the elite among the servile, some of them earning substantial amounts of money through their own work. They had their own families and their children were frequently regarded as free, although their fathers or mothers had not yet been formally manumitted. They were respected for their knowledge and thus commanded exceedingly high prices in the market, but they were rarely for sale. With almost the same status as freed slaves, a number of them actually owned small garden plots, and occasionally even slaves.[200] It appears that male slaves, because of their greater involvement in commercial activities, had more chance of gaining relative personal – and economic – autonomy than female slaves, who were mostly occupied in lowly positions, either in the household or in the fields and plantations.

In contrast to practices elsewhere in nineteenth-century Tanzania, slavery on the coast included formal, sometimes contractual arrangements between owners and slaves about its termination. According to prevailing Islamic ideas[201] concerning the proper role of slaves in society and, more vitally, in social practice, a large number of slaves received their 'freedom' (in ki-Swahili *uhuru*) from their owners through a formal act of declaration (that is, manumission). Though one could question the meaning of 'freedom' in a society which was (and still is) strongly based on hierarchical status distinctions between its members[202] – often the erstwhile slave became a client or dependant of his benefactor – it would be wrong to dismiss such practices as an insignificant 'ideological' prop of servility. According to the colonial *Freibrief* registers mentioned above, about two-thirds of the 17,243 slaves freed in Kilwa and Lindi districts between 1893 and 1912 received official certificates of emancipation because they were voluntarily manumitted by their owners. Over half of these manumissions involved a 'ransom' payment by the slave.[203]

The issue of the colonial *Freibriefe* was apparently modelled on local pre-colonial practice.[204] A few of these pre-colonial certificates have indeed survived.[205] Using Arabic script, they were written in ki-Swahili and given to the freed slave (in ki-Swahili, *huru*, pl. *mahuru*) as a protection against eventual claims by the owner's relatives and family. Manumission was thus an important feature of the social figuration of slavery on the coast, and it was probably already practised on a significant scale in the latter half of the nineteenth century.[206]

Slave owners freed their slaves mainly for three reasons, all of which were strongly supported by Islamic beliefs.[207] First, manumission was generally considered to be a virtuous act, regardless of the social relations between owners and slaves. Those who had sinned during their lives could free themselves from personal guilt by freeing their slaves.[208] Second, there were slaves who had obtained a position of trust within the owner's household (see above). As one source described it, such slaves received their freedom in recognition of the intimate personal relationship they had developed with their owners over the years.[209] Third, and more importantly, slaves could buy their freedom from their owners for an agreed sum of money that approximated their prevailing market value. As has already been pointed out, the act of manumission itself sometimes took effect after the owner's death. In elite households the freeing of slaves was an important part of the often lengthy and detailed written stipulations of the owner's last will.[210]

According to Islamic law, and actual social practice on the coast, those slaves whose owners had specifically allowed them to save some money from their work qualified for future manumission.[211] This was based on the assumption that they would eventually be able to offer their owners the required sum of money to buy their freedom. In this case, the legal stipulation that a slave's entire possessions belonged to the owner did not apply.[212] As far as urban adult male slaves were concerned, owners seem to have readily agreed to such arrangements as they could do little to prevent their slaves from taking up casual work.[213] According to one source, slaves tended to run away if owners tried to seize their possessions.[214] Furthermore, the sale of such slaves was prohibited.[215] Although contractual arrangements of this kind often lacked formality and the required approval by a local *kadhi* (Islamic jurist), it appears from colonial reports that they were indeed common all around the coast.[216] In some areas these semi-freed slaves were called *hadimu* (pl. *wahadimu*), especially by their former owners, but, according to Glassman, more often than not they called themselves *waungwana* or *waswahili*, depending on whether they wanted to accentuate their coastal communal identity or obscure their predominantly up-country origins.[217]

Crucially, arrangements of this kind blurred the line between those who were freed by their owners and those who worked towards their manumission. In effect, all slaves who had even minimal access to the commercial economy could potentially lay claim to being honourable autonomous clients rather than dishonourable personal dependants, as they were probably still regarded by the majority of their owners.[218] This included slaves who merely paid their owners fixed amounts of money and perceived their position to be similar to the free-born but indebted coastal people who repaid their debts in small instalments, whereas the owners considered them as their personal property that had been rented out for a certain period.[219] The slaves felt entitled to take up professions without their owners' explicit consent, for instance joining up-country caravans as porters and artisans or seeking casual employment in the towns.[220] Moreover, day labourers as well as artisans often withheld all or part of their owner's customary share of their earnings, some of them with a view to saving enough money to buy their freedom.[221] Finally, there was the group of semi-servile pawns. Their owners regarded them as potential slaves, but they themselves fiercely defended their perceived rights as free-born, which included the ability to retain part or all of the income they had earned for themselves. The overlap between slavery and freedom was a major source of political and social conflict in everyday life on the coast, sometimes erupting in violent clashes as has been forcefully argued by Glassman for the town of Pangani in the latter half of the nineteenth century.[222] However, it should be noted that the blurring of social distinctions primarily concerned slaves who were linked to or part of the commercial economy. In this respect the *mjinga* slaves were greatly disadvantaged, particularly women who worked permanently in the fields, as they usually obtained their 'wages' in kind. Their monetary sources of income were thus strictly limited.[223]

The relationship between the owner's family and the freed slave (and his or her family) did not cease after manumission.[224] The latter was still expected to show deference and respect in public; freed slaves also owed the owner's family political allegiance. At the same time, the former owner was expected to look after the freed slaves in times of distress and to show generosity by inviting them to private functions such as marriage festivities where they would receive a gift of perhaps small pieces of cloth.[225] In the eyes of the former owners, manumission was a way of acquiring autonomous clients with religious sanction, whose numbers bestowed great honour on the one who could command their loyalty.[226] For the slaves, manumission conveyed quite a different meaning. Although the relationship might develop along patron–client lines, it was determined by reciprocity rather than domination.[227] The manumitted slaves now had a measure of choice in the person they wanted to follow.

Utumwa (slavery) thus covered a whole range of different social configurations. There were those who were despised as *washenzi* (barbarians) and exploited in the fields as agricultural labourers. Then there were those who had managed to gain a measure of personal autonomy in their day-to-day affairs, be it as comparatively independent small-scale farmers and sharecroppers or as urban wage earners. Furthermore, there were the artisans who had a social standing akin to freed slaves. Finally, there were the comparatively few who had actually gained their freedom during their lifetime, many of whom subsequently became clients of their former owners.[228] Thus there was a social continuum between the kind of servility that the *washenzi* slaves had to endure and the relative freedom that skilled artisans and freed slaves – the self-made *waungwana* – proudly claimed.[229]

Yet, it should not be forgotten that despite the many gradations of relative freedom and dependency, in social terms slavery on the coast was as oppressive as anywhere else in late-nineteenth-century East Africa. As Berg writes, 'the best that the African slave population could hope for was assimilation into Swahili society'.[230] As there was no readily available alternative in the form of flight, slaves had to 'struggle for Swahili citizenship' (Glassman), whether they shared the dominant coastal ideology of patronage and patriarchy or not.[231] The distinction often made between coastal slavery as benign and slavery elsewhere as cruel probably reflects more the perspective of the Muslim owner than that of the slave.[232] As already indicated, the rights of slaves on the coast were severely restricted, even though they enjoyed minimal formal protection under Islamic law. The improvements, which some slaves experienced in their social circum-stances and fortunes, were not irreversible. Slave fathers, mothers and children were separated from each other, for instance, if owners wanted to settle their debts or required credit.[233] They could be imprisoned, beaten or put into iron chains for as long as their owner desired, or even killed. [234] Physical abuse of slaves was very much frowned upon on the coast, since it defied a stipulation of Islamic law which required owners to treat their slaves decently. However, in cases of physical maltreatment by individual owners there were no substantive regulations in Islamic law to provide slaves with assistance from other owners or the 'great and respected' of the community. Moreover, their material possessions legally belonged to their owners and, as long as they were slaves, they could not inherit the property of their fathers, mothers, brothers or sisters.[235] They could be sold, pawned or inherited. Furthermore, they were usually not allowed to marry without the consent of their owners and, more crucially, their offspring were also slaves.[236] 'Children born to slaves are, of course, the property of the master, and may be dealt with as he pleases', noted one observer, and 'these things are mentioned in deep shame and pity'.[237]

But, as in the case of Unyamwezi, the power of individual owners was limited by the exit option of rejecting the owners' claims altogether.[238] Flight, however, was predominantly undertaken by individual slaves or, at most, smaller groups since, as Burton put it, 'they hate and fear ... but they lack unanimity to free their necks from the yoke',[239] which, given their extremely different prospects, is hardly surprising. As in Unyamwezi, the majority of fugitive slaves on the coast were likely to be men. Running away in their hundreds in the 1870s and 1880s, fugitive slaves (in ki-Swahili *mtoro*, pl. *watoro*) managed to build up maroon com-munities in semi-permanent settlements, mostly in the more inaccessible parts of the coastal hinterland such as Makorora 25 miles south of Pangani.[240] Like other villages in the coastal hinterland these settlements were heavily fortified and sometimes able to withstand concerted attempts by slave owners to destroy them.[241] The fugitive slaves participated successfully in the commerce of the region, selling ivory, foodstuffs and slaves to the coastal towns.[242] Thus, the missionary Charles New, who had travelled along the coast and further inland to the Kilimanjaro area in the 1860s, noted in 1873 that in the northern hinterland of Tanga there was a sizeable *mtoro* community. He wrote

> In the woods about Jombo, a settlement of run-away slaves, called Muasangombe [sic], has been established. It numbers some thousands, but locked in as they are on all sides, expansion is scarcely possible.... We hear of slaves making their escape thither being delivered to their owners, when applied for, on the payment of a few dollars. The original settlers, finding it impossible to protect all that fly to them, yet anxious to make all they can out of their

position, accept a fee as a compromise, and so the settlement has become effete. It is likely that slaves are held and retained there, as they are everywhere else in this country.[243]

Individual slave owners were thus constantly faced with the threat of flight, particularly from those slaves to whom they had no close personal ties.[244] In the absence of coercive (state) institutions such as a regular police force, they had little means of preventing flight. The only hope of recovering fugitive slaves was to publicise the fact. Owners sent messages around their areas of residence containing a detailed description of the slave's physical appearance and his or her ethnic origin and name.[245] They then had to wait and see if the runaway slave would eventually be returned by other slave owners, by local office holders such as the *jumbe* of a neighbouring village, or by a local big man in expectation of a substantial reward, which, according to one source, ran to about one-third of the slave's market value.[246] When runaway slaves were forcibly returned, they were beaten or locked up for some time. They were also threatened with death if they attempted to run away again; it is difficult to ascertain whether this threat was ever actually carried out.[247]

Flight was a risky undertaking both on the coast and in Unyamwezi. If they could not find a protective community or a secure place to stay, fugitive slaves in the hinterland were often re-enslaved, so that their oppression continued.[248] As one acute observer noted, slaves would usually run away 'only ... when the slave knows of some place to which he can go with reasonable chance of escaping recapture'.[249] Yet there was no guarantee of personal safety in the hinterland, especially in the later nineteenth century, as a huge number of children found out to their peril after they were caught by slave traders and kidnappers and sold 'abroad'.[250] The precariousness of the hinterland also shows in the experiences of European travellers, for example, on approaching settlements there. They were not allowed inside the villages, and the women were heavily guarded by men 'lest any of our camp should fall upon, steal or seduce them', as the traveller Grant noted.[251] Moreover, slaves who thought about running away had to take into account how they were going to assure their basic physical survival after their flight. This is reflected in the following account by British Vice-Consul Smith, who visited the Kilwa hinterland in 1884:

> The day after this party [a slave caravan] had passed we found a Yao woman, who had escaped from it and had hidden herself in an almost dry watercourse. She had been three days without food, and how her rags hung on was a problem not to be solved by the casual observer. She had not been with us half an hour before a porter asked me her hand in marriage.... She was apparently happy with us, but after three days her fear and mistrust made her run away once more. I spent the greater part of the next day in hunting for her, but then gave up the search, for I think it may be reckoned an impossibility to find a person in the bush who wishes to hide.... There can be little doubt that this poor creature would shortly fall a prey to lion or leopard, or would die of hunger....[252]

It is therefore of little surprise that '[m]ost slaves eschewed flight, not because slavery was benign, but because the risks while running away were great, the penalties for capture harsh, and the security of maroon communities marginal in the best of times'.[253] This also explains why many runaway slaves fled to coastal towns. While the chances of being caught here and returned to their owners were higher compared to attaching themselves to fugitive slave communities, the general situation in terms of personal security was probably much better. In any case, these slaves joined the ranks of the urban poor, surviving as casual labourers or, if they were luckier, as caravan porters going up-country. The reports concerning the status of porters leaving the coast are mostly in agreement that the majority of them claimed to be free-born *waungwana*.[254] How many were actually fugitive slaves hiding their status is impossible to tell, but given the social division of labour on the coast, there were very likely quite a few.[255]

Slavery and Social Change

Comparing the main features of late-nineteenth-century servility in Unyamwezi with those prevalent on the coast, three distinct, albeit related and overlapping social processes need to be considered: how people became slaves; how people then sought to better their lives under the prevailing social and political conditions; and, finally, how some of them became free. This last question asks how people who had been despised by society as outsiders and treated as non-persons reached a social status similar to that claimed by free-born members of the society in question. Slavery both in Unyamwezi and on the coast was an indeterminate state, a fluid continuum of different social conditions and configurations of unequal power relations.[256] Importantly, these 'subtle gradations of unfreedom' were grounded in the minute arrangements of everyday life, particularly in the organisation of residence and work.[257]

In Unyamwezi this continuum of social relations was largely, but not exclusively, defined and expressed within kinship relations where the relative distance to the imagined descent group or immediate family of the owner was the main differentiating marker.[258] The majority of women slaves lived, ate and worked together with their owners, some even becoming 'proper' wives of their owners in the process. Over time, these women gained the recognised status of intimate kin group members of their owners' households. The position of male slaves in Unyamwezi was more ambivalent: in the process of absorption only a few became clients of powerful chiefs. The majority of male slaves, especially the older ones, remained in a social limbo. A few might have married free women and consequently become accepted into the owner's family.[259] But for most, that kind of social mobility did not exist. They could not become kin members of the household, nor could they achieve greater personal autonomy, as opportunities to participate in commerce and politics, and thus establish client relationships, were limited.

On the coast, social mobility was expressed in different terms. Here, the main marker was the degree of personal autonomy a slave achieved in his or her lifetime, more often than not at the price of becoming a personal client of the former owner in the process. In as much as slaves worked and lived in their owner's household, only the recognised concubines – the *masuria* – and a few trusted slaves crossed the threshold of the family. Even then, their position often remained ambivalent. All other slaves were strictly regarded as distant personal dependants who in most elite households got nowhere near working, eating or living together with their owners. Thus, unlike Unyamwezi, the coastal region recognised a clearly defined social boundary between those who were regarded as family members in the natal sense and slaves who were regarded at best as personal clients. In any case, on the coast the majority of slaves, again mostly women, worked and lived on plantations that most of their owners only visited sporadically.[260]

Yet, in contrast to Unyamwezi, a significant number of coastal slaves, predominantly the male *wazalia*, gained greater personal autonomy, some even their freedom, by participating on their own account in the commercial economy. The social configuration of slavery on the coast included arrangements, occasionally even formal contracts, concerning its very end. Manumission was not just an act of religious piety by the owner but a goal slaves strove to and could hope to achieve, even if only a minority of slaves actually experienced it.

Both in Unyamwezi and on the coast, absorption into kin or community was a contradictory process of peaceful acculturation and assimilation and of contestation, conflict and violence.[261] Slavery could not have succeeded as a system of social and work relations merely on the basis of permanent coercion; it needed a degree of consent from those who were enslaved. That consent was forthcoming partly because slaves were made to believe in the rectitude of their own marginality, for instance through their upbringing, through the imposition of a specific spatial order on their residence, and through restrictions governing social intercourse with their owners.[262] Yet slavery also depended on allowing slaves the perspective of potentially reducing their social marginality. Social mobility and the permeability of social boundaries, that is the feasibility of achieving the degree of personal autonomy free-born members of society claimed, was thus not the antithesis of slavery or quaint local customs. On the contrary, as slaves could not be replaced as a rule without incurring substantial social, political and economic costs, social mobility was the very condition on which slavery rested, given that other means of keeping slaves in their place or preventing them from running away, such as a strong police force, were largely lacking both on the coast and in Unyamwezi in the second half of the nineteenth century. The major deterrent to flight was the lack of alternatives. The exit option was only chosen if slaves felt they could escape immediate re-enslavement and somehow solve the problem of economic survival after the event. Dependence on their owners for protection and security was – as Frederick Cooper writes – a 'major underpinning of the slave owners' hegemony'.[263] However, it should be noted that the material and social opportunities open to female and male slaves differed a great deal, and widened as commercial expansion progressed.[264]

The actual and potential improvement in the life chances of individual slaves or groups of slaves was not irreversible. In adverse situations, as their life stories vividly demonstrate, slaves employed all the social and economic resources they could muster in order to defend what they had gained.[265] Moreover, a significant proportion of slaves in Unyamwezi and on the coast chose to cut off their ties altogether by flight, rather than to renegotiate their position within the household. Finally, slaves did not always suffer the pretensions and claims of their owners silently, but sometimes engaged in public displays of anger and discontent – as Jonathan Glassman has argued for the coastal town of Pangani in the latter half of the nineteenth century – especially when they perceived their owners' actions as endangering their precarious social and economic position within kin and community.[266]

In addition, the negotiation process that determined the actual life chances of slaves was embedded within a wider framework of the transformation of East African societies at large. As was pointed out in Chapter 2, the expansion of commerce in the nineteenth century and the increasing wealth it brought to local elites affected social relations in Unyamwezi and on the coast in different ways. Both regions experienced a substantial rise in locally resident slave populations, accompanied by an increasing reliance on slaves for the carrying-out of manual labour on plantations and farms. Yet, whereas the process in Unyamwezi was characterised by the partial militarisation of social relations, the coast experienced their partial commercialisation.

On the coast, this process was marked by the emergence of an export-oriented farm and plantation sector. During the course of the second half of the nineteenth century, agricultural production on the coast became increasingly geared towards translocal markets, and, as elsewhere in East Africa at the time, slaves felt the pressure from owners to enlarge farm production or increase their labour input on the owners' plantations. Moreover, especially in the north, an increasing number of non-agricultural slaves was transferred from towns to plantations and farms.[267] These pressures tended to undermine the social mobility of slaves. Commercial expansion thus brought both opportunities and constraints for slaves.[268] Instead of participating successfully in the prospering commercial economy, a significant and increasing number of slaves in the north experienced a decline in their potential fortunes and life chances. Slaves who saw themselves as autonomous clients were reduced by their owners to dependent farm hands whose access to a monetary income was strictly limited.[269]

Yet it should be noted that the intensity of the commercialisation of agricultural production, and thus of social relations, was highly uneven. It was most advanced in the northern parts of the coast, particularly around Tanga and Pangani, where the degree of commercialisation of social and economic relations had probably reached a level whereby the reproduction of society fully depended on the import and utilisation of slaves.[270] In these areas, working arrangements on plantations were designed to extract a much greater share of slave labour than was the case in the south. Agricultural slaves labouring on the sugar and rice plantations in the Pangani valley were made to work for longer periods of time than anywhere else on the coast.[271] Thus, in the north slaves were subjected to a harsher work regime, which sometimes included the beating and whipping of allegedly recalcitrant slaves.[272] Disciplinary methods of this kind – as far as is known – were not practised elsewhere on the coast on a comparable scale.

Moreover, commercial expansion rested both on the transformation of agricultural production and on the development of translocal trade networks. The prosperity of towns like Bagamoyo in the north or Kilwa and Lindi in the south was predominantly based on their profitable involvement in the translocal ivory, slave and grain trade. Consequently, the kind of marginalisation agricultural slaves experienced elsewhere on the coast was less pronounced. Finally, it should also be recognised that the great majority of coastal slaves actually lived in the south. For this reason, it would be wrong to assume that developments in the north necessarily represented the common experience of all coastal slaves.[273]

The reasons for this uneven development are not entirely clear. They can partly be explained by the nature of production of specific crops. Sugar cane, for instance, requires a tremendous amount of labour all year round through its stages of cultivation. It also has to be harvested in a comparatively short period of time, which requires a particularly high input of manual labour.[274] Moreover, land that could be used for the large-scale production of commercial crops was scarcer in the north, providing a strong incentive to use the land with a greater degree of labour intensity. Finally, it could be argued that work practices differed between the north and the south because many plantation owners in the north had only immigrated from Zanzibar and Pemba comparatively recently.[275] They probably modelled their farming techniques, and especially the organisation of servile farm labour, on those prevailing on the clove plantations of the islands.

Because of the paucity of historical sources, the analysis of slavery and nineteenth-century social change in Unyamwezi poses great difficulties for the historian. Some tentative suggestions, nevertheless, seem to be appropriate. The militarisation of Wanyamwezi society at the political level, subsequent to commercial expansion, and the rise of locally resident slave populations, advanced and underpinned the emergence of powerful warlords, particularly in Unyanyembe. These warlords sustained and enlarged their position at the cost of neighbouring chiefdoms, who were raided by armed bands of young men for cattle, ivory and women. At the social level, this development primarily involved the movement of people to stockaded villages and fortified settlements. At the same time, however, agricultural production expanded, not least because of the greatly increased use of slave labour on farms located near these new villages and settlements. As the security situation deteriorated in Unyamwezi in the second half of the

nineteenth century, village chiefs and household heads gained unprece-
dented control over subjects and family members, including slaves and
other dependants such as unmarried female relatives, changing the terms
but not necessarily the idiom of incorporation into kinship groups.[276] This
was also happening in other parts of East Africa at the same time.[277]

The actual living circumstances of slaves and dependants were determined to a considerable degree by their ability to reject the claims of
household heads, especially in periods of crisis. Now, in the second half of
the century, particularly in the 1870s and 1880s, the social position of
slaves deteriorated, as the few resources they and their female dependants
possessed in order to defend their perceived kinship rights were further
reduced.[278] Although kinship and patronage relations, according to Willis
and Miers, 'continued to provide some weapons of the weak as they sought
to improve the terms of their incorporation',[279] the social and material
conditions on which the incorporation into kinship groups and, thus,
effective social mobility rested, apparently declined as the second half of
the century progressed. Flight or the movement away from rapacious
chiefs, for instance, became a less viable option to better one's life. Moreover, as the number of slaves working on the farms and in the homesteads
increased, household heads, village headmen and chiefs were able to lessen
the constraints arising from kinship obligations. Their dependants became
increasingly less important as a means of sustaining or enlarging their
position *vis-à-vis* their neighbours. Moreover, wealth and prestige were
increasingly measured in the number of cattle, women and slaves a chief
could command.[280] This development was at its most pronounced in
Unyanyembe, the most prosperous but also the most militarised areas of
Unyamwezi where, in the early 1860s, chained gangs of slaves were
actually seen doing agricultural work in the fields under the supervision of
an overseer.[281]

As had happened on the coast, the disparities between the social and
economic opportunities for male and female slaves widened in the course
of the second half of the century. Chiefs increasingly recruited slaves and
other male dependants into armed bands of young men (*ruga-ruga*) to
defend and expand their chiefdoms.[282] In turn, these men were able to
extract not only wealth and status from their 'profession', but also the
ability to reject demands from chiefs and household heads for labour and
obedience. This is probably why European travellers were surprised to see
groups of armed young men in the villages and settlements who were
apparently doing little but smoking tobacco and hemp and amusing themselves by taunting elderly people, presumably household heads and their
dependents.[283] Such 'opportunities' were not available to women, at least
not on a comparable scale. Furthermore, in the second half of the century,
the status of women, including female slaves who had acquired fictive
kinship rights, generally declined, as it did in other parts of East Africa at
the time.[284] Women were no longer merely exchanged as wives in marriage
agreements between families but increasingly exploited as commercial and
political properties in transactions involving local officeholders. As the

second half of the century progressed, women and slaves were sold in rapidly increasing numbers to slave traders, given in exchange for goodwill from hostile neighbouring chiefs or pawned to local big men, village headmen and chiefs.[285] Thus, while the life chances of free-born women generally deteriorated, some even becoming a tradable commodity in the process, a significant number of male slaves gained the social position of free-born men.[286]

In summary, it appears that commercial expansion and the accompanying rise in the number of slaves resident in Unyamwezi and on the coast changed the patterns of mutual rights and obligations construed by locally defined sets of kinship and client relations.[287] This was the result of a process whereby one particular cluster of rules was not simply replaced by another but was rather the outcome of negotiations, disputes and even struggles between those who wished to defend and expand their perceived rights and those who wanted to do away with them. As far as the coast and Unyamwezi are concerned, but also in general terms, kinship and patronage relations should thus not merely be seen as a continuum comprising a variety of different social relations. They are, moreover, fields of social conflict whose substance and meaning were constantly reworked, particularly when the social, political and economic conditions by which they were shaped had undergone a change.[288]

Commercial expansion brought wealth to the few, but misery to the many, especially to dependants and slaves whose life chances of becoming respected members of kinship groups and patronage networks in the last decades of the nineteenth century declined. At the same time, the number of slaves resident not only in Unyamwezi and on the coast but elsewhere in East Africa had increased dramatically. The following chapter will show how the German colonial authorities dealt with that problem.

Notes

1   Coastal settlements in the interior will not be treated explicitly. According to descriptions of settlements such as Tabora, Ujiji and Kazeh, slavery here was very similar to the coast. Also, there is no evidence to suggest that in the matter of slavery Unyamwezi was influenced significantly by coastal practices, although *a priori* such influences cannot be completely ruled out. See, for instance, European travel accounts such as Burton 1860: 229 and Reichard 1892: 468, and descriptions in colonial records such as RHO Micr Afr 472 R.20/MF 44, Tabora District Book, 'Notes on an Interview with Jaba bin Zaid' by Assistant District Officer N. Burt, 24 May 1927.

2   Like the previous chapter, the following one has greatly profited from John Iliffe's study *A Modern History of Tanganyika* (1979: especially 40–87).

3   For an overview by contemporaries, see Le Roy 1890, Eberstein 1896: 177 and Velten 1903: 305ff. For a comparative perspective, see Meillassoux 1991: 143–56 and Kopytoff and Miers 1977: 12–14.

4   For examples, see Tippu Tip 1902 vol. I: 185, 216, 225, 232, 243.

5   For this argument, see Wright 1993: 7. For a detailed description, see the life story of Tatu Mulondyelwa in the same volume, p. 184. See also the 'trade biographies' of slaves in Colomb 1873: 28ff., Jones-Bateman (M. Furahani) 1891, Velten 1903: 306 and Nolan 1977: 141. For a different view, see, for instance, Coulbois (1901: 99–112), who describes nineteenth-century enslavement as an Arab '*razzia générale*'.

6   Reichard 1892: 462ff.
7   Reichard 1892: 462ff.
8   For a photograph of a man wearing a slave stick, see Blohm 1931 vol. I: 209, photograph no. 16. For a detailed description, see Cameron 1877 vol. I: 284. See also Morton 1990: 112.
9   See, for instance, Tippu Tip 1902 vol. I: 194, vol. II: 44 and RHO Micr Afr 472 R.19/MF 42, Tabora Regional Book, 'Extracts from Nyamwezi Law and Custom by H. Cory', 1952: 6. For this argument, see also Livingstone 1874: 149 (11 August 1871).
10 Blohm 1931 vol. II: 36 [extract from interview, n.d. (pre-1914)], Bösch 1930: 442.
11 See chapters 6 and 7.
12 Blohm 1931 vol. II: 63 [extract from interview, n.d. (pre-1914)]. See also Waller 1876, in Great Britain, *Parliamentary Papers. Royal Commission on Fugitive Slaves*, C. 1516, (vol. I, p. 35–8), cited in *Traite des esclaves* 1889: 132. See also Wright 1993: 151.
13 Reichard 1892: 484. See also the description of the journey to the coast by Jones-Bateman (M. Furahani) 1891: 18–20.
14 See, for instance, the highly biased description of the East African slave trade in Afrikaverein 1895, Baur and Le Roy 1886: 97–106 and Krenzler 1886–8: 71–4.
15 Reichard 1892: 484. For a similar view, see Burton 1860: 318, 326, Livingstone 1874: 345 (13 November 1868), 348 (19 November 1868) and 351 (27 November 1868), Cameron 1877 vol. II: 31, Tippu Tip 1902 vol. I: 208 and Velten 1898: 7, 1903: 306. See also Steudel 1895: 171–202 and RHO Micr Afr 472 R.20/MF 44, Tabora District Book, 'Notes on an Interview with Jaba bin Zaid by Assistant District Officer N. Burt', 24 May 1927 and Nolan 1977: 141. For a different description of a slave caravan on the move, see Elton 1874: 242ff., Toeppen 1885–6: 231, Pruen 1888: 661–5, 1891: 220ff. and the life story of Swema as recorded by Pater Horner in 1866 and translated by Alpers 1997 [1983]: 185–219. For a contraversial discussion of the origins of that life story, see Kollman 2005: 130f.
16 Iliffe 1979: 81.
17 Kopytoff (1988: 500) has argued that there is no substantive meaning to the term ' free', as slavery as much as kinship is embedded in a 'continuum of dependency'. Arguably, there are different kinds of dependency: for instance, only some forms of kinship in nineteenth-century East Africa allowed a person to become a commodity. Thus, the term 'free' is used here primarily to denote a status that precluded a person's outright sale under 'normal' circumstances.
18 The term 'family' is used loosely here in order to denote a kinship group or members of a household. Moreover, the status of freedom in opposition to enslavement is misleading to some degree, because it does not do justice to its fragility and ambiguity, as is argued in this chapter.
19 Bösch 1930: 444, Seibt 1910, cited in Gottberg 1971: 198 and Grant 1864: 48. See also RHO Micr Afr 472 R.20/MF 44, Tabora District Book, 'Records of Meeting Held from the 2nd October to 5th October 1932'.
20 Tippu Tip 1902 vol. I: 251, vol. II: 2.
21 For examples, see Burton 1860: 110, Velten (citing Baraka bin Shomari) 1903: 378, Löbner 1910, cited in Gottberg 1971: 161, 163, 166 and Seibt 1910, cited in Gottberg 1971: 193. For the original reports by Gottberg and Seibt, see BAB RKolA 4997/432, 'Beantwortung des Fragebogens über die Rechte der Eingeborenen in den deutschen Kolonien', Missionar Löbner, 1 March 1910 and BAB RKolA 4997/467, 'Beant-wortung des Fragebogens über die Rechte der Eingeborenen in den deutschen Kolonien', Missionar Seibt, 30 January 1910. I have used the texts reprinted in Gottberg (1971) for reference purposes since they are more easily accessible. For a more theoretical discussion of pawnship in Africa, see Roberts and Miers 1988: 46ff. and Falola and Lovejoy 1994: 1–26. See also the contributions by Morton 1994: 27–42 on coastal Kenya and Giblin 1994: 43–53 on north-eastern Tanzania in the same edition. For an enlarged version of that volume, see Lovejoy and Falola 2003. People in Unyamwezi were sometimes compelled to sell themselves into slavery because they had run up personal debts by playing *mbao* (a board game) for too high a stake. See Burton 1860: 462.
22 See Kirk to Granville 13 April 1885, in Great Britain, *Parliamentary Papers. Correspondence Relating to Zanzibar*, C. 4776, London 1886: 119, cited in *Traite des esclaves* 1889: 116ff. For a review of the vast literature on the household as a domestic production and

consumption unit, see Guyer 1981: 87–137.

23   Smith 1887: 103.

24   Bösch 1930: 445. For a slightly different perspective on pawning by household heads on the Kenya coast, see Willis 1993a: 47–59, 1993b: 132ff. and Morton 1994: 27–42.

25   Blohm 1931 vol. II: 38. Arguably, a distinction can be drawn between pawns and slaves depending on the distance between their place of origin and their new residence. However, European sources are frequently unspecific on this point, as differences of this kind were hardly discernible to the outside observer. For more details, see also the illuminating report concerning the practice in the Kilwa hinterland in BAB RKolA 4997: 497, 'Fragebogen über die Rechte der Eingeborenen in den deutschen Kolonien (Wakitu)', Bezirksamt Kilwa, 23 October 1910.

26   Blohm 1931 vol. II: 38.

27   For a description of the Ujiji slave market, see the report by Vycke [1888], cited in *Traite des esclaves* 1889: 106. See also Burton 1860: 318.

28   Reichard 1892: 475.

29   Cameron 1877 vol. I: 144. For a detailed description of a Zanzibar slave market, see Devereux 1869: 103–5.

30   See, for instance, the description of such 'relay' trade in Colomb 1873: 28ff., Jones-Bateman (M. Furahani) 1891 and the life story of Namwaga in Moravian Archives Herrnhut, 'Nachlass T. Bachmann', vol. III: 180ff. For comparative material, see also the life stories in Wright 1993.

31   For a detailed description of commercial transactions of slaves, see Reichard 1892: 472. See also Grant 1864: 48 and Blohm 1931 vol. II: 37 [extract from interview, n.d. (pre-1914)]. For the buying and selling of slaves by caravan porters, see Burton 1860: 154ff., 454 and Hermann 1893: 43ff.

32   Blohm 1931 vol. II: 37 [extract from interview, n.d. (pre-1914)]. As the text was translated by W. Blohm from ki-Nyamwezi into German and then by the author into English, it is likely that the more subtle meanings of some words have been lost in the process. It is probably worth noting that Blohm does not state in which part of Unyamwezi the person he interviewed had grown up. For a description of the outright sale of a person in the vicinity of Ujiji, see Joachim 1905–6: 109–15.

33   For the term 'rites of passage', see Van Gennep 1960.

34   For the phrase 'social death', see Patterson 1982.

35   Livingstone 1874: 93 (28 December 1870).

36   Nolan 1977: 49. Unfortunately, Nolan does not provide the ki-Nyamwezi words for 'foreigner' or 'stranger', which would have helped to compare their meaning with the appropriate ki-Swahili terms. The ki-Swahili word *mgeni* (pl. *wageni*) [stranger/foreigner] for instance, does not convey a derogative meaning.

37   Burton 1860: 299.

38   Burton 1860: 301. For the Unyoro–Buganda–Unyamwezi trade see also Jones-Bateman (M. Furahani) 1891: 17 and Baumann 1894: 243ff. Baumann states that in the early 1880s most slaves in Unyamwezi were from the Manyema region in the eastern Congo. Nyamwezi slave traders are also mentioned in the life story of Chisi-Ndjurisiye-Sichyajunga in Wright 1993: 100ff. See also the description of enslavement through capture following a raid by the soldiers of Mirambo in the life story of Anton as recorded by Krelle 1929: 9ff.

39   Bösch 1930: 442. See also Becker 1887: I: 220–2 and Grant 1864: 48. For a similar view, see RHO Micr Afr 472 R.19/MF 42, Tabora District Book, 'Extracts from Nyamwezi Law and Custom by H. Cory', 1952: 6.

40   RHO Micr Afr 472 R.19/MF 42, Tabora District Book, 'Extracts from Nyamwezi Law and Custom by H. Cory', 1952: 6.

41   Reichard 1890: 277.

42   BAB RKolA 7382/27: 88, 'Berichte der einzelnen Verwaltungsstellen in Deutsch-Ostafrika über die Sklaverei', Station Tabora, Berichterstatter: Hauptmann Puder, n.d. [1900].

43   See, for instance, the criticism of Reichard's estimate by Nolan 1977: 143. For a detailed compilation of population figures according to administrative district, see Hermann 1914: 172–6. These figures seem to suggest that Puder probably under-estimated the number of people resident in Tabora district. Hermann does not provide references to the sources he used for his study.

44 Professor A. Sheriff, personal communication.

45 Nolan 1977: 49, 143.

46 Other contemporary observers reported similar numbers not just for Tabora district, but also for the neighbouring districts of Ujiji and Mwanza. See *Stenographische Berichte des Reichstages: Anlagen*, 13. Legislaturperiode, 1. Session 1912–14, Aktenstück Nr. 1395, p. 2888 [abbreviated below as *RTA* 1912–14, no. 1395: 2888] 'Denkschrift über die Haussklaverei in Deutsch-Ostafrika' by Governor H. Schnee, 20 February 1914. See also BAB RKolA 7382/27: 82–4, 'Berichte der einzelnen Verwaltungsstellen in Deutsch-Ostafrika über die Sklaverei', Station Muanza, Berichterstatter: Hauptmann Schlobach, n.d. [1900].

47 Bösch 1930: 440 and Abrahams 1967b: 95. See also the short yet informative article by Spellig 1927–8: 212ff.

48 Blohm 1931 vol. I: 168, vol. II: 36 [extract from interview, n.d. (pre-1914)].

49 Reichard 1892: 474. See also Burton 1860: 383.

50 Pruen 1891: 235.

51 Nolan 1977: 49. For this argument, see also Kopytoff 1988: 490.

52 BAB RKolA 7382/27: 89, 'Berichte der einzelnen Verwaltungsstellen in Deutsch-Ostafrika über die Sklaverei', Station Tabora, Berichterstatter: Hauptmann Puder, n.d. [1900] and Blohm 1931 vol. II: 37 [extract from interview, n.d. (pre-1914)], 38. See also Löbner 1910, cited in Gottberg 1971: 142. It is unlikely that chiefs, important headmen or royal courtiers would be seen together with their agricultural slaves.

53 Löbner 1914: 12, Nolan 1977: 145. For a comparative perspective, see Robertson and Klein 1983, 2–25.

54 Burton 1860: 215. This quotation does not allow generalisation, because it is too unspecific about perceived gender roles in agricultural production in other neighbouring regions of Unyamwezi. But Burton also noted that 'Adults fetch no price, because they are notoriously intractable, and addicted to desertion.' Burton 1860: 355.

55 See, for instance, Burton 1860: 329, 355, 520 and Bösch 1930: 441. See also Roberts and Miers 1988: 39.

56 Nolan 1977: 146.

57 See, for instance, Burton 1860: 383.

58 For this argument see Wright 1993: 154.

59 Blohm 1931 vol. I: 89. See also Puder 1899, cited in Gottberg 1971: 237.

60 Nolan 1977: 147. See also Abrahams 1967a: 68.

61 Bösch 1930: 445.

62 Blohm 1931 vol. I: 3, vol. II: 36 [extract from interview, n.d. (pre-1914)]. See also Seibt 1910, cited in Gottberg 1971: 187. Arguably, from a structuralist perspective, kinship ties and the formal manumission of slaves exclude each other. As Kopytoff has argued (1988: 495) the former are acquired by birth and descent. These ties can be extended to non-natal kin, for instance to slaves, or reduced, but they cannot be broken except through the act of (re)-enslavement. Whether slaves and their owners saw this issue in a similar way, however, remains open to dispute.

63 Blohm 1931 vol. II: 36 [extract from interview, n.d. (pre-1914)], 64. See also Nolan 1977: 49. For a different view, see Stuhlmann 1894: 64.

64 Nolan 1977: 146. See also Abrahams 1967b: 95.

65 Blohm 1931 vol. II: 36 [extract from interview, n.d. (pre-1914)] and Abrahams 1967b: 95. Yet, see also Bösch 1930: 440ff., who states that all children of slaves were regarded as free. For a different view, see RHO Micr Afr 472 R.19/MF 42, Tabora District Book, 'Extracts from Nyamwezi Law and Custom by H. Cory', 1952: 6. Cory reports that all children of slaves had the same status as free-born children. On this issue, see also Abrahams 1967b: 95ff.

66 Blohm 1931 vol. II: 36 [extract from interview, n.d. (pre-1914)].

67 BAB RKolA 7382/27: 89, 'Berichte der einzelnen Verwaltungsstellen in Deutsch-Ostafrika über die Sklaverei', Station Tabora, Berichterstatter: Hauptmann Puder, n.d. [1900] and Löbner 1910, cited in Gottberg 1971: 152. See also Blohm 1931 vol. II: 36 [extract from interview, n.d. (pre-1914)]. It is unfortunate that Blohm does not provide a ki-Nyamwezi translation of these terms, as this would allow a comparison with other authors, such as Bösch. For comparative material, see BAB RKolA 7382/27: 82–4, 'Berichte der einzelnen Verwaltungsstellen in Deutsch-Ostafrika über die Sklaverei', Station Muanza, Berichterstatter: Hauptmann Schlobach, n.d. [1900].

68 For a description of female slave work duties, see the life story of Msatulwa Mwachitete in Wright 1993: 65. Whether female slaves actually worked for the free women of the household in daily life rather than for the male household head cannot be decided on the basis of the available sources, but it seems likely, given the gender division of labour. For this argument, see also Robertson and Klein 1983: 2–25.

69 BAB RKolA 7382/27: 89, 'Berichte der einzelnen Verwaltungsstellen in Deutsch-Ostafrika über die Sklaverei', Station Tabora, Berichterstatter: Hauptmann Puder, n.d. [1900].

70 For a comparative perspective, see Willis 1993a: 70.

71 Löbner 1910, cited in Gottberg 1971: 152. On this point, see also Ankermann 1929: 212ff.

72 Moravian Archives Herrnhut, R 15 M, 'Jahresbericht Urambo 1899', Löbner 1910, cited in Gottberg 1971: 153. See also Nolan 1977: 49. For a different view, see RHO Micr Afr 472 R.19/MF 42, Tabora District Book, 'Extracts from Nyamwezi Law and Custom by H. Cory', 1952: 6.

73 Bösch 1930: 441.

74 Blohm 1931 vol. II: 36 [extract from interview, n.d. (pre-1914)].

75 Löbner 1910, cited in Gottberg 1971: 154.

76 Wright 1993: 43.

77 Bösch 1930: 441.

78 Blohm 1931 vol. II: 36 [extract from interview, n.d. (pre-1914)].

79 Löbner 1910, cited in Gottberg 1971: 152 and Abrahams 1967a: 58. See also RHO Micr Afr 472 R.20/MF 44, Tabora District Book, 'Tribal Government' [1933].

80 Bösch 1930: 442ff. See also Reichard 1892: 479.

81 Blohm 1931 vol. II: 36 [extract from interview, n.d. (pre-1914)], 64. See also Grant 1864: 50 and RHO Micr Afr 472 R.20/MF 44, Tabora District Book, 'Tribal Government' [1933]. See also Wright 1993: 36.

82 See, for instance, BAB RKolA 7382/27: 88, 'Berichte der einzelnen Verwaltungsstellen in Deutsch-Ostafrika über die Sklaverei', Station Tabora, Berichterstatter: Hauptmann Puder, n.d. [1900].

83 Nolan 1977: 146.

84 Löbner 1914: 13.

85 Blohm 1931 vol. II: 124 and Grant 1864: 50, 61, 73.

86 Bösch 1930: 440. For a different view, see Löbner 1910, cited in Gottberg 1971: 152 and Löbner 1914: 13.

87 Blohm 1931 vol. II: 38 [extract from interview, n.d. (pre-1914)].

88 Blohm 1931 vol. II: 37 [extract from interview, n.d. (pre-1914)]. See also Löbner 1910, cited in Gottberg 1971: 152 and Reichard 1892: 462ff., 466ff.

89 Cameron 1877 vol. I: 184.

90 On the dangers of travelling alone in Unyamwezi, see Grant 1864: 102. See also Tippu Tip 1902 vol. I: 277.

91 See the life stories of Grandmother Narwimba and Chisi-Ndjurisiye-Sichyajunga in Wright 1993: 50–2 and 83–5.

92 Burton 1860: 259.

93 See Baumann 1894: 106. He describes how when he left Unyamwezi a number of women tried to join his caravan by attaching themselves to male porters. He does not state whether these women were slave or free. See also Rockel 2000b: 750ff. See also Wright 1993: 43.

94 For this argument see Wright 1993: 4. See also Robertson and Klein 1983: 18.

95 See, for instance, the life story of Sizia as recorded by Joachim 1905–6: 109–15.

96 Reichard 1892: 465.

97 See, for example Kopytoff and Miers 1977: 14–18 and Robertson and Klein 1983: 2–25. See also Willis and Miers 1997: 480ff.

98 For a striking example, Abrahams 1967b: 95ff.

99 Pruen 1888: 662ff., 1891: 217. See also Wright 1993: 25ff., 169. Whether kinship ideology was consciously used as a means of social control in lieu of coercion is a matter of debate. See, for instance, Meillassoux's (1991: 12–14) reading of Kopytoff and Miers (1977: 3–88).

100 Bösch 1930: 445. See also Broyon-Mirambo 1877–8: 32, cited in Gottberg 1971: 118.

101 Löbner 1910, cited in Gottberg 1971: 152, 168. See also Reichard 1892: 467.

102 Bösch 1930: 443.
103 Nolan 1977: 147.
104 For this argument see RHO Micr Afr 472 R.19/MF 42, Tabora District Book, 'Extracts from Nyamwezi Law and Custom by H. Cory', 1952: 6ff.
105 The Nyamwezi elders present at the meeting strongly favoured the reintroduction of this punishment for runaway wives. RHO Micr Afr 472 R.20/MF 44, Tabora District Book, 'Records of Meeting Held from the 12th to 14th October 1930'.
106 Wright 1993: 9.
107 This part of the chapter has greatly profited from the ideas and the perspectives to be found in the comparative literature on Zanzibar and the Kenya coast, especially Lodhi 1973, Cooper 1977, 1980, Strobel 1979, Romero Curtin 1983, Romero 1986, Morton 1990, Willis 1993a and Romero 1997. For a contemporary description of working practices on Zanzibar, see Fischer 1885: 63–70 and Mackenzie 1895: 69–96.
108 Sheriff 1987: 158–72. See also Chittick 1974.
109 For a description of the 'Nyasa' slave trade, see the life story of Ganisya as recorded by Klamroth 1927: 10–13 and Eberstein 1896: 175ff. Eberstein reports that in the early 1890s the price differentials between Lake Nyasa and Kilwa came to at least 400 per cent for slaves and at least 100 per cent for ivory. For the Nyasa–Rovuma–Kilwa/Mikindani slave trade in general, see Livingstone 1965: 67, 70, 73, 91, 97, 160–2 (14 September 1862, 17 September 1862, 18 September 1862, 27 September 1862, 30 September 1862, 'Despatch from David Livingstone to the British Foreign Secretary, 16 October 1862'), Livingstone 1865: 390–2, Livingstone 1874: 188 (14 July 1866), Waller 1876 (citing from a letter from Bishop Steere 1876), O'Neill 1895: 13ff., and Smith 1887: 101, 104–6. For a geographical description of the actual trade route, see Lieder 1894: 277–82. See also the detailed map of caravan routes in East Africa in *Deutsches Kolonialblatt*, 'Karte der Zollämter und Karawanenstrassen', 1892, annex.
110 See Chapter 2. For the clandestine slave trade between Pangani and Pemba and Dar es Salaam/Mbwamaji and Zanzibar, see also Kirk to Granville 19 and 20 December 1884 and Kirk to Sultan Barghash b. Said 12 March 1885, in Great Britain, *Parliamentary Papers. Correspondence Relating to Zanzibar*, C. 4776, London 1886: 90–3, 111, cited in *Traite des esclaves* 1889: 165, 215. See also BAB RKolA 7363: 182, extract from 'Correspondence relating to the Slave Trade, 1888–89', HMSO, London 1889: 27–29. The report states that between 1 July 1888 and 31 December 1889 some 69 dhows, carrying 951 slaves (273 men, 262 women, 228 boys, 188 girls) were captured. The great majority of these dhows had taken the slaves on board in the coastal harbours directly opposite Zanzibar.
111 Krapf 1858 vol. II: 186 [Nyasa slave trade to Kilwa], vol. II: 279 [Tabora slave trade to Pangani, Wazeguha trade] and University of Birmingham Library, Church Missionary Society, CA 50 16/179, 'Memoir on the East African Slave Trade', by J. L. Krapf, Rabai 1853. See also Kirk to Roseberry [northern slave trade] 12 March 1886, Great Britain, *Parliamentary Papers. Correspondence Relating to Zanzibar*, C. 5111, London 1887: 150, cited in *Traite des esclaves* 1889: 137 and Waller 1876 [Nyasa slave trade to Kilwa], in Great Britain, *Parliamentary Papers. Royal Commission on Fugitive Slaves*, C. 1516 (vol. I, p. 39), cited in *Traite des esclaves* 1889: 162. For the secondary literature on the subject, see Chapter 2.
112 Deutsch 1999: 124. The records on the issue of *Freibriefe* can be found in BAB RKolA 7410–7415, 'Sammlung der zur Mitteilung an das Spezialbüro in Brüssel bestimmten Nachweisungen', 1 October 1892–31 May 1915. For more detail, see Chapter 6.
113 On slavery in the Tanga hinterland, see, for instance, BAB RKolA 7382/27: 42, 'Berichte der einzelnen Verwaltungsstellen in Deutsch-Ostafrika über Sklaverei', Bezirksamt Tanga, Berichterstatter: Bezirksamtssekretär Blank n.d. [1899] and BAB RKolA 7382/27: 51ff., Bezirksamt Pangani, Berichterstatter: Bezirksamtmann Sigl n.d. [1899].
114 For a description of the capture of a female slave in 'Maniema' and her subsequent sale on the coast, see the life story of Anna as recorded by Krelle 1929: 13ff.
115 BAB RKolA 1004: 105, 'Bericht des Bezirksamts Lindi', 14 September 1897. According to that report, in the late 1880s and early 1890s Yao traders sold over 1,000 slaves in Mikindani and Lindi alone, a few hundred of whom were exported. The *Bezirksamt* did little to suppress the trade as the local German military forces were absent, having been relocated to the north following the coastal uprising of 1888.

116 Elton 1873: 237, 243. According to a report by Mackenzie to the British and Foreign Anti-Slavery Society in the late 1880s and early 1890s, Zanzibar and Pemba illegally imported about 6,000 slaves annually from the mainland, mostly from places opposite the islands. See Mackenzie 1895: 90. Lugard (1896: 343), however, estimated that their numbers were much smaller, accounting for 'only' about 4,000 annually.

117 For these numbers, see BAB RKolA 7382/27: 42–93, 'Berichte der einzelnen Verwaltungsstellen in Deutsch-Ostafrika über Sklaverei', especially BAB RKolA 7382/27: 42 Tanga n.d. [1899], BAB RKolA 7382/27: 48 Pangani n.d. [1899], BAB RKolA 7382/27: 57 Bagamoyo n.d. [1898], BAB RKolA 7382/27: 60 Dar es Salaam n.d. [1899], BAB RKolA 7382/27: 63 Rufiyi n.d. [1899], BAB RKolA 7382/27: 65 Kilwa n.d. [1900], BAB RKolA 7382/27: 68 Lindi n.d. [1900]. For the number of slaves resident in Lindi district, see also BAB RKolA 1004: 105, 'Bericht des Bezirksamts Lindi', 14 September 1897 ['three-quarters of the local population are slaves'], for Bagamoyo in the mid-1890s, see also BAB RKolA 1004/97: 1, 'Bericht des Bezirksamts Bagamoyo', 14 September 1897 [Bagamoyo 3,000 slaves, Kaule 1,000 slaves, Bueni 400 slaves]. See also *Deutsches Kolonialblatt*, 'Die Bevölkerung von Deutsch-Ostafrika', 1894: 106–9, where an anonymous correspondent notes that about 20 per cent (1,346) of the town population of 6,662 were slaves. The total population of Bagamoyo was said to exceed 10,000. Figures for other coastal towns were given as: Tanga 3,000–4,000, Pangani 10,000, Saadani 4,000, Dar es Salaam 10,000, Lindi 3,000, Kilwa [n.a.]. Further, more descriptive evidence can be found in BAB RKolA 4997/1–503, 'Beantwortung des Fragebogens über die Rechte der Eingeborenen in den deutschen Kolonien', various dates [1909–13]. For somewhat different figures, see Iliffe 1979: 129.

118 According to the detailed report by *Bezirksamtssekretär* Blank, two-thirds of all slaves residing in Tanga district lived directly on the coast. See BAB RKolA 7382/27: 42, 'Berichte der einzelnen Verwaltungsstellen in Deutsch-Ostafrika über Sklaverei', Bezirksamt Tanga, Berichterstatter: Bezirksamtssekretär Blank n.d. [1899]. As district offices were usually located in coastal towns, their knowledge of the hinterland was probably severely limited and very likely influenced estimates regarding the resident slave population in these areas. For the lack of knowledge about the hinterland, see, for example, BAB RKolA 7382/27: 69, 'Berichte der einzelnen Verwaltungsstellen in Deutsch-Ostafrika über Sklaverei', Bezirksamt Lindi, Berichterstatter: Bezirksamtmann Zache n.d. [1900]. See also BAB RKolA 1004/120: 3, 'Bericht des Bezirksamts Kilwa', 10 September 1897.

119 BAB RKolA 7382/27: 65, 'Berichte der einzelnen Verwaltungsstellen in Deutsch-Ostafrika über Sklaverei', Bezirksamt Kilwa, Berichterstatter: Bezirksamtmann von Rode n.d. [1900], BAB RKolA 7382/27: 69, Bezirksamt Lindi, Berichterstatter: Bezirksamtmann Zache n.d. [1900], BAB RKolA 7382/27: 51ff., Bezirksamt Pangani, Berichterstatter: Bezirksamtmann Sigl n.d. [1899], BAB RKolA 7382/27: 42, Bezirksamt Tanga, Berichterstatter: Bezirksamtssekretär Blank n.d. [1899].

120 BAB RKolA 1004: 105, 'Bericht des Bezirksamts Lindi', 14 September 1897 and BAB RKolA 7382/27: 68, 'Berichte der einzelnen Verwaltungsstellen in Deutsch-Ostafrika über Sklaverei', Bezirksamt Lindi, Berichterstatter: Bezirksamtmann Zache n.d. [1900]. For Mafia Island, see RHO Afr Micr R.8/MF 19, Mafia District Book, 'Domestic Slavery in German East Africa' by N. King, Mafia, April 1915: 18. See also King 1917: 120. In the article he gives the estimate that in 1915 slaves still accounted for about a third of the total population of 13,000.

121 The terminology changed according to region in ki-Swahili-speaking areas. See Middleton 1992: 25. For the use of ki-Swahili terms denoting slaves, see Tippu Tip 1902 vol. I: 189 (*watumwa wetu*), 192 (*watu wetu*), 199 (*wajakazi*), 214 (*wazalia, mtwana*), vol. II: 2 (*mtu suria*). One phrase he used was '*mzalia wa Unguja, mtumwa wa Ali bin Mohammed*', meaning 'the locally born slave, the slave of Ali bin Mohammed', which seems to indicate that he regarded *mtumwa* as a generic term. For the phrase, see Tippu Tip 1902 vol. I: 214. For other terms for slaves, see also BAB RKolA 1004/120: 1ff., 'Bericht des Bezirksamts Kilwa', 10 September 1897. According to *Bezirksamtmann* von Eberstein slaves were called *wajana, wazalia* or *watumwa wa assili* in order to describe the antiquity of their own, their parents' or their grandparents' arrival on the coast. For a discussion of the ki-Swahili terminology for slaves on the Kenya coast, see Berg 1971: 167–79, Morton: 1990: 3, Eastman 1994: 87–107; for Zanzibar, see Lodhi 1973; for female slaves, see

Bromber 2002. According to Morton (1990: 3) the term *waja* was used on the Kenya coast.

122 Pouwels 1987: 78, Glassman 1991: 289 and 1995: 22ff.

123 Middleton 1992: 90.

124 Glassman 1991: 296.

125 See BAB RKolA 7382/27: 42–93, 'Berichte der einzelnen Verwaltungsstellen in Deutsch-Ostafrika über Sklaverei', especially BAB RKolA 7382/27: 66, Bezirksamt Kilwa, Berichterstatter: Bezirksamtmann von Rode n.d. [1900], and BAB RKolA 7382/27: 42, Bezirksamt Tanga, Berichterstatter: Bezirksamtssekretär Blank n.d. [1899].

126 According to colonial reports, slaves were often the only wealth smaller slave owners possessed. See, for instance, BAB RKolA 1004/105: 14, 'Bericht des Bezirksamts Lindi', 14 September 1897.

127 BAB RKolA 1004/97: 1, 'Bericht des Bezirksamts Bagamoyo', 14 September 1897 and BAB RKolA 1004/103: 2, 'Bericht des Bezirksamts Dar es Salaam', 14 October 1897.

128 For an exposition of the normative framework of Islamic law and beliefs with regard to slavery, see Brunschvig 1960: 24–40. More detailed historical information can be found in Willis 1985 and Fisher 2001. For an overview, see McDougall 1998: 434–9 and Forte 1998: 497–7.

129 Leue 1900–1(c): 607ff. For an overview of the history of Islam in East Africa, see Trimingham 1964: 31–75. See also Nimtz 1980 and Pouwels 1987. The most useful contemporary source is Becker 1911: 1–48. For a discussion of the relevance of Islamic law in the context of slavery, see the article by Cooper 1981: 271–307. For examples of non-Islamic practices involving the change of ownership of slaves, see Eberstein 1896: 180 and Velten (citing Baraka bin Shomari) 1903: 385.

130 Niese 1902: 23.

131 When a slave received a *Freibrief*, the German district officer frequently recorded the name of the previous owner. There were only a few women among them. See BAB RKolA 7410–7415, Sammlung der zur Mitteilung an das Spezialbüro in Brüssel bestimmten Nachweisungen, 1 October 1892–31 May 1915. For the Kenyan coast, see Strobel 1979: 30–40.

132 A comprehensive listing of slave prices for the coast is not available. Burton (1860: 520), however, reports for Zanzibar town that the following prices were applicable in the late 1850s: boys before puberty (MT$15–30), youths (worth less than boys), men in their prime (MT$13–20), older men (MT$10–13), educated slaves (MT$25–70), trading agents ('fancy prices'). He also states that prices for female slaves were one-third higher than those for male slaves. For a list of export prices for slaves supplied from Zanzibar to different towns on mainland in 1874, see Cooper 1977: 123.

133 Velten 1898: 70, Niese 1902: 41.

134 Glassman 1995: 105.

135 Middleton 1992: 117. Note that *washenzi*, *washambala* and *wajinga* are not generic terms, but were probably used in a more descriptive sense. For the term w*ashambala*, see Berg 1971: 170. According to Velten (1903: 25ff.) 'imported' slaves could be distinguished from free coastal people by the absence of physical body marks, such as incisions on the temples.

136 Velten 1903: 306.

137 Krenzler (1886–8: 76) reports that sometimes plantations were sold along with slaves working on them, as if these were part of the property.

138 Burton 1860: 517. See also New 1873: 58: 'Slaves sometimes learn by rote sufficient of the Koran [sic] to take part with their betters in the religious exercises of the mosques.'

139 Velten 1898: 73, 1903: 307ff.

140 BAB RKolA 7382/27: 57, 'Berichte der einzelnen Verwaltungsstellen in Deutsch-Ostafrika über Sklaverei', Bezirksamt Bagamoyo, Berichterstatter: Bezirksamtssekretär Sperling n.d. [1898]. Velten (1903: 401) reports that adultery was also punished by enslavement if the offender could not pay his fine. According to Eberstein 1896: 174, the fine in the south (Kilwa) consisted of six slaves.

141 Compare, for instance, BAB RKolA 7382/27: 69, 'Berichte der einzelnen Verwaltungsstellen in Deutsch-Ostafrika über Sklaverei', Bezirksamt Lindi, Berichterstatter: Bezirksamtmann Zache n.d. [1900] and BAB RKolA 7382/27: 51ff., Bezirksamt Pangani, Berichterstatter: Bezirksamtmann Sigl n.d. [1899]. See also Velten 1903: 309.

142 Saadi 1941: 26.

143 Velten 1898: 50. S*hikamo* as a kind of salutation is only used today as a mark of respect, for instance when younger children greet people of their parents' or grandparents' age. It is also the expected greeting for elders.
144 Leue 1900–1(c): 608. On this point, see also Fair 1998: 63–94.
145 Velten 1903: 312.
146 Velten 1903: 312ff. For a detailed description of the public respect owed by the 'vulgar' [sic] to members of the coastal elite, see Burton 1858: 200.
147 See the numerous examples in Glassman 1995: 133–45.
148 See, for instance, New 1873: 59 and RHO Afr Micr 472 R.8/MF 19, Mafia District Book, 'Domestic Slavery in German East Africa' by N. King, Mafia, April 1915: 14. See also Glassman 1995: 85.
149 Velten 1903: 310.
150 Older female slaves were called *wajakazi* (sing. *mjakazi*) in ki-Swahili. See BAB RKolA 7382/27: 69, 'Berichte der einzelnen Verwaltungsstellen in Deutsch-Ostafrika über Sklaverei', Bezirksamt Lindi, Berichterstatter: Bezirksamtmann Zache n.d. [1900]. For an analysis of this and other term for female slaves, see Bromber 2002.
151 On female household work, see Velten 1903: 207–13, 310. See also New 1873: 64.
152 See, for example, the descriptive account of the mid-nineteenth century by the Sultan of Zanzibar's daughter Ruete 1989 [1886]: 133, 150ff. For Mombasa, see also Mirza and Strobel 1989: 50–5; for Lamu, see Romero Curtin 1983.
153 Leue 1900–1(c): 607. See also Velten 1903: 51, 138. For a comparative perspective, see Strobel 1997 [1983]: 111–29.
154 Velten 1903: 207.
155 Velten 1903: 310.
156 Velten 1898: 74.
157 BAB RKolA 7382/27: 50, 'Berichte der einzelnen Verwaltungsstellen in Deutsch-Ostafrika über Sklaverei', Bezirksamt Pangani, Berichterstatter: Bezirksamtmann Sigl n.d. [1899].
158 Velten (citing Baraka bin Shomari) 1903: 394. See also Sachau 1897: 5 and Niese 1902: 17ff.
159 RHO Afr Micr R.8/MF 19, Mafia District Book, 'Domestic Slavery in German East Africa' by N. King, Mafia, April 1915: 14. See also Karstedt [1912]: 103.
160 Velten 1903: 227 [translation by the author]. For the sexual abuse of men, see Velten 1903: 309. For a more general contemporary view on coastal women's subordination to men, see Werner and Hichens 1934.
161 Velten 1903: 315ff.
162 BAB RKolA 1004/97: 4, 'Bericht des Bezirksamts Bagamoyo', 14 September 1897.
163 See Sachau 1897: 24. It is noteworthy that marriages between male slaves and free women seem to have occurred only very rarely on the coast. See BAB RKolA 1004/94: 2, 'Bericht des Bezirksamts Pangani', 7 September 1897 and BAB RKolA 1004/105: 12, 'Bericht des Bezirksamts Lindi', 14 September 1897. For a different view, see Glassman 1995: 128.
164 Velten 1898: 73.
165 According to Morton (1990: 183), in coastal Kenya, especially Lamu, only the male children of *masuria* were regarded as free.
166 Velten 1903: 316. See also BAB RKolA 1004/125: 1, 'Bericht des Bezirksamts Tanga', 10 September 1897. See also Eberstein 1896: 180.
167 BAB RKolA 7382/27: 68, 'Berichte der einzelnen Verwaltungsstellen in Deutsch-Ostafrika über Sklaverei', Bezirksamt Kilwa, Berichterstatter: Bezirksamtmann von Rode n.d. [1900].
168 Leue 1900–1(c): 607.
169 BAB RKolA 7382/27: 50, 'Berichte der einzelnen Verwaltungsstellen in Deutsch-Ostafrika über Sklaverei', Bezirksamt Pangani, Berichterstatter: Bezirksamtmann Sigl n.d. [1899].
170 Glassman 1995: 74.
171 Velten 1898: 74, 1903: 310.
172 *Ibid.*
173 Glassman 1995: 96. See also Cooper 1977: 174.
174 BAB RKolA 1004/120: 2, 'Bericht des Bezirksamts Kilwa', 10 September 1897.
175 Beech 1916: 147. Glassman 1991: 291, 1995: 86.

176 Compare BAB RKolA 7382/27: 42–93, 'Berichte der einzelnen Verwaltungsstellen in Deutsch-Ostafrika über Sklaverei', particularly BAB RKolA 7382/27: 65, Bezirksamt Kilwa, Berichterstatter: Bezirksamtmann von Rode, n.d. [1899], BAB RKolA 7382/27: 69, Bezirksamt Lindi, Berichterstatter: Bezirksamtmann Zache, n.d. [1900] and BAB RKolA 7382/27: 48–56, Bezirksamt Pangani, Berichterstatter: Bezirksamtmann Sigl n.d. [1899].

177 BAB RKolA 7382/27: 63, 'Berichte der einzelnen Verwaltungsstellen in Deutsch-Ostafrika über Sklaverei', Bezirksamt Rufiyi, Berichterstatter: Bezirksamtssekretär Spieth n.d. [1899].

178 New 1873: 59–62. New also noted that slaves in towns were often not dressed much better than those working in the fields.

179 This description is based on RHO Afr Micr 472 R.8/MF 19, Mafia District Book, 'Domestic Slavery in German East Africa' by N. King, Mafia, April 1915: 11.

180 BAB RKolA 7382/27: 42–93, 'Berichte der einzelnen Verwaltungsstellen in Deutsch-Ostafrika über Sklaverei', particularly BAB RKolA 7382/27: 65, Bezirksamt Kilwa, Berichterstatter: Bezirksamtmann von Rode, n.d. [1899]. See also New 1873: 62.

181 Leue 1900–1(c): 607.

182 BAB RKolA 7382/27: 50, 'Berichte der einzelnen Verwaltungsstellen in Deutsch-Ostafrika über Sklaverei', Bezirksamt Pangani, Berichterstatter: Bezirksamtmann Sigl n.d. [1899]. For a map showing the locations of slave villages in the Pangani valley in the early 1890s, see Meinecke 1895a: 131. For a slightly different map, see Meinecke 1895b: 112.

183 BAB RKolA 7382/27: 43, 'Berichte der einzelnen Verwaltungsstellen in Deutsch-Ostafrika über Sklaverei', Bezirksamt Tanga, Berichterstatter: Bezirksamtssekretär Blank, n.d. [1899]. See also Glassman 1991: 290.

184 Compare BAB RKolA 7382/27: 42–93, 'Berichte der einzelnen Verwaltungsstellen in Deutsch-Ostafrika über Sklaverei', particularly BAB RKolA 7382/27: 65, Bezirksamt Kilwa, Berichterstatter: Bezirksamtmann von Rode, n.d. [1899] and BAB RKolA 7382/27: 48–56, Bezirksamt Pangani, Berichterstatter: Bezirksamtmann Sigl n.d. [1899], but see also BAB RKolA 7382/27: 43, Bezirksamt Tanga, Berichterstatter: Bezirksamtssekretär Blank, n.d. [1899]. For working arrangements in the south, see also BAB RKolA 1004/105: 11, 'Bericht des Bezirksamts Lindi', 14 September 1897.

185 Reichard 1892: 475. See also Glassman 1995: 4.

186 BAB RKolA 7382/27: 50, 'Berichte der einzelnen Verwaltungsstellen in Deutsch-Ostafrika über Sklaverei', Bezirksamt Pangani, Berichterstatter: Bezirksamtmann Sigl n.d. [1899]. See also Eberstein 1896: 179, who states that in the early 1890s male slaves paid Rs10 and female slaves Rs6 per year to their owner. On the Kenya coast, such payments are reported to have been much higher, averaging Rs5 per month, although Beech might have confused monthly and annual payments. See Beech 1916: 148. For Zanzibar, see Cooper 1977: 186.

187 For more details, see Pouwels 1987: 193. See also Glassman 1995: 4.

188 Reichard 1892: 475.

189 Glassman 1995: 4. This suggest that the origins of the informal urban economy in Tanzania in the twentieth century can be traced back in part to the movement of slaves into coastal towns in the latter half of the nineteenth century.

190 BAB RKolA 1004/97: 1, 'Bericht des Bezirksamts Bagamoyo', 14 September 1897. See also Beech 1916: 148, Cooper 1977: 184 and Glassman 1995: 61. In ki-Swahili such slaves were sometimes also called *hamali* (pl. *wahamali*). According to Cooper (1977: 184–6), in Zanzibar *hamali* slaves regarded themselves as having a higher status than *kibarua* or agricultural slaves.

191 BAB RKolA 7382/27: 43, 'Berichte der einzelnen Verwaltungsstellen in Deutsch-Ostafrika über Sklaverei', Bezirksamt Tanga, Berichterstatter: Bezirksamtssekretär Blank, n.d. [1899]. See also Glassman 1995: 87.

192 See BAB RKolA 7382/27: 43, 'Berichte der einzelnen Verwaltungsstellen in Deutsch-Ostafrika über Sklaverei', Bezirksamt Tanga, Berichterstatter: Bezirksamtssekretär Blank, n.d. [1899], BAB RKolA 7382/27: 52, Bezirksamt Pangani, Berichterstatter: Bezirksamtmann Sigl n.d. [1899] and BAB RKolA 7382/27: 59, Bezirksamt Bagamoyo, Berichterstatter: Bezirksamtssekretär Sperling n.d. [1898]. According to Glassman (1995: 73ff.) Indian creditors sometimes accepted slaves as repayment of a loan. On the actual registration and 'emancipation' of slaves owned by Indians under

British jurisdiction, see Elton's instructive report (1874: 235–52), dated 18 March 1874.
193   BAB RKolA 1004/125: 1, 'Bericht des Bezirksamts Tanga', 10 September 1897.
194   Schweinitz 1894a: 19 and Toeppen 1885–6: 230. For a biography of Sewa Haji, see Matson 1966: 91–4 and Brown 1971: 185–99.
195   Burton 1860: 104. For a copy of such a contract, see Meyer 1890: 303ff. See also Baumann 1884: 3ff., 7.
196   BAB RKolA 7382/27: 52, 'Berichte der einzelnen Verwaltungsstellen in Deutsch-Ostafrika über Sklaverei', Bezirksamt Pangani, Berichterstatter: Bezirksamtmann Sigl n.d. [1899]. See also BAB RKolA 1004/97: 1, 'Bericht des Bezirksamts Bagamoyo', 14 September 1897 and Velten 1903: 310ff. For an overview of the craft industry on the coast, see Prins 1961: 72–5. For a contemporary description, see Stuhlmann 1910, *passim*.
197   Thus, for instance the famous Mabruki who accompanied Burton on his travels was a slave from the coast. See Burton 1860: 104. For itinerant slave artisans, see Burton 1860: 229.
198   Burton 1860: 327, 517. According to Cooper (1977: 190), for instance, in the 1870s and 1880s the army of the Sultan of Zanzibar largely consisted of slaves. On slave mercenaries on the Kenya coast, see also Morton 1990: 19–51; for Mozambique, see Isaacman and Peterson 2003.
199   Velten 1903: 218.
200   BAB RKolA 7382/27: 63, 'Berichte der einzelnen Verwaltungsstellen in Deutsch-Ostafrika über Sklaverei', Bezirksamt Rufiyi, Berichterstatter: Bezirksamtssekretär Spieth n.d [1899]. See also Reichard 1892: 477 and Velten 1903: 311. For an account of a free man who sold himself into slavery and then bought slaves from the proceeds, see Livingstone 1865: 49.
201   For the various stipulations regarding the manumission of slaves in Islamic law, see Sachau 1897: 125–72.
202   For a discussion of the meaning of 'freedom' (*uhuru*) in Swahili society, see Willis 1993a: 55ff. See also Feierman 1990: 213 and Glassman 1995: 113. For the general argument, see Roberts and Miers 1988: 50 and Kopytoff 1988: 500.
203   Deutsch 1999: 117.
204   See below.
205   For an example, see Niese 1902: 45. This particular certificate was issued by the owner in 1901 and begins, after the usual introductory reference to 'God', with the words 'Yeye muungwana, hapana wa kumtaarrathi'. The phrase roughly translates as 'He/She is free and nobody can interfere with him/her', indicating that the person in question now has the same rights free-born coastal citizens could claim (that is, the rights of the *waungwana*; see Chapter 2). For another example, see Büttner 1892: 48ff. In this context it is interesting to note that there is a striking similarity between slaves who wanted to be free and married women who wished to get a divorce from their husbands. According to Islamic law both were required to pay their 'master' an agreed sum of money, which – at least in theory – he was free to accept or refuse. On this issue, see Sachau 1897: 10, 46–50 and Velten (citing Baraka bin Shomari) 1903: 397ff.
206   Velten 1903: 305–19. For a slightly different view, see Willis and Miers (1997: 480), who emphasise that legal ownership of slaves was the most important conceptual category defining coastal slavery. Yet, the concept and practice of manumission – the negation of ownership – was arguably of equal significance.
207   For the practice of manumission see Velten 1903: 318ff. and Eberstein 1896: 180. For the relevant legal stipulations in Islamic law, see Sachau 1897: 125–7. For a summary, see Cooper 1977: 242–5.
208   Velten 1903: 318. See also Sachau 1897: 131.
209   Velten 1903: 318.
210   For an example see, Büttner 1892: 48ff. See also BAB RKolA 7382/27: 53, 'Berichte der einzelnen Verwaltungsstellen in Deutsch-Ostafrika über Sklaverei', Bezirksamt Pangani, Berichterstatter: Bezirksamtmann Sigl n.d. [1899]. See also Niese 1902: 38ff. and Velten 1903: 319, 414.
211   For a description, see Velten 1898: 71 and BAB RKolA 1004/125: 5, 'Bericht des Bezirksamts Tanga', 10 September 1897. For the legal position of slaves in this respect, see Sachau 1897: 126, 132, 140, 150 and Niese 1902: 43.
212   Slave owners, and not the wife, husband or children of the deceased, often inherited the

material possessions of their slaves. The fact that slaves could not legally possess property was probably the main reason why some slaves spent their earnings on consumption items as quickly as possible − a recurrent theme in the contemporary literature and sources − thus thwarting potential demands from their owner. For this argument, see Reichard 1892: 475ff. For the legal position of slaves regarding their property rights, see Niese 1902: 13.

213 BAB RKolA 1004/97: 1, 'Bericht des Bezirksamts Bagamoyo', 14 September 1897.

214 BAB RKolA 1004/105: 12, 'Bericht des Bezirksamts Lindi', 14 September 1897.

215 For a slightly different view, see Glassman 1995: 89, who notes that such restrictions were only relevant for *mzalia* slaves.

216 See, for instance, BAB RKolA 7382/27: 44, 'Berichte der einzelnen Verwaltungsstellen in Deutsch-Ostafrika über Sklaverei', Bezirksamt Tanga, Berichterstatter: Bezirksamtssekretär Blank, n.d [1899] and BAB RKolA 7382/27: 61, Bezirksamt Dar es Salaam, Berichterstatter: Bezirksamtssekretär Michels n.d. [1899].

217 Glassman 1995: 62, 94ff.

218 Glassman 1995: 85.

219 Krenzler 1886−8: 69.

220 Krenzler 1886−8: 71 and Krenzler 1888: 39.

221 Eberstein 1896: 179ff. See also Glassman 1995: 62.

222 Glassman 1995: 89. See also Willis 1993a: 58.

223 For this argument, see Reichard 1892: 475−7. See also Glassman 1995: 90.

224 Beech 1916: 145−50. See also BAB RKolA 1004/120: 4, 'Bericht des Bezirksamts Kilwa', 10 September 1897.

225 For the post-manumission relationship between slaves and owners in Lamu (Kenya) in the later twentieth century, see Romero 1988: 140−58.

226 Sachau 1897: 143.

227 For the legal side of this relationship, see Sachau 1897: 140−50.

228 Velten 1903: 314. See also Middleton 1992: 24.

229 For a different view, see Glassman 1991: 297. Here, my only disagreement with Glassman is that he gives too little weight to manumission as an essential element in the working of slavery on the coast in the later nineteenth century. On this point, see also Cooper 1977: 252.

230 Berg 1971: 167.

231 Glassman 1995: 23. The contemporary evidence on slave consciousness in the later nineteenth and early twentieth centuries is extremely limited, but it appears that in the German colonial period the urgency of marginal groups to become respected members of coastal society seems to have declined as opportunities for flight increased. This does not mean that such urban struggles by slaves or other marginal groups did not happen, but no archival evidence has yet been found to indicate that this was an important issue. Similarly, the fact that so many slaves fled throws doubt on the assertion by Romero (1983: 882) that the most significant bond between slaves and their owners was the 'continuous belief held by both masters and slaves that their relationship was sanctioned by God and the Prophet Mohammed'. For a similar argument with regard to the Kenya coast, see Herlehy and Morton 1988: 256.

232 Morton 1990: 10.

233 BAB RKolA 1004/97: 1, 'Bericht des Bezirksamts Bagamoyo', 14 September 1897.

234 BAB RKolA 7382/27: 49, 'Berichte der einzelnen Verwaltungsstellen in Deutsch-Ostafrika über Sklaverei', Bezirksamt Pangani, Berichterstatter: Bezirksamtmann Sigl n.d. [1899]. For particularly brutal examples, see New 1873: 503 and Reichard 1892: 469ff. See also Morton 1990: 5−7.

235 Niese 1902: 43.

236 Velten 1903: 314ff.

237 New 1873: 67.

238 This and the following paragraphs have greatly profited from Cooper 1977: 200−10. See also Alpers 2004: 51−68.

239 Burton 1860: 522.

240 Behr 1891: 216f and Krenzler 1886−8: 71. For an overview, see Alpers 2004: 56, 61f. See also Iliffe 1979: 72ff. and Glassman 1991: 304ff., 1995: 106−13. For *mtoro* communities in the hinterland of Mombasa (Kenya), see Cooper 1977: 207ff., Cooper 1980: 50, and the more detailed accounts by Herlehy and Morton 1988: 254−81, Morton

1990: 19–51 (Gosha, Witu, Gasi), 86–98 (Fuladoyo); for the hinterland of Lamu (Kenya), see Romero 1997. For some evidence regarding fugitive slave communities in the southern part of the coast, see BAB RKolA 1004/105: 8, 'Bericht des Bezirksamts Lindi', 14 September 1897.

241 For a detailed description of a fortified village near Pangani, see Höhnel 1891: 48. For an 'Oukami' village, see Baur and Le Roy 1886: 175.

242 Glassman 1995: 109ff. The *watoro* communities in the hinterland thus contributed to the general insecurity prevalent in the coastal areas in the latter half of the nineteenth century. According to Morton (1990: 49) *watoro* communities in the Kenya coastal hinterland actively participated in slave raiding and kidnapping as 'part of the war for survival' obtaining guns and ammunition from coastal traders in order to be able to defend themselves against attacks by slave owners.

243 New 1873: 49. For more detail on Mwazangombe, see Morton 1990: 13–15.

244 BAB RKolA 1004/105: 9, 'Bericht des Bezirksamts Kilwa', 14 September 1897.

245 Velten 1903: 317.

246 Velten 1898: 71, 1903: 276, 317, 384ff. See also Büttner 1892: 55ff. and Eberstein 1896: 173.

247 Velten 1903: 317. There is no evidence to corroborate that runaway slaves were actually killed for the offence. Sachau (1897: 125) notes that some owners apparently regarded their slaves as a form of cattle and thus to kill them for running away was thought to be a rather inappropriate response. However, on the punishment of slaves by their owners, see Morton 1990: 5–7.

248 For slave raiding and trading in the hinterland, see Krapf 1858 vol. II: 279 (Pangani), Fischer 1885: 57 (Pangani), Kirk to Granville 22 December 1884 (Lindi, Kilwa), Kirk to Granville 14 February 1885 (Tanga), Kirk to Granville 13 April 1885 (Pangani) and Kirk to Salisbury 22 September 1885 (Uzaramo), in Great Britain, *Parliamentary Papers. Correspondence Relating to Zanzibar*, C. 4776, London 1886: 93, 105ff., 119, 156, cited in *Traite des esclaves* 1889: 115–7, 215. See also Burton 1858: 204 (Pangani), 1860: 172 (Usagara), Burton 1872: 148 (Pangani), New 1873: 494ff. (northern coast), Elton 1874: 233 (Rufiyi delta), Elton 1874: 250 (Kilwa), Smith 1887: 101ff. (Kilwa/Lindi/Lukuledi River/Rovuma River), Velten 1898: 74–6 (Uzaramo), Giblin 1992: 15 (Zigua), Willis 1993a: 130–4 (Bonde) and Feierman 1995: 367 (Usambara). According to these reports, in the period concerned insecure living conditions greatly increased in the hinterland because slavery was both the cause and the result of war and internal civil strife. For this argument, see also Feierman 1974: 176 and Cooper 1977: 126. For further, more descriptive evidence on slavery in the coastal hinterland, see BAB RKolA 4997/1–503, 'Beantwortung des Fragebogens über die Rechte der Eingeborenen in den deutschen Kolonien', various dates [1909–1913], particularly the reports by Klamroth on Uzaramo (BAB RKolA 4997/143), by Reuss on Uzeguha (BAB RKolA 4997/192) and by Wohlrab on Ushambaa (BAB RKolA 4997/390).

249 Pruen 1891: 236. Pruen was a missionary medical doctor. He was stationed in Mpwapwa in Ugogo – 'the Clapham Junction' of the East Central African caravan trade, as he called it (p. 224) – in the late 1870s and 1880s. During that time he evidently spent some time on the coast, as his comments on slavery and the slave trade reveal. See also Cooper 1977: 194ff.

250 Velten 1898: 76.

251 Grant 1864: 38 (Uzaramo). See also Burton 1860: 176 (Ugogo). Wright (1993: 27) argues that in the second half of the nineteenth century the importance of men as 'protectors' of women generally increased. As the personal dependence of women on men increased, their social position declined. As far as Unyamwezi and the coast is concerned, evidence regarding this particular aspect of the transformation of gender relations seemed to be absent, though it is indeed likely that such a change occurred.

252 Smith 1887: 105.

253 Morton 1990: 11. See also Morton 1990: 204. There he writes that runaway slaves 'lead a life of fear, loneliness, pain, and violence'. On the basis of the available evidence, it cannot be stated whether runaway slaves on the southern coast had similar experiences.

254 Höhnel 1891: 49. See also Rockel 1997: 48.

255 Glassman 1995: 4.

256 For a comparative perspective, see Kopytoff and Miers 1977: 14–20.

257 Iliffe 1979: 43. Glassman (1995: 23), following Pouwels (1987: 196), writes that on the

coast 'discursive struggle over [Islamic] ritual constituted a major forum for the contestation of power' between slaves and their owners in the late nineteenth century. However, whether this particular field of conflict was of equal importance to other fields – everyday disputes over working and living arrangements, for instance – might be a matter of debate. Moreover, written contemporary documentation is largely silent on this subject and, for this reason, a detailed discussion of the issue has not been attempted in this study.

258 For a completely different view on the relationship between kinship and slavery, see Meillassoux (1997 [1983]: 64, 1991 [1986]: 14ff., 99ff.), who argues that female slaves were used exclusively as agricultural workers. This might be a matter of definition, since he argues that the moment female slaves became kin, they were no longer slaves.

259 The sources are silent on this aspect.

260 Leue 1900–1(c): 618.

261 For these distinctions, see Willis and Miers 1997: 480, 485 and Glassman 1991: 283, 289, 297. See also Kopytoff 1988: 491.

262 For the observation that the upbringing and insecure circumstances of slaves explain their 'apathy', see Pruen 1891: 237ff. On the connection between spatial order, power and ideology, see Mitchell 1988: 34–62. For an excellent introduction to the literature on power and practice, see Lüdtke 1991: 9–63.

263 Cooper 1977: 195.

264 Wright 1993: 2.

265 Wright 1993: 7.

266 See, for instance Glassman 1995: 84. For lack of evidence, such a claim cannot be sustained for Unyamwezi. However, it is likely that because of their similar social position, some male slaves displayed their discontent in a similar way.

267 Glassman 1991: 291.

268 Willis and Miers 1997: 479. See also Glassman 1995: 91.

269 Glassman 1995: 91.

270 Whether the degree of commercialisation in the north justifies portraying the entire coastal economy as being dominated by a 'slave mode of production' (see, for instance, Sheriff 1985: 161–81) is debatable. Arguably, the term suggests a degree of uniformity of historical experience that probably never existed. On the other hand, there can be little doubt that both central Tanzania and the coast could be referred to as 'slave societies'.

271 Meinecke 1895b: 56–66, 108–44.

272 Glassman 1995: 103.

273 Except for the study by Aas (1989) and the thesis by Becker (2001) published work on the social history of the southern coast in the early colonial period is sadly lacking. The best contemporary descriptions of Lindi and its hinterland can be found in Behr 1892: 578–83, Fülleborn 1906: 33–124 and Adams n.d. [1903], all of whom have surprisingly little to say about slavery in the district.

274 Glassman 1995: 98. For a general description of the Pangani sugar plantations, see Meinecke 1895b: 56–66, 108–44. According to Meinecke, some plantation owners were already using steam engines on their plantations in the 1880s.

275 Glassman 1995: 100. For a similar argument concerning Malindi and Mombasa on the Kenya coast, see Cooper 1977: 86–8.

276 RHO Micr Afr 472 R.19/MF 42, Tabora Regional Book, 'Extracts from Nyamwezi Law and Custom by H. Cory', 1952.

277 Willis and Miers 1997: 481ff. See also Lonsdale 1992: 21.

278 On the subversive impact of the expansion of slavery on the ideology and practice of kinship relations in general, see Manning 1990: 119.

279 Willis and Miers 1997: 481ff., 485, 489.

280 Blohm 1931 vol. I: 168, vol. II: 35 [extract from interview, n.d. (pre-1914)]. See also, Willis and Miers 1997: 481.

281 Grant 1864: 61.

282 Shorter 1968: 252.

283 See, for instance, Grant 1864: 61.

284 Wright 1993: 152. See also Feierman 1995: 364.

285 Wright 1993: 152. See also Willis and Miers 1997: 485.

286 For a different view, see Rockel (2002b: 760), who argues that women in Unyamwezi

had 'a considerable degree of power and influence'. This is not necessarily a contradiction since the European nineteenth-century observers he cites made comments on the exceptional high-status women whom they encountered on their way through Unyamwezi, such as successful traders and office holders, but have little to say about the social situation of the female population at large in the region.

287 Iliffe 1979: 74 and Willis and Miers 1997: 481. For a different view, see Meillassoux 1991: 327.

288 Similar views on kinship relations have been expressed much more eloquently, for instance, by Cooper 1979: 119, Guyer 1981: 121, Comaroff 1987: 84, Kopytoff 1988: 495 and Godelier 1998: 4ff.

Part II

No Death for Slavery:
German Colonial Policy

Both when colonial rule was formally established (January 1889) and when it was coming to an end (February 1914), the German Reichstag became the centre of heated debates on the fate of the slaves in German East Africa. After twenty-five years of colonial rule, slavery and 'private' slave trading was still legal in German East Africa. In 1914 alone, hundreds, perhaps thousands, of slaves – men, women and children – were bought and sold under the watchful eyes of local administrative officers.[1] As will be seen below, these transactions were even taxed.[2] Arguably, government non-abolition policy was indicative of the general character of German colonial rule in East Africa. The German colonial authorities, perhaps more than other colonial powers in the region, sacrificed avowed moral principles all too easily to political expediency and economic interest. Even some contemporary observers regarded the government's policy as a veritable scandal.[3]

It should be pointed out, however, that in early 1914 government non-abolition policy was under strong parliamentary attack.[4] The colonial authorities' refusal to consider the abolition of slavery was no longer acceptable to the majority of the members of the Reichstag. Had the outbreak of war not interrupted its regular parliamentary proceedings, the Reichstag would most likely have succeeded in persuading the colonial secretary, Solf, to abolish slavery in the German colonies in Africa. At the very end of the debate in March 1914, Solf indicated to the Reichstag that he was prepared to seek a compromise between Parliament and the Governor of German East Africa, Schnee, who strongly opposed abolition.[5] Yet, there is no certainty whatsoever that the Reichstag initiative would have been immediately successful.[6] The political debate on the end of slavery in East Africa had dragged on for longer than two decades and, given the power and obstinacy of the local colonial authorities in this matter, this situation could have gone on for some years more. Nevertheless, it should be noted that slavery under German colonial rule was probably about to be abolished officially.

Still, the likelihood of the eventual success of the Reichstag initiative does not change the fact that for twenty-five years the relevant colonial authorities both in Berlin and in Dar es Salaam had steadfastly refused to yield to demands calling for the legal abolition of slavery in East Africa. Instead, the authorities adopted a piecemeal approach to the problem by gradually closing down commercial sources of supply for slaves and – ostensibly – regulating the legal relationship between owners and slaves in preparation for eventual abolition. The purpose of the following two chapters is to examine how and, perhaps more importantly, why that particular policy was pursued.

One could legitimately ask whether imperial debates in the German Reichstag should be investigated at all, as they seem to contribute little to the understanding of the history of the end of slavery in East Africa. As will be shown further on in this section, the outcome of the debate had a direct impact on colonial policy and practice and, indeed, consequently on the lives of slaves in German East Africa. Since the establishment of formal colonial rule in East Africa in 1890, the government had been heavily criticised in the Reichstag for its non-abolition policy. It will be argued that the legal regulations and administrative measures actually undertaken by the colonial authorities in this matter were largely a means of defending that very policy. At the same time, these measures were an attempt to create a novel form of slavery, one that was defined and supervised by the colonial state rather than created through social interaction between owners and slaves. It is thus all the more important to examine in detail the reasons why slavery was not abolished by the colonial authorities.

Both chapters investigate the political debate surrounding the problem of slavery in East Africa in two different, but overlapping arenas. Chapter 4 examines the debate between the imperial government and the parliamentary opposition in the Reichstag. The latter consisted mainly of members of the Social Democratic Party (Sozialistische Arbeiter-Partei, after 1891 Sozialdemokratische Partei Deutschlands), but they were joined on certain issues by individual members of the Catholic centre party (Zentrum) and the left-liberal party (Freisinn).[7] This had significant consequences for the non-abolition policy of the government. Other parties in the Reichstag such as the national-liberal party (Nationalliberale Partei) and the conservatives (Deutschkonservative Partei and Freikonservative Partei, after 1871 Deutsche Reichspartei) played only a minor role in the slavery debate. Their part in colonial as in many other affairs was mostly limited to supporting the government and attacking the opposition, which some of their members practised to considerable effect.[8] However, it should be noted that party politics in the Reichstag was highly fragmented. Members of Parliament did not always toe the party line. On controversial issues, the ruling parties – the conservatives and national-liberals – were forced to seek alliances with members of the opposition parties, particularly the Zentrum, in order to attain a comfortable majority vote in the Reichstag.

Chapter 5 explores the internal debate on the problem of slavery in German East Africa within government circles. This took place primarily in the Kolonialrat, a semi-official parliamentary advisory committee which consisted of a small number of hand-picked colonial 'experts' drawn mainly from the Christian Churches, commercial interests such as the German East Africa Company (Deutsch Ostafrikanische Gesellschaft or DOAG), political pressure groups such as the Deutsche Kolonialgesellschaft, and the colonial bureaucracy.[9] As will emerge from the debate in the Kolonial-rat, the imperial authorities in Berlin relied on information supplied by the various Governors of East Africa and, crucially, on reports and advice from district officers (in German *Bezirkschefs* or *Bezirksamtmänner*). Given the frequent changes of personnel in the governorship of East Africa, these *Bezirkschefs* and *Bezirksamtmänner* were regarded by the Kolonialrat as the 'true' authority on the question of slavery in East Africa, and their arguments and recommendations carried considerable weight. Their reports will also be reviewed in Chapter 5.

The debates on slavery and the slave trade held in the Reichstag and the Kolonialrat dealt with three of the four German colonies in Africa, that is Togo, Kamerun (Cameroon) and Deutsch-Ostafrika (mainland Tanzania). As far as the fourth African 'possession', Deutsch-Südwestafrika (Namibia), was concerned, the colonial authorities were convinced that this colony had no slaves. Thus, Südwestafrika was excluded from the discussions. The debate centred largely on German East Africa, which overshadowed the other German colonies in Africa in size, population and perceived economic importance, at least as far as the early colonial period (1890–1900) is concerned.[10]

Moreover, government policy with regard to slavery and the slave trade in East Africa was expressed in both imperial and local legislation. The former encompassed a parliamentary act (*Gesetz*) and two decrees (*Verordnungen*). The parliamentary act was signed by Kaiser Wilhelm II on 28 July 1895, outlawing slaving and slave trading within the imperial realm. This act was the only piece of legislation concerning slavery and the slave trade in East Africa in which the Reichstag was directly involved. Significantly, the 1895 act did not concern colonial subjects, that is 'natives' of German East Africa, but German citizens only. Its effectiveness was thus strictly limited.

As far as the population of German East Africa was concerned, the two *Reichskanzler Verordnungen*, signed by Chancellor von Bülow in 1901 and 1904, were of much greater importance than the 1895 act. The *Verordnungen* did not require parliamentary approval. The 1901 decree outlawed certain types of enslavement, notably pawning. Moreover, this decree contained a number of stipulations regarding the legal relationship between slaves and their owners, including the ransoming of slaves by themselves or by a third party.[11] The 1904 *Verordnung* declared that the children of slaves born after 31 December 1905 were to be regarded as free.

The local colonial legislation consisted of a series of instructions and ordinances (called *Runderlasse*, *Anweisungen* or *Verordnungen*) that the Governors of East Africa were entitled to enact in their own right, albeit, in the case of the *Verordnungen*, subject to subsequent approval by the government, that is the chancellor or his subordinate, the director of the colonial department of the Foreign Office.[12] Most of these ordinances concerned the suppression of large-scale slave trading and violent enslavement, but the very first ordinance, published in 1891, addressed the issue of official certificates of emancipation or *Freibriefe* to (ex)-slaves who had been ransomed by a third party. Third party here refers to 'non-natives' (*Nicht-Eingeborene*), that is, the European employers of ransomed slaves.

Finally, it is important to note that the legal and constitutional structure of the Reich determined the scope of parliamentary control over colonial policies. The Kaiserreich was a (semi-)constitutional monarchy in which the power of Parliament was severely curtailed.[13] Thus, for instance, the chancellor and his subordinates (and thus the 'government') were directly appointed (or indeed dismissed) by the Kaiser. There was only one further qualification. These appointments had to be approved by the Bundesrat, the council of German states, whereas parliamentary approval was not required. Moreover, the government had to seek authorisation from the federal state council in all legislative and a number of executive matters. The autocratic and ultra-conservative Bundesrat thus represented a powerful counterweight to the democratically elected Reichstag.[14]

Formally, the members of the Reichstag had very little direct influence on colonial affairs. Their constitutional rights were restricted to casting their vote on the government's annual colonial budget bill. The proposed financial assistance to be received by local colonial governments from the imperial treasury in Berlin formed what was perhaps, politically speaking, its most significant section. It may be worth noting that, in this respect, the Reichstag's constitutional powers actually exceeded those of the British Parliament at the time, but it should also be recognised that the colonial authorities in Britain were ultimately accountable to Parliament. The Reichstag obtained the right to scrutinise the colonial budget in 1892 after more than generous agreements had been reached with the Deutsch Ostafrikanischen Gesellschaft regarding compensation it was to receive from the colonial government for 'loss' of its East African 'possessions' to the Reich.[15]

In contrast to the situation in the Reich, Parliament's legislative powers did not extend to the colonies. To all intents and purposes, the German colonial empire in Africa was ruled by decrees and ordinances enacted by the Kaiser and his appointees – the chancellor, the colonial director, the Governors and local administrative officers.[16] Apart from the afore-mentioned budgetary restrictions, the *Kaiser's* executive and legislative power – the so-called *Kommandogewalt* or *Schutzgewalt* – in the colonies was all-embracing, which meant that the Reichstag was excluded from the administrative decision-making process to a great extent.[17] Other groups, as will be shown further on in this section, had far greater say in colonial affairs, above all the colonial bureaucracy, commercial interests, organised political pressure groups, and the Christian Churches.[18] Yet, these groups were not equally successful in pursuing their particular interests. On the whole, it appears that apart from the colonial bureaucracy, the organised political pressure groups – in particular, the Deutsche Kolonialgesellschaft (founded in 1887) – probably had the greatest influence.[19]

In political terms, nevertheless, Parliament was far from powerless in colonial affairs. The Reichstag had the right to obtain information from the government on administrative matters, including colonial policy; this was used by the opposition with increasing frequency and effectiveness as time progressed. Thus, administrative scandals, brought up by the opposition, played a large role in parliamentary proceedings, with the government feeling compelled to publicly defend its colonial record and policy.[20] Furthermore, with the important exception of military appropriations, the government could not pass acts such as colonial budgets without approval from the Reichstag. On a number of occasions that approval was in fact denied.[21] In retrospect, it appears that although its rights remained formally curtailed by the constitution, by threatening to make use of its veto power the informal parliamentary influence of the Reichstag over government policy, including colonial affairs, gradually increased, especially after the turn of the century, and reached its height just before the outbreak of the First World War in 1914.[22] Whether these subtle developments can be regarded as the beginning of full-scale parliamentary control over colonial and other government affairs is still a matter of historiographical debate.[23]

Four

Imperial Politics [24]

The suppression of the slave trade in Africa was one of the main arguments used by the German government to legitimise colonial expansion and conquest in East Africa.[25] The anti-slave-trade rhetoric of the late 1880s brought various interest groups together, forging a powerful pro-expansionist coalition between the government, a significant part of the opposition in the Reichstag, commercial interests and the Christian Churches. This coalition proved to be highly effective in overcoming parliamentary resistance to committing the Reich to the assumption of formal colonial rule in East Africa. This coalition was also highly successful in defending and propagating government colonial policy in general.

In the early 1880s, both Chancellor von Bismarck and the vast majority of the Reichstag had shown little interest in directly involving the German Reich in the administration of African territories.[26] Up until 1884/5 financial support for the colonial (ad)ventures of private companies was thought to be incompatible with the doctrines of 'Manchester' liberalism that were prevalent at the time. This attitude changed in 1884/5 when the European 'Scramble for Africa' reached its first peak. Now colonial undertakings received official blessing and financial assistance, but the support was still rather limited in scope and substance. Chancellor von Bismarck believed that the commitment of the Reich should be kept to the bare minimum, and that it was up to German private chartered companies to establish a rudimentary form of colonial presence; the Reich was to protect and defend German commercial interests diplomatically, although it would be prepared to use military means if these interests were thought to be threatened. In any case, when the German Reich committed itself to direct involvement in East Africa in 1889, following the breakdown of the Deutsch Ostafrikanische Gesellschaft, the suppression of slavery and the slave trade was one of the main arguments used to justify the expense of sending German military officers abroad.

The DOAG was a chartered company that had been active in the coastal hinterland since the mid-1880s, but its financial means were exceedingly limited. On the basis of fraudulent treaties with some village

102

headmen of little local standing who were made out to be powerful 'sultans' reigning over a vast African empire, the company had managed to obtain a *Schutzbrief* from the Kaiser for their 'possessions'. Nevertheless, business was slow and the company's meagre profits did not even suffice to recoup the costs of maintaining the few trading posts it had established in the coastal hinterland.[27] As far as the long-distance slave trade and slavery were concerned, the company had neither the intention nor the resources to intervene.[28] The area under the company's effective control was exceedingly limited and the power of the company's officers did not extend far beyond the view from their trading station's veranda.[29]

However, the company, especially its director, Peters, had bigger plans in mind. Possibly in order to save the company from bankruptcy, Peters and his financial backers embarked on a programme of expansion. With the help of the German navy, the Sultan of Zanzibar was forced to cede the tax revenue and the administration of his internationally recognised mainland possessions to the company.[30] Yet, when in mid-1888 the German East Africa Company attempted to actually establish its administrative presence in the coastal towns, it sparked off an uprising that brought its imperial pretensions and ambitions to a sudden halt.[31] The company officials were forced to retreat hastily from all but a few posts on the coast. The coastal uprising of 1888 created a situation Chancellor von Bismarck had probably hoped to avoid. A decision had to be taken on whether to abandon support for colonial ventures in East Africa altogether or to transform the chartered possessions of the German East Africa Company into a formal colony of the *Reich*.[32] Bismarck was no friend of the DOAG, and certainly not of its megalomaniacal director, Peters. However, for political reasons that had nothing to do with the uprising itself, he chose the latter option.[33]

Although in possession of a parliamentary majority, Chancellor von Bismarck sought to create a broader coalition of political forces in Germany and in the Reichstag itself to support colonial expansion in East Africa. Up to 1889, colonial ventures in Africa had required comparatively little government expenditure. Committing the Reich financially to recapturing the East African coast and establishing colonial rule was an entirely different political and, indeed, fiscal matter. A number of legislative measures, involving far less government expenditure than the support of colonial ventures in Africa, had previously failed to find a parliamentary majority. Thus, stiff opposition in the Reichstag against the enabling bill was to be expected,[34] despite the fact that in a public speech on 22 November 1888 the new Kaiser Wilhelm II had given his wholehearted support for intervention by declaring that the suppression of slave trading and raiding in East Africa was one of the first priorities of 'his' colonial policy.[35]

The government's main political strategy for overcoming parliamentary opposition was to portray the resistance against the DOAG as an uprising of 'Arab' slave owners and traders against the 'civilising' effects of European colonial rule, as an Islamic movement against supposedly dearly held

Christian values.[36] This move must be seen in the context of anti-slavery propaganda by the Catholic and Protestant Churches at the time.[37] They had their own agenda as their often barely hidden anti-Islamic undertones reveal. The anti-slavery campaigns of both Churches had reached a high in the second half of the 1880s. For instance, the founder of the Congréga-tion de Pères Blancs and anti-slavery campaigner Cardinal Lavigerie, the Bishop of Algiers, travelled through Belgium, Britain, France and Germany at the time to address several anti-slavery meetings.[38] In Germany, these meetings were coordinated by the Afrika-Verein der deutschen Katholiken. Similar meetings were held by the Evangelische Afrikaverein.[39] The height of the German anti-slavery movement was a meeting in Cologne in October 1888 in which both Churches took part. Its motto was 'Against Slavery!' (*Wider die Sklaverei!*) and it demanded the government's immediate and sustained intervention in East Africa. Significantly, this particular meeting was organised and financed with the help of the German East Africa Company.[40]

Chancellor von Bismarck's indifferent attitude towards slavery in Africa is well documented. In 1885, for instance, when Consul Rolfs asked the Foreign Office if he was entitled to 'liberate' slaves who had sought refuge in the German Consulate in Zanzibar, he was told brusquely by von Bismarck not to get involved in such matters (*'die Sklaven gehen Sie nichts an!'*).[41] Nevertheless, von Bismarck seized the momentum of the anti-slavery movement, arguing that in presenting the bill he was simply ful-filling a popular call for humanitarian intervention.[42] The military officers who were to be sent to East Africa, he wrote, were not merely to fight for national pride and the commercial interests of the German East Africa Company but primarily to spread 'civilisation' and combat 'Arab' slavers and slave traders.[43] Accordingly, when the German Parliament voted on a motion by Windthorst in favour of appropriating RM2,000,000 to send Hauptmann von Wissmann as *Reichskommissar* to East Africa to reoccupy the coast, the final enabling act of 1889 was entitled 'Law to combat the slave trade and to protect German interests in East Africa'.[44] The declared purpose of colonial expansion was to suppress the slave trade and not to abolish slavery, as Chancellor von Bismarck had made absolutely clear in the Reichstag.[45] However, in the subsequent debate, this very issue was frequently and perhaps deliberately fudged by other members of Parlia-ment, possibly in order to drum up support for the bill.[46]

Another group that seized the momentum of the anti-slavery agitation of the late 1880s was the German Anti-Slavery Committee (Deutsche Anti-Sklaverei-Komite).[47] It was formed in 1890 and became active in the following year. The Anti-Slavery Committee largely consisted of members of the Deutsche Kolonialgesellschaft (German Colonial Society), but also included prominent representatives of various church groups, especially Catholic anti-slavery activists from southern Germany.[48] The committee took up a suggestion, which was first made by the German Colonial Society in one of its publications, to establish an 'Auxiliary Fund for the Rescue of Africa' (Hilfsfonds zur Rettung Afrikas).[49] For this purpose the

Komite gained permission from the government to set up an anti-slavery lottery. Its surplus would be used as a '*fonds perdu*' for 'the development of the colonies', 'the advancement of culture', and the 'fight against the slave trade'. According to the Komite, the funds generated by the lottery would be employed to improve the commercial conditions for German private companies in East Africa; they would be also used for the purpose of supporting Governor Wissmann and his *Schutztruppe* officers in their endeavour to establish effective rule in the interior, which so far – for the lack of resources – they had been unable to achieve.[50]

The lottery was a highly successful undertaking, not least because of the effective distribution of leaflets through church organisations and various advertisements in newspapers, all of which dramatically appealed to the prevalent anti-slavery sentiment.[51] In the second half of 1891 the anti-slavery lottery sold about 400,000 tickets that netted the Komite almost RM2,000,000.[52] However, choosing the right kind of anti-slavery projects was an entirely different matter. On the whole, it proved to be a disaster. The Komite financed a number of expeditions into the interior of East Africa, of which only the smallest one, led by the geographer Baumann, was judged to be a success.

The bulk of the money generated by the lottery was spent on trying to transport two steam boats – the *Wissmann-Dampfer* and the *Peters-Dampfer* – to Lake Victoria. Both attempts failed miserably. The *Peters-Dampfer* never actually left the coast while the *Wissmann-Dampfer* finally ended up in Lake Nyasa, where its usefulness was strictly limited.[53] In order to facilitate the use of the steamers on Lake Victoria, the Komite decided, before it was clear that the steamers would never reach their destination, to fit out a number of expeditions to the Lake. The first expedition, led by Baron Fischer, actually reached Lake Victoria, but he then died of blackwater fever. He was succeeded by Lieutnant Meyer, who lacked the scientific training to carry out the expedition's task to explore the south-eastern Lake region.[54]

The third and most lavishly equipped expedition was initially led by Herrn Borchert, but he soon fell ill, to be replaced by the more energetic and enterprising Lieutnant Schweinitz. This expedition consisted of nine German officers and privates, a hundred 'Sudanese' troops and about four hundred porters, carrying with them several artillery pieces as well as 'luxury guns'.[55] Schweinitz was supposed to built a wharf on Lake Victoria for the *Peters-Dampfer*. However in Tabora, on his way to the lake, he became involved in a military campaign against Isike of Unyanyembe. It is not entirely clear to what extent Schweinitz took part in the campaign unwillingly, but he and Lieutnant Meyer, who had waited at Tabora for Schweinitz, made their troops available to the local district officer, Amtsarzt Schwesinger, who was eager to use the opportunity of the presence of the anti-slavery expeditions to fulfil his long-standing aspiration to crush Isike's resistance to the German occupation.[56] The two attacks on Isike's residence took place in June and August 1892, but they failed to achieve their objective.[57] Both Schweinitz and Meyer were wounded in the fighting, but, more importantly, by becoming involved in the two-month campaign, they allowed the expedition's own resources to be critically depleted.[58] Though Lieutnant Meyer subsequently built a wharf on Ukerewe island, he was only able to do so on a much-reduced scale.[59] In any case, his efforts were ultimately fruitless since neither the *Peters-Dampfer* nor the *Wissmann-Dampfer* actually reached the Lake.

The three other, much smaller, expeditions, led by Lieutnant Werther, Kapitän Germer, and Hauptmann Langheld, also achieved very little for the anti-slavery cause. Even on their own terms, they were judged to be ineffective.[60] They seem to have played havoc on the caravan routes by terrorising those who encountered them. Both Schweinitz and Langheld, for instance, were known for forcing villagers near the caravan routes to sell provisions to them at gunpoint.[61] Perhaps the most successful project supported by the Komite was an expedition led by the geographer Baumann, who explored the north-eastern parts of German East Africa. Originally this expedition was instigated by the DOAG, but it was then transferred to the Anti-Slavery Committee's accounts after a payment of RM35,000.[62] The expedition resulted in the publication of one of the best-known colonial explorers' accounts of north-eastern Tanzania, Baumann's *Durch Massailand zur Nilquelle. Reisen und Forschungen der Massai-Expedition des deutschen Antisklaverei-Komites in den Jahren 1891–1893*, which appeared in 1894.

The activities of the Anti-Sklaverei-Komite thus had no direct impact on the end of slavery or the slave trade in German East Africa. The Komite itself ran into financial difficulties in early 1893 and was already defunct by 1894. However, the political importance of the Komite should not be entirely dismissed. Its formation was part of a wider political realignment in Germany, which provided a durable platform for the government's 'anti'-slavery policy. This realignment largely concerned the rapprochement between Catholic groups in Germany and the government.

It was mentioned above that Windthorst – who was a leading member of the Catholic opposition, the Zentrum party – proposed the initial parliamentary motion, which, in its amended form, later became the enabling government act of 1889. This motion is widely regarded as a turning point in the parliamentary history of German colonial expansion.[63] In previous years, the Catholic centre party had followed a strictly anti-colonial course. It now appeared that even the opposition in the Reichstag was supporting the government initiative. Importantly, the Windthorst motion signalled the end of the *Kulturkampf*, the bitter long-drawn-out struggle between the Catholic Church and its political ally the Zentrum party, on the one hand, and the government as represented by Chancellor von Bismarck and his mainly northern German Protestant supporters on the other.[64] For many years, practically since the establishment of the German Reich in 1871, the centre party had been treated as a political outcast. In the late 1880s, supporting the government and its colonial policy meant that the centre party could expect political concessions from the government in the field of domestic politics, and indeed these were forthcoming in the following years.[65] Yet, it would be wrong to portray the Zentrum party as a political monolith bent on supporting government colonial policy out of political opportunism. The Zentrum was above all a confessional party that combined different, even opposing ideological interests such as a left-wing Catholic labour movement and the ultra-conservative leadership of the Catholic Church.[66] However, due to its political heterogeneity, the party was able to support both sides of the argument, and, apparently, voting for or against the government depended on issues which were not even remotely connected with the debate at hand. The fact that the Zentrum party's support for the government attitude towards slavery in the colonies was crucial to maintaining that policy was probably neither anticipated nor actually realised by the parliamentary leadership at the time.

The coalition of interest forged in 1889 between the conservative government parties and the former Catholic opposition had a strong impact on colonial policy in subsequent years, particularly on the question of slavery in East Africa. The Zentrum support was vital to maintaining a comfortable government majority in the Reichstag. Opposition to government non-abolition policy came from members of the left-liberal Freisinn party and the Marxist Social Democratic Party, the SPD, at least up to the end of the first decade of the twentieth century. Some members of the centre party also held strong humanitarian anti-slavery convictions.

It appears that in the 1890s and 1900s, the colonial authorities in Berlin successfully balanced contradictory interests. The government never seriously contemplated discarding its non-abolition policy. But in the interest of keeping a broad Reichstag majority for that policy, the government ostensibly gave in to demands for amelioration and reform, particularly when such demands were supported by or originated from individual members of the Zentrum party. Whether such a bifurcated policy had any real impact on slavery in German East Africa was, as far as the government was concerned, probably of secondary importance. Reforming slavery was a political strategy in order to avoid more fundamental change.

Debating Slavery in the Reichstag

The debate in the Reichstag began in late 1891, less than a year after the government had assumed formal responsibility for the East African territories.[67] Having ratified the Brussels Anti-Slavery Conference Act of 1890, the government presented a draft bill to the Reichstag proposing to outlaw slave trading by German citizens in Africa.[68] Against the background of the history of slavery and abolition in Africa, it is difficult to imagine an anti-slavery bill that could have been more irrelevant to the actual issues at hand.

The background to this remarkable government legislative initiative needs some further explanation. Worried by the seemingly overwhelming success of the international anti-slavery movement, the British government approached the Belgian monarch, King Leopold II, in late 1889 with a suggestion to convene an international conference to discuss common measures against slaving, slave trading and the export of slaves from Africa.[69] Significantly, despite the conference title, the abolition of slavery itself was not on the agenda. Each of the participants – the major maritime and colonial powers as well as the Ottoman Empire, Persia and Zanzibar – had its own interest in taking part in the conference. The German government supported the idea of an international anti-slavery conference with great enthusiasm, yet did not believe that it would eventually lead to effective measures.[70] The conference fitted exceedingly well into the strategy of opposing the slave trade for propaganda purposes following the coastal uprising of 1889. In order to broaden the base of support for colonial expansion, Chancellor von Bismarck sought political allies not only within the Reichstag, but also abroad. Thus he persuaded the British and Italian authorities to participate in a naval blockade of the coast, the ostensible purpose of which was to prevent the export of slaves and the import of firearms.[71] Taking part in the Brussels conference was merely a further element in that strategy.[72] The signatories bound themselves to suppress slave raiding and trafficking on land and sea. As far as the coastal and the ocean-going trade was concerned, they reaffirmed various, mostly British, treaty rights to search vessels suspected of carrying slaves, though only in a designated 'slave trade zone'. They also agreed to emancipate 'foreign' fugitive slaves and to repatriate freed slaves, if possible to their place of birth or former residence.[73] The conference also resolved to curb the trading of arms to areas that were believed to be under the control of slave traders, and to set up information-gathering bureaux in Brussels and Zanzibar.

The results of the Brussels conference were highly ambiguous. While humanitarian concerns gained international recognition for the first time, the actual measures agreed to be undertaken by the signatories legitimised colonial conquest and rule, since implementing the suppression of slave trading and raiding required the establishment of colonial administration in the interior of Africa, especially East Africa, and the restructuring of African societies.[74] Significantly, while the Brussels Act was teeming with anti-slavery and slave trade rhetoric, it did not stipulate any tangible measures against signatory powers that failed to fulfil their obligations arising from the Act.

Nevertheless, Article V proclaimed that within a year of signing the Brussels Act, signatories would seek to change their national legislation in compliance with the spirit of the conference.[75] As far as German criminal law was concerned, this stipulation concerned slave trading only, which was not explicitly forbidden to German citizens outside the territory of the Reich. In July 1891, the government proposed to Parliament an appropriate amendment of the penal code – a *Sklavenhandelsgesetz* – that would render slave trading by German citizens illegal.[76]

The ensuing discussion in the Reichstag took place on 17 November

1891. It was an important debate, not because it yielded any tangible results, but because of the arguments used by the government to introduce the bill. The director of the colonial department at the time, Kayser, discussed at length measures that the then Governor of East Africa, von Soden, had undertaken to suppress 'native' slave trading in German East Africa. He also outlined future government policy.[77] It is worth examining Kayser's speech in some detail, as its main arguments were repeated again and again in the years to come.

Kayser argued that slavery in East Africa was a 'benign', even 'beneficial' (*segensreich*) institution that could not be abolished without triggering a dramatic upheaval of economic life. Abolition would result in slaves refusing to work.[78] Enormous changes had already taken place, he claimed, as the authorities in East Africa did not recognise the institution and abstained from getting involved with it officially in court. He went on to quote at length a report by Governor von Soden from 30 August 1891.[79] According to Kayser, the crucial passage in the report stated that

> from the very beginning (of my governorship), I have taken the view and made it known, that slavery will not be recognised as a legal institution and that no legal consequences can thus arise from it, but that for the time being ... we will tolerate the current state of slavery....
>
> Accordingly, I have instructed ... the district military commanders to steer clear of becoming involved in slave matters if possible, in order to avoid the impression ... that slavery exists as a recognised legal institution.[80]

Elaborating on the report, Kayser told Parliament that though great progress had already been made, the buying and selling of individual slaves would continue for the time being. Kayser also mentioned a decree, which von Soden had issued in September 1891, to the effect that slaves sold to 'non-natives' automatically received a certificate of emancipation (*Freibrief*). He also stated that the decree regulated agreements on the ransoming of slaves, either by themselves or by a third party. By this he mainly meant German or other European 'employers' of ransomed slaves. These agreements had to be made in the presence of local district officers who were charged with establishing their legal validity, ostensibly in order to safeguard the interests of the 'freed' slave.[81] Kayser ended his long speech by re-emphasising the government's eagerness to abolish slavery, even if, for the moment, it was unable to solve the problem. In his view, abolition would eventually come about as a result of the civilising influence of the Christian Missions.

Kayser's speech is remarkable because it managed to reconcile several contradictory positions. While he stressed that government would like to see the end of slavery, he also contended that nothing should actually be done to achieve this goal. On the one hand, Kayser portrayed slavery as a 'benign' institution, as a form of 'serfdom', which, in his view, had existed in Germany in the Middle Ages. Since slaves did not even benefit from receiving their freedom, he argued, there was no humanitarian need to intervene in slavery matters. On the other hand, he stated that abolition would gravely harm local economies. 'Free Africans', he claimed, 'only work voluntarily for themselves; only a slave can be forced to work for another person.'[82] It is difficult to see how the assertion of the supposedly favourable social position of slaves can be reconciled with the argument that slavery was necessary to compel people to work for others.[83] A similarly inconsistent line of argument was presented as regards the official (non-) recognition of slavery. Kayser stated that the government did not legally recognise slavery but, at the same time, admitted government acceptance of its existence. In fact, the issuing of certificates of emancipation by administrative officers depended on their tacit endorsement of slavery. During the debate, the colonial director had pointed out that local administrative officers were charged with establishing the legal validity of ransoming contracts, which necessarily entailed establishing the legal validity of the slave–master relationship. Moreover, he said, the buying, selling and pawning of slaves would continue without official hindrance or interference. Again, it is difficult to see how that statement can be reconciled with the government's anti-slavery rhetoric. In any case, the crucial contradiction was that the government proposed to tolerate social and commercial practices in East Africa that would have been illegal in the German Reich.[84]

The government would probably have convinced the majority of the Reichstag, were it not for Rintelen, a member of the Zentrum party, who argued that government policy amounted to perpetuating slavery in its current form. He, for one, was not prepared to accept the government's ineffective attempts to achieve the abolition of slavery in German East Africa.[85] He suggested that government should rethink the issue. Without any further discussion, the Reichstag followed Rintelen's suggestion and referred the proposed 1891 draft bill to a commission for further deliberation. The commission dealt only briefly with the issue, and as early as 1892 submitted a report stating that the Reichstag should pass the bill without any further alteration. However, the commission, apparently adhering to Rintelen's intervention in the Reichstag, agreed on a motion proposing that the chancellor settle the entire question of slavery in the German colonies by 1 October 1895.[86] Thus as far as the Reichstag was concerned, the subject was left to the government to resolve, at least for the time being.

In accordance with the motion, the government asked the Kolonialrat to gather information about slavery in the German colonies and make suitable recommendations (see Chapter 5), but otherwise the government remained largely inactive for the next two years. This state of affairs was unacceptable to Parliament. In January 1894, the parliamentary budget commission agreed to prepare a motion for the Reichstag in which the government was to be urged to submit the 1891 anti-slave trade bill to Parliament once more. Subsequently, the motion was discussed in the Reichstag on 16–17 February 1894.

The debate was opened by von Arensberg (Zentrum) who reported the views of the budget commission members.[87] According to von Arensberg, the conservatives (that is, the government) had argued that slavery could not be abolished in the German colonies at that time. The only feasible policy would be to enable slaves to work for their freedom through (self-) purchase. Moreover, slaves should receive legal status in court. These arguments prompted Bebel, the leader of the SPD, to restate the general attitude of the Social Democrats towards colonial affairs.[88]

Without concerning himself too closely with the issue at hand, Bebel made it clear that on principle the SPD would not participate in a discussion about aspects of colonial policy. In his view, colonialism could not be justified on any grounds. He believed that colonialism was fundamentally wrong for moral, political and economic reasons. Thus, the SPD would reject the budget bill as a whole.[89] For Bebel, slavery in the German colonies merely represented another form of exploitation by 'Christian capitalists'. He closed his speech by saying that there was basically no difference between 'house slavery' in the colonies and 'wage slavery' at home.[90]

It was left to another member of the Social Democratic Party, Ehni, to offer more constructive criticism.[91] Ehni stated that he agreed with much of what the government had said about the state of slavery in the colonies. However, he argued that for humanitarian and practical reasons the government should introduce an amendment to the proposed 1891 bill that would make the ownership of slaves illegal.[92] The colonial authorities, however, brushed Ehni's suggestion lightly aside. They stated that the ownership of slaves by German citizens was already forbidden by law and that, moreover, the 1891 draft bill concerned 'whites' only, that is, the 'non-natives' of German East Africa.[93] The Reichstag accepted these arguments and thus promptly rejected Ehni's intervention. However, Parliament was still unsatisfied with the government attitude towards the 1891 draft bill. Consequently, in February 1894, the Reichstag passed with a large majority the budget commission motion urging the government to present the anti-slave trade bill to Parliament.[94]

The 1891 *Sklavenhandelsgesetz* finally reached the Reichstag in May 1895. The ensuing debate was dominated by the confrontation between the government and the SPD, which on this occasion was apparently much better prepared. However, in contrast to the previous debate, the national liberals (Nationalliberalen) and, significantly, the Zentrum now also joined the fray. The debate was opened by Rimpau, a member of the National Liberal Party, who restated the government's arguments that slavery could only be abolished by gradual means, otherwise the peaceful development of the colony would suffer enormously.[95] Von Bernstorff, a member of the conservative Deutsche Reichspartei, continued the debate. Speaking for himself rather than his party, he urged the government to be more active in the matter. His statement probably indicated that even members of the conservative party thought the government was not doing enough for the abolition of slavery.[96]

The government responded immediately.[97] The colonial director, Kayser, reported that the government had received new information from the colonies. He argued that the 'African social question' of slavery could not be resolved at one stroke, but that conditions in the colonies would have to change in such a way that the abolition of slavery would not have a negative effect on the economy or political stability. He also reassured the Reichstag that the government did not intend to recognise slavery as a legal institution.[98]

In any case, it should be noted that Kayser introduced two new arguments to the debate. First, he argued that slavery was the 'African social question'. Importantly, the phrase 'social question' had a specific meaning in the German political context.[99] In the second half of the nineteenth century, Germany had become a rapidly industrialising country. This process was accompanied by the destitution of a substantial part of the working population. Vast numbers of people had left the countryside and its semi-feudal 'traditions' of political and social control and had moved to the cities in search of work and, perhaps, a better life.[100] The 'social question' was thus basically the question of the emergence of a new pauperism, the abject misery of the living conditions and life chances of the floating, unattached urban working class.[101] The political system of the Kaiserreich had little to offer this group. The conservatives and the bourgeois liberal parties felt exceedingly threatened by this development, especially since it was accompanied by the rapid rise of a new political force, the Social Democratic Party.[102] By alluding to the 'social question', Kayser invoked the threat that the abolition of slavery would lead to the emergence of an unattached African working class and thus, in his view, political instability. One could dispute whether this argument was even remotely related to the social, political and economic realities of colonial rule and slavery in German East Africa. But it was evidently believed to be pertinent, since it was brought up again and again in subsequent discussions in the Reichstag and elsewhere.[103]

Second, Kayser redefined the government's approach to abolition. Whereas previously it was argued that abolition was simply impracticable, now Kayser seems to suggest that social and economic conditions in German East Africa had to be changed before abolition could be contemplated seriously. The key words here were 'preparation for abolition'.[104] The kind of preparation he envisaged, however, was expressed in a perhaps deliberately vague manner.

However, these arguments did not convince the speakers of the Social Democratic Party.[105] They pointed out that the proposed law – a slightly revised version of the 1891 anti-slave trade act – was not effective against the buying and selling of slaves in the colonies. After all, the proposed bill only concerned German citizens, not 'natives' of East Africa. The Social Democrat Stadthagen, in particular, criticised the government sharply for its non-abolition approach. He implored Parliament not to allow the government to override all humanitarian concerns.[106]

Stadthagen's powerful rhetoric and emotional plea apparently had considerable effect. At least the ruling parties felt the need to defend themselves against their critics. The conservative von Buchka gave the debate a new direction by introducing a motion from the Zentrum party. This was a novelty, since parliamentary motions were usually introduced into the actual debate by the parties that had submitted them for discussion. In any case, it appears that this motion rescued the government from embarrassment. It urged the latter to submit a bill to the Reichstag in which 'slavery and pawnship as practised by the natives of the colonies were to be subjected to preparatory regulations leading to their eventual abolition'.[107] This motion, obviously based on the 1891 budget commission motion (see above), contained a slight, but vital modification. Whereas the 1891 motion had demanded that the government 'regulate all aspects of slavery', the government was now urged merely to pass 'preparatory regulations' for abolition. This was, in fact, government policy at the time, as shown by the colonial director's statement cited above. After reading the motion, Buchka claimed that it contained all that Stadthagen and the SPD could reasonably expect from the government. Abolition, he said, would only lead to 'intolerable social relations'.[108] He did not specify the intolerable social relations he had in mind.

In the end, it was the speech by Gröber (Zentrum), the author of the motion, that turned the tide in Parliament.[109] Slavery, he argued, was part of customary African life and deeply imbedded in religion and polygamy (*Vielweiberei*). In his view, to demand the suppression of slavery amounted to advocating the use of force against 'natives'. He repeated that the colonial authorities did not legally recognise slavery and, thus, administrative officers were not involved in upholding it in any conceivable way. He ended his speech by explaining the rationale behind the motion. The first aim of government policy should be to abolish slavery as quickly as possible. In order to achieve that end, it would be necessary to create some kind of statutory intermediate state between slavery and 'freedom', regulated and controlled by the colonial authorities. Regulations were to be enacted which would specify the mutual rights and obligations of owners and slaves, and define the rules by which slaves could purchase their liberty, or work for their freedom.[110]

The Social Democratic Party was at a loss for an appropriate answer to Gröber's speech. Its members had urged the government to abolish slavery, but as far as practical suggestions were concerned they had little to offer. The SPD had obviously concentrated its preparations only on criticising the government's 1891 anti-slave trade act. Suggesting constructive alternatives would have been tantamount to validating the colonial project, which was an anathema to the party leadership at the time.[111] Nevertheless, Stadthagen rejected Gröber's argument that the colonial authorities were not involved in slavery matters on the grounds that administrative officers had already participated in the buying and selling of slaves by recording the legal validity of the transactions. He also drew attention to the fact that motions urging the government to undertake specific legislative measures were ineffective – with the government sometimes delaying them *ad infinitum*. At the conclusion of his speech, he once again implored the Reichstag not to pass the anti-slave trade bill or to accept the motion of the Zentrum. 'As long as Parliament does not move against slavery itself,' he said, 'members of Parliament will only have achieved decorative window-dressing.'[112] Ultimately, the SPD intervention proved fruitless. At the end of the day's proceedings, Parliament accepted Gröber's motion with a substantial majority.[113] Two days later, at the next meeting of the Reichstag, the SPD tried to delay the matter, but its demand was rejected by a majority of the house without much further discussion. Thus the bill was finally passed on 22 May 1895.[114] Since the *Sklavenhandelsgesetz* concerned German citizens only, the German colonial governments in Africa were subsequently instructed by the Foreign Office to enact similar legislation for the colonies. The relevant decree for German East Africa was issued in August 1896 and largely followed the example of the 1895 act.[115]

The significance of the 1895 debate lies in the fact that it was the only occasion on which Parliament was directly involved in the making of anti-slave trade legislation, even if it concerned German citizens only. Moreover, the debate revealed the alliance between the government parties and the Zentrum in colonial affairs, which was crucial to defending government non-abolition policy. Gröber's speech probably saved the day for the beleagured government, by challenging the opposition where it was probably weakest, that is the SPD's refusal to offer constructive alternatives to government policy. Gröber's motion urging the government to undertake preparatory measures for the abolition of slavery was a pre-emptive strategy to disarm the opposition and assure government supporters that the colonial authorities were actively engaged in the matter. Nonetheless, nothing happened, at least not until 1901 when the matter was again raised in the Reichstag.

The 1901 Debate and Its Aftermath

The discussion in 1901 began with a front-page article in the *Ostafrikanische Zeitung*, a small, privately owned newspaper, published and printed in Dar es Salaam, which enjoyed significant financial support from the government at the time.[116] In the debate on the colonial budget for 1901/2, Bebel, the parliamentary leader of the SPD, first attacked the government on general grounds. Colonialism, he claimed, was a total economic failure and nothing had been achieved by the administration. He then asked Stuebel, the colonial director at the time, whether the report in the *Deutsch-Ostafrikanische Zeitung* of 2 July 1900 regarding a meeting of the district *Jumben* (lower African government officials) in Dar es Salaam was true. According to this report, the district *Jumben* were told by the government that the buying and selling of slaves was to be effected in Dar es Salaam, as only the Dar es Salaam district office was officially allowed to validate the transfer of slaves between owners. The *Jumben* were instructed that inherited slave mothers and children should not be separated from each other, but always sold together.[117] Bebel was apparently appalled by this report. How is it possible, he exclaimed, that after ten years of German colonialism in East Africa, slavery is being officially sanctioned?[118] Stuebel's reply was less than adequate. Expressing his own surprise about the article, he maintained that the report was just a misunderstanding and that Governor von Liebert's policy was designed to minimise certain excesses of slavery. He assured Parliament that after reading the article he had immediately sent a telegram to Governor von Liebert, urging that local government should avoid giving the appearance that slavery was a legal institution under German law.[119]

In retrospect, it is somewhat surprising to note that Bebel – unlike some of the other members of the Reichstag, including von Hertling (Zentrum) – was apparently satisfied with this reply to his question. However, he continued the debate by declaring that he had previously believed slavery to be slowly dying out because the average age of slaves had risen significantly. Referring to the buying and selling of slaves in Dar es Salaam, Bebel now felt compelled to ask himself where the new slaves were coming from. The colonial director was apparently at a loss for an answer. He could only point out that slavery in East Africa was 'of course' reproduced by birth. This answer did little to deflect criticism from the government. The Social Democrat von Vollmar immediately seized the opportunity to point out that it was attempting to gloss over the fact that people were still enslaved in German East Africa. Newborn children of slaves, he demanded, should be declared free.[120] This demand was subsequently taken up by Bebel, the leader of the party.[121]

The members of the conservative alliance and the Zentrum party (Hasse, von Stolberg-Wernigerode, von Karrdorf, von Arensberg) responded to these demands by restating their now well-worn arguments.[122] The government, they maintained, did not recognise slavery and both the government and the Reichstag favoured abolition, but for the time being its implementation would only lead to political instability. Moreover, von Arensberg argued, owners lacked the means to prevent their slaves from running away. They would not get any help from the colonial administration, and government intervention was thus not required.[123] With somewhat unusual openness, the conservative party member von Stolberg-Wernigerode added that even if the government wanted to implement abolition, it lacked the material resources and military means to do so. Effecting abolition would, in his view, actually entail increasing the colonial army, the *Schutztruppe*, by a factor of ten. Alternatively, he suggested that the opposition should agree to finance the construction of railways in the colonies, as economic development was the best way of throttling slavery.[124] The meeting of the Reichstag of 11 March 1901 ended before the issue could be settled.[125]

The debate was continued a week later at the Reichstag meeting on 19 March 1901. In the meantime, both the SPD and the Zentrum had filed parliamentary motions, the former demanding a declaration from the government that the children of slaves be regarded as free, while the latter urged the government to regulate the state of slavery.[126] To a large extent, the speakers of the various parties merely repeated points they had already made. However, some novel arguments did crop up. Bebel began the debate with an explanation of his party's motion, arguing that the government's supposedly gradual approach to abolition had failed since slavery was reproduced by the birth of slave children. This, he argued, was intolerable since no definite end to slavery in East Africa was in sight; the SPD, therefore, would reject the Zentrum motion.[127]

The response to Bebel was led by Gröber, the member of the Zentrum party who had taken up the government position in 1895 (see above) and was now again coming to its assistance.[128] Restating the argument that abolition would inevitably lead to political instability, he claimed that a declaration concerning the freedom of slave children would have the same effect. Though he sympathised with Bebel's motion, he believed that the development of the colony had not yet reached a stage that warranted contemplating such a radical measure. Moreover, he argued, there was no great urgency in this matter, as slavery in East Africa had already changed so much for the better that slaves should no longer be referred to as such. In retrospect, it is difficult to understand how this argument could carry any credibility: if Gröber was right in thinking that slaves in East Africa did not in fact have slave status, why should it be difficult to have them or their children declared free?[129]

Gröber continued his speech by clarifying some aspects of his motion. He introduced this section by stating that the principles the motion sought to express were actually those already practised by the colonial authorities. The central aim of the motion, he claimed, was to overcome the intermediate state of slavery in which slaves were neither 'free' nor 'slaves' in the true sense of the words, and thus to pave the way for eventual abolition. While the first three paragraphs of his motion were designed to define the rights and obligations of slaves and owners, the last and, in his view, most important paragraph endeavoured to make it easier for slaves to gain freedom from their owners.[130] This last paragraph stated that slaves should be afforded the opportunity to purchase their freedom. Again, in retrospect, it is difficult to understand why this reasoning should convince the Reichstag. If the principles of the motion were by and large already practised by the administration, a parliamentary motion to that effect was rather pointless. In any case, the motion was warmly welcomed by the colonial director, Stuebel, who reaffirmed Gröber's statement that the principles of the motion were already being practised by the colonial government.[131]

As in 1895, the SPD found it difficult to counter these arguments. Moreover, the Social Democrat members of Parliament seem to have abandoned their demand for abolition. Bebel stated that the party had finally realised that, given the cultural peculiarities of the 'native' population, slavery in East Africa could not be abolished with a stroke of the pen. Instead, abolition would come as a result of development. However, he still strongly urged the Reichstag to support the Social Democrat motion that the government should at least regard the children of slaves as free.[132]

However, the conservative majority was not prepared to give in to such a demand. The final blow to the SPD motion came from Oriola, a member of the national liberal party.[133] He argued that by freeing the children of slaves, the Reichstag would be legally recognising the servile state of their parents! Consequently, district officers would, in fact, be obliged to intervene by law and to return fugitive slaves. This kind of reasoning obviously impressed the Reichstag. Thus, when Gröber repeated the old argument that the colonial authorities lacked the (military) means to liberate slave children, and the colonial director insisted that the liberation of slave children would have the gravest political consequences, the Social Democratic Party could only muster the feeble reply that the introduction of the hut tax had sparked off more 'native' uprisings than the freeing of slave children was ever likely to cause.[134]

When the debate of 19 March 1901 was brought to a close, both motions were put to the vote. Not surprisingly, the Social Democratic Party lost its vote by a large majority, whereas the Zentrum motion was passed. Consequently, the then Chancellor, von Bülow, issued a decree in November 1901 that seemed to reflect the motion passed in the Reichstag. As the decree will be discussed in detail in Chapter 5, it is sufficient at this point to draw some conclusions from the debate itself. First, it appears that the Zentrum was instrumental in drumming up support for the government's non-abolition policy and that its motion was basically a defence mechanism to prevent change. When the government came under severe criticism on 11 March 1901, especially from the SPD, the Zentrum quickly produced a motion that ostensibly promised a measure of reform.[135] Arguably, the motion was simply a means to outmanoeuvre the opposition. After all, during the debate the Zentrum and the colonial director both admitted that the motion had expressed both government policy and actual administrative practice. However, it is perhaps worth noting that the SPD had modified its political position towards German colonial rule in Africa. For the first time, it suggested practical measures to change government colonial policy in East Africa, and that in itself was a significant change from its previous policy of total opposition.[136] Second, it should be noted that the constant repetition of the argument that the government was unable to abolish slavery for political and other reasons, finally seems to have convinced even the members of the opposition. Thus, the gradual approach to abolition was the victorious political argument in the end, at least for the time being.

Still, the 1901 debate did have a positive long-term effect. Without any parliamentary discussion, Chancellor von Bülow issued a decree in December 1904 that actually realised the 1901 motion of the Social Democratic Party.[137] The decree declared that children born after 31 December 1905 be regarded as free. It is curious that, three years on, neither the public nor the Reichstag seem to have noticed that connection: it was not mentioned in any of the comments that appeared at the time.[138] It should also be noted that slave owners in German East Africa showed no discernible political reaction to the enactment of this decree, and that

Gröber's central argument regarding the likely political consequences of the Social Democrat motion of 1901 turned out to have been a figment of his imagination.

Abolition at Last?

It was 1912 before the slavery issue finally reappeared in a parliamentary debate. The political set-up of the Reichstag had changed tremendously over the intervening eleven years.[139] The SPD was now the largest party in the Reichstag, while the conservatives and national-liberals had lost their overall parliamentary majority. In order to enact laws, the conservative Chancellor, von Bethmann-Hollweg, needed votes from other parties. Moreover, the Zentrum no longer principally supported the government, especially not on colonial questions. Finally, a new generation of parliamentarians, such as Noske (SPD) and Erzberger (Zentrum) had become influential party representatives in the Reichstag, and they were no longer prepared to accept the verities of the established colonial order. The colonial secretary, Solf, thus came frequently under attack.

On the occasion of the 1912 colonial budget debate, Erzberger asked the Reichstag to endorse a motion by the budget commission that slavery finally be abolished in the German colonies in Africa.[140] He suggested January 1920 as a possible date for abolition, in order to leave an eight-year period for the government to undertake appropriate preparatory measures. The reason Erzberger chose to adopt the slavery issue at this point in time is not entirely clear. He mentioned in his speech that he had received information according to which slave prices in East Africa were rising fast, and that slaves thus found it increasingly difficult to purchase their freedom from their owners through their own labour.[141]

Erzberger's initiative was well received from all sides in the Reichstag. The SPD signalled its support and even the ex-Governor of German East Africa, von Liebert, a member of the ultra-conservative Deutsche Reichspartei, welcomed it but suggested extending the final date of formal abolition by another three to five years.[142] The colonial secretary stated that he principally agreed with the motion, although on the advice of the new Governor of German East Africa, Schnee, who happened to be in Berlin at the time, he asked Parliament to refrain from setting a specific date for abolition.[143] The Reichstag did not heed his request and passed the budget commission motion urging the government to abolish slavery on 1 January 1920.[144]

A year later, in March 1913, again on the occasion of the colonial budget debate, Erzberger strongly criticised Governor Schnee's labour policy. Schnee had evidently tried to solve with decrees the long-standing scarcity of wage labour that had now become particularly pressing. He had allowed a number of district officers to enact local ordinances forcing substantial parts of the male population of the district to work for European employers for forty days every three months. News of this policy had reached the Reichstag. It was in this context that Erzberger raised the question of what the government had done about the previous year's motion on the abolition of slavery. In response, Solf defended the government's non-abolition approach.[145] His speech was probably the most radical statement ever made by a colonial secretary (or colonial director for that matter) in the German Reichstag, revealing an undercurrent of racism that had informed government policy over the years.

Solf argued that the notion of equality of humankind was misguided and that Africans should rather be regarded as 'children' under the tutelage of Europeans. He said that he would not like to repeat the dictum (but did so anyway) that Europeans were a master race (*Herrenvolk*) and the 'natives' a mere subservient race (*dienende Rasse*). Yet he declined to accept responsibility for labour affairs in the colonies. The decision on whether 'native' African labour should be harnessed by 'persuasion' rather than other methods (meaning physical force) should be left entirely to the Governors of the colonial territories in Africa. The colonial secretary added that this policy should take the old proverb into account that 'one should not kill the goose that lays the golden eggs'. In answer to Erzberger's question, he stated that he had asked Governor Schnee to put a report together on the actual state of slavery in the colony. He fervently assured Parliament that the government would do everything in its power to exterminate slavery in German East Africa ('*Sklaverei ... mit Stumpf und Stil auszurotten*') but that, on the whole, both the imperial government and the local colonial authorities favoured a gradual approach to abolition.[146]

The Reichstag had to be content with this answer, but members of the Social Democratic Party, especially Noske, made it clear that they would stick to the 1920 abolition date.[147] The 1913 debate was largely concerned with government colonial labour policy. In this context, the issue of abolition was of secondary importance. However, the debate ended with a motion in which the majority of the Reichstag demanded that the chancellor instruct the colonial authorities in Africa to abstain from issuing decrees forcing Africans to work involuntarily for German or other European employers in the colonies.[148]

One year later, the slavery issue was again raised in the annual budget debate, where particular attention was paid to the annual report of German East Africa and Governor Schnee's *Denkschrift* about slavery in the colony.[149] In the *Denkschrift*, after a lengthy description of the history of slavery in East Africa and its decline under German colonial rule, Governor Schnee argued that slavery would vanish rapidly in the coming years so that government intervention was unnecessary. Consequently, a specific date for abolition was not required.[150] Outright abolition, on the other hand, would have serious political and economic consequences, including local uprisings. Furthermore, he argued, it would even destroy the small African-owned plantations employing slaves, let alone the large ones. The African plantation owners would inevitably be driven into the camp of the dissatisfied, whereas they now had a direct, vested interest in the continuation of colonial rule. He also argued that the cost to human life of suppressing anti-government uprisings would far outweigh the possible benefits of abolition![151]

As in 1913, the discussion focused on the 'Forced Labour Question'. Both the Social Democratic Party and the Zentrum mounted a sustained attack on the colonial secretary. For them, the forced labour policy and the refusal by Governor Schnee to fix a date for abolition were just two sides of the same shameful attitude towards 'native' subjects. The debate was opened by the social democrat Dittmann, who described the situation in East Africa. Forced and 'voluntary' contract labour had depopulated large parts of the colony. Labourers who tried to leave their employers were caught, beaten up and returned to the plantations in order to fulfil their contracts. He concluded that 'the terrible form of slavery now practised by the authorities had never existed in the colony before'.[152]

Dittmann's arguments were seconded by Erzberger, the leading spokesperson of the Zentrum party.[153] Like Dittmann, he stated that he had read Governor Schnee's report as a validation of slavery in East Africa. The Governor portrayed slavery as a welfare institution for slaves, as if even the slaves themselves had no interest in abolition. Erzberger announced that his party would not tolerate this approach, and subsequent speakers, including a member of the left-liberal party, agreed with him.[154] Both the colonial secretary and the conservative parties in the Reichstag that had supported this policy in the preceding years were now in trouble, as the majority of the Reichstag threatened to vote for abolition and reject the colonial budget. The defence was thus designed to limit potential damage to government abolition policy.

The more liberal-minded conservatives tried to play down the rift between the government and the opposition by arguing that their disagreement merely concerned the speed of abolition, and not the principle of its eventual enactment.[155] However, the ultra-conservative Paasche restated the old arguments and attitudes. He suggested that slavery, like forced labour, was a method of making people work for others and argued that since (male) Africans were lazy by nature and preferred 'to hang out in front of their huts', a measure of force was necessary in order to achieve economic and social 'development'.[156] These racist diatribes, however, were of little help to the government.

The next speaker was the Social Democrat Noske, who began by recounting the history of colonialism and slavery since the assumption of colonial rule in 1890. He went on to assert that although the vote on the first millions for East Africa had been passed ostensibly to combat slave trading and slavery, after twenty-five years of colonial rule slavery still existed in the colony.[157] Moreover, he accused the colonial administration of participating in slave trading by legally validating the transfer contracts for slaves between owners. As proof for this assertion, he read to Parliament the text of a slave transfer contract from Tabora, which had been signed by the district officer. The Social Democratic Party, he stated, would thus vote against the proposed colonial budget. Noske then went on to attack Governor Schnee's forced labour policy. The day ended with the acceptance of an SPD motion in which the chancellor was urged to issue a decree that included the requirement by local administrations specifically to outlaw all forms of forced labour in the German colonies in Africa, and to regulate the working conditions of African labourers on European farms.[158]

The debate came to an end on 19 March 1914. It was the third day of parliamentary debate on this issue and few new arguments were introduced. However, in a last minute attempt, the colonial secretary tried to mollify the Reichstag opposition, probably in order to ensure that the government would win the vote for the colonial budget – which, eventually, it did.[159] With regard to the embarrassing Tabora transfer contract, Solf argued that Noske had merely drawn the wrong conclusion. The government and the colonial authorities had a clear conscience on this account. Slave trading, he asserted, did not exist in German East Africa. Local district officers were merely required to supervise slavery, which happened to entail the legal validation of transfer contracts between owners. These transfers were only officially certified if the slave agreed. Moreover, district officials had to make sure that all three – the old and the new owner, and the slave – resided in the same administrative district. Thus, the Tabora contract was not a document of 'cruel slave trading' but an 'instrument of a humanitarian policy' which sought to improve the living conditions of the economically weak.[160] In retrospect, it is difficult to understand how the colonial secretary, Solf, could have believed that these arguments would convince the opposition.

The colonial secretary continued his speech by indicating to the Reichstag that he would seek a compromise. He repeated that he would not instruct Governor Schnee to accept the Reichstag's anti-slavery policy, but he would ask him, nevertheless, to consider the suggestion that, as of 1920, the colonial courts should no longer accept complaints by slave owners regarding the 'establishment, reconstitution, recognition or continuance' of slave–master relationships. However, as compensation for their losses, owners should be allowed to file civil suits against their slaves for remuneration of services rendered to the slave. Finally, he suggested that slave-ransoming prices should be fixed for each district.[161]

These proposals did not receive the welcome the colonial secretary had probably hoped for. In reply to Solf, Noske made it clear that the SPD would reject any suggestion to extend the legality of slavery in German East Africa beyond the date laid down in the Reichstag resolution of 1912, that is 1 January 1920. He inferred that the colonial secretary had not understood the essence of his, Noske's, argument that after twenty-five years of colonial rule in East Africa, human beings were bought and sold under the eyes of the administration 'as if they were nothing but cattle'.[162] For this reason his party would not consider making concessions on the issue, and he urged the Reichstag to pass the SPD motion that the colonial secretary should report to Parliament in a year's time on the progress made in preparing for the abolition of slavery in 1920. The Reichstag accepted this motion by a great majority.[163] Thus, at least as far as the parliamentary vote was concerned, the political battle for abolition in the Reichstag had been won. However, the answer to the question as to whether the Reichstag would have succeeded in forcing the colonial secretary and the Governor of East Africa to effect abolition on 1 January 1920 is an entirely different matter; since the outbreak of war prevented any further discussion, it remains open to speculation.[164]

Three of the features in the long parliamentary debate on slavery in the German colonies in Africa, particularly East Africa, are relevant for an understanding of the history of government anti-slavery policy. First, government legislative measures regarding slavery and the slave trade – the then-much-celebrated 1901 decree regulating the slave–owner relationship and the 1904 decree declaring children of slaves to be free – were not the result of an enlightened policy but of political pressure applied by the opposition to achieve abolition. The enactment of these decrees was a defensive strategy, designed to accomplish as little substantive change as possible.

Second, the government carried out this policy with the active support of the Catholic Zentrum party, which – in its own narrow interests – gave up its pre-colonial anti-slavery stance to gain acceptance and recognition by the political establishment. This policy apparently silenced the Catholic Missions, which had so vocally and so successfully put slavery and the slave trade on the national agenda in the years immediately preceding the formal establishment of colonial rule. Their voice became less than a whisper during the colonial period.

Finally, the debate on slavery reveals that the members of the Reichstag had very limited knowledge of colonial affairs. Already in 1901, the leader of the Social Democratic Party, Bebel, complained that discussions in the Reichstag depended on information supplied either by the government or by colonial interest groups, both of whom propagated highly biased views.[165] Colonial debates in the Reichstag were thus often rather limited in scope and substance. The slavery debate in the Reichstag presents a good case for this argument. The recurring statement that colonial authorities did not legally recognise slaves apparently lulled many members of the Reichstag into thinking that slavery was not a pressing colonial problem, that slavery indeed had somehow vanished. Thus in 1907, for instance, even an informed colonial secretary like Dernburg evidently had no qualms in writing that slavery had already been abolished in the German colonies.[166] This statement was manifestly untrue, but it could only have been contradicted by someone who had access to information showing that, on the contrary, the colonial administration was pursuing an entirely different course of action. The colonial authorities, for example, were actually supervising the buying and selling of slaves. Information of this kind was certainly available in Germany at the time, as the next chapter in this section will demonstrate, but only to the colonial bureaucracy and a tiny group of selected government advisers who constituted the Kolonialrat.

Notes

1 Karstedt 1912: 105. See also RHO Afr Micr 472 R.8/MF 19, Mafia District Book, 'Domestic Slavery in German East Africa' by N. King, Mafia, April 1915: 14. For a different view, see Roberts and Miers 1988: 17. They state that 'the colonial powers could not tolerate open slave ... trading' because the ideology of the anti-slavery movement became part and parcel of the European mission to civilise Africa. The German example seems to contradict that argument.

2 For more detail, see below. Few local administrative records dealing with the purchase and sale of slaves under government supervision have survived. For an example, see Tanzania National Archives (henceforth TNA) G38/7, 'Bezirksamt Kilwa: Verzeichnis über Sklavenkäufe und Verkäufe, 1911–1914'. See also Sunseri 2002: 30, 46, note 32.

3 See, for instance, the emotional appeal by Noske (Social Democratic Party) in *Stenographische Berichte über die Verhandlungen des Reichstages*, 13. Legislatur Periode, 1. Session 1912–14, 236. Sitzung, 19. März 1914: 8105 (in the following abbreviated as *RT* 1912–14, 19 March 1914: 8105).

4 See *RT* 1912–14, 19 March 1914. Here, it is interesting to note that after the First World War, the fact that the German authorities had not abolished slavery was seen as proof for the argument that 'the Germans' were morally 'unfit' to have colonies in Africa. See Dundas 1923: 35.

5 For the motion by the budget commission (Kommission für den Reichshaushalts-Etat), demanding the abolition of slavery, see *RTA* 1912–14, no. 385: 336. For Colonial Secretary Solf's position on the question, see *RT* 1912–14, 19 March 1914: 8102 and BAB RKolA 1007: 57, Solf to Schnee, 6 May 1914.

6 The then Governor of German East Africa, Schnee, strongly opposed the active emancipation of slaves. See *RTA* 1912–14, no. 1395: 2885, 'Denkschrift über die Haussklaverei in Deutsch-Ostafrika' by Schnee, 20 February 1914. For another copy of the 'Denkschrift', see BAB RKolA 1006/201, 'Denkschrift über die Haussklaverei in Deutsch-Ostafrika', 28 October 1913.

7 Spellmeyer 1931: 3. See also Schwarz 1999: 305–25. For a concise overview on party politics in the Kaiserreich, see Schwarz 1965: 115–36, Wehler 1995: 1045–63 and Nipperdey 1992 vol. II: 311–58, 514–76. For an African historian it is somewhat surprising to note that despite the abundance of literature on the Kaiserreich and German imperialism (see, for instance, the detailed bibliography in Wehler 1995: 1463–5) no comprehensive study has been undertaken on colonial party politics in the Reichstag. Contemporary accounts, such as Noske (1914) and Erzberger (1907), or the more scholarly works by Spellmeyer (1931) and Lackner (1939), are now very dated. The study by Schröder (1968) and the new book by Schwarz (1999) on the Freisinn and the Social Democratic Party do not entirely fill the gap, since they are mainly interested in the changing attitudes of the parties towards colonialism and/or imperialism as a whole. Thus, particular aspects of colonial policy tend to receive only minor attention.

8 See, for instance, the intervention by Graf von Kardorff, *RT* 1888–9, 26 January 1889: 623. See also Spellmeyer 1931: 4.

9 For a history of the Kolonialrat, see the unpublished theses by Westphal 1964 and by Pogge von Strandmann 1970.

10 See, for example, BAB RKolA 6992: 60, 'Bericht des Ausschusses zur Beratung der Sklavenfrage', 5 November 1901. For the debate with regard to Cameroon, see Harding 1995: 280–308, Eckert 1998: 133–48. For Togo, see Maier 1987: 73–92.

11 The decree will be discussed in detail further on in this section.

12 *Anweisungen* or instructions were primarily issued for internal administrative purposes while *Verordnungen* (ordinances) had full legal status. The line between the two was often blurred. See Sippel 2003: 297–311. Note that the colonial department became a full government ministry in 1907. It was then headed by a secretary of state (*Staatssekretär*). The first, and in many respects most important office holder was Dernburg.

13 For an overview on the constitutional rights of the Reichstag, see Wehler 1985: 60–72, Baumgart 1986: 114–22, Mommsen 1990: 39–65 and Nipperdey 1992 vol. II: 85–109.

14 For more detail, see Schwarz 1965: 115–36, Mommsen 1990: 52ff., 62 and Wehler

1995: 1043. In this context it is perhaps worth noting that women were denied the right to vote in parliamentary elections. Thus, even if the Reichstag was democratically elected, it only represented the political will of the male electorate.

15 For more detail, see Pogge von Strandmann 1970: 73ff.

16 The power of the Kaiser was only limited by the stipulation that his decrees had to be countersigned by the chancellor. Karlowa 1911: 11, Karstedt 1912: 5, Schack 1923. See also Trotha 1988: 317–46, Naucke 1988: 297–315 and Sippel 1995: 466–94.

17 On the *Kommandogewalt* of the Kaiser, see Mommsen 1990: 57 and Wehler 1995: 1016, 1285. The legal basis for the *Schutzgewalt* of the Kaiser in the colonies was the *Schutzgebietsgesetz* of 17 April 1886, modified by the *Schutzgebietsgesetz* of 10 September 1900. Paragraph 1 of the *Schutzgebietsgesetz* states that all executive and legislative matters were to be decided by the Kaiser in the name of the Reich. It reads: 'Die Schutzgewalt in den deutschen Schutzgebieten übt der Kaiser im Namen des Reiches aus'. For more detail, see the entry 'Schutzgebietsgesetz' in Schnee 1920 vol. III: 317–19.

18 On political decision-making processes in the Kaiserreich, see Wehler 1995: 1002–4, 1042ff.

19 Wehler 1995: 1071–3. On the Kolonialgesellschaft, see also Pierard 1987: 19–34.

20 For a full list of these scandals, see Noske 1914: *passim*.

21 The military budget was not subject to parliamentary approval. In the 1880s, the military accounted for about 80 per cent of total government expenditure. See Schwarz 1965: 122.

22 For more detail, see Nipperdey 1992 vol. II: 85–109. See also Wehler 1995: 1286ff.

23 Wehler 1995: 1038–45.

24 This and the following chapter have greatly profited from Bley 1991, Harding 1995: 280–308 and Eckert 1998: 133–48.

25 Various authors have recounted the history of the assumption of formal colonial rule in Africa by the German Reich. For a short and concise summary and an excellent bibliography, see Gründer 1995: 51–109. For a comparative perspective, see Miers 1999: 16–37.

26 This paragraph draws heavily on Mommsen 1990: 109–39. For the 'classical' statement by Chancellor von Bismarck on his colonial policy, see BAB RKolA 7230: 53, 'Denkschrift über die deutschen Schutzgebiete' by von Bismarck, 2 December 1885.

27 For the activities of the German East Africa Company, see Müller 1959: 220–44. See also Bückendorf 1997: 290–317.

28 BAB RKolA 7363: 132, 'Bericht über die Vorstandssitzung der Deutschen Kolonial-gesellschaft. Rede des Präsidenten Fürst zu Hohenlohe-Langenburg', 19 January 1889.

29 Sippel 1995: 470. See also BAB RKolA 7363: 171, extract from *Kölner Volkzeitung*, 26 November 1889, 'Bericht von Premier-Lieutnant Giese, Stationschef der Station Mpwapwa'.

30 See Deutsch 1995: 210–19.

31 For a detailed history of the coastal uprising and its social origins, see Glassman 1995: 177–98. For a highly critical report by a contemporary observer, see Hamburger Staatsarchiv, 132–5/4, 'Bericht über die Unruhen an der Küste' by O'Swald, 22 October 1888. See also the instructive article in the British military journal *Jane's Gazette*, 2 November 1888, cited in BAB RKolA 7362: 146. The article was based on British consular reports from Zanzibar.

32 It is worth noting that the DOAG strongly favoured the takeover of its East African 'possessions' by the Reich. See the report in *Deutsche Kolonialzeitung*, 2 (1889), 1.

33 Chancellor von Bismarck's change of heart in colonial matters is still a subject of historiographical debate. See, for instance, Gründer 1995: 68, 87 and Koponen 1994: 45–86. For a summary of the more recent debate, see Mommsen 1990: 182–213, Nipperdey 1992 vol. II: 445–53 and Wehler 1995: 985–90. For the older debate, see, for instance, Müller 1959, Turner 1967 and Washausen 1968.

34 Previous parliamentary debates concerned the proposed financial support by the government for a steamship connection with East Africa in the context of the so-called *Samoa Dampfervorlage* that did not find a parliamentary majority. For the devastating critique of the 1889 bill by Richter, a member of the Freisinn, see *RT* 1888–9, 29 January 1889: 656–63. For a detailed discussion of the Social Democratic Party's position concerning intervention in East Africa, see Schwarz 1999: 259–68.

35 Jacob 1938: 153.

36 See *RTA* 1888–9, no. 41, 'Sammlung von Aktenstücken, betreffend den Aufstand in Ostafrika', 6 December 1888.
37 This paragraph is based on Miers 1975: 201–6. For further detail, see Renault 1971, particularly vol. II: 147–87, Gründer 1977: 210–24, Bade 1977: 31–58 and Bade 1982: 124–32.
38 For a letter from Cardinal Lavigerie to Chancellor von Bismarck, see *RTA* 1888–9, no. 41/23: 34, Lavigerie to von Bismarck, 24 August 1888. The original of this letter can be found in BAB RKolA 7362: 27, Lavigerie to von Bismarck, 24 August 1888. In this letter Lavigerie seems to advocate the inauguration of a 'new crusade' in order to 'emancipate' Africa both from slavery and from Islam. He argued that for this purpose only 500 armed men were needed. Chancellor von Bismarck did not reply. See BAB RKolA 7362: 40, 'Memorandum betreffend die Eingabe des Kardinal Lavigerie' by Krauel, 31 August 1888. For further detail, see Müller 1959: 421–2. For an example of the fusion of anti-slavery and anti-Islam propaganda at the time, see Saget 1889 and Anonymous, *Gott will es! Wer bleibt zurück im heiligen Kampf für Christentum und Menschenrechte*, 1889. For a similar attitude, see von Wissmann 1888: 352. Von Wissmann suggested that all 'Arabs' should be deported from East Africa. He also proposed that those who refused to leave should be killed. This seems to be a late-nineteenth-century example of what is known today as the politics of 'ethnic cleansing'. See BAB RKolA 7362: 102, 'Auszug aus einem Gutachten', by von Wissmann, 13 October 1888.
39 The anti-slavery activities of the Protestant and Catholic Churches have been described by Bade 1982: 124–32 and Bade 1977: 31–58. For further detail, see Anonymous, 'Das Deutsche Reich und die Sklaverei in Afrika. Stenographischer Bericht der am 18. Januar 1895 in der Tonhalle zu Berlin auf Veranlassung des evangelischen Afrikavereins abgehaltenen Versammlung', 1885. See also 'Eingabe der Vertreter der Cöllner Versammlung zur Unterdrückung des afrikanischen Sklavenhandels vom 27 Oktober 1888' and 'Eingabe des Vorsitzenden der Versammlung zu Freiburg im Breisgau vom 19 Nov. 1888' in *RTA* 1888–9, no. 41 'Sammlung von Aktenstücken, betreffend den Aufstand in Ostafrika', no. 24: 37, No. 25: 38 and the report 'Die Sklavenfrage auf der 35. Generalversammlung der deutschen Katholiken in Freiburg' in Humanus, *Sklavenhandel in Afrika*, 1888: 42–52. See also Anonymous, *Wider die Sklaverei. Bericht über die Verhandlungen der Vollversammlung in Gürzenich zu Köln am 27 Oktober 1888*, 1888 and the declaration of a meeting of the board of the Deutsche Kolonialgesellschaft, entitled 'Against the Slave Trade!' (*Gegen den Sklavenhandel!*) in *Deutsche Kolonialzeitung*, 2 (1889), 25ff., 28ff. For a discussion of the problem in the press, see Buchner 1886 and the report in *Hamburgische Börsenhalle*, 17 December 1888. Further information, including press reports, can be found in BAB RKolA 7362, 'Sklavenfrage in Afrika. Allgemeines'.
40 Bade 1982: 128. The Deutsche Kolonialgesellschaft had taken the anti-slavery issue fully on board in November 1888, a few months after the outbreak of the 'Arab Uprising' in the *Schutzgebiet*. See the lengthy report 'Anti-Sklaverei-Bewegung und Deutsch-Ostafrika' in *Deutsche Kolonialzeitung*, 1 (1888), 349–55. For further detail, see the article about the 1889 annual general meeting of the Deutsche Kolonialgesellschaft and the subsequent meeting of its board of directors in *Deutsche Kolonialzeitung*, 2 (1889), 25–8. The *Kolonialzeitung* reports that motions were passed in both meetings that strongly urged the government to suppress the slave trade in East Africa, arguing that commercial development in the region depended on it. The *Kolonialzeitung* was the mouthpiece of the Kolonialgesellschaft and the Deutsch-Ostafrikanischen Gesellschaft. See also BAB RKolA 7363: 127, von Hohenlohe-Langenburg to von Bismarck, 22 November 1888 and BAB RKolA 7363: 132, 'Bericht über die Vorstandssitzung der Deutschen Kolonialgesellschaft', 19 January 1889.
41 See BAB RKolA 1002: 14, 'Vermerk', 10 June 1885. For more detail, see Zanzibar National Archives (henceforth ZNA) G2/47/1, Foreign Office to Konsul Arndt, 20 August 1886. See also his comment 'certainly' on the report by Consul Michahelles who argued that abolition was impracticable. See BAB RKolA 7363: 96, Michahelles to von Bismarck, 17 December 1888.
42 For a contemporary critique, see the speech by Bamberger in *RT* 1888–9, 26 January 1889: 606–14. See also Noske 1914: 46–8. Colonial enthusiasm was in fact limited to a tiny but well-organised and highly vocal minority of political activists, as the study by Soénius (1992) shows. For the opportunistic change in von Bismarck's attitude, see BAB RKolA 7362: 101, 'Notiz', by von Rothenburg, 13 October 1888. See also von

Bismarck's telling comment in BAB RKolA 7362: 113 on a report about slavery in East Africa by the *Berliner Politische Nachrichten* (25 October 1888): 'kann man nicht schaurige Details über Menschenquälerei auftreiben?' ['is it not possible to come up with some gruesome details on human suffering?']. For further detail see BAB RKolA 7387: 87, 'Notiz', by von Rothenburg, 30 November 1888.

43 Müller 1959: 392–427. For the way in which the German Colonial Society hijacked the German anti-slavery movement and their sentiments for their own purposes, see 'Die Antisklaverei-Bewegung und Deutsch-Ostafrika' in *Deutsche Kolonialzeitung*, 1 (1888), 349–55.

44 *RTA* 1888–9, no. 71, 'Entwurf eines Gesetzes, betreffend Bekämpfung des Sklaven-handels und Schutz deutscher Interessen in Ostafrika', 22 January 1889. See also Müller 1959: 427. The only two groups, who voted against the bill in Parliament, were the Social Democratic Party and the left-liberal Freisinn party.

45 For Chancellor von Bismarck's statement, see *RT* 1888–9, 15 January 1889: 433 and *RT* 1888–9, 26 January 1989: 514. See also *RTA* 1888–9, no. 71, 'Entwurf eines Gesetzes, betreffend Bekämpfung des Sklavenhandels und Schutz deutscher Interessen in Ostafrika', 22 January 1889, especially p. 4, 'Begründung'.

46 For an example of confusing the problem of slavery and slave trading, see the speech by Stöcker, who belonged to the conservative party, in *RT* 1888–9, 15 January 1889: 679. For more on the detail of von Bismarck's colonial politics, see Bückendorf 1997: 378–81 and Gründer 1995: 63–78.

47 This and the following three paragraphs are based on Gottberg 1971: 69–91, Schweinitz 1897: 161–71 and BAB RKolA 1030: 67–77, 'Bericht des Lieutnants Prince über die Niederwerfung und Vernichtung des Häuptlings Sike von Tabora', cited in Gottberg 1971: 370–83. See also BAB RKolA 6988/98: 35, 'Anlage VII: Unter-nehmungen der deutschen Antisklaverei-Lotterie für Deutsch-Ostafrika', in 'Denk-schrift, betreffend Deutsch-Ostafrika [for the year 1891–2]', n.d. [1892], 'Die Expeditionen des Antisklaverei-Komites', *Koloniales Jahrbuch*, 1892: 141–80, and Gondorf 1991. For a slightly revised version of von Prince's report, see Prince 1893: 198–204.

48 For a list of the members of the German Anti-Slavery Committee, see BAB RKolA 1007: 50, Anti-Slavery Lottery Committee to Kaiser Wilhelm, 15 April 1891.

49 See *Deutsche Kolonialzeitung*, 4 (1891), 91. The anti-slavery committee saw itself as successor to the various groups, who had previously tried to organise financial support for colonial enterprises, such as the *Emin-Pasha*-Komite, the *Peters-Dampfer*-Komite and the *Wissmann-Dampfer*-Komite. Only the Wissmann committee had been moderately successful in collecting donations.

50 See BAB RKolA 1007: 46, Anti-Slavery Lottery Committee to Kaiser Wilhelm, 15 April 1891.

51 See, for instance, the advertisement in *Gott will es*, 3 (1891) 14: 421. See also Schweinitz 1897: 170.

52 BAB RKolA 1007/1: 42, 'Bericht des geschäftsführenden Ausschuss des deutschen Anti-Sklaverei-Lotterie-Komites', 8 May 1891. For the accounts of the Anti-Sklaverei-Komite, see BAB RKolA 1008: 92, 'Nachweis der Einnahmen und Ausgaben des Deutschen Anti-Sklaverei-Komites für die Jahre 1981 und 1892, abgeschlossen am 31. Dezember 1892'.

53 Schweinitz 1897: 161. The failure to bring the *Wissmann* steamer to Lake Victoria attracted considerable attention at the time. The internal correspondence of the anti-slavery committee was subsequently made available to the Colonial Office. The documents reveal that the project basically failed because of deep personal rivalries between the persons involved as well as their inaptitude to properly plan and carry out a project of such magnitude. The report also hints that a certain amount of graft and corruption permeated the whole undertaking. See BAB RKolA 1015: 22, 'Die Akten der Ausführungskommission des Deutschen Anti-Sklaverei-Komites betreffend das Wissmann-Dampfer-Unternehmen', 14 January 1893. See also *Deutsche Kolonialzeitung*, 6 (1893), 115–17.

54 Subsequently, Kapitän Spring was attached to that expedition to undertake the scientific work. In any case, as Stuhlmann reports (1894: 749), Fischer and his successor had few guidelines regarding the purpose of their expedition.

55 Schweinitz later stated that in his view the expedition was 'completely useless'. See

Imperial Politics

Schweinitz 1897: 166.

56 BAB RKolA 1008: 14, 'Bericht des Grafen Schweinitz über seine Tätigkeit bei dem Sturm auf Quikuru kwa Sikki', 12 July 1892. See also BAB RKolA 1030: 17–20, Schwesinger to von Soden, 11 June 1892 and BAB RKolA 1014: 73, Spring to Reichskolonialamt, 25 August 1906, and *Deutsche Kolonialzeitung*, 5 (1892), 126. Isike was accused of being a slave trader, bent on murdering all Europeans in the region. Little evidence was offered for these assertions.

57 Apart from participating in the attacks on Isike, Schweinitz and Meyer also ordered their troops to burn several villages near Isike's residence. See Gottberg 1971: 87. Schwesinger undertook a third attempt to raze Isike's residence to the ground, but again he failed. He was subsequently relieved of his post. Isike's resistance was finally broken in January 1893 by T. von Prince, who succeeded in overrunning the fortifications of the village. Isike and his son were shot on the spot. See BAB RKolA 1030: 67–77, 'Bericht des Lieutnants Prince über die Niederwerfung und Vernichtung des Häuptlings Sike von Tabora', January 1893, cited in Gottberg 1971: 370–83. For the burning of villages by the Emin Pasha expedition, see Stuhlmann 1894: 46.

58 BAB RKolA 1008: 100, 'Promemoria über den Stand der Unternehmungen des Deutschen Anti-Sklaverei Komites und deren Zukunft', 28 February 1893. The whole affair seems to be a prime example for the use of anti-slavery rhetoric as a 'heaven-sent excuse for campaigns which otherwise might have raised a storm of criticism at home'. See Miers 2003: 23.

59 The Schweinitz expedition carried three disassembled sailing boats to Lake Victoria. They were put together on the Peters Werft, later renamed Neuwied. The boats were subsequently transferred to Bukoba on the western side of the Lake. For a plan of the Peters Werft, see *Deutsche Kolonialtzeitung*, 6 (1893), 34.

60 BAB RKolA 1008: 100, 'Promemoria über den Stand der Unternehmungen des Deutschen Anti-Sklaverei Komites und deren Zukunft', 28 February 1893.The reports on the activities of Langheld can be found in BAB RKolA 242: 32, 37, 44, 47, 'Forschungsreisen: Expedition Langheld', 20 September–10 November 1893. For the reports by Fischer, Borchert and Baumann, see BAB RKolA 1007/4: 36, 'Veröffentlichungen der Geschäftsleitung der Ausführungskommission der Deutschen Anti-Sklaverei-Lotterie', Koblenz 1892.

61 See, for instance, the scathing critique by Lieutnant Herrmann in BAB RKolA 1007/4: 5, Herrman to Gouvernement, 22 March 1892 and BAB RKolA 1007/4: 7, Herrman to Gouvernement, 12 March 1892.

62 See BAB RKolA 1008: 92, 'Nachweis der Einnahmen und Ausgaben des Deutschen Anti-Sklaverei-Komites für die Jahre 1981 und 1892, abgeschlossen am 31 Dezember 1892'. According to the accounts, the total cost of Baumann's expedition was RM63,275.

63 *RTA* 1888–9, no. 27, 'Antrag Windthorst', 27 November 1888. The Reichstag passed the motion on 14 December 1888. For Protestant mission support of colonial intervention, see BAB RKolA 7362: 136, Fabri to von Bismarck, 29 October 1888. See also Müller 1959: 392–427.

64 On the *Kulturkampf*, see Nipperdey 1992 vol. II: 364–81.

65 Spellmeyer 1931: 12, 24ff., 28–34.

66 Wehler 1995: 1055–60.

67 See *RT* 1890–2, 17 November 1891. There had already been some parliamentary discussion in 1884, but the debate referred to West Africa only and apparently had no bearing on the parliamentary debate on slavery in East Africa.

68 *RTA* 1890–1, no. 501, 'Entwurf eines Gesetzes, betreffend die Bestrafung des Sklavenhandels, nebst Begründung', 2 July 1891. The Brussels Act itself was approved by Parliament in May 1891. At the time, there was some discussion in Parliament about slave trading by German commercial companies in West Africa, a fact that had been made public by the traveller Krause. The bill was not, however, connected to that issue. For further detail on Krause, see Sebald 1972.

69 The Berlin conference of 1884–5 had already discussed measures against slavery and slave trading in Africa. Yet, the participants could not agree on a common policy. The act states rather vaguely that the signatories would strive to 'participate in the suppression of slavery and of the slave trade'. See BAB RKolA 7362: 47, 'Generalakte der Berliner Konferenz', 26 February 1885, Chapter I, Article VI. The following

account is based on Miers 1967: 83–118, Miers 1975: 236–91. For more details with regard to the 'humanitarian' issues discussed at the 1884–5 Berlin conference, see Miers 1988: 333–45, and Gann 1988: 321–31.

70 Miers 1975: 206–9, 229–35.

71 Italy also participated in the blockade. On the political usefulness of the blockade, see *RT* 1888–9, 26 January 1889: 619. See also Müller 1959: 421–2 and Miers 1975: 209–16.

72 See *RTA* 1888–9, no. 71: 4, 'Entwurf eines Gesetzes, betreffend Bekämpfung des Sklavenhandels und Schutz deutscher Interessen in Ostafrika', 22 January 1889.

73 See Articles LXIII and LXIV of the Brussels Act. For a German translation of the act, see Kaiserliches Gouvernement 1911: 39–66. For an English translation, see Miers 1975: 346–63.

74 Miers 1999: 19.

75 See Article V of the Brussels Act. For a detailed discussion of the Brussels Conference Act and its consequences, see 'Denkschrift betreffend die Ausführung der Beschlüsse der Brüsseler Antisklaverei-Konferenz vom 2. Juli 1890, nebst Anlagen', in *Documents relatifs* 1892: 1–100. The Brussels Act also bound the German government to inform the other signatory powers about legislative anti-slavery measures. Moreover, the Act required the German authorities to keep statistical records regarding the number of slaves officially emancipated by the administrative authorities in the German colonies and the penalties they had imposed on slave traders, and to send these records to the 'bureau' in Brussels.

76 *RTA* 1890–1, no. 501: 3, 'Entwurf eines Gesetzes, betreffend die Bestrafung des Sklavenhandels, nebst Begründung', 2 July 1891.

77 See *RT* 1890–2, 17 November 1891: 2892ff.

78 See *RT* 1890–2, 17 November 1891: 2892.

79 For the report, see BAB RKolA 6987/179: 33, 'Bericht des Kaiserlichen Gouverneurs von Deutsch-Ostafrika' by von Soden, 30 August 1891.

80 See *RT* 1890–2, 17 November 1891: 2892.

81 For the text of the decree, see Kaiserliches Gouvernement 1911: 329–31, 'Gouverneurs-Verordnung, betreffend den Freikauf von Sklaven. Vom 1. Sept. 1891'.

82 See *RT* 1890–2, 17 November 1891: 2892 [translation by the author].

83 For this argument, see Roberts and Miers 1988: 28.

84 For this argument, see BAB RKolA 1002: 4, 'Denkschrift: Betrifft die Frage der Sklaverei in den deutschen Schutzgebieten in Afrika', by Kayser, 6 June 1885. This was the first official memorandum concerned with the problem of slavery in East Africa.

85 *RT* 1890–2, 17 November 1891: 2895.

86 See *RTA* 1894–5, no. 138, 'Begründung' by von Hohenlohe-Schillingsfürst, 31 January 1895.

87 *RT* 1893–4, 16 February 1894: 1286.

88 For Bebel's arguments, see *RT* 1893–4, 16 February 1894: 1291 and 17 February 1894: 1309–12, 1317–8.

89 *Ibid.*

90 *RT* 1893–4, 17 February 1894: 1318.

91 For Ehni's arguments, see *RT* 1893–4, 17 February 1894: 1314.

92 This was the first time that a Member of Parliament actually demanded the abolition of slavery.

93 See Arensburg's reply in *RT* 1893–4, 17 February 1894: 1319. For the racist structure of German colonial law, see below.

94 *RT* 1893–4, 17 February 1894: 1319.

95 *RT* 1893–4, 20 May 1895: 2339.

96 *RT* 1893–4, 20 May 1895: 2340.

97 *RT* 1893–4, 20 May 1895: 2341.

98 *Ibid.*

99 Nipperdey 1990 vol. I: 335–73.

100 For a slightly different analysis, see Sunseri 2002: 26ff., 47 note 51. According to Sunseri, German official policy was inspired by an idealised version of the *Gesindewesen*. He argues, that the *Gesindewesen* policy was a deliberate attempt by the government to uphold 'patriarchal authority' of rural employers in the face of rapid industrialisation by preserving the personal relationship between masters and servants, which supposedly

had emerged on rural estates and farms in eastern Germany after the end of serfdom in the early nineteenth century. However, the term *Gesindewesen* was hardly ever mentioned in the discussions about the possible dangers of abolition. Instead the expression *Dienstverhältnis* (service relationship) was used, which had a much wider meaning as it also encompassed industrial relations.

101 Interestingly, the opponents of abolition in Britain invoked a similar argument. See Cooper 1980: 29.

102 The perceived threat of social upheaval by unfettered capitalism was probably the single most important reason why Germany failed to abolish slavery in its East African possession. Apparently, the articulation and promotion of social and moral values necessary to promote capitalist expansion were much weaker in Germany than in Britain. Here is not the place to explore this theme any further, but I hope to return to the subject in a separate publication.

103 For a discussion of the British case, see Cooper 1980: 24–34.

104 *RT* 1893–4, 20 May 1895: 2341.

105 *RT* 1893–4, 20 May 1895: 2342–4, 2347ff.

106 *RT* 1893–4, 20 May 1895: 2447ff.

107 The German text of this motion is difficult to translate because of its bureaucratic style. It reads 'die Verbündeten Regierungen um Einbringung eines Gesetzentwurfs zu ersuchen, welche die in den deutschen Schutzgebieten unter den Eingeborenen bestehende Hausklaverei und Schuldknechtschaft eine ihrer Beseitigung vorbereitenden Regelung unterwirft'. *RT* 1893–4, 20 May 1895: 2349. See also *RTA* 1893–4, no. 356, 'Änderungsantrag' by Gröber, 20 May 1895.

108 *RT* 1893–4, 20 May 1895: 2349.

109 *RT* 1893–4, 20 May 1895: 2349ff.

110 *Ibid.*

111 Schwarz 1999: 275.

112 *RT* 1893–4, 20 May 1895: 2351 [translation by the author].

113 *RT* 1893–4, 20 May 1895: 2358.

114 *RT* 1893–4, 22 May 1895: 2420. For the text of the 1895 act, see Kaiserliches Gouvernement 1911: 328.

115 For the decree, see BAB RKolA 7382/22: 3–5, 'Runderlass an sämtliche Bezirksämter, Bezirksnebenämter und Stationen', 19 August 1896 and 'Anweisung betreffend die Bestrafung des Sklavenhandels zu befolgenden Grundsätze', 19 August 1896. The decrees were signed by von Bennigsen, who was the acting Governor at the time since von Wissmann was on sick leave in Germany and his successor, von Liebert, had not yet arrived in Dar es Salaam. The differences between the 1895 *Sklavenhandelsgesetz* and the *Anweisung* of 1896 concerning the definition of commercial slave trading are extensively discussed in Wege 1914: 3–15. For further detail, see Chapter 5.

116 For the article, see *Deutsch-Ostafrikanische Zeitung*, 'Der Jumbentag in Daressalam', 28 July 1900. The article had already been criticised in the social democratic press. See, for instance, 'Sklavenverkäufe in Dar es Salaam' in *Vorwärts*, 25 August 1900.

117 See *Deutsch-Ostafrikanische Zeitung*, 'Der Jumbentag in Daressalam', 28 July 1900.

118 *RT* 1900–3, 11 March 1901: 1780.

119 *RT* 1900–3, 11 March 1901: 1784. For this telegram see below.

120 *RT* 1900–3, 11 March 1901: 1786.

121 *RT* 1900–3, 11 March 1901: 1787.

122 *RT* 1900–3, 11 March 1901: 1786 –8.

123 Arguably, this was indeed a core issue. As will be shown below, the statement was probably at best a half-truth.

124 *RT* 1900–3, 11 March 1901: 1788.

125 *Ibid.*

126 See *RTA* 1900–3, no. 199, 16 March 1901 and *RT* 1900–3, 19 March 1901: 2006.

127 *RT* 1900–3, 19 March 1901: 1997.

128 At the time, the Zentrum was one of the main pillars of parliamentary support for Chancellor von Bülow. This only changed in 1907, towards the end of von Bülow's chancellorship. For an overview on party politics in this period, see Schwarz 1965: 130ff. On the relationship between the Zentrum and Chancellor von Bülow, see also Wehler 1995: 1008–11.

129 For this argument, see Harding 1995: 293.

130 *RT* 1900–3, 19 March 1901: 1999.

131 *RT* 1900–3, 19 March 1901: 2001.

132 *RT* 1900–3, 19 March 1901: 2003.

133 *RT* 1900–3, 19 March 1901: 2004.

134 *RT* 1900–3, 19 March 1901: 2004ff.

135 Two years later, Stolle, a member of the Social Democratic Party, stated in a speech at the Reichstag that he had believed that after the 1901 debate, Gröber's motion would actually change slavery in German East Africa 'for the better'. See *RT* 1900–3, 21 March 1903: 8786.

136 It is tempting to interpret the Social Democratic Party's change of mind in the wider context of the evolution of parliamentary politics in the Kaiserreich, which, according to some observers, was marked by an increasing integration of the SPD into the political system of the Reich. However, to elaborate on this aspect is beyond the scope of this book. For more detail, see Schwarz 1999: 272ff. For the actual change of position by the SPD in colonial matters, see the speech by Barth, *RT* 1900–3, 21 March 1903: 8801ff.

137 For the decree, see Kaiserliches Gouvernement 1911: 332, 'Verordnung des Reichskanzlers, betreffend die Haussklaverei in Deutsch-Ostafrika', 24 December 1904.

138 See, for instance, the report in *Deutsch-Ostafrikanische Zeitung*, 25 February 1905.

139 For an overview, see Schwarz 1965: 131ff. For more detail, see Nipperdey 1992 vol. II: 748–57.

140 *RT* 1912–14, 29 April 1912: 1529. For the resolution by the budget commission, see BAB RKolA 1006: 174, 'Reichstag, Budget Kommission, Etat für das ostafrikanische Schutzgebiet, Anlage 1, Resolution', 25 April 1912.

141 *RT* 1912–14, 29 April 1912: 1529.

142 *RT* 1912–14, 30 April 1912: 1546.

143 *RT* 1912–14, 30 April 1912: 1561.

144 *RT* 1912–14, 1 May 1912: 1588.

145 *RT* 1912–14, 6 March 1913: 4334–7.

146 *RT* 1912–14, 6 March 1914: 4337.

147 *RT* 1912–14, 7 March 1914: 4350.

148 *RT* 1912–14, 8 March 1913: 4379.

149 For the report, see *RTA* 1912–14, no. 1395: 2885, 'Denkschrift über die Haussklaverei in Deutsch-Ostafrika' by Schnee, 20 February 1914.

150 See *RTA* 1912–14, no. 1395: 2890, 'Denkschrift über die Haussklaverei in Deutsch-Ostafrika' by Schnee, 20 February 1914.

151 See *RTA* 1912–14, no. 1395: 2889, 'Denkschrift über die Haussklaverei in Deutsch-Ostafrika' by Schnee, 20 February 1914.

152 *RT* 1912–14, 7 March 1914: 7903.

153 *RT* 1912–14, 7 March 1914: 7912ff.

154 *RT* 1912–14, 7 March 1914: 7925.

155 See the statement by Arndt, *RT* 1912–14, 7 March 1914: 7927ff.

156 *RT* 1912–14, 10 March 1914: 7974.

157 *RT* 1912–14, 10 March 1914: 7985.

158 *RT* 1912–14, 10 March 1914: 7995.

159 *RT* 1912–14, 19 March 1914: 8101ff.

160 *RT* 1912–14, 19 March 1914: 8102.

161 *RT* 1912–14, 19 March 1914: 8102ff.

162 *RT* 1912–14, 19 March 1914: 8105ff.

163 *RT* 1912–14, 19 March 1914: 8106.

164 For a different interpretation, see Sunseri 2002: 27.

165 *RT* 1900–03, 11 March 1901: 1779. For an example, see the informative but in some ways highly misleading article by the former *Bezirksamtmann* of Dar es Salaam, Leue, who claimed that there were no slaves in the interior of German East Africa. See Leue, 1900–1(c): 606–8, 617–25.

166 Dernburg 1907: 6.

Five

The Politics of the Administration

The issue of slavery was discussed at length at various levels of government and the local colonial administration. Some of these discussions were secret. Their examination reveals an approach to the problem of slavery in East Africa strikingly different from the one presented to the Reichstag in 1891 by the colonial director, Kayser, when he emphasised the imperial government's eagerness to abolish slavery. The debate within the colonial administration came to an early conclusion with the enactment of Chancellor von Bülow's 1901 decree. The making of that decree was marked by long, probably deliberate, delays in the political decision-making process, particularly at the higher government level. Rather than 'making preparations for the eventual abolition of slavery' as the colonial director had promised the Reichstag in May 1895,[1] the colonial authorities introduced administrative regulations that effectively legalised the subordinate status of slaves. This chapter examines the internal discussions on the problem of slavery in German East Africa at the higher government level. Yet these discussions largely depended on information supplied by the 'men on the spot', the Governors and district administrative officers in German East Africa. Their views will receive particular attention in this chapter.

When the Reich assumed formal control of overseas territories in 1890, the newly established colonial department of the Foreign Office had no ready-made blueprint for its administrative policy, major elements of which still needed to be drafted. In the early years of colonial rule, these were largely made up 'on the hoof' by the colonial director and the Governors of the colonies concerned. Certain aspects of colonial policy and administrative practice, especially the more important ones, were subsequently reviewed in the light of experience. This review took place in the Kolonialrat, the all-important advisory council to the colonial department (Kolonialabteilung) in the Foreign Office (Auswärtiges Amt).[2]

The Kolonialrat was inaugurated by imperial decree on 10 October 1890 and supplied the government with sorely needed expertise on colonial affairs. However, this was not the sole reason for its establishment. At the time, the government was facing strong criticism from political pressure groups concerning the Heligoland (Helgoland) treaty with Great Britain, which limited German colonial expansion in East Africa.[3] In order to defuse this criticism, the colonial authorities developed a forward strategy whereby major colonial interest groups were invited to participate in shaping future government colonial policy.[4] In addition, commercial and political groupings involved in overseas and colonial affairs, such as the Kolonialverein and the Deutsche Kolonialgesellschaft, had been lobbying the government for an advisory body in which they could present their views to the administration with the explicit aim of influencing colonial policy.[5] Be that as it may, when the first meeting of the Kolonialrat was convened in 1891, leading members of the German colonial movement and the business community readily agreed to participate. Although the powers of the Kolonialrat were exceedingly limited – it had no formal legislative or executive functions within the government – its influence should not be underrated, as the colonial department rarely disregarded or overruled its motions or recommendations.

The main activity of the Kolonialrat was to scrutinise the annual colonial budget before it was tabled in Parliament. It also discussed a host of other matters ranging from major colonial issues such as the construction of railways or the question of slavery in Africa to more mundane subjects such as the purchase of a rowing boat for the harbour master of Dar es Salaam and the desirability of street lighting for the town of Tanga.[6] Initially, the Kolonialrat consisted of twenty members but, after the turn of the century, this increased to forty. Meetings were also attended by members of the colonial department. The colonial director was an *ex officio* member who presided over the affairs of the Kolonialrat, but neither he nor any other government official from the colonial department who attended the meetings of the Kolonialrat had the right to vote. Thus, the decisions of the Kolonialrat – that is, the official advice given to the government – were taken on the basis of a simple majority vote by the appointed members. Although the Kolonialrat discussions were regarded as confidential, both government and non-government members regularly informed the press about the issues addressed at the meetings. The Kolonialrat usually met two or three times a year, sometimes more often if the need arose.[7]

The colonial advisory council was disbanded in 1907 after the reorganisation of the imperial colonial administration and the establishment of a full-scale colonial office (Reichskolonialamt).[8] Its function was then taken over by more specialised *ad hoc* committees.[9] The dissolution of the Kolonialrat was politically motivated. After the turn of the century, it had become increasingly involved in political controversies with the Reichstag, which, itself largely excluded from the decision-making process, was apparently no longer prepared to accept that a secretive, non-elected body representing specific interests should have such a strong influence on government colonial policy.[10] The Kolonialrat was dissolved because it lacked the minimum degree of legitimacy necessary to fulfil its political role as a clearing-house for colonial interest groups.[11] Moreover, events in the colonies – the Maji Maji uprising in German East Africa (1905–6) and the Herero and Nama wars in German South-west Africa (1904–7) – added to the criticism that government colonial policy – framed as it was by the Kolonialrat – had failed to achieve its self-proclaimed aim of bringing 'peace and prosperity' to the colonies. Finally, after the turn of the century, even the members of the Kolonialrat themselves became increasingly doubtful about their own political role.[12] Colonial issues had become so complex that a single government advisory council meeting twice a year was no longer considered an adequate framework within which to debate all aspects of colonial policy. Yet it should not be forgotten that despite its ultimate political failure, the Kolonialrat was instrumental in forging a political alliance between potentially opposing interest groups, as well as in shielding government colonial policy from public scrutiny and criticism during the first decade of German colonial rule in Africa. Up to the beginning of the twentieth century, all relevant political groupings – apart from the social democratic and liberal opposition in the Reichstag – were involved in Kolonialrat debates in Berlin and, thus, in the making of colonial policy. Even the representatives of the Protestant and Catholic missions had their say, which probably explains why internal opposition to the government attitude towards slavery in East Africa did not develop at the upper administrative level.

Because of its decisive role in the making of government policy, it is worth examining who the participants actually were in the Kolonialrat discussions. Between 1890 and 1907, the chancellor appointed a total of 64 people to the colonial advisory council, most of whom represented specific business interests. In contrast to other members of the Kolonialrat, commercial members were directly nominated by the various companies and banks involved in colonial affairs, members such as A. Lucas (Deutsch-Ostafrikanische Gesellschaft, Berlin), K. van der Heydt (Deutsch-Ostafrika Linie, Deutsch-Ostafrikanische Bank, Berlin), W. von Oechelhäuser (Deutsche Bank, Berlin), A. von Hansemann (Diskonto-Gesellschaft, Berlin), J. K. Vietor (Vietor and Söhne, Bremen), J. Thormählen (Kamerun-Land-Plantagengesellschaft, Hamburg), W. Hernsheim (Jaluit-Gesellschaft, Hamburg) and A. Woermann (Woermann-Linie, Hamburg).[13]

Other less well-known members were directly appointed by the chancellor, such as the geographer Professor G. Schweinfurth and the linguist Dr Büttner from the Friedrich-Wilhelm-Universität (Berlin), R. Kraetke, the director of German postal services (Reichspostamt, Berlin), and government officials, such as Vizekonsul C. Weber from the Foreign Office or T. von Hoffmann, the influential head of the chancellery (Präsident des Reichskanzleiamts) who, apart from being a Member of Parliament for the national liberal party, also happened to be a member of the board of directors of the Südwest-Afrikanische Gesellschaft.[14]

In addition, the chancellor appointed influential colonial activists and politicians to the Kolonialrat, such as the lawyer J. Scharlach (Hamburg), General H. von Hohenlohe-Langenburg (Deutscher Kolonialverein), J. A.

zu Mecklenburg, Vizeadmiral G. Valois (both Deutsche Kolonialgesellschaft, Berlin) or the publisher E. Vohsen (Berlin). Finally, the Kolonialrat included representatives from the Catholic and Protestant Missions whose opinions carried a great deal of weight as far as discussions on the question of slavery in Africa were concerned, since they were seen as representing the 'native' point of view.[15] These were Domkapitular K. Hespers (a member of the Zentrum party, founder of the African Association of German Catholics, and adviser to the Archbishop of Cologne), Staatssekretär B. von Jacobi (former Prussian Minister of Trade, closely connected to the Protestant Berliner Missionsgesellschaft), and, from 1901 onwards, W. Buchner, director of the Moravian Mission (Herrnhuter Brüdergemeine) in Herrnhut.

Policy Making in the Kolonialrat

The Kolonialrat discussed the problem of slavery at considerable length on four different occasions – in 1892, 1893–4, 1896 and in 1901 – all of which came about as a result of the parliamentary motions discussed above. The outcome of the long debate was the all-important Verordnung des Reichskanzlers, betreffend die Hausssklaverei in Deutsch-Ostafrika, which was issued by Chancellor von Bülow in November 1901. The decree regulated, *inter alia*, the legal relationship between slaves and owners in German East Africa, ostensibly in preparation for the eventual abolition of slavery.

As has been pointed out above, the parliamentary commission set up to discuss the draft anti-slave trade bill (*Sklavenhandelsgesetz*) of 1891 was dissatisfied with the fact that the proposed measures addressed German citizens only. Thus in 1892 it passed a motion urging the chancellor 'to regulate all matters relating to slavery in the German colonies' by 1 January 1895.[16]

The government, however, lacked any expertise in this matter. Consequently, the colonial director decided that the colonial governments should be asked to send reports to the authorities in Berlin on the state of slavery in the colonies. However, before making this request, the government sought the advice of the Kolonialrat on the kind of information required. For this purpose, the colonial department prepared a set of documents, including a departmental memorandum, a draft questionnaire, and an appendix containing various reports, all of which were sent to the Kolonialrat on 10 April 1892.[17]

The memorandum spelled out in great detail how the colonial department approached the problem. It conceived slavery basically as a legal issue and was thus divided into two parts. The first part examined the current civil law practice with regard to slavery in German East Africa, that is the servile relationship between 'non-natives' and 'natives' on the one hand, and those between the 'natives' themselves on the other hand. The second part focused on existing criminal law stipulations that circumscribed colonial government actions and, again, also contained a 'non-native' and a 'native' section. With this approach, the question of slavery became entangled with the type of law that was applied in the colonies.

German criminal law explicitly prohibited both enslavement and the ownership of slaves.[18] Yet racist assumptions about the 'barbaric' and 'child-like' nature of Africans and other non-Europeans meant that German criminal law was not applied to the East African 'coloured population (locally born Africans, Arabs, Indians, Goans, Afghans, Banyans, etc.)' as the 'native' category was defined at the time.[19] An imperial decree issued 1 January 1891, which supposedly sought to regulate the legal status of the 'natives' in German East Africa, formed the legal basis for excluding non-Europeans from enjoying the same rights as Europeans in East Africa. The decree stipulated that Africans and other non-European residents fell under German civil and criminal law only if the Governor issued a decree to that effect.[20] However, no such decree was ever enacted.[21] Thus in the early 1890s the colonial authorities operated in a kind of *terra incognita*, as 'colonial law' – which may be defined here as a loosely coherent set of regulations and institutional practices – had not yet been developed. These legal ambiguities complicated the slavery issue and, in many instances, delayed the political and administrative decision-making process considerably.

The letter written by the colonial director asking the Kolonialrat for advice contained an appendix, part of which consisted of an official report by a Governor of East Africa on the subject of slavery, the first of many that were to follow.[22] It also contained the copy of a decree, which Governor von Soden had issued on 1 September 1891, regulating the ransoming of slaves by 'non-natives' (Europeans) and the certification of their freedom by the government.[23]

In political terms, Governor von Soden's report of August 1891 was of vital importance. The colonial director, Kayser, quoted a substantial part of it in the Reichstag debate on 17 November 1891 to prove that the colonial government did not intend to recognise slavery as a legal institution, which had the immediate effect of silencing criticism of government policy. The report itself went even further. Governor von Soden stated that local authorities would not return fugitive slaves to their owners. 'Whoever does not want to be a slave,' he wrote, 'can reject the state of slavery without hindrance from the colonial authorities; as far as the German administration is concerned, such a person will be regarded as a free man.'[24] However, von Soden also stated in his report that, for the time being, the government would not interfere with the 'customary' selling, pawning and bequeathing of slaves.[25] As far as government policy towards slavery was concerned, he apparently believed that nothing more should be done than, as he put it, 'to instruct the district military commanders ... to stay clear of becoming involved in slave matters'.[26]

Yet Governor von Soden did not explain how district officers were supposed to achieve this goal. In fact, quite the opposite was expected of them. In May 1891, one month before he wrote his report, von Soden had issued a decree to the effect that both civil and criminal law cases involving Africans were to be decided by district officers.[27] One section of this decree contained three examples, apparently authentic cases, of how district officers were to record civil law cases in the district office files.[28] Two of them concerned pronouncements in slave cases! In the first example, a slave owner (an 'Arab') was said to have brought a complaint to the district officer involving the ownership of a slave child. The *Bezirksamtmann* was asked to ensure that the 'free' husband of the owner's female slave returned his, that is the husband's, child to the owner. According to the example, the child was returned to the slave owner. The second example concerned a female runaway slave. She was said to have given birth to a child by the owner. The plaintiff (the owner) was said to have asked the district officer to establish the woman's legal status as a slave, presumably in order to sell her. In this case, the district office rejected the complaint.[29]

The contradiction between the May 1891 law decree and the August 1891 slavery report to the colonial department is difficult to reconcile. From the beginning of colonial rule, district officers had evidently given verdicts in slave matters, yet – at the same time – the Governor wrote that his officers did not recognise slavery at all.[30] Could it be that, in writing the August 1891 report, von Soden was aware of addressing a quite a different audience to the one his law decree was supposed to reach?

In any case, the essence of the report was that the government was neither greatly concerned by, nor actively involved in, the slavery issue and that, consequently, no further administrative action was needed. It is therefore not surprising that in the discussion on the report on 20 April 1892, the members of the Kolonialrat agreed that the 1 January 1895 deadline, set by the parliamentary commission for the regulation of all slave matters, was 'impossible' to meet. There was no particular urgency for government intervention and the problem of slavery itself was compli-cated enough, not least because of the legal considerations involved.[31] However, the Kolonialrat took up a suggestion by the colonial director, Kayser, that a 'beginning to the end of slavery' should be made for international, but more importantly for national political reasons.[32] As Kayser subsequently explained, the prime purpose of the government initiative at this stage was to 'strengthen our supporters and to win over new ones' for the colonial project. He was obviously referring here to members of the Reichstag.[33]

Having considered the matter, the Kolonialrat decided that a com-mission should review the draft questionnaire in greater detail. The commission was dutifully elected the next day, 21 April 1892, and con-sisted of the Kolonialrat members Domkapitular Hespers, Staatssekretär von Jacobi, Fürst von Hohenlohe-Langenburg, Kaufmann Thormählen, and Konsul Weber. They reported back to the council that the draft required only minor alterations.[34] However, the commission also discussed closely related issues that, significantly, included the problem of labour in the colonies.[35] Unfortunately, the records of the discussion are incomplete but they do reveal that the Kolonialrat was divided on this issue. One of its members, Woermann, had argued that the problems of labour and slavery should be discussed and solved as one and the same issue if possible. In his opinion, the Kolonialrat should take note of the possibility that abolition would diminish the number of labourers in the colonies, by which he did not necessarily mean only those who worked for German or European employers.[36]

The other members of the Kolonialrat shared Woermann's concerns but argued that to link the problem of slavery to the labour question would make it appear as if a 'new form of slavery was about to be introduced through the back door' and that would certainly lead to 'undesirable' press reports.[37] In the end, the Kolonialrat decided not to include the labour question in the slavery questionnaire that was to be sent to the German colonial governments in Africa.[38] In fact, it was decided that the matter should not be raised at all.

The Kolonialrat discussed wage labour – or rather the lack of it – for quite some time at the meeting on 22 April 1892. Unfortunately, little is known about this discussion, but it illustrates that even at this early stage of colonial rule in East Africa, the labour question loomed large in the minds of those who felt responsible for framing government policy. The labour question was a recurrent theme, touched on time and again in subsequent Kolonialrat discussions on slavery and its abolition in German East Africa. Although the issue of the relationship between labour and the abolition of slavery was never fully explored, the labour question was a hidden agenda in subsequent debates.

The Kolonialrat agreed with the government that more information was needed about the state of slavery in the colonies and that, in good time, a report should be made to the colonial department. The question-naire sent out to the Governors was phrased in such a way as not to specify the colonial advisory council's preferred policy.[39] However, the accom-panying letter from the colonial director left no doubt about the govern-ment approach to the slavery issue. He wrote that owing to lack of effective power in the colonies, 'this generation will be deprived of finding a satisfactory solution' to the problem of slavery, but that it should not prevent the government from making a start.[40] He thus indicated that a demand for the abolition of slavery was not what the government expected as a response from the colonial administrations in Africa. Whether that hint influenced the German East African Governor's report is difficult to ascertain. In any case, Kayser wrote that he did not expect the various Governors to report immediately on the state of slavery in the colonies, as filling out the questionnaire would obviously take some time.[41]

It took more than a year for the first full-length report from East Africa to arrive.[42] Meanwhile, the governorship of German East Africa had changed. The comparatively liberal-minded von Soden, who had been a civilian diplomat before he became a colonial Governor of German East Africa, had been replaced by the hawkish Colonel von Schele, the commander of the *Schutztruppe*, the colonial defence force. Von Schele's report from October 1893 is of interest, because it describes both the development of the legal system in German East Africa and important changes in the official approach to the slavery problem.

Von Schele wrote that he favoured the continuance of the legal system introduced by Reichskommissar von Wissmann in 1890.[43] Arguably, this legal system was a more dignified form of martial law. District officers were endowed with great personal powers. In the vast majority of cases there was no recognised means of appeal against their decisions.[44] Both civil and criminal law cases were tried in public and therefore, as a rule, no detailed written records of the proceedings were kept. District officers did not rely on written law or established legal practice for their *ad hoc* judgements but, as von Schele wrote in his report, on 'the German sense of justice and on local customary law, if the latter was not in conflict with the former'.[45] Thus, local African dignitaries thought to be well versed in customary law were involved in the judicial decision-making process, since they were often asked for their opinion. However, their views were not binding for the district officer. Von Schele's phrase was significant because it expressed in one sentence for the first time the principle to be applied in legal proceedings, with minor modifications, where Africans were concerned. This was to continue until the end of German colonial rule and included hundreds, if not thousands, of civil law cases dealing with slave matters.[46]

With regard to the slavery question itself, von Schele's report was equally telling. He first reiterated his predecessor's position that the colonial government did not legally recognise slavery. But he then added that it regarded the relationship as similar to that between masters (*Herren*) and servants (*Dienstboten*) at home in Germany, and that he and his officers were treating slave matters accordingly.[47] Thus, slaves and owners would be allowed to sue each other in court (that is, in the district office) if they felt that their rights had been violated. These rights consisted of the obligation by owners to feed, clothe and house their slaves, while the slaves were expected to work for between three and five days for their masters. Slave owners had no right to discipline their slaves, but had to go to the district office in order to have their slaves punished, which at the time meant 'moderate' whipping.[48] Although he avoided stating it explicitly, von Schele indicated that he regarded runaway slaves in the same light as African workers who left their European employers before the end of an agreed period of work.[49] Runaway slaves would thus be returned to their owners, apparently not because they were slaves, but presumably because they had broken their involuntary 'labour contract'. Perceiving slavery as a master–servant relationship was a novel idea and provided the blueprint for Chancellor von Bülow's all-important 1901 decree.[50]

With regard to the abolition of slavery, von Schele stated unequivocally that for economic reasons such a measure should be avoided. Most of the agricultural producers in the colony were slaves, he argued, and agriculture thus would suffer greatly from the end of slavery. In his view, there was no need for abolition since, as he put it, 'humanity will be served more than enough by rooting out slave raiding and overseas slave trading'.[51]

Finally, he expressed his belief that slavery would gradually decline in the future and that a peaceful transformation to agricultural production based on free labour would eventually take place.[52]

Not surprisingly, the colonial department in the Foreign Office did not see any reason to respond to von Schele's statement and simply filed the report away. The Kolonialrat was not greatly concerned either and did not receive the report until 23 October 1895. As it happened, the Kolonialrat was occupied with quite a different matter in 1893 and 1894.[53] In September 1893, the colonial director had sent a lengthy *Denkschrift* entitled 'Housing, Education and Alimentation of Liberated Slaves' to the Kolonialrat.[54] The background to this request was that the signatories of the Brussels Conference Act had agreed in Article VI and Article XVIII to free slaves if they had been imported from 'abroad', that is from areas outside the effective control of the colonial power concerned. Moreover, they had decided that if such slaves could not be returned to their place of birth or former residence, the liberating colonial administration was to provide for them. In 1892 and 1893, the government had stopped a number of slave-carrying ships and caravans, giving rise to the question of what was to be done with liberated slaves.

According to the *Denkschrift* of 1 September 1893, the German navy had found 39 slave girls on slave ships plying the Zanzibar route in February 1892, and had sent them to the Catholic and Protestant mission stations in Bagamoyo and Dar es Salaam.[55] A further group of 54 slaves had been liberated on the south coast near the administrative posts of Kilwa, Lindi, and Mikindani. They had also been transferred to the missions. In April 1893, the missions were looking after altogether 51 slave children under eight years of age.[56]

The *Denkschrift* further explained that the Kolonialrat had already debated the issue.[57] The representative of the Catholic missions, Dom-kapitular Hespers, had then asked the Kolonialrat to sanction a formula that had already been agreed to by Chancellor von Caprivi. Subject to this accord, local administration was to pay the missions Reichsmark 25 annually for each slave child under eight years of age. According to the *Denkschrift*, the Protestant missions had made similar demands. Yet the question of who should provide for liberated adult slaves had not been solved. The missions were reluctant to take on the burden without re-imbursement. On the whole, their experience with adult freed slaves was negative, since they made neither 'good converts' nor 'good labourers'.[58] In fact, adult freed slaves tended to leave the mission stations at the first opportunity.[59]

The Kolonialrat discussed the problem at great length at the meetings of 20 and 21 September 1893, agreeing that the colonial government should be asked to provide the missions with the means of setting up villages for liberated adult slaves in which they were to be taught to work and to pray.[60] The request made by the missions that villagers should enjoy their day of rest on Sundays was heavily emphasised. The requested financial support was awarded in due course.[61]

In retrospect, it is difficult to understand why the Kolonialrat and the general public were so intrigued by this question. The matter concerned a comparatively small number of slaves, perhaps less than three hundred adults altogether.[62] One possible explanation for the publicity surrounding the issue was that it afforded an opportunity to be seen to improve the life of some of the slaves in East Africa, while the problem of slavery remained unresolved. In any case, financial support for the missions to feed and house adult freed slaves was already superfluous a year later. According to a report on the matter given by Domkapitular Hespers at the meeting of the Kolonialrat on 20 October 1894, adult 'freed' slaves who preferred not to be returned to their place of birth or former residence were now being transferred to European plantations instead of being sent to the missions.[63]

The Kolonialrat did not return to discuss the problem of slavery in East Africa for another year and would very likely not have done so for some time, if the Reichstag had not passed a motion in May 1895 asking the government to submit a bill whereby 'slavery and pawnship as practised by the natives of the colonies were to be subjected to preparatory regulations leading to their eventual abolition'.[64] The colonial director instantly approached members of the Kolonialrat with a request to advise the government on the matter, probably because the colonial advisory council had already been involved in this issue.

At the meeting on 10 June 1895, the colonial director indicated in his introductory remarks that, despite the Reichstag's motion, no immediate action was required, since, as far as the colonies were concerned, Parliament had no legislative powers. He also told the Kolonialrat that none of the reports yet received from the German colonial Governors in Africa favoured abolition. In this situation the Kolonialrat felt that the best way forward would probably be to ask the Governors for further information and to elect a commission to review the expected incoming reports during the next session of the Kolonialrat.[65] The debate on the subject was put on hold until then. Before closing the subject, the Kolonialrat elected the members of the future commission. It consisted of Herzog von Mecklenburg (representing the Deutsche Kolonialgesellschaft), Domkapitular Hespers and Staatssekretär von Jacobi (representing the Catholic and Protestant missions), Kaufmann Thormählen (representing commercial interests) and Regierungsrat von Tucher.[66]

In October 1895, three months later, the Kolonialrat and its slavery commission received the first set of detailed reports, entitled *Materialien zur Beurteilung des Standes der Sklavenfrage in den deutschen Schutzgebieten*. Apart from other documents, the set contained lengthy reports by the Governors of Togo, Cameroon and East Africa, the latter being the statement by Governor von Schele in 1893 mentioned above.[67] Yet the slavery commission of the Kolonialrat waited for another year before deciding to review the matter in October 1896.

Meanwhile, in September 1896, another two sets of information had arrived.[68] The documents contained the copies of two decrees, which the Governor of East Africa had enacted in August 1896.[69] Moreover, the

Kolonialrat received further reports from the Governors of Togo, Cameroon and German East Africa and extensive summaries of British, Portuguese, French and Dutch colonial legislation and administrative practice. Significantly, this time the documents also included memoranda by mission representatives, Superior Acker of the Catholic Holy Ghost Fathers and Missions Inspector Merensky of the Protestant Berlin Mission.[70]

The decrees issued by Acting Governor of German East Africa, von Bennigsen, in September 1896 were largely modelled on the 1895 slave trade act that had outlawed slave raiding and trading by German citizens. There was, however, one vital difference. Paragraph two of the 1895 act had outlawed all forms of slave trading.[71] The 1896 decree was much more limited in scope. Article II of the *Anweisung* only mentioned *commercial* slave trading as a punishable offence.[72] The *private* transfer of slaves between individual slave owners was thus legally permitted and, by implication, officially recognised. As will be shown in Chapter 6, this enabled district officers to supervise the buying and selling of slaves without being required by this *Anweisung* or any other decree to intervene. Moreover, it should be mentioned that the prime purpose of this legislation was to give district officers some guidance on how they should deal with slave cases.[73] According to the introductory letter by Acting Governor von Bennigsen, the lack of detailed legislation had led to a situation whereby each district officer applied his own understanding of the 'law'. Thus, slave trading in all its forms was forbidden in some districts, while slaves could be bought and sold freely in others.[74]

The Governors' reports were brief and very much to the point. Governor of German East Africa (former Reichskommissar) von Wissmann simply stated that for political and economic reasons the abolition of slavery was neither desirable nor practical, arguing that administrative measures against the *Haus- and Schambensklaverei* (house and *shamba* or field slavery) were bound to fail. In his view, only future generations of district officers – and not the current one – would be charged with introducing some form of change whereby slavery would slowly be replaced by a more moderate master–servant relationship.[75] He concluded his memorandum by stating that 'time' would eventually solve the problem of slavery; its demise should not be unduly hastened by artificial means.[76]

Both memoranda from representatives of the mission took an entirely different approach. After examining the humanitarian and economic side of slavery and abolition, Father Acker strongly favoured government intervention.[77] How long, he asked, will the government tolerate slave owners selling men, women and children? He recognised that the abolition of slavery would probably lead to the economic decline of coastal plantations. But, as far as the political consequences of abolition were concerned, he did not foresee any major problems. Slave owners, he reported, had been expecting government measures against slavery for years and were 'mentally' prepared for abolition, even if they would abandon the practice with reluctance.[78] Acker also contradicted the argument that abolition would harm slaves because their livelihood depended on their owners, pointing out that, in his experience, most slaves lived separate lives from their owners, within a relationship that was frequently reduced to surrendering part of their earnings to them.

Distinguishing between slavery in the interior and on the coast, Father Acker suggested that, although slavery should be outlawed in both areas forthwith, slave owners on the coast should be compensated by a law requiring slaves to work as servants for their former owners for an agreed period of time, such as five years, at half pay. They should then be allowed to leave. He also recommended that children under sixteen years of age should be declared free by the government.

The position held by the Protestant missionary Merensky was less coherent in substance but just as determined.[79] Like Father Acker, he favoured the immediate abolition of slavery for humanitarian reasons, but since he did not suggest a specific period within which it should be abolished, also indicated that he would be prepared to accept a longer 'compensation period' for slave owners. He did not expect abolition to create major political or economic problems for the government. On the contrary, he argued that after abolition former slaves would flock to European plantations in search of work. Though he acknowledged that abolition was likely to hurt the political and economic position of slave owners on the coast, he argued that in the interest of combating 'Arab influence' in German East Africa, their downfall should be welcomed rather than feared by the administration.

The members of the slavery committee (Ausschuss) of the Kolonialrat met in October 1896 to review both sets of information.[80] The colonial director, Kayser, and two other officials from the colonial department were also present. Domkapitular Hespers, adviser to the Archbishop of Cologne, began the meeting with an outline of the problem at hand. Right from the beginning, he stated that abolition of slavery was completely out of the question, thereby disregarding the opinion of the missions. He argued that abolition was impracticable and besides, would 'endanger the civilisational progress' (*Gefährdung der bisherigen Kulturarbeit*) that, in his view, had been made in the colonies.[81]

As none of the other participants at the meeting disputed the validity of the arguments, the Ausschuss had then to decide how to proceed. First of all, it was agreed that certain preparations for the eventual abolition of slavery should be made. These were, however, not to be legislated by the Reichstag or the Bundesrat, but by the Governors of the colonies concerned. It was argued that each colony required its own solution and local administration was in the best position to judge what was needed.[82]

The meeting then discussed a memorandum by Regierungsrat von Tucher on the current legal position of slaves in East Africa, which he had evidently prepared in advance.[83] This report consisted of a list of legal principles currently adhered to by German colonial administrations in Africa. First, he emphasised that the colonial government still did not officially recognise slavery as a legal institution, but treated slaves as if they were in contractual personal service (*Dienstverhältnis*).[84] Second, he claimed that slave owners were denied the right to 'discipline' their slaves.[85] Third, he stated that, independently of their subordinate status, slaves were recognised by the administration as legal subjects who were fully responsible as far as civil law was concerned. In criminal law, however, slaves were treated differently, allowing for the consideration that they were bound to obey their owners' wishes. Finally, he maintained that as far as the actual dispensation of civil and criminal law was concerned, district officers frequently applied the stipulations of customary law that prevailed locally. According to Regierungsrat von Tucher, the latter implied that the existence of slavery was accepted 'in reality' by the administration.[86]

These arguments might appear to be a mere exercise in legal sophistry. Yet, Regierungsrat von Tucher's distinction between 'legally not recognising slavery' and 'actually accepting its existence' is crucial for the understanding of German colonial administrative practice and, indeed, colonial propaganda. Until the enactment of the 1901 decree, this distinction enabled colonial administration to maintain that it 'stayed clear of becoming involved in slave matters' – at least officially – while at the same time it was free to pursue whatever policy it liked on the grounds that it was merely applying local customary law.

As administrative practice will be discussed in greater detail in Chapter 6, it is sufficient to point out here that the distinction between the actual and the legal recognition of the subordinate status of slaves was – to say the least – fraught with difficulties. We have seen that civil and criminal law were to be dispensed by district officers, relying on 'the German sense of justice and on local customary law, if the latter was not in conflict with the former'.[87] Since recognising slavery by applying stipulations of local customary law was clearly in conflict with fundamental aspects of German criminal law, the distinction made by Regierungsrat von Tucher regarding the acceptance of slavery was invalid. Moreover, to argue that the government regarded slavery as a form of contractual personal service did not take into account that these services were rendered involuntarily by the slave.

After briefly discussing the legal arguments spelled out by Regierungsrat von Tucher, the Kolonialrat-Ausschuss passed a motion that the colonial governments in Africa should be asked to provide further details on how they dealt with the problem of slavery. They were to receive Regierungsrat von Tucher's 'list of legal principles' for comment.[88] In order to codify the different slavery policies in the German colonies in Africa, the Kolonialrat required specific information, particularly on the administrative policy applied by individual colonial Governors with regard to slavery.[89]

In the second half of the Ausschuss meeting in October 1896, members discussed the measures they thought would help to bring about abolition. The discussion centred mainly on East Africa, since the Kolonialrat believed that there was little difference between the German colonies in Africa. Distinguishing between the coast and the interior of

German East Africa, Domkapitular Hespers suggested that, as far as the latter was concerned, more military posts should be established and a railway line built to link the interior with the coast.[90] With regard to the coast, he proposed that the government should no longer accept enslavement as a consequence of debt or punishment for adultery. He also wanted the government to outlaw the practice of people selling themselves or their kin in times of hardship. Moreover, he proposed that slaves should be allowed to ransom themselves even against their owners' stated will.[91] However, he also made clear that he expected the buying and selling of slaves to continue on the coast and elsewhere in the colony for some time to come.

Most of the Hespers proposals found support from other members of the Ausschuss, but no formal resolution was passed. Thus it might appear as if little was decided in the 1896 Ausschuss meeting. It was, nevertheless, far from insignificant and turned out later to be an important stepping stone towards the enactment of the 1901 legislation. First, the committee resolved that abolition was 'out of the question'. Importantly, the members of the Kolonialrat-Ausschuss who were supposed to speak for the missions failed dismally in this task. The reports by Father Acker and Missions Inspector Merensky urging the government to intervene were simply brushed aside. In fact, at the very beginning of the meeting Domkapitular Hespers removed any doubt about the position of the Catholic Church in this matter and, according to the minutes of the meeting, the representative of the Protestant missions, Staatssekretär von Jacobi, obviously had nothing to add to this statement.[92] Moreover, the 1896 meeting introduced the process of codifying the legal position of slaves in the German colonies in Africa. The aforementioned 'list of legal principles', which Regierungsrat von Tucher presented to the Kolonialrat in 1896, was to become the blueprint for the *Verordnung* enacted by Chancellor von Bülow in 1901. Finally, it should be noted that although he accepted the existence of slavery in German East Africa and elsewhere in the German colonial empire, Domkapitular Hespers put forward the proposal that local government should outlaw the enslavement of free people. Again, this principle was subsequently included in the 1901 decree. Significantly, Domkapitular Hespers did not express his opinion as to whether the colonial administration should regard the children of slaves as slaves or free people who could not be sold, at least not under the supervision of the local district officer.

The meeting ended without a formal decision on the key issue being taken. The Kolonialrat-Ausschuss had ruled out abolition but refrained from stating the fact. Instead, the committee agreed to ask the colonial governments for further information, most likely in the interests of delaying the issue for a protracted period. To this end, the relevant documents, including the minutes and resolutions of the Kolonialrat, were sent to the colonies for the Governor's comments.[93] As there was no great urgency in the matter, it took almost five years for the Kolonialrat to return to the subject.

The Legalisation of Slavery

When the Kolonialrat held one of its regular meetings in late June 1901, the then colonial director, Stuebel, asked the colonial advisory council to examine the information that the colonial department had received since 1896.[94] He promised that these would soon be forwarded to the Kolonialrat. The background to this somewhat sudden request was the Reichstag debate of March 1901, already discussed in Chapter 4. At the end of that debate, the Reichstag passed a motion asking the chancellor to regulate slave matters in the colonies, particularly the relationship between slaves and owners. Moreover, slaves should be given the opportunity to buy their freedom from their owner.[95] Following the Reichstag debate, the colonial department prepared a memorandum on the proposed legislation, which was sent to the Governors in Africa for comment.[96]

The Kolonialrat-Ausschuss received the new set of documents on 1 October 1901.[97] This set was the most comprehensive yet. It contained hundreds of narrowly printed pages of reports, included memoranda from Togo, Cameroon and German East Africa, the minutes of past meetings of the Kolonialrat and its slavery committee, and an undated 'draft decree' by the former Governor of German East Africa, von Liebert. Furthermore, there were lengthy reports on the British and French colonies in Africa, particularly on the current situation on the islands of Zanzibar and Pemba.[98] The information on German East Africa was the most detailed, and contained various reports by district officers about how they had approached the question of slavery in their district and their recommendation regarding what should be done about the problem.[99] Further documents, including a memorandum by Governor von Götzen dated 9 September 1901 and a government draft for the proposed legislation, were presented to the new Kolonialrat-Ausschuss when it finally met on 24 and 25 October 1901.[100]

In many ways, the district reports and von Götzen's memorandum were the most important documents ever reviewed by the Kolonialrat in the matter. The former show how the administration dealt with the situation at local level, while von Götzen's memorandum spelled out the rationale of the colonial government's non-abolition policy. The government draft for the proposed legislation basically summarised the district officers' and von Götzen's approach. However, as von Götzen frequently refers to von Liebert's 'draft decree', mentioned above, this document needs to be examined first.

Governor von Liebert's so-called 'draft decree' was in fact a secret decree issued in March 1899.[101] In some respects, this particular piece of legislation was a follow-up of an earlier *Runderlass* concerning the suppression of 'commercial' slave trading and slave raiding in the colony, which the previous Governor, von Bennigsen, had issued in August 1896. At the time, von Bennigsen had stated that the prime purpose of his decree was to unify the various administrative approaches to the problem of slave trading.[102] Governor von Liebert seems to have had a similar purpose in mind when he was planning future policy, having received the first reports from district officers who had been requested by the Kolonialrat in 1896 to provide further information on how the administration actually dealt with the problem of slavery at local level.[103]

The reports concerned the administrative districts of Tanga, Pangani, Bagamoyo, Dar es Salaam, Kilwa and Lindi; they were sent to Governor von Liebert in late September and early October 1897. They revealed that the *Bezirksamtmänner* employed different policies. Thus, for instance, in some districts, fugitive slaves were forcefully returned to their owners, while in others the district officers absolutely refused to deal with cases involving slave matters.[104] Governor von Liebert, who was of the opinion that reform was urgently needed, prepared a draft decree in which he took into account both Regierungsrat von Tucher's 'list of principles' from 1896, defining slavery as a form of personal service, and the reports mentioned above. This draft decree was sent to the colonial department on 23 October 1897.[105]

As abolition had been ruled out, von Liebert proposed that the colonial authorities accept the existence of slavery under German colonial rule, albeit in a somewhat modified form. He claimed that his proposals did not contradict the spirit of the Brussels Act, in which the signatory powers had agreed to suppress slave trading and to undertake measures towards the eventual abolition of slavery. The relationship between owners and slaves in German East Africa could not be described as 'slavery', he argued, but should more correctly be called 'serfdom' (*Hörigkeit*).[106] Thus, the Brussels Act could not really be applied. With regard to slave trading, Governor von Liebert suggested that there was an essential difference between the commercial and the private purchase of slaves. It would be wrong to summarily suppress the latter, since it was individual owners and not slave traders who were involved in the transaction. He admitted that the social position of female slaves posed a special problem, as they were in his opinion often required to provide sexual services to their new owners. However, nothing could be done about it because the abolition of the institution 'would hit slave owners at their weakest spot' (*würde durch die Aufhebung des Instituts, die Sklavenherren an ihrer empfindlichesten Stelle getroffen werden*) – and this was to be avoided.[107]

Governor von Liebert's comprehensive 'draft decree' consisted of seven parts containing 32 paragraphs.[108] Part A declared that from now on slavery in German East Africa was to be regarded as 'serfdom' (*Hörigkeit*). Part B then defined who was to be regarded a 'serf' for the purpose of the decree.[109] Serfs were the children of 'unfree mothers' – unless the mother was married to a free-born man – as well as those who rightfully bore the status of unfree by 'custom' (*Gewohnheit*) at the date of the enactment of this decree (that is, the current slave population). Those who became serfs through self-enslavement or pawnship were to be regarded in future as free, as far as the administration was concerned, and, accordingly, owner claims based on enslavement of this kind were to be rejected by the local district officer.[110]

Parts C and D regulated the mutual rights and obligations of the serfs and their owners.[111] Basically, the regulations consisted of a list summing up the owner's right to a fixed amount of the serf's labour, ranging between four and six days per week, according to whether a serf was employed in the fields or in the house. Alternatively, owners had the right to halve a slave's earnings if he or she was employed by somebody else. If these rights were transgressed, owners were allowed to sue their serfs in court; in other words, fugitive serfs were to be returned to their owners or punished for 'laziness' by the district officer. In exchange, the owner or his family was to provide for the serf and his family as long as the serf lived. Moreover, the serf was free to marry whomever she or he chose.[112] Owners were permitted to buy and sell their serfs if these transactions were carried out under the supervision of the district officer, who had to make sure that the serf was unfree by custom or birth, and that she or he had not recently become a serf. These transactions were to be registered by the district office.

Part E specified under what conditions the serfdom of an individual would come to an end.[113] On the whole, these comprised manumission by the owner, ransoming, and official emancipation – the latter, for instance, in the case of maltreatment of the serf by the owner. Finally, parts F and G contained regulations concerning the legal position of slaves in court.[114] As far as criminal law was concerned, serfs were considered fully responsible, unless they had been ordered to break the law by their owners and had obeyed that order for fear of recrimination. In civil law cases, owners were supposed to pay for any offence committed by their serf up to the amount of the market value of the serf. Part F specified the punishment for those who broke the stipulations of the decree. According to paragraph 31 of the decree, district officers were permitted to fine offenders up to Rs3,000. Alternatively, they were allowed to send offenders, both owners and slaves, to jail or put them in chains (*Kettenhaft*), the latter for a period not exceeding one year.

The secret decree ended with a brief but significant explanation of the reasons why Governor von Liebert thought it advisable to specify the punishment for offenders in such general terms. He wrote that, in the past, fugitive and 'lazy' slaves were sentenced by district officers without any legal basis. The decree would change that, but, at the same time district officers should be free to choose the punishment they thought fit in such cases, without the burden of *a priori* stipulations.[115]

The archival records do not reveal how Governor von Liebert arrived at his views on the appropriate form of slavery for German East Africa. It is likely that they were based on information he had received from northern coastal district officers who, at the time, were the most involved in this matter. The decree was almost a modified 'customary law', attempting to combine various elements of perceived actual practices with colonial visions of the correct order for African societies.[116] Von Liebert conceptualised slavery as a fixed legal status rather than a variety of negotiable dependencies, so that, to an extent, the 1899 decree seemingly reflected the views and interests of slave owners rather than those of slaves. However, until further evidence comes to light, it is difficult to ascertain that this was indeed the case.

The colonial department gave permission to pass the decree, albeit with the provision that under no circumstances should it be made public.[117] Thus, from the enactment of the March 1899 decree onwards, slavery was actually recognised as a legal institution in German East Africa and, moreover, backed up by the local administration. Furthermore, it should be pointed out in this context that a comparison between Governor von Liebert's secret decree and the subsequent government draft for the proposed legislation reveals that the latter was largely based on the former, except for one significant alteration. While paragraph 1 of Governor von Liebert's secret decree explicitly stated that slavery was to be legally recognised by the colonial government in the form of 'serfdom', that very paragraph was removed from the government draft for the proposed legislation.[118] By removing this paragraph the colonial authorities in Berlin successfully shielded themselves from parliamentary criticism; the omission enabled the colonial government in East Africa to recognise slavery as a legal institution without actually admitting the fact to the wider public. It also explains the considerable confusion in the Reichstag debates on this issue.

Importantly, the Kolonialrat never received the original 1897 reports from the district officers, nor a full copy of Governor von Liebert's secret decree. On the contrary, in October 1901 the Kolonialrat-Ausschuss was merely told that the former Governor, von Liebert, had prepared a 'draft decree' that the Ausschuss might like to see. The exact legal status of the *Runderlass* was deliberately kept secret because the Kolonialrat had not been informed that von Liebert's 1899 decree had already been sent to the district administrations.[119] The second document of importance dealt with by the Ausschuss in its October 1901 meeting was a memorandum from Governor von Götzen that had been sent to the colonial department in the previous month.

In the memorandum, Governor von Götzen stated that the government draft decree for the proposed legislation, sent to him by the colonial department for comment, was largely in accordance with both actual administrative practice as well as former Governor von Liebert's supposed 'draft decree'. Given that the government draft decree was an abridged version of Governor von Liebert's secret decree, this was hardly surprising.[120] Much more important was his statement that the official policy of not recognising slavery had failed, since local circumstances had forced local administration to become involved with slave matters. As slaves represented the most important part of the wealth of the propertied classes (*Vermögen der besitzenden Klasse*), district officers could not avoid arbitrating civil disputes over the bequest of slaves to the sons and daughters of deceased slave owners or sorting out insolvency cases that required the selling of the debtor's slaves.[121] This development, he claimed, had prompted Governor von Liebert to prepare his supposed 'draft decree'.[122]

As to the suggestion that local administration should regard children of slave parentage as free, von Götzen strongly argued that while he favoured the proposal in principle, he believed that for political and economic reasons such a measure should be postponed for some time to come. He claimed that, in the interior, colonial administration lacked the political and military power to bring about even such limited reform, let alone effect total abolition. As far as the coast was concerned, he believed that declaring slave children to be free would completely alienate the local elite from the German administration. In any case, he was convinced that the presumably negative economic consequences of abolition were of far greater importance than the political ones. With regard to the coast, he argued that abolition would amount to depriving the propertied classes of their wealth.[123] Both agricultural production and trade would suffer accordingly, and – in the current economic depression – this should be avoided at all costs. He closed his memorandum with the argument that railway lines linking the interior with the coast were essential for the economic development of the colony, and until such time as they were built he felt unable to agree to any administrative measure towards the abolition of slavery.[124] Incidentally, four years later, noting that the Reichstag had agreed to finance the construction of the central railway line, Governor von Götzen suggested to the colonial authorities in Berlin that slave children born after 1 January 1906 should be officially declared free. Chancellor von Bülow agreed and thus enacted the 1904 decree.[125]

The 1901 the Kolonialrat-Ausschuss took two full days to discuss the various memoranda, reports and draft proposals.[126] There is no detailed record of the discussions on 24 and 25 October 1901, which were chaired by Staatssekretär von Jacobi, but the subsequent report of the Ausschuss reveals that its members basically accepted Governor von Götzen's position. Domkapitular Hespers seems to have dominated the discussion. He proposed that the Ausschuss desist from making any detailed recommendations. However, the Governors should be advised to pass legislation in preparation for abolition according to local circumstances. Other members of the slavery committee accepted these suggestions and, apparently, the committee went on to debate for quite some time whether slave children should be declared free. In the end, the majority seems to have followed Domkapitular Hesper's advice, echoing Governor von Götzen's position, that as far as German East Africa was concerned, the right moment for this measure was yet to come. However, since Governor Köhler (Togo) had welcomed such a declaration, he (Köhler) should be permitted to enact the appropriate local legislation in his own right. And since Governor von Puttkamer (Cameroon) had strongly opposed this measure, he (von Puttkamer) should not be forced by the colonial authorities in Berlin to undertake the freeing of slave children 'prematurely'.[127]

The Kolonialrat-Ausschuss examined the documents at hand in detail, particularly Governor von Götzen's memorandum and the government's proposed draft legislation. No substantial alteration had been made to the latter except for the insertion of a paragraph that specifically outlawed the pawning of free people, the selling of relatives, self-enslavement, and judicial enslavement in cases of adultery or unpaid debts.[128] On the whole, the slavery committee seems to have followed the government line of argument. Thus, as far as German East Africa was concerned, abolition was ruled out. Even the freeing of slave children was thought to be an inappropriate administrative measure at the time. In line with von Liebert's 1899 secret decree, it was decided that government legislation was to specify the mutual rights and obligations of slaves and their owners.[129] This included the following stipulations: slaves had the right to buy their 'freedom' from their owners by paying a ransom; their owners were to allow them to work for themselves for at least two days a week; owners were to provide for their slaves in old age and in the case of ill-health; and the transfer of slaves between owners was to be supervised by the local district officer, who was to ascertain the legality of slave status and to make sure that families were not separated from each other as a result of these sales. Furthermore, in the case of maltreatment, owners would lose their rights over their slaves. The latter were to be freed by the local district officer. In other words, the Kolonialrat-Ausschuss agreed that owners should have a lawful right to the labour of their slaves for five days a week, that individual owners should be allowed to sell and bequeath their slaves as they pleased (provided they did not separate slave families from each other), and that the colonial government should oversee the lawful buying and selling of slaves and the proper treatment of slaves by their owners.

When the Ausschuss presented its report to the colonial advisory council meeting of 21 November 1901, not all of the Kolonialrat's members were prepared to accept the results. Vizeadmiral von Valois, the chairman of the Deutsche Kolonialgesellschaft, expressed his regret that the children of slaves were not to be declared free by the government.[130] Moreover, he disputed that the buying and selling of slaves should be conducted under government supervision.[131] Apparently, he was in a minority in holding this opinion. Both Domkapitular Hespers and the colonial director, Stuebel, repeatedly stated that while they would also like to end slavery as soon as possible in East Africa, they believed that the right moment for this ultimate government intervention had not yet arrived. They claimed that, for economic reasons, the colonial government could afford neither abolition nor the freeing of slave children. This argument seems to have ultimately won the day.[132]

Thus, on 21 November 1901, the Kolonialrat passed an only slightly revised version of the government draft decree. The substance of this draft decree was based on Governor von Liebert's secret decree of 1899, which, in turn, was based on Regierungsrat von Tucher's 'list of legal principles' of 1896. This is probably the main reason why the government draft decree was accepted with no great opposition from the Kolonialrat. Much more difficult to explain is the fact that, by passing the draft decree, the members of the Kolonialrat, including the representatives of the Catholic and Protestant Churches, agreed to legalise the subordinate status of slaves (and their children) in German East Africa. Ostensibly, the decree aimed at restricting legal forms of enslavement, and at the 'betterment' of the lives of slaves. Yet, just as the rights of slaves were codified, so, too, were the rights of their owners.[133] There are some indications that the Kolonialrat had hoped for further reforms in the future, but – apart from the 1904 declaration that slave children should be regarded as free – they never materialised.[134] The decree, signed by Chancellor von Bülow on 29 November 1901, remained essentially unchanged in the statue book up to the very end of German colonial rule in East Africa.[135]

The View from Below

In the administrative debate on the problem of slavery in East Africa, all Governors of German East Africa stated that abolition was out of the question in their view, that for economic and political reasons it was both undesirable and impracticable.[136] Governor von Götzen was the best informed and most outspoken among them.[137] Listing the reasons why he opposed abolition, he argued that slavery underpinned the power and reputation of the 'sultans' and 'big men' in the interior.[138] As regards the coast, slaves constituted most of the wealth of the 'propertied classes'. Abolition, he claimed, would ruin the ruling elites and alienate them from the colonial administration.[139]

Governor von Götzen's 1901 memorandum was basically a summary of the reports that he and his predecessor, von Liebert, had received from local administrative officers in the preceding years. These reports spell out even more clearly why von Götzen opposed abolition in German East Africa. Regarding the political consequences of abolition, the *Bezirksamt-männer* wrote that they anticipated armed resistance, particularly in Unyamwezi but also elsewhere, if slaves were to be actively emancipated by local administration, adding that whatever merit abolition possessed, they plainly lacked the military power to repress such resistance.[140]

Moreover, several district officers argued that abolition would greatly weaken the power and prestige of the local slave-owning elites,[141] precisely the group of people through which the administrators wished to rule the population and organise their local labour supply.[142] 'The *majumbe* do not have the power to impose their will on the free born', wrote one district officer, '... now all major government projects are being carried out at the same time by slaves on the order of the *majumbe* and the slave owners.'[143] It thus appears that, in the early colonial period, at least some district officers believed that abolition would reduce their access to unpaid 'political' labour, because the principal means whereby the local African representatives of the colonial state – known in German as *Jumben* and *Akiden* on the coast and the *Sultane* in the interior – could mobilise this kind of labour was not their supposedly 'charismatic' or 'traditional' form of political authority and legitimacy, but the dependent status of slaves.[144] In this connection it might be noted that contrary to the policy pursued by other colonial powers, notably Britain and, to a lesser extent, France, the German colonial authorities set up a system of local governance which to a great extent relied on salaried employees to enforce government policy. In local terms, these employees often lacked even a modest degree of political legitimacy.[145] In the absence of data, it is difficult to assess to what extent the initial development of the colonial state actually depended on the availability of slave labour, but there is little doubt that, at least in the minds of the colonial administration, this particular political problem provided a strong, if not compelling, reason for the perpetuation of slavery.

The second, equally important motive for rejecting abolition was based on the expectation that government intervention would greatly harm the economy, particularly agricultural production.[146] This argument largely concerned the commercial rice, coconut and sugar plantations in the northern coastal districts that were worked by slaves.[147] It was believed that abolition would destroy these plantations and thus the wealth of their African owners, since government compensation for their losses was ruled out on grounds of the great costs it would entail.[148]

Moreover, there was the argument that freeing slaves would greatly damage the commercial interests of German trading companies, as the African slave-owning elites were the target group for imported luxury goods, a profitable and important business at the time.[149] It was also pointed out in this context that much of the trade on the coast was done on credit. In the past, slave ownership had provided the necessary security for loans given to certain members of the coastal elite. Abolition would immediately destroy their creditworthiness and endanger the credit already extended to them.[150] In brief, abolition was bad for business. Yet in these reports there was a notable absence of arguments concerning the business interests of big German plantation companies, for instance that abolition would affect their labour supply negatively.[151] At the turn of the century, when the discussions on the abolition of slavery in German East Africa took place, their presence and their interests evidently did not play a major role in the debate.[152]

Finally, one should mention that some (but not all) of the anti-abolitionists shared certain ideological beliefs. A number of district officers expressed the opinion that slavery was the only means available to make Africans work. 'Laziness and liberty are just the same thing for them', claimed one district officer.[153] Others, including Governors von Liebert and Schnee, were evidently of the same opinion.[154] This racist attitude was linked to the belief that abolition would greatly expand the already existing 'proletariat' – that is, according to one statement, the floating urban working class that could only be controlled by the rigorous application of criminal law and the deployment of police.[155] This was the background to what some commentators called 'the African social question', already mentioned in the previous chapter. Abolition would lead, as one very outspoken author of a report claimed, to an increase in crime, particularly theft.[156] The 'proletariat' would expand beyond control and consequently, he argued, the population would die of hunger and disease.[157]

Admittedly, not all district officers shared these somewhat hysterical ideological beliefs. Furthermore, it should be noted that some district officers actually favoured abolition, arguing that, as far as their districts were concerned, no negative effects were to be expected from the freeing of slaves. Yet, as they presided over districts which contained only marginal slave populations or that were thinly populated, their views did not carry any weight.[158] Like the aforementioned pro-abolition memoranda of the Protestant and Catholic missionaries, their opinions were brushed aside, first by the Governors – in this instance von Götzen – and later by the Kolonialrat, and were, thus, of no significance in the debate.

Colonial records do not reveal any one – simple – answer to the question of why the great majority of the *Bezirksamtmänner* and, in turn, the Governors of German East Africa opposed abolition so vehemently at the turn of the century. However, some tentative general observations can be made. First, the arguments against abolition seem to vary according to the societies and polities the administrative officers claimed to have observed. The way in which colonial officers described slavery and the likely consequences of abolition were not just figments of the colonial imagination, but represented an attempt to come to terms with African social realities at the local level.[159] There was a tendency to portray slavery as a 'benign' institution, while denying the harsh reality of the buying and selling of men, women and children. Yet there was more to the diversity of the analyses of slavery and abolition. As has been argued in Chapter 3, slavery comprised a wide range of negotiated dependencies, involving complex, locally defined figurations of social domination and marginality, such as patronage and clientship. Moreover, these dependencies began to change as slavery declined. In an attempt to understand these fluid and variable relationships, district officers invoked different labels to fit certain key aspects of this relationship in their locality at a particular point in time. This is why district officers referred to slaves as 'personal dependants', 'servants', 'serfs' and 'proletarians', without feeling any obvious need to explain their use of these particular terms to describe people they believed to be slaves. The potential effects of abolition were perceived in a similar way. In areas where vast numbers of slaves worked as agricultural labourers on plantations, such as the coast, slaves were regarded as potentially dangerous 'proletarians'. In other areas, such as Unyamwezi, slaves tended to be seen as personal dependants of chiefs, or as distant family members who had somehow fallen on hard times. Here it was believed that abolition would terminally weaken the power of the local chiefs and headmen who were perceived to be essential to the working of colonial rule in that particular area. Thus, the variety of reasons for a non-abolition stand matched the variety of social situations in which slaves were believed to make their living.

Second, on a more abstract level, it appears that the colonial administration was faced with profoundly conflicting demands, which it found difficult to reconcile.[160] On the one hand, there was great pressure from the imperial government to make the colonies pay their way as soon as possible and to relieve the imperial treasury of the financial assistance it gave to local colonial governments. For this reason, the colonial administration, apart from supporting European-owned plantation companies, sought to nurture African agricultural production and local commerce, since the latter generated the greater part of the local tax revenue. On the other hand, the colonial administration was charged with suppressing social practices deemed to be incompatible with colonial rule at the time, such as slave holding and trading. Given the choice between accomplishing one or other of these goals, the administration opted for the former, perhaps recognising that the power of the colonial state to transform African societies fundamentally was indeed rather limited.[161] In any case, the German colonial administration did not just turn a blind eye to slavery, as most other colonial powers at the time apparently chose to do.[162] On the contrary, in the guise of ameliorating the social lives of slaves in East Africa, the colonial authorities legalised their subordinate status.

Thus it appears that not one but two distinct strands existed in the making of German non-abolition policy. They came together in Chancellor von Bülow's 1901 decree and were expressed in an ambivalent and reoccurring phrase: 'enacting preparatory regulations for the eventual abolition of slavery'.[163] Whereas the emphasis was on the second part of the phrase and its seeming promise of abolition in the political debate in the Reichstag, the administrative debate reveals that the first part was of much greater significance. Enacting regulations effectively meant official recognition of the rights of ownership, which was precisely the aim of Governor von Liebert's secret decree of 1899. In more ways than one, the politicians in the Reichstag and the public in general were thus deceived by the colonial authorities about the true aims of its anti-slavery/non-abolition policy. However, the same cannot be said for the members of the Kolonialrat, some of whom, like Domkapitular Hespers, were specifically elected to represent humanitarian concerns but manifestly failed to do so.

Yet it should be recognised that colonial policies and blueprints such as the 1901 decree often differed markedly from administrative practices. More importantly, colonial subjects had their own interests and strategies to improve their lives under colonial rule, irrespective of the intentions, visions and actions of their colonial overlords. These two themes will be addressed in more detail in the final part of this book.

Notes

1   *RT* 1893–4, 20 May 1895: 2340.
2   The first paragraphs of this chapter largely follow Westphal 1964: 29–38 and Pogge von Strandmann 1970: 34–82. See also the entry 'Kolonialrat' in Schnee 1920 vol. II: 338ff.
3   The contemporary literature on the Heligoland treaty is vast, because it generated

considerable controversy. For a brief review of that literature, see Bückendorf 1997: 428–37 and Fröhlich 1990: 67–95.

4   Pogge von Strandmann 1970: 48.

5   See 'Aufruf' in *Deutsche Kolonialzeitung*, 3 (1890), 288.

6   For an overview, see BAB RKolA 6975/4: 9, 'Sachregister zu den Verhandlungen des Kolonialrats der I. - V. Sitzungsperiode, 1891/2–1898/1901', 1902. See also Pogge von Strandmann 1970: 203–328.

7   *Ibid.*

8   On the dissolution of the Kolonialrat, see Pogge von Strandmann 1970: 386–410.

9   These *ad hoc* committees are of no concern here, as none of them was asked to deliberate the problem of slavery,

10 Westphal 1964: 144–9.

11 For this argument, see Pogge von Strandmann 1970: 257.

12 Westphal 1964: 144.

13 K. van der Heydt was also a leading member of the Flottenverein and the Alldeutscher Verband, an ultra-imperialist political pressure group, which greatly influenced German foreign policy, especially after the turn of the century. See Wehler 1995: 1073. It should be noted that J. K. Vietor was closely connected to the Norddeutsche Misionsgesellschaft in Bremen, while A. Woermann was also a Member of Parliament for the national liberal party. According to Westphal (1965: 38) and Pogge von Strandmann (1970: 83–92) most of the commercial members of the Kolonialrat held several directorships in colonial companies and banks, as was the case with K. van der Heydt and A. Woermann, whose interests encompassed shipping firms, banks, plantation companies and industrial concerns.

14 For biographical information on the members of the Kolonialrat, see Westphal 1964: 156–79 and Pogge von Strandmann 1970: 85ff., 93–120.

15 *Ibid.*

16 BAB RKolA 7382: 2, Kayser to Kolonialrat, 10 April 1892. On the background of the 1892 parliamentary motion, see BAB RKolA 7365/209: 5ff., 'Verhandlungen des Kolonialrats', 20 April 1892.

17 BAB RKolA 6987: 180, 'In welchem Umfange und welchen Richtungen hin gestatten die Verhältnisse der Schutzgebiete, an eine gesetzliche Regelung der gesamten, die Sklaverei betreffende Materie heranzutreten?', 10 April 1894. For the revised questionnaire, see BAB RKolA 6957: 31, 'Anlage I: Fragebogen zu Nr. 10', 22 April 1892. Another set of the printed documents can be found in BAB RKolA 7382: 18.

18 See articles 234 and 239 of the German penal code. They are cited in *Documents relatifs* 1893: 16ff.

19 The crucial passage reads as follows: 'Die Gerichtsbarkeit über die farbige Bevölkerung (Eingeborene, Araber, Inder, Goanesen, Belutschen, Banianen u.s.w.) eines Bezirks wird vom Bezirkshauptmann ausgeübt.' See Kaiserliches Gouvernement 1911: 198, 'Verordnung, betreffend die Gerichtsbarkeit und die Polizeibefugnisse der Bezirkshauptleute', 14 May 1891. It is noteworthy that later certain exceptions were made for Goans, Persians and non-Muslim Syrians. Reflecting racist attitudes of the time, they were believed to be of equal civilisational status to Europeans, thus deserving special consideration. The absurdity of the 1900 legislation is revealed by the fact that the chancellor thought it necessary to specifically exempt people of Japanese origin from being counted as 'natives'.

20 For the discussion of the 1891 decree, see BAB RKolA 6960: 133, 'Denkschrift betreffend das in den deutschen Schutzgebieten bei den Eingeborenen zur Anwendung kommende Strafrecht und 'Strafverfahren', 25 May 1895. The decree was replaced by the more detailed *Schutzgebietsgesetz* of 10 September 1900, which in this respect, however, was similar in design.

21 For a concise summary of the legal position of 'natives' and 'non-natives' in German East Africa, see the entry 'Eingeborenenrecht' in Schnee 1920 vol. I: 507–14. See also the entries 'Strafrecht' und 'Strafverfahren' in Schnee 1920 vol. III: 417–19, 420–5. For the text of the *Schutzgebietsgesetz*, see Kaiserliches Gouvernement 1911: 162–6, 'Schutzgebietsgesetz', 10 September 1900.

22 For the letter by Kayser, see BAB RKolA 7382: 2, Kayser to Kolonialrat, 10 April 1892. The original of von Soden's report can be found in BAB RKolA 6987/179: 33, 'Bericht des Kaiserlichen Gouverneurs von Deutsch-Ostafrika' by von Soden, 30

August 1891.

23 BAB RKolA 6987/179: 7, 'Verordnung, betreffend den Freikauf von Sklaven', 1 September 1891. The practical consequences of the decree are discussed in greater detail in Chapter 6. There is little indication that this decree was actually modelled after the British 1890 decree, passed in the name of the Sultan of Zanzibar, which outlawed the buying and selling of slaves and regulated the purchase of freedom by slaves within the islands and coastal Kenya. For more detail see, Cooper 1980: 47 and Morton 1990: 119–44, especially 141ff.

24 BAB RKolA 6987/179: 33, 'Bericht des Kaiserlichen Gouverneurs von Deutsch-Ostafrika' by von Soden, 30 August 1891 [translation by the author]. Note that Governor von Soden used exclusively the male form for slaves here, although he must have been aware that the majority of slaves were actually women.

25 *Ibid.*

26 *Ibid.*

27 See Kaiserliches Gouvernement 1911: 198, 'Verordnung, betreffend die Gerichts-barkeit und die Polizeibefugnisse der Bezirkshauptleute', 14 May 1891.

28 For more detail, see Chapter 6.

29 The reason for the rejection was not given, but it is clear from later reports that the basis for this decision was coastal Islamic practice according to which female slaves who had children by their owners were regarded as free and thus could not be sold. For more detail, see Velten 1903: 316.

30 For further detail, see Chapter 6.

31 BAB RKolA 7365/209: 5ff., 9, 'Verhandlungen des Kolonialrats', 20 April 1892.

32 See BAB RKolA 7365/209: 9, 'Verhandlungen des Kolonialrats', 20 April 1892, especially the summing-up of the position of the Kolonialrat by von Jacobi.

33 BAB RKolA 7382: 18, Kayser to *Lokalbehörden*, 27 April 1892.

34 BAB RKolA 6957/27: 3, 'Verhandlungen des Kolonialrats', 22 April 1892.

35 The report on the meeting of the Kolonialrat on 22 April 1892 does not reveal why a discussion on labour problems took place. It is likely that there had been a disagreement in the committee about linking slavery with the labour question, but the surviving records are not entirely clear on this point.

36 BAB RKolA 6957/27: 5, 'Verhandlungen des Kolonialrats', 22 April 1892. As will be shown below, this was a widely held belief. It was often expressed in racist terms – the 'lazy native' was a typical expression at the time. The argument probably carried a certain weight because it seemed to have a rational core. Woermann and many of his contemporaries believed that slavery was a work regime producing a surplus over and above the amount necessary to feed, house and clothe the direct producer. This surplus could be taxed by the colonial state or appropriated by private companies and was thus one of the few means of sustaining the colonial project from locally generated resources.

37 BAB RKolA 6957/27: 6, 'Verhandlungen des Kolonialrats', 22 April 1892 [translation by the author].

38 *Ibid.*

39 See especially questions 18 and 19 in BAB RKolA 6382/18: 38, 'Anlage I: Fragebogen zu Nr. 10', 22 April 1892. It is noteworthy that the *Fragebogen* was made available to the French and British governments at the time. See *Documents relatifs* 1893: 28–31.

40 BAB RKolA 7382: 18, Kayser to Lokalbehörden, 27 April 1892 [translation by the author].

41 *Ibid.*

42 BAB RKolA 7382/18: 43, 'Eingereicht mit Bericht des Gouverneurs Freiherrn von Schele aus Dar es Salaam', 30 October 1893. On 25 November 1892, Governor von Soden sent a report to the colonial department in which he briefly described how the legal system had developed since he took over the governorship in 1891. He mentioned that a full report on the slavery question was to follow, but it is uncertain whether that particular report was ever written. See BAB RKolA 7382/18: 40, von Soden to von Caprivi, 25 November 1892.

43 BAB RKolA 7382/18: 43, 'Eingereicht mit Bericht des Gouverneurs Freiherrn von Schele aus Dar es Salaam', 30 October 1893. Further copies of this document can be found in BAB RKolA 1003: 162, BAB RKolA 7366: 101A and *Documents relatifs* 1894: 43–54. The actual report by Governor von Schele to which the document cited above was apparently attached has not yet been found.

44 For more detail, see Deutsch 2002: 93–104. See also Sippel 2003: 297, 311.

45 Von Schele wrote: 'Das für die Entscheidung massgebende Recht war kein Gesetzbuch, sondern das deutsche Rechtsbewusstsein und, soweit es sich hiermit vertrug, die Rechtsgewohnheiten oder Gesetze der in Betracht kommenden Stämme.' See BAB RKolA 7382/18: 43, 'Eingereicht mit Bericht des Gouverneurs Freiherrn von Schele aus Dar es Salaam', 30 October 1893. In a sense, von Schele elaborated here a decree that his predecessor von Soden had issued on 14 May 1891. It contained the statement that 'judgements [of district officers were] to be based on the legal principles of the civilised nations, common sense and local customs and traditions'. The original text reads as follows: 'Für die Entscheidungen sind die unter gebildeten Völkern geltenden Rechtsgrundsätze, der gesunde Menschenverstand und die landesüblichen Gewohnheiten und Überlieferungen massgebend.' See Kaiserliches Gouvernement 1911: 198, 'Verordnung, betreffend die Gerichtsbarkeit und die Polizeibefugnisse der Bezirkshauptleute', 14 May 1891. On this issue, see also Raum 1965: 185 and Iliffe 1979: 118ff.

46 These cases are briefly reviewed in Chapter 6.

47 BAB RKolA 7382/18: 43, 'Eingereicht mit Bericht des Gouverneurs Freiherrn von Schele aus Dar es Salaam', 30 October 1893.

48 For more detail, see Chapter 6.

49 The report, in fact, had two sections. In the first section, Governor von Schele described the development of the relationship between African workers (whether free or unfree) and European employers. In the second section he dealt with the slavery question. He used exactly the same wording and terms in both sections, except that in the second section he did not explicitly state what he considered to be the correct treatment of runaway slaves. He had explained that 'runaway workers' would be returned to their employers because they had broken their contract. See BAB RKolA 7382/18: 43, 'Eingereicht mit Bericht des Gouverneurs Freiherrn von Schele aus Dar es Salaam', 30 October 1893.

50 For the 1901 decree, see Appendix A.

51 BAB RKolA 7382/18: 43, 'Eingereicht mit Bericht des Gouverneurs Freiherrn von Schele aus Dar es Salaam', 30 October 1893 [translation by the author].

52 *Ibid.*

53 BAB RKolA 7382: 18, 'Material zur Beurteilung der Sklavenfrage', 23 October 1895.

54 See BAB RKolA 7365: 29, Kayser to Kolonialrat, 27 August 1893. See also BAB RKolA 7382: 14, Kayser to Kolonialrat with 'Denkschrift über die Unterbringung, Erziehung und Versorgung befreiter Sklaven', 1 September 1893. The issue had been discussed – despite its comparative insignificance – in various publications prior to the Kolonialrat meeting. See, for instance, Reichard 1889, Back 1890, Soden 1892. See also Merensky 1894, Müller 1894 and Otto 1903. The *Denkschrift* of 1 September 1893 was also published in *Documents relatifs* 1894: 22–8.

55 BAB RKolA 7382: 14, Kayser to Kolonialrat with 'Denkschrift über die Unterbringung, Erziehung und Versorgung befreiter Sklaven', 1 September 1893.

56 *Ibid.*

57 *Ibid.*

58 Iliffe 1979: 85.

59 *Ibid.* and BAB RKolA 1003: 204, 'Bericht', Gesellschaft zur Beförderung der evangelischen Mission unter den Heiden to Foreign Office, 7 March 1894. For a detailed description, see Moravian Archives Herrnhut, 'Nachlass T. Bachmann' vol. II: 43ff. For the history of Protestant Missions in East Africa, see Wright 1971b. For the history of the Holy Ghost Fathers in Bagamoyo, see Kollman 2005 and the doctoral theses by Kieran 1966 and Brown 1971. See also the masters thesis by Prein 1995.

The history of the missions' attitude towards the end of slavery in German East Africa has yet to be written. In this book the missions are not treated in greater detail because their contribution to the decline of slavery was comparatively small. Thus, for instance, in the period 1901–5, the total number of slaves redeemed by the Catholic Missions amounted to less than 350 slaves, most of whom were children. The Protestant missions did not redeem slaves at all. For some numerical information, see BAB RKolA 6533/3: 31, 'Denkschrift über die Entwicklung der deutschen Schutzgebiete in Afrika und Übersee 1902/1903', n.d. [1903], BAB RKolA 6534/2: 97, 'Denkschrift über die Entwicklung der deutschen Schutzgebiete in Afrika und Übersee 1903/1904', n.d.

[1904] and BAB RKolA 6535/3: 50, 'Denkschrift über die Entwicklung der deutschen Schutzgebiete in Afrika und in der Südsee 1904/1905', n.d. [1905]. See also Versteijnen 1968: n.p.[12]. He states that in 1896 the Bagamoyo Holy Ghost Fathers had an overall intake of forty slaves, twenty of whom were sent to the Mission by the German administration and ten by the British Consul of Zanzibar; nine were redeemed by the Mission at an average price of Rs35 per head and one slave had run away from his owner. Some further information can be found in Kollman 2005: 45f, note 3.

60   BAB RKolA 7365: 33, 'Verhandlungen des Kolonialrats', 20 and 21 September 1893. These *Verhandlungen* were also published in *Documents relatifs* 1894: 29–43.

61   BAB RKolA 6528/2: 15–8, 'Bericht des Dr. Stuhlmann' in 'Denkschrift betreffend das ostafrikanische Schutzgebiet 1893/1894', n.d. [1894].

62   An analysis of the issue of official certificates of emancipation shows that between 1890 and 1914 only a few slaves were actually sent to mission stations. For more detail, see Deutsch 1999: 109–32. It is noteworthy that government financial support for the missions to look after liberated slaves remained constant after 1894, irrespective of the number of slaves sent to the missions. The missions received a total of RM30,000 for 'expenses in the interest of liberated slaves' from the government. See, for instance, BAB RKolA 6961/82: 13, 'Titel 5k' of the 'Entwurf zum Etat des ostafrikanischen Schutzgebiets 1896/97', n.d. [1897].

63   BAB RKolA 6960/23: 7, 'Verhandlungen des Kolonialrats', 20 October 1894.

64   *RT* 1893–4, 20 May 1895: 2349 [translation by the author].

65   BAB RKolA 6961/9: 9, 'Verhandlungen des Kolonialrats', 10 June 1895.

66   I have been unable to find an explanation reasons for *Regierungsrat* von Tucher's appointment in the *Kolonialrat*. He belonged to the Nuremberg Tucher von Simmelsdorf family, who owned breweries and a major stake in the Nuremberg *Vereinsbank*. *Regierungsrat* von Tucher bore the title of *Kammerherr* (senior adviser) to the Bavarian king. From his contributions to the discussions of the *Kolonialrat*, it appears that he was a trained lawyer and probably represented the *Bundesrat* in the *Kolonialrat*.

67   A full set of these documents can be found in BAB RKolA 7382: 18. The statements by the Governors of Togo and Cameroon will not be discussed here.

68   See BAB RKolA 7382: 19. This set was called 'Weiteres Material zur Beurteilung des Standes der Sklavenfrage in den deutschen Kolonien', 7 September 1896.

69   BAB RKolA 7382/22: 3–5, 'Runderlass an sämtliche Bezirksämter, Bezirksnebenämter und Stationen', 19 August 1896 and 'Anweisung betreffend die Bestrafung des Sklavenhandels zu befolgenden Grundsätze', 19 August 1896. The text of von Bennigsen's 1896 decree was published in *Documents relatifs* 1897: 2–5.

70   See BAB RKolA 7382/19: 8, 'Äusserung des Superiors der Kongregation der Väter vom heiligen Geist und unbefleckten Herzen Mariä zu Knechtsteden', 18 August 1896 and BAB RKolA 7382/19: 12, 'Äusserung des Missionsinspektors Merensky zu Berlin', 4 September 1896.

71   For the text of the 1895 act, see Kaiserliches Gouvernement 1911: 328, 'Gesetz, betreffend die Bestrafung des Sklavenraubs und des Sklavenhandels', 28 July 1895.

72   BAB RKolA 7382/22: 4ff., 'Anweisung betreffend die Bestrafung des Sklavenhandels zu befolgenden Grundsätze', 19 August 1896.

73   BAB RKolA 7382/22: 3, 'Runderlass and sämtliche Bezirksämter, Bezirksnebenämter und Station', 19 August 1896.

74   *Ibid.*

75   Von Wissmann wrote: 'erst einer späteren Generation wird es vorbehalten sein, hier eine Änderung zu schaffen und die Begriffe allmählich so zu leiten, dass an Stelle der Sklaverei ein blosses Dienstverhältnis tritt'. BAB RKolA 7382/19: 3, 'Bericht des Gouverneurs von Wissmann aus Dar es Salaam', 15 February 1896.

76   *Ibid.*

77   BAB RKolA 7382/19: 10, 'Äusserung des Superiors der Kongregation der Väter vom heiligen Geist und unbefleckten Herzen Mariä zu Knechtsteden', 18 August 1896.

78   According to Father Acker, all coastal slave owners were devout Muslims and their attachment to the institution of slavery was largely dictated by their religion (and their 'laziness'). Arguably, this view echoes the general anti-Islamic propaganda of the missions at the time, particularly of the Catholic Church. See BAB RKolA 7382/19: 10, 'Äusserung des Superiors der Kongregation der Väter vom heiligen Geist und unbefleckten Herzen Mariä zu Knechtsteden', 18 August 1896.

79 BAB RKolA 7382/19: 12, 'Äusserung des Missionsinspektors Merensky zu Berlin', 4 September 1896. In 1889, Merensky had argued that abolition was impracticable, but apparently then changed his mind. See BAB RKolA 7363: 132, 'Bericht über die Vorstandssitzung der Deutschen Kolonialgesellschaft', 19 January 1889.

80 BAB RKolA 7382/27: 1, 'Sitzung des Kolonialrat-Ausschusses zur Prüfung der Frage der Abschaffung der Haussklaverei und Schuldknechtschaft in den deutschen Schutzgebieten', 16 October 1896.

81 BAB RKolA 7382/27: 2, 'Sitzung des Kolonialrat-Ausschusses zur Prüfung der Frage der Abschaffung der Haussklaverei und Schuldknechtschaft in den deutschen Schutzgebieten', 16 October 1896.

82 *Ibid.*

83 BAB RKolA 7382/27: 3, 'Sitzung des Kolonialrat-Ausschusses zur Prüfung der Frage der Abschaffung der Haussklaverei und Schuldknechtschaft in den deutschen Schutzgebieten', 16 October 1896.

84 As has already been mentioned above, this entailed the return of fugitive slaves to their owners on the pretext that they had broken their 'contracts'.

85 For more detail, see Chapter 6.

86 BAB RKolA 7382/27: 3, 'Sitzung des Kolonialrat-Ausschusses zur Prüfung der Frage der Abschaffung der Haussklaverei und Schuldknechtschaft in den deutschen Schutzgebieten', 16 October 1896.

87 BAB RKolA 7382/18: 43, 'Eingereicht mit Bericht des Gouverneurs Freiherrn von Schele aus Dar es Salaam', 30 October 1893.

88 The district officers' comments on Regierungsrat von Tucher's list of legal principles later appeared in a special report. See BAB RKolA 7367: 20, 'Anhang zu den Berichten der einzelnen Verwaltungsstellen', n.d. [1899/1900].

89 BAB RKolA 7382/27: 3, 'Sitzung des Kolonialrat-Ausschusses zur Prüfung der Frage der Abschaffung der Haussklaverei und Schuldknechtschaft in den deutschen Schutzgebieten', 16 October 1896.

90 *Ibid.*

91 Note that part of these demands were later included in the 1901 decree.

92 In this connection, it is noteworthy that at the time a number of pro-abolition articles appeared in Protestant mission journals, probably known to Staatssekretär von Jacobi. See, for instance, ' Der deutsche Reichstag und die afrikanische Sklaverei', *Afrika*, 1895: 119–20 and 'Die Behandlung eines Sklaven in Ostafrika', *Afrika*, 1896: 148. However, it should also be noted that prominent Protestant missionaries, such as Klamroth, opposed abolition. See Berliner Missionsarchiv, Berliner Missions-Gesellschaft, IV/10 vol. VI: 27, 'Bericht über die Beratungen des Gouvernement-Rats' by Klamroth, 29 June 1914. I owe this reference to Frank Raimbault whom I would like to thank. For a similar view by a Catholic missionary, see Adams n.d. [1903]: 58.

93 For these comments, see BAB RKolA 7367: 20, 'Anhang zu den Berichten der einzelnen Verwaltungsstellen', n.d. [1899–1900].

94 BAB RKolA 6991: 11, 'Verhandlungen des Kolonialrats', 27 June 1901.

95 See *RT* 1900–3, 19 March 1901: 2006.

96 BAB RKolA 7382/28: 29, 'Entwurf einer Verordnung betreffend die Haussklaverei in Ostafrika', n.d. [April? 1901].

97 BAB RKolA 7382: 27, 'Ferneres Material zur Beurteilung des Standes der Sklavenfrage in den deutschen Schutzgebieten', 1 October 1901. Another copy can be found in BAB RKolA 6992: 5.

98 Except for reports from Zanzibar, which served as vindication for the view that abolition spelled economic disaster, information received from other parts of Africa seems not to have influenced the debate in the Kolonialrat. Governor Schnee also used the Zanzibar argument. See BAB RKolA 1006/201: 8, 'Denkschrift über die Haussklaverei in Deutsch-Ostafrika', 28 October 1913.

99 For these reports, see BAB RKolA 7382/27: 42–115, 'Berichte der einzelnen Verwaltungsstellen in Deutsch-Ostafrika über die Sklaverei' and 'Anhang zu den Berichten der einzelnen Verwaltungsstellen in Deutsch-Ostafrika', 1 October 1901.

100 BAB RKolA 6992: 60, 'Bericht des Ausschusses des Kolonialrats zur Beratung der Sklavenfrage', 5 November 1901. Domkapitular Hespers und Staatssekretär von Jacobi signed that report.

101 For this decree, see BAB RKolA 1004: 185, 'Runderlass' by von Liebert, 5 March

1899. Apparently there were not many secret decrees of this kind as, for instance, neither Tetzlaff (1970), Bald (1970), Iliffe (1979) nor Koponen (1995) mention their existence. For the legal status of this decree, see the exchange of letters between Governor von Liebert and the colonial department in BAB RKolA 1004: 208, Kayser to von Liebert, 8 June 1899, BAB RKolA 1004: 211, von Liebert to Foreign Office, 21 July 1899. There seems to have been a disagreement between Governor von Liebert and the colonial department on this matter. The issue is not entirely clear, but, according to the colonial department, decrees issued by the Governor had no legal status unless they were published. Consequently, Governor von Liebert enacted a *secret* decree that, as far as the local administration was concerned, had of course the same effect as a published one.

102 BAB RKolA 7382/22: 3, 'Runderlass and sämtliche Bezirksämter, Bezirksnebenämter und Station', 19 August 1896.

103 BAB RKolA 1004/85, Kayser to Liebert, 3 July 1897 and BAB RKolA 1004: 90, von Liebert to Foreign Office, 23 October 1897.

104 For the reports, see BAB RKolA 1004: 94–125. The different administrative practices are examined in more detail in Chapter 6.

105 BAB RKolA 1004: 90, von Liebert to Foreign Office, 23 October 1897.

106 It is noteworthy that some years earlier Lugard, the Governor of Uganda, used a similar argument. See Lugard 1893: 171. On Lugard's policy when he was employed by the Imperial East Africa Company, see Morton 1990: 121–7 and Lovejoy and Hogendorn 1993: 99–101.

107 BAB RKolA 1004: 90, von Liebert to Foreign Office, 23 October 1897.

108 BAB RKolA 1004/194: 1, 'Grundsätze, welche bei der Entscheidung von Sklavensachen zu befolgen sind' by von Liebert, 3 March 1899. For another copy of the *Grundsätze*, see BAB RKolA 1004/194.

109 BAB RKolA 1004/194: 1, 'Grundsätze, welche bei der Entscheidung von Sklavensachen zu befolgen sind' by von Liebert, 3 March 1899.

110 *Ibid.*

111 BAB RKolA 1004/194: 2–6, 'Grundsätze, welche bei der Entscheidung von Sklavensachen zu befolgen sind' by von Liebert, 3 March 1899.

112 *Ibid.*

113 BAB RKolA 1004/194: 6ff., 'Grundsätze, welche bei der Entscheidung von Sklavensachen zu befolgen sind' by von Liebert, 3 March 1899.

114 BAB RKolA 1004/194: 7ff., 'Grundsätze, welche bei der Entscheidung von Sklavensachen zu befolgen sind' by von Liebert, 3 March 1899.

115 BAB RKolA 1004/194: 8, 'Grundsätze, welche bei der Entscheidung von Sklavensachen zu befolgen sind' by von Liebert, 3 March 1899.

116 For a general exposition on the invention of 'customary law', see Chanock 1985: 3–24. See also Roberts and Mann 1991: 3–58. For an example of German colonial ideas about the proper order of colonial society with special regard to the role of slaves, see the entry 'Sklaverei' in Schnee 1920 vol. III: 364–6.

117 BAB RKolA 1004: 185, 'Runderlass', 5 March 1899. For a brief discussion of the legal status of the decree, see BAB RKolA 1004: 208, Kayser to von Liebert, 8 June 1899, BAB RKolA 1004: 211, von Liebert to Foreign Office, 21 July 1899 and BAB RKolA 1006: 16, 'An alle Bezirksämter und Bezirke des Inneren', 20 July 1900.

118 See BAB RKolA 1004: 194, 'Grundsätze, welche bei der Entscheidung von Sklavensachen zu befolgen sind' by von Liebert, 3 March 1899 and BAB RKolA 7382/28: 29, 'Entwurf einer Verordnung betreffend die Haussklaverei in Ostafrika', n.d. [April? 1901].

119 See BAB RKolA 7382/27: 33, 'Grundsätze, welche bei der Entscheidung von Sklavensachen zu befolgen sind' by von Liebert, in 'Ferneres Material zur Beurteilung des Standes der Sklavenfrage in den deutschen Schutzgebieten', 1 October 1901.

120 For Governor von Götzen's memorandum, see BAB RKolA 6992/60: 9–12, von Götzen to Foreign Office, 9 September 1901. For the original draft version of the 1901 decree, see BAB RKolA 7382/28: 29, 'Entwurf einer Verordnung betreffend die Haussklaverei in Ostafrika', n.d. [April? 1901].

121 BAB RKolA 6992/60: 10, von Götzen to Foreign Office, 9 September 1901. It thus appears that the deep involvement of the local administration in slave matters in the 1890s was the main reason why in 1901 the German authorities did not consider

adopting the British 'Indian' model of legal abolition. On the British 'Indian' model, see Miers 2003: 30.

122   *Ibid.*

123   BAB RKolA 6992/60: 11, von Götzen to Foreign Office, 9 September 1901. It should be noted that Governor von Götzen based his view on the arguments advanced in the district reports. These will be examined in some detail in the last part of this chapter.

124   BAB RKolA 6992/60: 12, von Götzen to Foreign Office, 9 September 1901.

125   For Governor von Götzen's arguments, see BAB RKolA 6533/2: 15, 'Denkschrift über die Entwicklung der deutschen Schutzgebiete in Afrika und Übersee, 1902/1903', n.d. [1903] and BAB RKolA 1006: 131, 'Runderlass' by von Götzen, 26 July 1904 and BAB RKolA 1006: 123, von Götzen to Foreign Office, 20 December 1904. For the actual 1904 decree, see Kaiserliches Gouvernement 1911: 332, 'Verordnung des Reichskanzlers, betreffend die Hausssklaverei in Deutsch-Ostafrika', 24 December 1904.

126   BAB RKolA 6992/60: 1–8, 'Bericht des Ausschusses zur Beratung der Sklavenfrage', 5 November 1901. In addition to the elected members of the Kolonialrat, the Ausschuss meeting was attended by Dr Stuebel (colonial director), Governor Köhler (Togo), Legationsrat von der Decken, and Legationsrat Seitz.

127   BAB RKolA 6992/60: 3, 'Bericht des Ausschusses zur Beratung der Sklavenfrage', 5 November 1901.

128   BAB RKolA 6992/60: 4, 'Bericht des Ausschusses zur Beratung der Sklavenfrage', 5 November 1901.

129   It is worth noting that the idea to specify the rights and obligations of slaves and owners was first raised by Staatssekretär von Jacobi in the Kolonialrat meeting of 20 April 1892. It thus appears that it took more than nine years to come to a final agreement about their content. See BAB RKolA 7365/209: 8, 'Verhandlungen des Kolonialrats', 20 April 1892.

130   BAB RKolA 6992/18: 3, 'Verhandlungen des Kolonialrats', 21 November 1901. It is likely that the influence of Vizeadmiral Valois helped to convince the government to issue the 1904 decree. It is noteworthy that Valois, the president of the Deutsche Kolonialgesellschaft, basically restated the arguments advanced by the Social Democrat Bebel (see Chapter 4).

131   BAB RKolA 6992/18: 5, 'Verhandlungen des Kolonialrats', 21 November 1901.

132   BAB RKolA 6992/18: 1–3, 'Verhandlungen des Kolonialrats', 21 November 1901.

133   Nolan 1977: 266.

134   BAB RKolA 6992/18: 3, 'Verhandlungen des Kolonialrats', 21 November 1901. In 1903, the government told the Kolonialrat that no money would be available for colonial reforms in the future and that, of course, included compensation to slave owners for losses in the event of abolition. See BAB RKolA 6978: 50, 'Verhandlungen des Kolonialrats', 18 May 1903.

135   For the 1901 decree, see Kaiserliches Gouvernement 1911: 331ff., 'Verordnung des Reichskanzlers, betreffend die Hausssklaverei in Deutsch-Ostafrika', 29 November 1901. For an English version of the decree, see the translation in the appendix.

136   BAB RKolA 7382/13: 33, 'Bericht des Kaiserlichen Gouverneurs von Deutsch-Ostafrika' by von Soden, 30 August 1891, BAB RKolA 7382/18: 43, 'Bericht des Gouverneurs Freiherrn von Schele', 30 October 1893, BAB RKolA 7382: 19, von Wissmann to Foreign Office, 15 February 1896, BAB RKolA 1004: 90, von Liebert to Foreign Office, 23 October 1897, BAB RKolA 1006: 56, von Götzen to Foreign Office, 9 September 1901, BAB RKolA 1006/110, von Götzen to Foreign Office, 12 January 1904, BAB RKolA 1006/159, von Rechenberg to Colonial Office, 8 August 1910, BAB RKolA 1006/201: 17, Schnee to Colonial Office, 28 October 1913. For Schnee's arguments, see also *RTA* 1912–14, no. 1395: 2885, 'Denkschrift über die Hausssklaverei in Deutsch-Ostafrika', 20 February 1914. For the position of the colonial department, see BAB RKolA 7365: 154, 'Denkschrift, betreffend Sklavenfrage', 11 January 1895. For a comparative perspective, see Roberts and Miers 1988: 49.

137   BAB RKolA 1006/56: 1–7, von Götzen to Foreign Office, 9 September 1901. For the district reports, see BAB RKolA 7382/27: 42–115, 'Berichte der einzelnen Verwaltungsstellen in Deutsch-Ostafrika über die Sklaverei' and 'Anhang zu den Berichten der einzelnen Verwaltungsstellen in Deutsch-Ostafrika [1898–1900]', 1 October 1901 and BAB RKolA 1004: 94–133, 'Berichte der Bezirksämter...' [1897], 13 October 1897.

138 BAB RKolA 1006/56: 5, von Götzen to Foreign Office, 9 September 1901.

139 BAB RKolA 1006/56: 6, von Götzen to Foreign Office, 9 September 1901. For a
similar view, see BAB RKolA 1004: 158, 'Bericht von Dr. Bumiller', n.d. [1897] and
the article by Leue 1900–1(c): 624ff., both of whom had served as district officers in
German East Africa. Leue's article was particularly influential. Subsequently, it was
widely cited as proof of the supposedly 'benign' character of slavery in German East
Africa. See, for instance, Fülleborn 1906: 7.

140 For Unyamwezi, see BAB RKolA 7382/27: 88, 'Berichte der einzelnen Verwaltungsstellen in Deutsch-Ostafrika über die Sklaverei', Station Tabora, Berichterstatter:
Hauptmann Puder, n.d. [1900]. See also 'Bericht des Leutnants Sigl, Stationsvorsteher
in Tabora, an den Kaiserlichen Gouverneur, über den Sklavenhandel', 31 August
1891, *Documents relatifs* 1893: 85 and *Deutsches Kolonialblatt* 1891: 509. For other districts,
see BAB RKolA 1004: 125, 'Bericht des Bezirksamts Tanga', 10 September 1897, BAB
RKolA 1004: 94, 'Bericht des Bezirksamts Pangani', 7 September 1897 and BAB
RKolA 7367/20: 114, 'Anhang zu den Berichten der einzelnen Verwaltungsstellen',
Bezirksamt Wilhelmstal, n.d. [1899/1900]. It is noteworthy that almost 15 years later
these arguments reappeared in Governor Schnee's *Denkschrift*. See BAB RKolA
1006/201: 18, 'Denkschrift über die Haussklaverei in Deutsch-Ostafrika', 28 October
1913.

141 In this context, it may be worth noting that subsequent observers attributed the
surprising popularity of German colonial rule among the local elite to the handling of
the slavery question. After the British had taken over Mafia Island, a well-informed
member of the occupying forces claimed that 'the German attitude to the slavery
question and ... their system of jurisdiction over the natives are one of the main factors
which attach Arabs and better-class Swahili to the German cause in the war.' RHO Afr
Micr R.8/MF 19, Mafia District Book, 'Domestic Slavery in German East Africa' by N.
King, Mafia, April 1915: 19. For this argument, see also Harding 1995: 281.

142 BAB RKolA 1004/125, 'Bericht des Bezirksamts Tanga', 10 September 1897, BAB
RKolA 7382/27: 69, 'Berichte der einzelnen Verwaltungsstellen in Deutsch-Ostafrika
über Sklaverei', Bezirksamt Lindi, Berichterstatter: Bezirksamtmann Zache n.d. [1900]
and BAB RKolA 7382/27: 77, 'Berichte der einzelnen Verwaltungsstellen in Deutsch-
Ostafrika über Sklaverei', Bezirksamt Kilosa, Berichterstatter: Lieutnant Abel n.d.
[1900]. See also BAB RKolA 7367/20: 95ff., 'Anhang zu den Berichten der einzelnen
Verwaltungsstellen', Bezirksamt Lindi, n.d. [1899–1900]. For a similar argument, see
also the report in BAB RKolA 1006: 178, extract from *Frankfurter Zeitung*, 8 September
1912. For a comparative perspective, see Lonsdale 1985: 737ff.

143 BAB RKolA 7382/27: 78, 'Berichte der einzelnen Verwaltungsstellen in Deutsch-
Ostafrika über Sklaverei', Bezirksamt Kilosa, Berichterstatter: Lieutnant Abel n.d.
[1900].

144 BAB RKolA 7367/20: 110, 'Anhang zu den Berichten der einzelnen Verwaltungsstellen', n.d. [1899–1900]. For a comparative perspective, see Roberts and Miers 1988:
43.

145 For this argument, see Gann 1987: 1–17.

146 See Governor von Götzen's statement in BAB RKolA 1006/56: 5–7, von Götzen to
Foreign Office, 9 September 1901. See also BAB RKolA 1006/110: 6, von Götzen to
Foreign Office, 12 January 1904. For a comparative perspective, see Harding 1995:
295ff.

147 BAB RKolA 7382/27: 54, 'Berichte der einzelnen Verwaltungsstellen in Deutsch-
Ostafrika über Sklaverei', Bezirksamt Pangani, Berichterstatter: Bezirksamtmann Sigl
n.d. [1899] and BAB RKolA 7382/27: 59ff., 'Berichte der einzelnen Verwaltungsstellen
in Deutsch-Ostafrika über Sklaverei', Bezirksamt Bagamoyo, Berichterstatter: Bezirksamtssekretär Sperling n.d. [1898] and BAB RKolA 7382/27: 65, 'Berichte der
einzelnen Verwaltungsstellen in Deutsch-Ostafrika über Sklaverei', Bezirksamt Rufiyi,
Berichterstatter: Bezirksamtssekretär Spieth n.d. [1899]. It is noteworthy that after the
turn of the century the importance of southern food crop farms probably increased.
These farms were also worked by slaves. According to a report published in the
Frankfurter Zeitung in 1912, the southern coastal farms contributed significantly to feeding
the ever-growing number of wage labourers working on the European-owned export
crop plantations in the north and north-east of the colony. See BAB RKolA 1006: 178,
extract from *Frankfurter Zeitung*, 8 September 1912.

148 BAB RKolA 7365: 154, 'Denkschrift, betreffend Sklavenfrage', 11 January 1895. In 1913, Governor Schnee estimated that abolition would cost just over Rs4 million or about RM5.6 million. This is not a particularly large sum, considering that in 1890 the shareholders of the Deutsch-Ostafrikanische Gesellschaft had received RM10 million from the government for the loss of their fictive East African 'possessions'. See BAB RKolA 1006/201: 17, 'Denkschrift über die Haussklaverei in Deutsch-Ostafrika' by Governor Schnee, 28 October 1913. For a somewhat lower estimate of the cost of abolition arising from compensation payments to slave owners, see Karstedt 1913: 619.

149 For this (almost Marxist) statement, see BAB RKolA 1004/125, 'Bericht des Bezirksamts Tanga', 10 September 1897.

150 For this argument, see BAB RKolA 1004: 105, 'Bericht des Bezirksamts Lindi', 14 September 1897. For a similar statement, see BAB RKolA 1006/110: 6, von Götzen to Foreign Office, 12 January 1904.

151 Arguments that the abolition of slavery would help the plantation companies to solve their perennial labour problems are notably absent from the debate.

152 It might be argued that statements regarding the interests of the big plantation companies were deliberately suppressed, but there is no evidence to support that suggestion. For a different view, see Sunseri 1993(a): 130, 137.

153 BAB RKolA 1004/97, 'Bericht des Bezirksamts Bagamoyo', 14 September 1897.

154 BAB RKolA 7382/27: 60, 'Berichte der einzelnen Verwaltungsstellen in Deutsch-Ostafrika über Sklaverei', Bezirksamt Bagamoyo, Berichterstatter: Bezirksamtssekretär Sperling n.d. [1898]. For Governor Schnee's position, see BAB RKolA 1006/201: 17, 'Denkschrift über die Haussklaverei in Deutsch-Ostafrika', 28 October 1913; for von Liebert's approach, see his notes on the report by the Bezirksamt Tanga in BAB RKolA 1004/125: 14, 'Bericht des Bezirksamts Tanga', 10 September 1897 and BAB RKolA 7367/20: 95ff., 'Anhang zu den Berichten der einzelnen Verwaltungsstellen', Bezirksamt Lindi, n.d. [1899–1900]. Some members of the colonial department as well as some eminent colonial 'experts' such as Baumann appear to have agreed with this view. See Baumann 1890: 216. For the views of members of the colonial department, see BAB RKolA 7365: 55, von Gravenreuth to Bergrath, 10 September 1891 and BAB RKolA 7365: 154, 'Denkschrift, betreffend Sklavenfrage', 11 January 1895. Von Gravenreuth wrote: 'Die Sklaverei mit einem Schlage abschaffen zu wollen heisst ungefähr für Afrika dasselbe was für Europa der Sozialismus mit Güterteilung und Gleichberechtigung ist. Wenn es nicht Blödsinn wäre, wäre beides ja ideal schön!' ('To abolish slavery with one stroke means for Africa approximately what for Europe is the introduction of socialism with an equal division of material goods and equal rights for men and women. If this were not rubbish, it would be ideal!') [translation by the author]. See BAB RKolA 7365: 55, von Gravenreuth to Bergrath, 10 September 1891. For further detail, see Koponen 1994: 323–39 and Sippel 1996b: 311–33.

155 See BAB RKolA 7382/27: 43, 'Berichte der einzelnen Verwaltungsstellen in Deutsch-Ostafrika über Sklaverei', Bezirksamt Tanga, Berichterstatter: Bezirksamtssekretär Blank, n.d. [1899] and BAB RKolA 7382/27: 60, 'Berichte der einzelnen Verwaltungsstellen in Deutsch-Ostafrika über Sklaverei', Bezirksamt Bagamoyo, Berichterstatter: Bezirksamtssekretär Sperling n.d. [1898]. See also Karstedt 1912: 99.

156 For more detail, see Deutsch 1996.

157 BAB RKolA 7382/27: 68, 'Berichte der einzelnen Verwaltungsstellen in Deutsch-Ostafrika über Sklaverei', Bezirksamt Kilwa, Berichterstatter: Bezirksamtmann von Rode n.d. [1900]. See also BAB RKolA 7367/20: 95ff., 'Anhang zu den Berichten der einzelnen Verwaltungsstellen', Bezirksamt Lindi, n.d. [1899–1900].

158 BAB RKolA 7382/27: 73, 'Berichte der einzelnen Verwaltungsstellen in Deutsch-Ostafrika über Sklaverei', Bezirksamt Wilhelmstal, Bezirksamtmann Meyer, n.d. [1899], BAB RKolA 7382/27: 74, 'Berichte der einzelnen Verwaltungsstellen in Deutsch-Ostafrika über Sklaverei', Bezirksamt Mpapua, Bezirksamtmann Langfeld, n.d. [1899], BAB RKolA 7382/27: 76, 'Berichte der einzelnen Verwaltungsstellen in Deutsch-Ostafrika über Sklaverei', Bezirksamt Kisaki, Bezirksamtmann von Reitzenstein, n.d. [1898] and BAB RKolA 7382/27: 82, 'Berichte der einzelnen Verwaltungsstellen in Deutsch-Ostafrika über Sklaverei', Bezirksamt Muanza, Bezirksamtmann Schlobach, n.d. [1900].

159 For this argument, see Methner 1938: 45. For a more theoretical statement, see Pels 1994: 321–51.

160 Roberts and Miers 1988: 17, 19.
161 For a similar view, see Harding 1995: 296 and Sunseri 2002: 31ff. See also Cooper 1980: 18.
162 For this argument, see Miers and Klein 1999: 1–15.
163 For this phrase, see *RT* 1893–4, 20 May 1895: 2349. In a slightly abbreviated form, the phrase also introduced the 1901 decree. For the 1901 decree, see Kaiserliches Gouvernement 1911: 331ff., 'Verordnung des Reichskanzlers, betreffend die Haussklaverei in Deutsch-Ostafrika', 29 November 1901. For an English version of the decree, see the translation in the appendix.

Part III

The Decline of Slavery
under German Colonial Rule

At the turn of the century the resident slave population was estimated to have exceeded 400,000 people, roughly 10 per cent of the population of German East Africa, excluding Ruanda and Urundi.[1] Less than fifteen years later, their numbers were believed to have fallen to around 165,000 (see Table 1) or roughly 4 per cent of the population.[2] Even if these estimates were incorrect by a considerable margin, they would still indicate that slavery was decidedly on its way out, particularly in districts that had previously harboured the biggest slave populations. In Tabora, for instance, the number of slaves living in the district was believed to have fallen from about 233,000 in 1890 to 70,000 in 1914.[3] On the coast, that is in the districts of Tanga, Pangani, Bagamoyo, Dar es Salaam, Rufiyi, Kilwa and Lindi, the decline was thought to be somewhat smaller, yet equally impressive: from over 150,000 to perhaps less than 50,000 slaves.[4] The last part of this book seeks to explain how and why this happened.

Chapter 6 assesses the role of the colonial administration in this process, exploring how administrative officers actually dealt with the problem of slavery in their districts. The previous two chapters have already examined the development of government non-abolition policy and the making of the 1901 decree. It should be recognised that, although this decree legalised slavery in principle, in fact it merely regulated certain aspects of servility. Moreover, district officers were still largely free to apply their own approaches to the problem if they thought that local circumstances warranted other measures than those stated in the decree. The 1901 decree stipulated, for example, that slaves had the right to work for themselves for two out of seven days per week.[5] At the same time, district officers were told to apply local customary regulations if these were more favourable to the slave. Importantly, whether to return fugitive slaves to their owners or not was left to the district officer to decide. The crucial passage in the decree simply stated that disagreements between slave owners and their slaves were to be settled by the 'competent authorities': in other words, the district officer.[6] What constituted a disagreement, and how it was to be settled was not specified. As will be shown below in Chapter 6, throughout

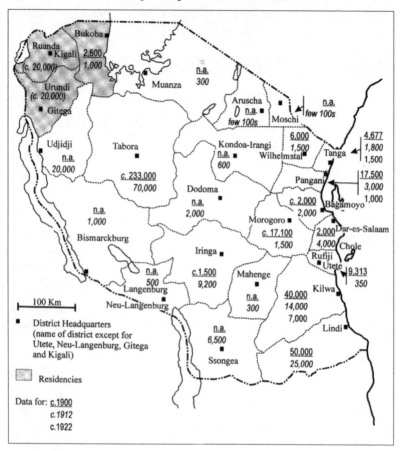

Map 3: The Decline of Slavery in German East Africa and Tanganyika, c. 1900–1922

Sources: As in Table 1.

Note: The archival spelling of place and district names has been retained in this map.

Table 1: *The Decline of Slavery in German East Africa and Tanganyika, c. 1900–1922*

Districts	c. 1900	1912–1913	1922
Aruscha	n.a.	few 100	
Bagamoyo	c. 2,000	2,000	
Bismarckburg	n.a.	1,000	
Bukoba	2,500	320	
Dar es Salaam	c. 2,000	4,000	
Dodoma	n.a.	2,000	
Iringa	c. 1,500	9,200	
Kilwa/Chole	40–50,000	14,000	4,000
Kondoa-Irangi	n.a.	600	
Langenburg	n.a.	500	
Lindi	50–100,000	25,000	
Mahenge	n.a.	300	
Morogoro	c. 17,100	1,500	
Moschi	n.a.	few 100	
Muanza	n.a.	300	
Pangani	17,500	3,000	1,000
Rufiji	9,313	350	
Ssongea	n.a.	6,500	
Tabora	c. 233,000	70,000	
Tanga	4,673	1,800	1,500
Udjidji	n.a.	20,000	
Wilhelmstal	5–6,000	1,500	
All	over 400,000	c. 165,000	6,500

Source: c. 1900: BAB RKolA 7382/27: 42-93, 'Berichte der einzelnen Verwaltungsstellen in Deutsch-Ostafrika über die Sklaverei', n.d. [c. 1900]. 1912–13: BAB RKolA 1006:201, 'Denkschrift über die Haussklaverei in Deutsch-Ostafrika' by Governor Schnee, 28 October 1913. 1922: PRO CO 691/45: 414, Governor Byatt to Secretary of State for the Colonies, 19 July 1921; RHO Mss. Afr. s275, 'History of Mafia' by W. Page, 1924.
Note: The archival spelling of district names has been retained in this table. n.a.: not available

the German colonial period administrative practice within the broad confines of the decree varied greatly from one district to another, and it was this same variety that became a pillar of colonial policy on slavery.

Chapter 7 investigates the strategies employed by slaves in order to take advantage of the social and political changes that occurred after the imposition of colonial rule. This chapter will focus on the rapid decline of the local slave population in two particular areas, the coast and Unyamwezi, taking up the story of the transformation of owner–slave relationships where it was left off in Chapter 3. It was argued there that the social mobility of slaves – the promise of a better life – was the very condition on which the owner–slave relationship rested, given that there was a large absence of other means of preventing them from running away, such as a strong police force. In Chapter 7, it will be shown that in the early colonial period social mobility greatly increased, tearing apart the kinship and patronage relations which until then had kept the 'evil institution' alive.

Six

Colonial Intervention

Colonial administrative practices affected slavery at various points. First, the colonial government suppressed the export of slaves, which was of particular interest to the coast.[7] Second, the colonial government closed down internal sources of supply for slaves: first, it suppressed the more violent methods of enslavement, particularly slave raiding and the kidnapping of women and children; later, but more gradually, it reduced enslavement by non-violent means, such as the pawning of free-born people, self-enslavement, enslavement through judicial procedures, and the sale of children and relatives into slavery by household heads.[8] As has already been mentioned in the previous chapter, the government finally declared in 1904 that children of slaves born after 31 December 1905 should be regarded as free.[9] Thus, all forms of legal enslavement were outlawed by 1906, and it appears, indeed, that after that date the number of newly enslaved declined significantly.

Third, the government attempted to regulate the relationship between owners and slaves.[10] This primarily involved the legal buying and selling of slaves and the fulfilment of putative mutual rights and obligations.[11] If these were transgressed, the colonial administration was expected to intervene. Slaves would be punished for their ostensible 'laziness' or absence from work without consent of the owners, while owners were to be punished if they were found guilty of 'neglect' or maltreatment of slaves.[12]

Last, the government sought to control the emancipation of slaves.[13] Under certain conditions, slaves were to receive official certificates of emancipation or *Freibriefe,* protecting them against subsequent claims by their former owners. Between 1891 and 1912, the government issued 51,632 of these certificates. Given that the years 1913 and 1914 are not included in this calculation, it is likely that the total number exceeded the 60,000 mark (see Table 2).

Initially, the government had believed that German East Africa could be divided neatly into two parts, one where slave matters could be decided on the basis of Islamic law (the coast) and another where customary law was to be applied (the interior). However, much to their surprise, district

Table 2: Issue of 'Certificates of Emancipation' in German
East Africa, 1891 [1893]–1912

District Office/ Sub-Office	Certificates of Emancipation 1891–3	Year 1893–1912	Redm.	Manu.	Eman. (Official)	Others	Total
Kilwa	9,835	1893	74	93	210	91	468
Lindi	7,408	1894	150	142	391	98	781
Pangani	4,141	1895	209	274	281	97	861
Tanga	3,550	1896	229	207	1,043	111	1,590
Bagamoyo	3,546	1897	283	624	818	467	2,192
Tabora	3,276	1898	369	603	906	156	2,034
Dar es Salam	3,000	1899	389	617	1,088	86	2,180
Rufiji	2,354	1900	365	665	440	34	1,504
Udjidji	2,146	1901	691	783	830	100	2,404
Iringa	2,005	1902	723	673	965	59	2,420
Morogoro	1,909	1903	738	922	901	70	2,631
Mikindani	1,904	1904	781	983	690	60	2,514
Saadani	1,018	1905	1,052	1,093	633	42	2,820
Handeni	641	1906	1,525	9,40	353	262	3,080
Muanza	576	1907	1,642	1,332	474	56	3,504
Bukoba	556	1908	1,782	1,358	362	52	3,554
Kilimatinde	526	1909	1,922	1,464	476	8	3,870
Kilossa	492	1910	1,980	1,338	754	11	4,083
Mpapua	463	1911	2,186	1,534	368	6	4,094
Usumbura	446	1912	2,221	1,729	280	4	4,234
Wilhelmsthal	351						
Bismarckburg	290	1893–1912	19,311	17,374	12,263	1,870	50,818
Ssongea	256						
Kondoa-Irangi	172						
Moschi	137						
Kisaki	135						
Mahenge	106						
Langenburg	102						
Urundi	100						
Dodoma	47						
Rutschugi	41						
Schirati	36						
Ussuwi	19						
Ssingidda	11						
Aruscha	9						
Mkalama	8						
Mkondua	7						
Kifumbiro	6						
Ruanda	5						
Ubena	2						
All	51,632						

Source: BAB RKolA 7410-15, 'Sammlung der zur Mitteilung an das Spezialbüro in Brüssel bestimmten Nachweisungen', 1 October 1892–31 May 1915.
Note: The archival spelling of place and district names has been retained in this table.
Redm. = Redemption Manu = Manumission Eman = Emancipation

officers found that matters were more complicated.[14] They realised that, first, many coastal inhabitants paid little regard to the written stipulations of Islamic law and, in fact, followed their own local customs.[15] Second, while Islamic law is particularly specific about some aspects of civil law such as family law, it says nothing about the more mundane but arguably more important areas that were constant sources of dispute between slaves and their owners. The length of a working day, the right of slaves to establish a family with or without consent of the owner, and how much of a slave's earnings was to be surrendered to the owner were some of these sensitive areas. Thus, district officers invented their own version of Islamic law, even in areas believed to be predominantly inhabited by devoted Muslims.[16]

The Suppression of Slave Raiding

From the onset of colonial rule, local administration was charged with rigorously suppressing slave raiding and 'commercial' wholesale slave trading. The intensity of administrative intervention followed the pattern of the conquest of the colony.[17] The northern coast was the first to come under full administrative control. Thus, the first person to be convicted of slave trading was sentenced in April 1890 in Bagamoyo, the capital of the colony at the time.[18] With the advance of the administrative frontier, the repression of wholesale slave trading and raiding moved further inland.[19] From the mid-1890s, most cases tried in court involving violent enslavement and similar matters were offences that had been perpetrated in the interior.[20] By about 1900, the area geographically defined as German East Africa was under effective military control. Colonial intervention in slave raiding and trading matters was swift and often brutal – particularly in the early colonial period when many of the accused were hanged without a proper trial.[21] From the turn of the century on, occurrences of 'commercial' slave raiding, large-scale kidnapping and wholesale slave trading seem to have been on the wane.[22]

This argument is illustrated in a ki-Swahili account translated by Velten, which describes contemporary African views on the decline of slavery on the coast in the second half of the 1890s.[23] According to this text, many of the slave raiders had already died in poverty, since they were no longer able to enslave people. Those who were still alive were now forced to cultivate the fields on their own. In contrast to earlier times, slave raiders were now (*c.* 1898) immediately brought to the district office by their neighbours who were afraid of the 'punitive devastation' district officers were likely to inflict on villages suspected of harbouring the raiders. The villagers are reported to have told slavers that 'former customs have been abolished'.[24] Whether the text is accurate in all aspects is open to question, but it suggests that, to a large extent, government measures to suppress slaving were effective and experienced as drastic. Another indication of the effectiveness of government policy in this respect is the fact that, at the turn of the century, the annual, colony-wide number of people convicted of slave raiding and trading dwindled to about five.[25]

In addition, coastal district officers were instructed to make sure that no slaves left the colony by sea.[26] For this purpose, all 'native' travellers had to obtain special departure passes from the nearest district offices. These passes were normally refused when the district officer suspected that the prospective travellers were slaves accompanying their owners.[27] It is worth noting that there was one exception to this rule. In 1891 Tippu Tip, the well-known ivory and slave merchant, returned to Zanzibar. He obtained a special permit from Governor von Soden to leave Bagamoyo with his entourage of about eight hundred slaves and dependants. In clear breach of the stipulations of the Brussels Conference Act of 1890, Tippu Tip was allowed to send a hundred of his 'house slaves' to Zanzibar in advance, on the understanding that they would not be sold on the island.[28] In any case, control of slave exports was first achieved in the northern part of the coast. In the south, slave exports seem to have continued well into the late 1890s.[29]

From very early on, controlling the caravan routes was the principal means employed by the colonial government to suppress the 'commercial' slave trade. Caravans were frequently stopped, particularly in the southern interior, and, if found carrying slaves, disbanded.[30] Their leaders were arrested and tried, while the slaves, having been issued with certificates of emancipation, were usually sent to nearby mission stations, although it should be noted that only some of these slaves, mainly children and younger women, actually arrived at the mission stations, since younger male slaves usually took to flight.[31] In 1895, the government embarked on more intensive and bureaucratic forms of control of the caravan routes, first on the coast and later in the interior.[32] Caravan leaders had to obtain from the local district office travel permits stating the number of people travelling with the caravan and their loads. These permits had to be presented to each district office on the way to the ultimate destination of the caravan.[33] Finally, as a further measure, the government banned the hitherto legal 'transfer' of slaves from one district to another in 1902.[34] Thus, as far as regional slave trading was concerned, even legal loopholes that had previously been used to trade slaves over longer distances were now sealed.

Yet, it should be recognised that there was no blanket control of slave exports or the caravan trade. Even in the later colonial period, local administration was only thinly spread. This was particularly the case in the southern and north-western areas of the colony. In many cases, administrative influence in these areas did not extend much beyond the district offices, of which there were only a few. After all, in the early colonial years the south and north-west of the colony had little to offer in terms of economic prospects for colonial settlers and plantation companies. Thus, up to about the turn of the century when the administration finally managed to control riverside outlets, slaves continued to be exported in considerable numbers from the villages located in the Rovuma delta, for example, and on the banks of the Rufiyi River.[35] Even more tightly policed regions, such as the north-east corner of the colony, continued to export slaves, albeit to a lesser degree. In the early colonial period, slave traders repeatedly tried to export slaves clandestinely from the north coast, as the distance to the Zanzibar and Pemba markets was comparatively short.[36] Again, by the turn of the century these small-scale commercial exports seem to have been almost entirely suppressed.

Finally, it should be noted that in certain circumstances administrative officers were prepared to turn a blind eye to violent enslavement. Admittedly, the evidence concerning such instances is extremely rare. According to one report, during the conquest period (1890–8) and the Maji Maji uprising (1905–7), some local chiefs in the more remote areas of the south-west who had sided with the colonial authorities were allowed, probably in return for their support, to enslave the subjects of neighbouring chiefs believed to have joined the uprising.[37] These slaves were known in ki-Swahili as *mateka* (booty or war captives).[38] However, based on the available evidence, it is impossible to come to a firm conclusion about the significance of such enslavements. They did not occur on a large scale, because non-government observers such as the missions would very likely have raised their voice against such a practice.

While it appears that on the whole the government succeeded in repressing violent enslavement and the export of slaves soon after colonial occupation, the same cannot be said of other types of enslavement. Up until the enactment of von Liebert's secret 1899 decree, non-violent enslavement was regarded as legal and as legitimate customary practice.[39] The selling of children during famine periods, for instance, was officially condoned in many districts until then, while from then on government gradually began actively to suppress these practices. Thus in 1899 district officers were ordered by the Governor to intervene in both the selling of relatives and the pawning of children and debtors.[40]

Furthermore, von Liebert's 1899 secret decree instructed district officers no longer to recognise claims to slave ownership in cases where enslavement had taken place by non-violent means after the date of issue of the decree. Enslavement by birth, however, continued to be recognised until finally outlawed by the 1904 decree. Thus it appears that the colonial government slowly sealed off the sources of supply, at first by suppressing violent forms of enslavement and later on, much more gradually and hesitantly, the non-violent forms. It is impossible to estimate the effectiveness of these measures precisely. According to a report written in 1910, for instance, slave children under the age of five in the Kilwa hinterland were still often regarded as 'property' by their parents' owners.[41] However, the same report claims that the pawning of children leading to enslavement had sharply declined, evidently a general pattern at the time.[42]

Still, it is unlikely that the ongoing decline of resident slave populations was greatly hampered by the supply of new slaves. It appears that while enslavement still occurred right up to the end of German colonial rule, particularly in areas that were only thinly controlled by the administration,[43] the impact of new supplies was comparatively insignificant.

The Buying and Selling of Slaves

Local administrative authorities had already begun to supervise the buying and selling of slaves by individual owners in the early 1890s.[44] According to a report from Pangani, the district office began to register slave purchases in 1894.[45] The reason for the new policy was a dramatic increase in the number of slaves imported to the district.[46] In the 1890s, several ecological catastrophes, particularly the devastating rinderpest of 1891, caused severe famine in north-eastern and central Tanganyika. Many people died, in some extremely hard-hit areas probably as much as three-quarters of the local population.[47] Furthermore, large numbers of women and children were sold into slavery, principally in the coastal hinterland and in north-central Tanzania, and subsequently brought to the coast by slave traders for resale.[48] Faced with a massive influx of slaves, the administration in Pangani district decided to monitor and register their growing numbers in 1894. Because of their reputed origin, the district officer referred to the newly arrived as 'Massai' slaves. Slave owners already in possession of Massai slaves received an official letter showing that they had obtained them legally.[49] The registration of slave sales was subsequently extended to cover all slave purchases within the district. The purpose of this policy is not entirely clear, but it was probably instituted in order to assure the new owners' cooperation and also to protect them from being wrongfully accused of slave trading. A similar policy was pursued in the neighbouring district of Tanga.[50]

With regard to the supervision of buying and selling slaves, von Liebert's 1899 secret decree and von Bülow's 1901 decree merely reaffirmed a policy that had already been employed in some districts before their enactment.[51] Basically, district officers were instructed by the decrees to ascertain the legal validity of the transfer – that is, to establish the legal enslavement of the person in question. This meant that claims to ownership were rejected if enslavement had taken place by violent means after 1890, by non-violent means after 1899, and by birth after 1905.[52] Moreover, to be rightfully considered a slave, a person had to have been in continuous 'employment' with the prospective seller for at least five years.[53] Only then had the owner the right to claim the person in question as a slave. If within these five years people had worked for themselves continuously for longer periods, they were regarded as free, provided they had not left their owner without his or her consent. The effect of this stipulation was that fugitive slaves could still be bought and sold as long as their owners had regained effective possession of them within a five-year period.

According to administrative regulations, all purchases of slaves had to be registered by the district officer.[54] Yet only one of these registers seems to have survived in the archives.[55] According to this register, the Kilwa district officer alone supervised the sale of 996 slaves in the period between 1 April 1911 and 2 March 1914. For each transaction, the *Bezirksamt* (local government) received a fee of 1.5 per cent of the sale price.[56] Presumably the buyer paid this fee, since he had an interest in having the sale registered. Without registration, he ran the risk of being accused of illegal slave trading, resulting in the loss of his newly acquired 'property'.[57] The Kilwa register shows that between one and six slaves were sold at a time by individual owners, which suggests that the term 'private slave trading' was interpreted somewhat loosely. Judging from the names of the slaves involved, probably as many as two-thirds of those sold were men. The age of the slaves was not recorded. The fees paid ranged from Rs1 to Rs5 and varied with the slave's selling price. The highest fee recorded (Rs5.10, corresponding to a selling price of about Rs340) was paid for a woman, presumably a *suria*.[58]

The 1901 decree stated that district officers had to make sure that the slaves agreed to their sale, but it is doubtful that this stipulation was observed regularly.[59] Moreover, children under the age of twelve were not supposed to be sold.[60] As with the other stipulations in the 1901 decree, much was left to the discretion of the district officer. There is some evidence to suggest that small children were sold by their owners in the presence of German officials, but it is unlikely that this happened frequently.[61] After all, the 1901 decree stipulated that both the parents and the child had to agree to such sales. There were probably limits to what even the most unscrupulous district officers believed to be the proper 'transfer of slaves'.[62]

The district office was also charged with fixing the purchase price for slaves in case of disagreement between buyers and sellers.[63] In doing so, they were to take into account the peculiarities of local customs. It appears that between 1890 and 1900 official sale prices increased significantly.[64] According to Leue, the district officer of Dar es Salaam, young slave women fetched Rs80–100 around the turn of the century, while younger men sold for only Rs60–80. Older slaves could be bought more cheaply, but buyers had to pay 'fancy' prices for concubines (*masuria*) and highly skilled artisans.[65] The former were female slaves who were particularly valued for their 'beauty' or sexual attractiveness to the prospective buyer.[66] In this connection, it should be mentioned that there is some evidence to show that German administrative officers as well as non-officials habitually bought, redeemed or rented female slaves as 'concubines', sometimes for exorbitantly high prices, far in excess of the usual market 'value'.[67] These purchases were not registered, but there are a few instances in which German district officers manumitted *masuria*, and these cases were certainly recorded officially (see below).[68]

Until 1902, individual slave owners in the coastal hinterland were legally entitled to sell their slaves to the coast. However, the number of sales seems to have already declined by the late 1890s. This was probably due to the fact that colonial administration rigorously suppressed the outbreak of armed disputes between neighbouring villages and polities. Previously, these conflicts had been a major source of supply for slaves.[69] Moreover, slave owners who sold their slaves outside their resident district had to show some evidence that they were legally entitled to them. Since direct proof of ownership was only rarely possible, coastal district officers often refused to certify the saleability of the imported slaves, and in some cases actually emancipated the slaves instead. The transfer of slaves between districts, particularly from the interior to the coast, was thus strongly discouraged, as owners realised that by exporting their slaves they ran the risk of losing their property.[70] Finally, in 1902, the sale of non-resident slaves was generally banned. Since then, at least as far as the legal selling of slaves was concerned, slaves could only be sold within the same district. However, as some districts harboured tens of thousands of slaves, especially the southern districts of Lindi, Kilwa and Tabora in the interior, these measures had only a limited effect on 'private' slave trading as a whole. Moreover, it is not entirely clear to what extent this regulation was observed.[71]

As in the case of the suppression of enslavement, it is impossible to determine the precise effectiveness of the registration of slave purchases. According to a report from 1910, despite regulations to the contrary, some district officers do not seem to have supervised the sale of slaves thoroughly in outlying areas. This would have included supervising imports of substantial numbers of slaves into the district.[72] Thus, for instance, the *Bezirksamtmann* of Lindi district reported in 1897 that about 1,000 slaves were brought annually to the coast and that he had no power to suppress these sales.[73] According to this report, a good many of these slaves were exported to Zanzibar, Madagascar and southern Arabia, but the majority were probably sold locally or sent to Kilwa further on.[74] From there, many of the slaves were probably taken to Mafia Island, where food crop and coconut plantations thrived in the early colonial period.[75] It also appears that administrative control was never extensive enough to be able to monitor clandestine sales of slaves within towns or villages.[76] Finally, it should be noted that, as the German administration ruled through a local elite whose leading members included large-scale slave owners, control of the buying and selling of slaves through that elite was a hopeless endeavour. The evidence on this aspect of colonial rule is exceedingly limited, but some reports suggest that colonial chiefs, *akida* and *majumbe*, and local big men in the more peripheral areas of the districts, routinely broke colonial rules and regulations in slave matters, and that their wrongdoing was simply overlooked by the local administration.[77]

It seems reasonable to conclude that slave sales outside the administrative centres were not registered in the early colonial period, and that, although registration of slave sales had increased with the internal advance of colonial control, comprehensive monitoring of these sales was never fully achieved. It is difficult to estimate the number of slave sales carried out under government supervision, but it is clear that these sales must have amounted to several thousand each year.[78]

Crime and Punishment

Slave owners were allowed to punish their slaves whatever way they liked within the limits set by the district office.[79] The administrative officer of Tanga, for instance, thought that fifteen strokes would be the appropriate maximum punishment slave owners should be allowed to mete out to their slaves.[80] Another *Bezirksamtmann* wrote that he had instructed slave owners in his district to 'only' beat their slaves with a light stick, quoting its ki-Swahili name *bakora*, which was used for this purpose.[81] In the majority of the districts, however, slave owners were required to bring their slaves, both male and female, to the district office to have them 'disciplined'. If the latter were found guilty of offences such as 'laziness, cheekiness, and insubordination' or repeated flight, they were beaten by the district police force, the *askari*, or put in chains.[82]

Granting slave owners limited rights to discipline their slaves was most probably a matter of administrative convenience. It is worthwhile noting, however, that this particular policy had a strong ideological undercurrent. There seems to have been a widespread belief that since servants could be disciplined by their employers in Germany, it would be 'unjust' (*ungerecht*) to deny slave owners in East Africa the right to punish their slaves.[83] In any case, slave owners in the vicinity of district offices usually preferred to have their slaves disciplined by the district *askari* in order to avoid the risk of being accused of brutality towards them.[84]

Slaves who felt mistreated by their owners had the right to bring their complaints to the district office. If an owner was found guilty of having over-stepped his disciplinary rights, of having denied the slave the 'rightful' share of his wages or product of his or her labour, or of having failed to provide material support when the slave was ill, the district officer was free to issue a *Freibrief* to the slave that effectively barred owners from raising claims against the slave in the future. However, there is some evidence that not all known cases of maltreatment were actually punished by the district officers.[85] More-over, in this as in many other slave matters, the effectiveness of administra-tive policy depended on the disposition of slaves and owners to bring their complaints to the district office. While it is certain that not all slaves (or owners for that matter) brought their disagreements to the attention of the district officer, on the basis of the evidence available it is impossible even to guess to what extent such conflicts were resolved by other individuals, such as local chiefs, or were left undecided. Still, district officers constantly complained that much of their time was taken up with slave matters, by which they largely meant complaints by slaves against their owners.[86]

'Sharing' the Fruits of Labour

The portion of wages and working time owed by slaves to their owner varied a great deal from one district to another, and even within the districts themselves. It was a matter of constant disagreement between owners and slaves, and the district officer was sometimes asked to settle the argument.[87] As in the case of whether to return fugitive slaves, each district officer apparently devised his own policy. On Mafia Island, the attempt of the district administration to fix the amount of piecework slaves had to accomplish within a day apparently failed.[88] The *Bezirksamtmann* in Kilwa decided that slaves should work for themselves for two days a week, while the district officer in Tanga believed that slaves should be given at least three days off.[89] Still others insisted that, depending on their individual status, slaves should be allowed to work their own plots for up to four days a week.[90]

Some district officers apparently helped owners to recoup part of the wages slaves received for work done for European and other employers. In Tabora district, for instance, the administrative officer insisted that slaves hand over a third of their earnings to their owner, if they were employed outside the latter's village.[91] The district officer reported that the majority of these slaves worked as agricultural labourers or as porters. If they failed to honour what was due to the owner by 'customary law', the administrative officer sent the district *askari* to the slave in order to enforce such payments.[92] The administrative officer in charge of Dar es Salaam district seems to have pursued the same policy.[93] Yet, in Tanga district and on Mafia Island, slaves were made to surrender half their earnings to the owner.[94] Finally, it should be remarked that the administrative officer in charge of Kilwa district, von Eberstein, thought that owners were adequately remunerated if they received an annual payment of Rs6 from their female slaves and Rs10 from their male slaves. His successor, von Rode, insisted that owners should obtain between one-third and two-thirds of a slave's earnings, which very likely yielded a higher return.[95]

Especially in the early years of colonial rule, owners frequently rented their slaves out to European employers, mostly Germans, for an agreed amount of the slaves' wages.[96] These arrangements mostly involved working as labourers on European plantations in the north-eastern part of the colony or as servants in European households in town. The employers officially paid their workers and servants wages. They could thus not be accused of 'owning' slaves or 'using' slave labour. Slave owners were often found lingering around the plantation office buildings on payday, eagerly waiting to obtain their 'rightful' share of their slaves' wages.[97] Given that adult male slaves were sold for about Rs60 to Rs80, renting out slaves for Rs4 to Rs6 per month was an excellent business proposition, as the capital outlay could be recouped within two years.[98]

The disputes between slaves and owners mentioned above seem to have been mostly about these arrangements.[99] Slaves were keen to retain a larger share of their wages, while the owners hoped for a larger return from their 'property'. For this reason, the arrangements were notoriously unstable. Another reason was that slaves who were rented out for periods of time quickly discovered that the power of their owners to obtain half their monthly earnings of about Rs8–12 was somewhat curtailed.[100] If slaves were dissatisfied with their work or their wages, they tended to leave without their owners' or employers' consent.[101] Thus European plantation owners, having found renting agreements to be unsatisfactory, began very early on to advance money to their ostensible 'wage labourers' so that the latter could pay the ransom to their owners and work off their debts afterwards. Alternatively, plantation owners ransomed their 'slave wage labourers' themselves (see below).[102]

The Restitution of Fugitive Slaves

Significantly, one of the first locally enacted decrees concerned the return of fugitive slaves to their owners. In August 1890, acting Reichskommissar Schmidt instructed district officers that, whereas they were to suppress the export of slaves rigorously, they should abstain from interfering in internal slave matters. They were informed that slave owners were free to buy and sell their slaves and that they should only intervene when they suspected 'commercial' or wholesale slave trading. The Governor also instructed the *Bezirksamtmänner* to return fugitive slaves in their employment to their rightful owners: 'I do not wish to hear any further complaints of this kind' he admonished the district authorities.[103] If they wanted to retain a slave, they were told to 'buy' the person. Such purchases had to be vetted by the Governor.[104]

The question of whether to return fugitive slaves to their owners subsequently even became an international issue for a brief period. In September 1890 a proclamation was published in Bagamoyo, which read:

> Be it known to all that we give permission to everybody who has land in Bagamoyo ... to recover and retain their slaves, and everybody who possesses slaves has permission to sell his slaves to the people of Bagamoyo, but it is forbidden to ship the slaves by sea. We desire that the shamba owners should begin working their shambas without delay, because it will be good for all the people and the town.
>
> 6 September 1890.[105]

This proclamation was an attempt to resuscitate agricultural production in the area, which had suffered greatly during the conquest of the coast in 1888–9. Many slaves had fled from coastal plantations, and the local administrative officers apparently tried to help slave owners to recover their slaves.[106] The British Consul in Zanzibar sent a report to the Foreign Office in London, which, in turn, made inquiries to the authorities in Berlin about the proclamation. The Brussels Anti-Slavery Conference of 1890 had just ended, and the proclamation contradicted if not the letter then plainly the spirit of what the signatory powers had agreed upon at that conference. The issue raised considerable international interest. Two long articles appeared in *The Times* of London on 15 and 16 September 1890,[107] which were followed by similar accounts in several German newspapers and an official inquiry by the British embassy in Berlin and the British consulate in Zanzibar.[108] The colonial government as well as the colonial authorities in Berlin were greatly embarrassed by these reports, as the flurry of activities in the German Foreign Office shows.[109] The Foreign Office reacted to the accusation that the colonial authorities were aiding and abetting slavery in East Africa by denying that the Bagamoyo district office had anything to do with the proclamation of 6 September 1890, and claimed at the same time that it was just a private initiative of the *liwali* of Bagamoyo, Suleiman bin Nasr al-Lemki.[110] It is worth noting that in early October 1890, almost a month after the event, Liwali Suleiman bin Nasr al-Lemki submitted a statement claiming he had composed a draft proclamation that had somehow ended up on the notice board of the Bagamoyo district office. How this could have happened, he wrote, he did not know. It is difficult to ascertain whether he had volunteered this statement or not. In any case, it was probably a great help to the Bagamoyo district officer who had come under severe criticism from the higher authorities for publishing the proclamation.[111] According to Acting Reichskommissar Schmidt, no further action needed to be taken in the matter.[112]

Whether Schmidt's statement was true or not cannot be decided with certainty. It seems unlikely that the *liwali* had issued the proclamation of 6 September 1890 without permission by the Bagamoyo district office. Nevertheless, the importance of the 'Bagamoyo Affair' lies probably more in the fact that the colonial government was extremely anxious to avoid any impression of supporting slavery in the aftermath. This could be the reason why, in the following year, the then Governor, von Soden, so adamantly emphasised that the administration did not recognise the legal status of slaves.[113] As has been mentioned, he wrote a report in August 1891 stating that he had instructed 'the district military commanders ... to steer clear of becoming involved in slave matters'. This passage was read out in the Reichstag and was taken as the official policy of the colonial authorities, although at the time the principle had already been more honoured in its breach than its practice.[114]

The issue of what the administration should do about fugitive slaves was never officially addressed, as neither the 1890 decree mentioned above nor any subsequent decree actually spelled out how district officers should approach the problem. Consequently, each district officer devised his own local policy so that in some districts fugitive slaves were forcibly returned to their owners, while in others such extreme measures were only applied to 'vagrant' slaves who had no gainful wage employment or fixed residence.[115] Finally, there were districts in which local administration refused to listen to the complaints of slave owners. In such cases, fugitive slaves were not returned to their owners, and could thus live wherever they wanted in the district or leave the district altogether.[116] The long-serving Mwanza district officer (1906–16), Gunzert, claimed in his memoirs that he even 'abolished' slavery unofficially in his district and had no interest in returning runaway slaves.[117]

The colonial government denied slave owners the power to repossess their slaves by personal force, but they had the right to appeal to the district office to take the necessary steps on their behalf. In Bagamoyo and Tabora districts, for instance, fugitive slaves were forcibly returned to their owners if they were caught within the boundaries of the district.[118] Matters became more complicated if a runaway slave lived outside the area of jurisdiction of the district office. Some owners were given a special permit to bring their case to the administrative officer in charge of the district in which the fugitive slave was suspected of living. The local administrative officer then had to decide how to proceed in the matter. According to the district reports, slave owners rarely applied for a permit of this kind, as the chances of ultimately repossessing the fugitive slave were judged to be quite slim, with district officers in remote districts usually not inclined to pay attention to such demands.[119] This was due to the fact that while slave owners had the right to bring their claims to the district office, the *Bezirksamtmann* was not legally bound to act on them. Slave owners first had to ascertain the whereabouts of fugitive slaves before they could apply for a 'repossession' permit. They often had no knowledge of the residence of their fugitive slaves and thus abstained from officially pursuing their return.[120]

If there was a universally accepted rule, then it concerned fugitive slaves who worked for European employers. In this case, the district officer generally declined to return slaves to their owners. If they intervened in these cases at all, they tended to broker an agreement between owner and slave. The slaves were made to pay a certain amount of their wages or a lump sum – a ransom – to their owners. In the latter case the required amount was often borrowed from the slave's employer. There is some evidence indicating that only vagrant slaves were routinely given back to their owners. If slaves of this kind were found to have left their owners more than once without the latter's consent, they were often severely punished, either beaten or locked up in chains.[121] However, these were probably individual cases. According to the *Bezirksamtmann* of Dar es Salaam, Leue, the majority of runaway slaves remained unaffected by government intervention, since district officers were either unwilling or unable to return fugitive slaves to their 'rightful' owners.[122]

There seems to be no clearly discernible pattern regarding the kind of policy individual district officers applied. In this context, it should also be mentioned that, with a few notable exceptions such as Mwanza and Bukoba districts, the administrative personnel of the district office was subject to fluctuation. Thus, a long-term policy did not emerge, even though many *Bezirksamtmänner* seem to have continued their predecessors' line of practice.[123]

Arguably, there was method in this peculiar administrative policy. As mentioned in the previous chapter, the colonial government had decided that all civil and criminal law cases involving Africans were to be judged by district officers on the basis of the 'legal principles of the civilised nations, common sense and local customs and traditions'.[124] Slave matters were regarded as civil law cases. It was thus up to the district officer whether he wanted to apply 'local customs and traditions', which meant the forceful return of fugitive slaves, or 'the legal principles of the civilised nations', which would have entailed the refusal to act on claims of ownership.

The systemic incoherence of the government's fugitive slave policy is brought out in a widely read article by the district officer of Dar es Salaam, A. Leue, who lamented that

> Nobody knows what the score is. Neither slave owners nor district officers have a clear idea of what they have to do or what is forbidden to them. Likewise, slaves are ignorant of their rights and duties.[125]

The policy of leaving slave matters for the district officers to decide lacked the bureaucratic rationality and efficiency usually associated with colonial administration, particularly with German colonial rule,[126] but it possessed definite advantages for the imperial government. As there was no 'official' policy, the opposition at home or, for that matter, even other colonial powers could not easily accuse the colonial authorities in Berlin of condoning or abetting slavery, which for political and economic reasons was believed to be indispensable to the working of German colonial rule.

Certification of Emancipation

The certification of emancipation was not peculiar to German administrative policy, but rather had its origin in the stipulations of the Brussels Act of 1890. According to this Act, fugitive slaves who crossed the borders of one of the signatory powers were to be issued with official certificates of emancipation (*Freibriefe*). Moreover, the signatory powers had agreed that all those who had been violently enslaved should be set free by the local administrative authorities.[127] The German colonial government made use of this device when it was faced with the problem of how to regulate the relationship between European, mainly German, employers on the one hand and African slaves and their owners on the other. As European ownership of slaves was ruled out, some form of semi-contractual relationship had to be found to take its place.[128]

The solution was to allow European employers to redeem slaves for an agreed sum of money. The crucial administrative regulations are contained in a decree that Governor von Soden enacted in September 1891.[129] This decree banned the purchase of slaves by 'non-natives' (*Nicht-Eingeborene*), including not only Zanzibaris and people of Indian origin, but also Europeans, especially German nationals. Slaves bought by 'non-natives' were immediately to be issued with certificates of emancipation. Yet, at the same time, the decree specifically allowed the 'temporary acquisition' or ransoming of slaves. In order to satisfy the ever-increasing European demand for African labour, plantation owners were granted the right to conclude redemption agreements with slaves and their owners.[130] These contracts had to state the sum of money which the redeemer agreed to pay to the slave's owner and the length of time for which a slave had to work for the new employer in order to pay off the ransom. The money was then deducted monthly from a previously agreed wage.[131] The contract sometimes also specified the type of work the slave was expected to do.

According to these agreements, slaves had to work for about two or three years to repay the sum of money they owed. A number of slaves, however, incurred further debts. In some areas, such as Mafia Island, this seems to have happened quite commonly, as the wage left to the slave after deducting the redeemer's share was sometimes insufficient to satisfy even the most basic needs.[132] Slaves thus asked for advances from employers, using their already meagre future earnings as security. Consequently, they were caught in a debt trap. In such cases, relief from slavery had turned into a new form of bondage. However, there is some evidence to show that not many slaves were heavily indebted to their European redeemers.[133] Indebtedness (like slavery) depended to a considerable extent on the debtors' (or slaves') ability to cut ties to their employers by taking flight. Wherever escape was feasible, the plantation owners' ability to exploit their indebted ex-slave labourers was severely limited.[134] Thus these arrangements were found more in places where flight was almost impossible, such as Mafia Island, and only rarely elsewhere.[135]

Both the original labour contract and the certificate of emancipation were registered by the local district officer who kept the certificate in his office until the debts were actually worked off.[136] Only then would the slave receive his or her *Freibrief*. In this context, it should be recalled that fugitive slaves were returned to their European employers not because they were their property, but on the pretext that they had broken their work contracts.[137]

The 1891 decree mentions in passing that *Freibriefe* could also be issued for other reasons. The decree itself is rather vague as to what these were, but an accompanying *Runderlass* specifically names 'manumission' (by the owner), 'death of the owner', 'freed on a military campaign', 'birth of children' (to the owner) and 'unknown'.[138] Moreover, in their local law making and enforcing capacity, district officials were free to issue certificates of emancipation to slaves whose owners they believed were morally unfit to own slaves.[139] Thus, there were basically three broad headings under which *Freibriefe* were issued: third party redemption, manumission by the owner and official emancipation.

All certificates of emancipation had to be recorded by the district officer. At the end of each financial year, district officers were required to forward statistical summaries to the colonial government, which, in turn, sent these records to the authorities in Berlin. After these records had been thoroughly scrutinised, an edited version was forwarded to a special bureau in Brussels, set up after the signing of the Brussels Act in order to facilitate communication on slave matters between the signatory powers.[140]

While the 1891 decree only regulated third party redemption, slaves seem to have tried from very early on to redeem themselves from their owners.[141] Owners, however, often refused to accept this. Slaves or their relatives then went to the district office to argue their case. Initially, the majority of district officers were reluctant to force owners to release their slaves for ransom, but the aforementioned 1901 decree established the right of slaves to purchase their freedom by paying the ransom themselves

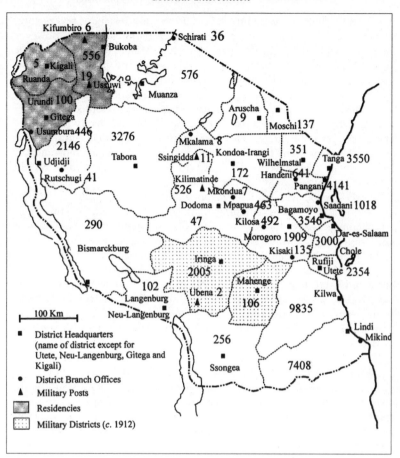

Map 4: Issues of 'Certificates of Emancipation' in German East Africa, 1891–1912

Sources: As in Table 2.
Note: The archival spelling of place and district names has been retained in this map.

Table 3: Issue of 'Certificates of Emancipation', 1891–1912 (Selected Districts and Main Reasons o*

	1891	1892	1893	1894	1895	1896	1897	1898	1899	1900	1901
Kilwa	5	103	64	121	185	654	445	471	1122	447	538
Redm.	n.a.	n.a.	3	8	29	25	46	41	n.a.	61	86
Manu.	n.a.	n.a.	6	26	102	59	284	286	n.a.	270	296
Eman.	n.a.	n.a.	41	74	52	554	114	144	n.a.	116	156
Lindi	7	66	95	100	113	61	451	88	104	109	167
Redm.	n.a.	n.a.	30	76	69	13	21	17	n.a.	10	41
Manu.	n.a.	n.a.	13	19	11	8	41	54	n.a.	54	55
Eman.	n.a.	n.a.	12	5	25	29	107	16	n.a.	42	61
Pangani	3	22	24	56		43	130	97	49	162	144
Redm.	n.a.	n.a.	4	24		16	19	35	n.a.	91	84
Manu.	n.a.	n.a.		6		5	11	15	n.a.	43	48
Eman.	n.a.	n.a.	20	26		22	99	44	n.a.	24	12
Tanga	7	270	97	168	78	186	268	122	91	63	190
Redm.	n.a.	n.a.	17	11	14	42	90	48	n.a.	31	85
Manu.	n.a.	n.a.	29	16	21	50	54	45	n.a.	27	73
Eman.	n.a.	n.a.	47	99	43	87	119	17	n.a.	5	32
Bagamoyo	16	174	72	172	90	110	97	68	60	74	221
Redm.	n.a.	n.a.	5	9	2	21	21	10	n.a.	15	104
Manu.	n.a.	n.a.	28	50	29	33	34	20	n.a.	25	65
Eman.	n.a.	n.a.	27	89	55	41	13	24	n.a.	11	56
Tabora						96	64	46	80	30	23	84
Redm.						43	5	13	10	n.a.	11	18
Manu.						3				n.a.	1	5
Eman.						50	59	21	60	n.a.	8	52
Dar-es-Salam		131	72	113	150	264	184	152	58	116	85
Redm.		n.a.	4	20	25	26	21	42	n.a.	46	25
Manu.		n.a.	7	25	72	29	113	52	n.a.	60	28
Eman.		n.a.	49	49	17	178	39	33	n.a.	3	23
Mohorro-Rufiji									59	121	112
Redm.									n.a.	8	13
Manu.									n.a.	76	78
Eman.									n.a.	37	21
Udjidji						14		134	74	36	117
Redm.						6		22	n.a.	16	85
Manu.								1	n.a.		5
Eman.						8		108	n.a.	20	27
Iringa							162	262	114	67	80
Redm.							9	32	n.a.	35	33
Manu.								1	n.a.		
Eman.							152	178	n.a.	27	47
Others	0	10	44	51	149	194	409	560	419	286	666
Total	38	776	468	781	861	1,590	2,192	2,034	2,180	1,504	2,404

Redm.: Redemption   Manu.: Manumission   Eman.: Emancipation   n.a.: not available
Source: BAB RKolA 7410- 7415, 'Sammlung der zur Mitteilung an das Spezialbüro im Brüssel bestimmten Nachweisungen',
1 October 1892–31 May 1915. Note: The archival spelling of district names has been retained in this table.

)2	1903	1904	1905	1906	1907	1908	1909	1910	1911	1912	Total
39	535	611	327	379	565	505	506	473	700	590	9,835
92	56	88	64	103	79	106	101	122	320	232	1,762
06	304	307	221	256	449	349	267	317	350	325	4,680
01	175	216	42	20	37	50	138	34	30	33	2,117
00	219	347	380	608	362	623	818	973	499	1118	7,408
21	38	132	99	412	183	350	409	402	254	535	3,112
35	67	116	145	112	145	220	302	255	138	452	2,239
30	101	99	128	56	22	53	100	316	107	131	1,440
52	264	178	574	436	372	348	177	186	522	92	4,141
48	139	92	314	124	270	226	105	114	243	49	1,997
33	86	73	206	95	102	113	72	66	279	39	1,292
31	39	13	54	17		5		6		4	566
71	172	118	157	173	215	224	200	208	216	156	3,550
53	52	52	65	97	117	100	86	114	92	62	1,236
73	86	42	87	76	98	123	114	90	124	94	1,322
33	34	16	4			1		4			541
36	217	108	243	158	339	156	289	202	290	204	3,546
51	54	55	79	69	177	90	131	74	98	99	1,164
01	94	41	134	85	155	58	144	110	186	97	1,486
34	69	12	30	4	7	8	14	14	6	8	516
42	114		150	242	223	274	371	265	581	591	3,276
4	45		92	188	159	201	229	197	363	340	1,918
3			42	38	19	50	62	48	125	231	627
35	69		16	16	38	23	80	20	93	20	660
75	114	127	126	108	184	118	162	203	152	206	3,000
58	17	51	53	60	95	64	62	66	81	106	922
59	64	48	43	42	78	28	86	128	60	89	1,111
40	14	10	20	3	11	15	14	9	11	11	549
55	207	248	105	199	196	183	137	197	245	190	2,354
5	20	35	24	66	66	67	76	133	140	102	755
73	105	172	55	24	82	107	59	61	103	88	1,083
77	82	41	26	109	48	8	2	3	2		456
59	124	65	53	101	187	196	293	236	197	250	2,146
38	47	36	24	57	157	126	128	142	142	166	1,192
4	8	12	8	29	14	24	148	61	44	65	423
27	66	8	21	15	16	46	17	33	11	18	441
71	196	113	65	190	182	123	73	65	94	48	2,005
22	161	89	46	167	8	102	51	59	64	25	1,003
	7	10	1	8	3	4	12	2	20	22	90
49	13	11	13	5	170	6	10	2	10	1	694
00	469	599	640	486	679	804	844	1,075	598	789	10,371
20	2,631	2,514	2,820	3,080	3,504	3,554	3,870	4,083	4,094	4,234	51,632

or having it paid by a relative and, thus, gain the desired certificates of emancipation, even if the owner had explicitly refused the offer.[142] In such cases, the district office was expected to intervene on behalf of the slave and issue a *Freibrief*.

Unfortunately, the statistical records kept by the district offices for the period from 1891 to 1912 concerning the issue of certificates of emancipation do not distinguish between third party redemption by European employers and self-redemption by slaves or their relatives.[143] Other evidence, however, seems to suggest that while very few slaves bought their freedom themselves in the early years of colonial rule, their numbers increased substantially from the turn of the century onwards. This apparently reflects both the growth of money-earning opportunities in the colonial economy and an administrative policy change.[144] A further marked increase took place in the late 1900s and early 1910s.[145] In this context it should also be noted that 'official emancipation' could take place for a variety of reasons, ranging from mistreatment of a slave and non-residence of the owner within the boundaries of the colony to emancipation following 'punitive expeditions' against local chiefs who had resisted the establishment of colonial rule in their areas.[146] Frequently, however, no specific reason was given as to why the district officer emancipated a particular slave. Thus, both categories – 'redemption' and 'official emancipation' – are open to interpretation.[147]

Looking at the overall number of slaves who received *Freibriefe*, there was a steady increase between 1893 and 1912 (see Table 2). Only a few hundred were issued up to the mid-1890s, but the numbers increased to 2,000–3,000 in the second half of the 1890s and early 1900s. In 1909 the 4,000 mark was reached. Thus, although there are no data available for the years 1913 and 1914, one can safely assume that in the period 1890–1914 about 60,000 *Freibriefe* were issued by the local administration, since according to the records 51,632 slaves had received such a certificate by the end of 1912.

Detailed records for the years 1891 and 1892 are missing, but for the period 1893–1912 the available figures (see Table 2) show that of the total of 50,818 slaves freed in this period 19,311 were redeemed (38 per cent), 17,374 were manumitted by their owners (34 per cent), and 12,263 were officially emancipated (24 per cent). All other reasons, such as 'death of the owner' and 'freed on a military campaign' (that is, a punitive expedition) accounted for only a total of 1,870 *Freibriefe* (4 per cent).[148]

The records also show the development of the certification of slaves within the various *Freibrief* categories over time. In the period 1893–1912 the number of slaves who were manumitted by their owners, redeemed themselves or were redeemed by others, steadily increased, while the number of slaves who were officially emancipated slowly declined from about the turn of the century on. This was largely because the period of colonial conquest had by that time come to an end. Up to about 1900, members of the coastal elite or chiefs further inland who had resisted or were suspected of having opposed the establishment of colonial rule in their area were often relieved of their slaves. This policy was also a subtle but highly effective strategy to exert a strong measure of political control. Local 'big men' and chiefs often owned large numbers of slaves and their loss meant their immediate financial, social and, thus, political ruin. In the event, after the turn of the century the number of slaves who received a *Freibrief* for that particular reason declined.[149] The relative absence of 'punitive expeditions' was probably the main reason why the overall number of *Freibriefe* dropped so sharply in 1900. This decrease was almost entirely due to a decline in the number of official *Freibriefe* issued that year.[150]

According to the *Freibrief* records, the geographical distribution of certification varied a great deal between districts (see Map 4). Between 1893 and 1912 about half the slaves who received *Freibriefe* lived in or near the four coastal districts of Kilwa, Lindi, Pangani and Tanga. This is hardly surprising since these particular districts harboured large numbers of slaves and were effectively controlled by the German colonial government much earlier than the inland districts.[151] Yet there are certain important local variations in this pattern. In the inland districts where, according to administrative reports, huge numbers of slaves could be found, especially in Tabora and Ujiji districts, only a few slaves obtained their freedom by certification (see Table 3).[152] In these districts, the unmaking of slavery followed a different historical trajectory.[153]

The reasons for issuing *Freibriefe* varied noticeably between regions, too. Manumission by the owner, for instance, played a major role only on the coast, particularly in Kilwa, Bagamoyo and Dar es Salaam districts, where many Muslim slave owners lived.[154] As mentioned in Chapter 3, manumission was considered a pious act of the highest order according to the teachings of Islam, and bestowed considerable *heshima* (social prestige/honour) on the slave owner.[155] In the inland districts, the number of slave owners who were devout Muslims was much smaller. Yet, it would be wrong to attribute the increase in the number of manumissions after 1900 entirely to an increase in religious piety on the coast, since manumission was probably also a means of purchasing some form of social benefit from a situation that had to all intents and purposes become politically and socially untenable. The development of the colonial economy had slowly eroded the grip owners had on their slaves. The increase in the number of manumissions was an indication of this development (see Chapter 7).

It is also worth mentioning that in Tabora district, which was said to have harboured more than 200,000 slaves in the 1890s, the number of redemption *Freibriefe* only began to increase steadily in the second half of the 1900s and early 1910s (see Table 3). By that time, however, the local slave population is believed to have already declined to about 70,000 (see Table 1).[156] Finally, it should be noted that the number of fugitive slaves who received their *Freibriefe* in accordance with the stipulations of the Brussels Act was quite small, 36 to be precise. But this figure is probably misleading. There were certainly several hundred, probably even thousands, of both male and female slaves who received *Freibriefe* because their owners resided abroad and they had run away from them.[157] However, since these slaves had already lived in German East Africa for some time, many district officers did not regard them as fugitives in the narrow sense of the Brussels Act and, therefore, abstained from issuing *Freibriefe* under this category.[158] Instead, these slaves received 'official emancipation' certificates. For instance, of the 171 *Freibriefe* issued in Tanga in the year 1894, 89 bore that heading. A closer inspection of these *Freibriefe* reveals that 86 were issued because the owner of the slave resided on the island of Pemba, which at that time belonged to the British Protectorate of Zanzibar.[159]

While the aggregate numbers concerning the issue of *Freibriefe* in the period 1891–1912 provide at best a broad outline of major trends, the more detailed district records concerning the years 1893–6 allow a more subtle interpretation of the statistics.[160] They contain detailed information on several aspects of slavery under German colonial rule, particularly on slavery as it was practised on the coast. Nevertheless, it would be wrong to suppose that slaves who received *Freibriefe* between 1893 and 1896 are representative of the entire slave population of German East Africa at the time; nor can it be safely assumed that the interpretation of the data for this period is equally valid for the entire period 1890–1914. However, despite these restrictions, some cautious observations can be made.

Between 1893 and 1896, most owners whose slaves received certificates of emancipation were men, though there were also a few women.[161] These men and women usually owned only one or two slaves, though there were others, certain colonial chiefs and 'big men' in the interior and on the coast, for instance, who apparently owned hundreds. These men were often part of the local social and political elite, and it was from among them that the German administration chose their local representatives (the aforementioned *Sultane, Akiden* and *Jumben*). As has already been indicated in the previous chapter, this was one of the main reasons why the German administration was so reluctant to abolish slavery outright in the colony, since this would have greatly diminished the social and political power of those through whom the administration wished to rule the country.

Most freed slaves, male and female, were previously employed as agricultural labourers, but not all slave owners were big landowners, at least not on the coast. A few slave owners seem to have acquired slaves solely for entrepreneurial purposes: long-distance trade, for instance, for which mostly male slaves were employed as trusted agents or caravan porters. Moreover, it appears that some owners deliberately diversified the employment of their slaves. For instance, when in 1894 Abdallah bin Sef, resident on the island of Mafia, was 'relieved' of his 55 slaves for political reasons, his workforce included 41 agricultural labourers as well as seven seamen, three blacksmiths, two agricultural overseers, one carpenter and one personal servant.[162]

According to *Freibrief* records between 1893 and 1896, only a few Europeans or German nationals manumitted slaves. Ownership of (female) slaves was probably much more widespread, but neither their purchase nor their emancipation was recorded. One notable exception is the case of a *Hauptmann* of the *Schutztruppe*, Hermann Sigl, after whom Sigl Gorge in Tanzania is still named today. In 1895 he manumitted his female slave Sassonsi, a 25-year-old woman who stated that she was born in Tabora.[163] But such instances were exceedingly rare, since all 'non-natives', especially members of the German civil administration and the *Schutztruppe*, were strictly forbidden to own slaves. More common were the cases in which owners of Indian origin manumitted slaves, although as British subjects they were not allowed to own slaves either. Thus, according to the classification system employed in the records, the vast majority of slaves belonged to 'Arab', 'Swahili', or 'African' owners, although it is not entirely clear how the administration in towns like Tabora or Lindi, for instance, defined these three groups. As far as the owners' profession is concerned, it is noticeable that many African owners carried official titles, such as *Jumbe* or *Akida*. Finally, it appears that a certain number of female slaves who were manumitted or redeemed had previously been owned by *askari* of the *Schutztruppe*, especially non-commissioned officers, although slave ownership was forbidden to them as well.[164]

As already mentioned, the majority of slaves who received *Freibriefe* in the period 1893–6 were previously employed in agriculture. Most of them worked on their owners' farms or plantations. Some district officers made a distinction between slaves who were only employed as agricultural labourers and those who farmed on their own. It appears that, especially on the southern coast, some slave owners had settled slaves on their land not because they were interested in their labour, but in order to obtain a portion of the vegetables and grain they produced. The social prestige of these *shamba* slaves was considered to be much higher than that of agricultural labourers, since their status was almost similar to share-croppers and other clients and dependants of the local elite.[165]

A minority of freed slaves had occupations outside agriculture.[166] These varied with the structure of the local economy and thus included such diverse professions as seaman, fisherman, net maker, trader, blacksmith, carpenter, butcher, bricklayer, porter, hunter, herdsman, mat maker, basket maker, dressmaker, shoemaker, tailor, potter, stone carrier, domestic servant and 'native doctor'.[167] The majority of these 'professional' slaves were men. Women apparently dominated only the mat-making business.[168]

There was, however, one 'profession', as it was called in the *Freibrief* records, which was exclusively the domain of women. These female slaves were bought by prosperous men as concubines (*masuria*), usually without bridewealth payment or the performance of an Islamic or other marriage ceremony.[169] Most of them were between fifteen and twenty-five years of age, and their redemption prices often exceeded those of female agricultural labourers in the same age group by a factor of two to three. They were frequently ransomed by *askari*,[170] though there were also a few instances of these women being redeemed by German nationals.[171] However, it should be noted that the fact that European men redeemed

African *masuria* is in itself no direct proof of the existence of more than a casual sexual relationship between African slave women and European men in this period. Still, one might speculate why these men paid such extraordinarily high redemption prices for these women and, combined with more incidental evidence regarding such relations (see above), it indeed appears that European, particularly German men, exploited African slave women sexually on a regular basis.

Only a small number, perhaps less than 10 per cent of all freed slaves, worked in their owners' households.[172] This surprisingly low figure seems to contradict much of the contemporary writing about slavery in East Africa. According to this literature most of the slaves in German East Africa were employed as domestic servants.[173] However, there is probably a bias in the records here, since, for instance, older slaves, especially those born in their owner's household, were less likely to be redeemed than other slaves because of their firmer attachment to their owner's family. Conversely, slaves who remembered where they had been enslaved or had recollections of their birthplace were more likely to seek redemption than second- or third-generation slaves. It should also be noted in this context that the great majority of slaves who received *Freibriefe* were not born in the location of certification or in the area of their owners' residence. It seems, nevertheless, that the incidence of 'house slavery' was exaggerated to some extent in the official portrayal of slavery in East Africa at the time, probably because it allowed slavery to be painted as a 'benign' institution, the abolition of which, for supposedly humanitarian reasons, was not desired.[174]

The overall majority of freed slaves, including those who had previously been employed in agriculture, were female. There is thus reason to suggest that the majority of slaves in East Africa were indeed women. The records show that almost two-thirds of all manumitted slaves and over half of all redeemed slaves were female, most of whom were less than twenty-five years old. But as with the uneven regional distribution of certification and the variable professional status of the slaves, the place of certification is significant in this respect. While in some districts the gender balance of the freed slave population was almost even, in other districts the number of freed female slaves greatly exceeded the number of freed male slaves. There is, moreover, some evidence to suggest that women played a far greater role in agriculture in general than colonial reports published at the time acknowledged. As mentioned above, a number of coastal 'big men' were relieved of their slaves because they opposed German administration. In the case of Abdallah bin Omari of Kilwa Kivinji, whose slaves were officially emancipated in 1896, it appears that of the 226 slaves concerned, 120 were women, most of whom were less than thirty years old and employed as agricultural labourers.[175]

The *Freibrief* register also provides a glimpse into the gender, age and price structure of slaves in coastal East Africa in the early colonial period (see Table 4). The records show that at the turn of the century younger female slaves were more highly valued than their male counterparts in the

Table 4: Slave Redemption Prices on the East African Coast, 1894–6 (in Rs)

Age Groups	Male slaves			Female slaves			All slaves	
	No.	Range (Rs)	Average (Rs)	No.	Range (Rs)	Average (Rs)	No.	Average (Rs)
0–5	4	32–50	37	2	37–80	58	6	48
6–10	8	14–50	33	11	25–80	45	19	39
10–15	9	20–90	42	17	40–160	88	26	65
16–20	24	25–150	58	30	20–160	90	54	74
21–25	5	58–200	88	10	30–200	80	15	84
26–30	3	40–100	80	3	60–80	70	6	75
31–35	4	60–140	100	2	36–105	71	6	86
35+	3	30–40	36	2	12–35	24	5	30
All	60		68	77		75	137	72

Source: BAB RKolA 7410–412, 'Sammlung der zur Mitteilung an das Spezialbüro bestimmten Nachweisungen', October 1892–November 1901. In the preparation of this table I was greatly helped by Vincent Ovaert (Berlin).

Note: In 1895, the Mikindani district officer applied a flat redemption rate of Rs50 for male slaves and Rs55 for female slaves, irrespective of their age, origin, or profession. Overall, 62 slaves were redeemed in this way in that year. Their details were not included in the table above. See BAB RKolA 7412: 10, 'Verzeichnis der im Jahre 1895 erteilten Freibriefe des Bezirksnebenamtes Mikindani', n.d. [January 1896].

same age group. For instance, for younger women in the 16–20 age group the redeemer usually had to pay about Rs90, while male slaves in the same age group fetched only Rs60. Older females, aged 35 and above, were apparently redeemed at a discount, fetching only about Rs25 a head, a price markedly lower than that of female slave children. In this age group the differences in the prices between male and female slaves narrowed considerably. Compared with selling prices, it appears that redemption prices were on the whole somewhat lower than the local 'market rate' for slaves.[176] The price was fixed – as has already been pointed out above – by the district officer after consulting local opinion.[177] It should also be noted that the redemption prices quoted above only represent averages.[178] They do not take local variation into account. It appears that slaves were generally more highly valued on the coast than in the interior, although for highly priced slaves, such as *masuria*, redemption costs tended to be similar everywhere.[179]

The fact that the difference between the redemption price for male and female slaves of the same age group and profession was greatest in the 15–25 age group, and that redeemed female slaves were generally younger than their male counterparts, suggests that female slaves were valued for other reasons than just their productive capacity.[180] It is impossible to ascertain the reason for these differences on the basis of the *Freibrief* records alone, but younger female slaves were in greater demand because they could be more easily controlled after redemption than young men. Younger women were probably also more highly valued for their putative reproductive capacities. After redemption, they usually remained with their redeemers. Thus it appears that in the guise of redeeming young women, a clandestine small-scale female slave trade was conducted in which African men, largely the *askari* of the *Schutztruppe*, as well as German plantation owners, military officers and members of the civilian administration, all seem to have had their share. Finally, there is some circumstantial evidence to suggest that younger female slaves conferred considerable higher social prestige on their redeemer than young men.[181]

As to the question of who redeemed slaves in the period 1893–6, five distinct groups can be identified. About half of the 662 freed slaves in this category were ransomed by Europeans, mostly German nationals.[182] The other half were nearly all redeemed either by Africans or by so-called Arabs; a few were redeemed by people of Indian origin; while, finally, only a tiny minority of slaves redeemed themselves. Altogether, these cases constituted less than 10 per cent of all redemptions listed in the *Freibrief* records in 1893–6, although their numbers may have been higher as the name of the African redeemer was not always included in the registers. European redeemers comprised two plantation owners, two priests acting on behalf of the Catholic Missions in Bagamoyo and Lindi, and a number of individuals, mostly members of the civil administration.

The largest single group of slaves was redeemed by the manager of a coffee plantation called Nguelo in the vicinity of the Usambara Mountains in 1895.[183] Sixty-one slaves of all age groups (30 women and 31 men) were redeemed from an almost equal number of different slave owners. The plantation paid Rs55 for each female slave and Rs50 for male slaves. This was not a very large sum of money considering that at that time domestic servants usually received wages of between Rs8 and Rs12 per month from their European employers. Most of the slaves were said to be Nyassa, Makonde or Yao. The freed slaves were supposed to work for 18 months on the plantation, after which they were to receive their *Freibriefe*. During this period, food and shelter were to be provided by the plantation. Interestingly in this case, all freed slaves were already living on the plantation at the time of their redemption. This suggests that the plantation owner had previously rented slaves from local slave owners and now redeemed them in order to turn these slaves into his permanent wage labour force. A year later, the plantation redeemed another sixty slaves, 26 men and 34 women, most of whom belonged to the 15–25 age group and none of whom had previously lived on the plantation.[184] In both 1895 and 1896, the great majority of African and so-called Arab owners 'sold' one or, at most, two slaves to the plantation.

A further 40 slaves (14 women and 26 men) had already been redeemed in 1894 by G. Rowehl, who owned rubber and cotton plantations near Lindi and Mikindani.[185] The freed slaves came from all age groups. Most of them were believed to have come from northern Mozambique. As in the 1895 Nguelo case, these slaves apparently already lived on the plantation. Unfortunately, little more is known about this transaction. Thus, altogether 161 slaves were explicitly redeemed by plantation owners in the period 1893–6. There may have been a few unrecorded or unidentified cases, but the overall picture shows that about half the number of slaves redeemed by Europeans and about a quarter of all redeemed slaves were ransomed in order to employ them on European owned plantations. Even assuming that there might have been a handful of cases where European plantation owners had not been recorded as redeemers in the *Freibrief* registers, it seems implausible to argue that redemption was a means by which the European plantation owners substantially reduced their perennial labour shortage problems.[186] First, the number of slaves redeemed by the European plantations was too small in comparison with the total workforce employed by them, even at that early stage of the development of the European-owned plantation sector. Second, large-scale redemption by plantations seems to have been limited to the southern coastal area and a few individual plantation owners.[187] It was thus a locally specific phenomenon and very unlikely to have been a general pattern.[188] On the whole, in contrast to other redeemers, European redeemers seem to have preferred male to female slaves. It is also noteworthy that Europeans usually paid higher prices than other redeemers, especially for female slaves.[189]

Missionary redemption constituted a special case of European redemption. In 1895, the Catholic mission in Lindi redeemed 60 male and eight female slaves, most of whom were less than ten years old.[190] To the great embarrassment of the mission, some of these boys had to be given back to their parents later on, since it turned out that they had been enslaved by some local entrepreneurs for the purpose of obtaining redemption money from the mission.[191] All in all, it appears that slave redemption by the Catholic missions was not as widespread as one might have expected, probably amounting to less than 2,000 cases for the whole period 1890–1914.[192]

One of the most intriguing aspects of the *Freibrief* records concerns the age and gender composition of the freed slaves. If one compares the vital statistics of the slaves who were manumitted by their owners with those who were redeemed or officially emancipated, it seems that the former were considerably older. Moreover, the records suggest that redeemed younger women were generally more highly valued in monetary terms than older women. This suggests that the 'intersection between extra-familial and intrafamilial stratification', the social interplay between slavery and patriarchy, is slightly more complicated than the secondary literature suggests.[193] There, it is argued that since both women and slaves were socially marginal to the societies in which they lived, female slaves occupied the very bottom of the local social order. Implicit in such accounts is the assumption that gender roles and slave status reinforced each other. Yet, at least in East Africa in the 1890s and particularly on the East African coast, gender roles as well as slave status apparently changed during the life cycle of female slaves. Thus, the relationship between gender and slavery should rather be seen as the intersection of different sets of life chances that varied according to the age of the female slave.

Finally, it should be mentioned that in the few cases of emancipation in which district officers took care to note that the slaves were freed because they had actively fled from their 'foreign' owners, the proportion of female slaves was remarkably high. For instance, of the 96 slaves who were handed out certificates of emancipation from the district office in Tanga in 1893, a group of 14 were clearly identified as fugitives from the neighbouring island of Pemba.[194] In this particular case, the majority of the runaway slaves were men. But there were also five, mostly younger women. While some were probably fleeing with their spouses, others fled individually or with other women, as far as one can judge from the records. This belies the stereotype of the docile female household slave. Female slaves were as eager as male slaves to 'break their chains', if and when the occasion arose, though in comparison to male slaves their ability to do so was severely restricted, not least because they often had small children to look after.

Assessment

This chapter has examined the impact of administrative policies on the decline of slavery under German colonial rule. As regards the suppression of wholesale slave trading, large-scale violent enslavement, and the export of slaves, it appears that the colonial government to a large extent succeeded in achieving its self-proclaimed aims. As far as regulating the relationship between owners and slaves is concerned, however, a different picture emerges. As intended by the colonial authorities, administrative practice varied a great deal between districts and over time. On the whole, it appears that the stipulations of the 1899 and 1901 decrees were only partly enforced. This underlines the well-known argument that the publicly stated aims of colonial policy should never be confused with local administrative practices, especially when colonial legislation is as ambivalent as the 1901 decree.[195] As far as the official freeing of slaves is concerned, records reveal that only a minority of the certificates of emancipation, probably as few as a quarter, were issued as a result of direct administrative intervention. About three-quarters of the 60,000 slaves who received the *Freibrief* between 1890 and 1914 did so because they themselves or their owners had asked the district office to issue them.

In conclusion, it thus appears that the impact of colonial policies and administrative practice was strongest on the 'supply side' of slavery. Wholesale slave trading and large-scale enslavement were almost thoroughly suppressed. However, the colonial administration did little to actively help slaves to become free, nor, it seems, did district officers spent much of their time on actually improving the lives of slaves. On the contrary, there is considerable evidence to show that district officers tried to keep slaves in their place. The unmaking of slavery was, therefore, largely left to the slaves themselves. As will be shown in the next and final chapter of this book, they succeeded in doing so to a significant and, as far as the historiography of East Africa is concerned, hitherto unrecognised extent.

Notes

1 For population figures for the early 1900s, see Kjekshus 1996: 24.
2 The total population of German East Africa, excluding Ruanda and Urundi, was officially estimated to be 4,145,000 with an estimated margin of error of 100,000. See *Die deutschen Schutzgebiete in Afrika und der Südsee 1912/13*, 1914: 8.
3 See Table 1. For a different set of figures, see Raum 1965: 168. Note that the figures for Tabora district might be particularly inaccurate. The estimates for the number of slaves living in other districts in the interior are considerably lower.
4 The slave population figures for the coast and Tabora district should be seen as broad estimates, which might not be accurate. The figure of 150,000 for the number of slaves living on the coast in 1898–1900 was calculated as a mean average of the figures presented in Table 1.
5 See Kaiserliches Gouvernement 1911: 331ff., 'Verordnung des Reichskanzlers, betreffend die Hausklaverei in Deutsch-Ostafrika', 29 November 1901, paragraph 2.
6 See Kaiserliches Gouvernement 1911: 331ff., 'Verordnung des Reichskanzlers, betreffend die Hausklaverei in Deutsch-Ostafrika', 29 November 1901, paragraph 3.
7 The relevant decree was issued by acting Governor Schmidt. See BAB RKolA 1002: 78, 'Erlass des stellvertretenden Reichskommissars Schmidt', 10 August 1890.
8 For the relevant decrees, see BAB RKolA 7382/22: 3–5, 'Runderlass an sämtliche Bezirksämter, Bezirksnebenämter und Stationen', 19 August 1896, BAB RKolA 1004: 194, 'Grundsätze, welche bei der Entscheidung von Sklavensachen zu befolgen sind' by von Liebert, 3 March 1899 and Kaiserliches Gouvernement 1911: 331ff., 'Verordnung des Reichskanzlers, betreffend die Hausklaverei in Deutsch-Ostafrika', 29 November 1901.
9 Kaiserliches Gouvernement 1911: 332, 'Verordnung des Reichskanzlers, betreffend die Hausklaverei in Deutsch-Ostafrika', 24 December 1904.
10 These regulations were part of the aforementioned decrees, that is BAB RKolA 1004: 194, 'Grundsätze, welche bei der Entscheidung von Sklavensachen zu befolgen sind' by von Liebert, 3 March 1899 and Kaiserliches Gouvernement 1911: 331ff., 'Verordnung des Reichskanzlers, betreffend die Hausklaverei in Deutsch-Ostafrika', 29 November 1901.
11 See BAB RKolA 1004/120: 7ff., 'Bericht des Bezirksamts Kilwa', 10 September 1897.
12 BAB RKolA 1004/125: 3, 'Bericht des Bezirksamts Tanga', 10 September 1897. In cases of owners' 'neglect' or maltreatment of slaves, the latter were often issued with certificates of emancipation. For an example, see BAB RKolA 7410: 352, 'Verzeichnis der im Jahre 1893 im Bezirk Lindi erteilten Freibriefe', n.d. [1894].
13 Kaiserliches Gouvernement 1911: 329ff., 'Verordnung, betreffend den Freikauf von Sklaven', 1 September 1891.
14 BAB RKolA 1004/97: 7, 'Bericht des Bezirksamts Bagamoyo', 14 September 1897 and Karstedt 1912: 97. For a similar argument, see Raum 1965: 184 and Cooper 1981: 271–307.
15 BAB RKolA 1004/97: 7, 'Bericht des Bezirksamts Bagamoyo', 14 September 1897.
16 St. Paul-Illaire 1895: 192. See also BAB RKolA 7382/27: 44, 'Berichte der einzelnen Verwaltungsstellen in Deutsch-Ostafrika über die Sklaverei', Bezirksamt Tanga, Berichterstatter: Bezirksamtssekretär Blank, n.d. [1899] and BAB RKolA 7382/27: 49, 'Berichte der einzelnen Verwaltungsstellen in Deutsch-Ostafrika über die Sklaverei', Bezirksamt Pangani, Berichterstatter: Bezirksamtmann Sigl, n.d. [1898].
17 For a chronology of the German conquest of mainland Tanzania, see Kjekshus 1996: 143–51, 186–90.
18 Few German records concerning this early period of colonial rule have survived. The British consul in Zanzibar, however, closely monitored developments on the coast. For the hanging of the suspected slave traders in Bagamoyo, see PRO FO 881/6039, Euan-Smith to Salisbury, 21 March 1890 and PRO 881/6123, Euan-Smith to Salisbury 3 October 1890.
19 For an example of the retreating slave raiding frontier, see BAB RKolA 1006: 92, 'Runderlass', 10 December 1902.

20 See the various scattered entries concerning the punishment of slave traders in BAB RKolA 7410–15, 'Sammlung der zur Mitteilung an das Spezialbüro bestimmten Nachweisungen', October 1892–May 1915 and *Documents relatifs* 1892–1913.

21 BAB RKolA 6527/2: 10, 'Denkschrift betreffend Ostafrika 1891/92', n.d. [1892]. It appears that, in the later 1890s, punishment for offences such as slave trading or slave exporting was somewhat reduced. The death penalty was increasingly replaced by long-term imprisonment and/or severe beatings. In one particularly gruesome case, the district officer sentenced a slave trader to five years' hard labour in chains and 250 lashes. It is unlikely that the person in question could have survived either of these punishments. See BAB RKolA 7411/253, 'Verzeichnis der im Jahre 1895 wegen Sklavenraub oder Verschiffung von Sklaven über See verurteilten Personen im Bezirk Dar es Salaam 1995', n.d. For detailed information on individual cases of slave trading and the punishment of slave traders in various districts in 1893, see, for instance, BAB RKolA 7410: 321, 381, 382, 383, 385, 386, 'Verzeichnis der im Jahre 1893 verhängten Strafen wegen Menschenraub im Bezirk... [Bagamoyo, Pangani, Saadani, Kilwa, Tanga, Lindi]', 31 May 1894. It is worth noting that most of these cases concerned the kidnapping of children. According to these reports, sometimes both the buyer and the seller (slave trader) were punished.

22 See BAB RKolA 6527/2: 10, 'Denkschrift betreffend Ostafrika 1891/92', n.d. [1893] and BAB RKolA 6534/2: 8, 'Denkschrift über die Entwicklung der deutschen Schutzgebiete in Afrika und Übersee 1903/04', n.d. [1904]. The relevant extract of the *Denkschrift* was also published in *Documents relatifs* 1905: 26.

23 Velten 1898: 77. It should be noted that two of the three authors (Baraka bin Shomari, Mwenyi Hija bin Shomari and Muhamedi bin Madigani) worked for the colonial government and thus their testimony might be biased.

24 *Ibid.* (translation by the author).

25 See, for instance, BAB RKolA 6536/2: 15, 'Denkschrift über die Entwicklung der deutschen Schutzgebiete in Afrika und der Südsee 1905/1906', n.d. [1906]. According to a detailed report in the *Frankfurter Zeitung* of 8 September 1912, in the seven-year period 1905–11 less than 40 people were actually punished for slave raiding, exporting or kidnapping. For the report, see *Frankfurter Zeitung*, 8 September 1912, an extract of which can be found in BAB RKolA 1006: 178.

26 See BAB RKolA 1002: 78, 'Erlass des stellvertretenden Reichskommissars Schmidt', 10 August 1890 and BAB RKolA 1004/97: 1, 'Bericht des Bezirksamts Bagamoyo', 14 September 1897. The 'Erlass' was further amended by the 'Verordnung, betreffend die Sklavenausfuhr' of 31 May 1899. For the *Verordnung*, see Kaiserliches Gouvernement 1911: 329.

27 Leue 1900–1(c): 619.

28 See BAB RKolA 1003: 71, von Soden to Foreign Office, 15 July 1891.

29 BAB RKolA 1004/105: 2, 'Bericht des Bezirksamts Lindi', 14 September 1897. See also Becker 2002: 76.

30 See, for instance, BAB RKolA 7411: 43, 'Verzeichnis der im Jahre 1894 im Bezirk Bagamoyo erteilten Freibriefe' n.d. [1895], BAB RKolA 7410: 331, 'Verzeichnis der im Jahre 1893 im Bezirk Kilwa erteilten Freibriefe' n.d. [1894] and BAB RKolA 7411: 200, 'Verzeichnis der im Jahre 1895 im Bezirk Tabora erteilten Freibriefe' n.d. [1896].

31 In 1893, Baron von Eltz, the district officer of Langenburg, intercepted a slave caravan of 216 slaves. Of these only 99 slaves, mainly women and children, were actually moved to nearby mission stations, as the other 117 slaves had run away. For further detail, see BAB RKolA 1003: 204, 'Bericht der Gesellschaft zur Beförderung der evangelischen Mission unter den Heiden', 7 March 1894. The Protestant missionaries, stationed at Wangemann's Höh on the Makonde plateau, immediately gave the younger slave women in marriage to local men, on the condition that their 'husbands' had only one wife, that the couple would live on mission grounds and that their children would be allowed to attend the mission school. The missionaries reported that female slaves were much sought after as wives. See *ibid.*

32 BAB RKolA 1004: 23, 'Runderlass', 17 December 1895.

33 For an example of such a travel permit, see ZNA G1/36: 2, 'Erlaubnisschein Nr. 475', 3 May 1897. This particular caravan consisted of eight men and one woman carrying guns, powder and lead from Bagamoyo to Irangi. For more detail, see BAB RKolA 1003: 215, 'Bericht des Gouverneurs von Schele', 25 May 1894. See also Leue

1900–1(c): 618.

34 BAB RKolA 1006: 92, 'Runderlass an sämtliche Bezirksämter, betreffend Massnahmen zur Bekämpfung des Sklavenhandels', 10 December 1902. The *Runderlass* was published in *Documents relatifs* 1903: 324–6. See also BAB RKolA 6533/2: 15, 'Denkschrift über die Entwicklung der deutschen Schutzgebiete in Afrika und Übersee 1902/1903', n.d. [1903] and *Documents relatifs* 1904: 8f. According to *Bezirksamtmann* Leue, the colonial government felt unable to require slave owners to travel without their servants. Thus, despite the ban on the selling of slaves outside the district of their residence, a number of clandestine slave transfers seem to have occurred under the pretence that the respective slaves had simply accompanied their owners. See Leue 1900–1(c): 618.

35 BAB RKolA 1003: 104, von Soden to Foreign Office, 25 May 1892, BAB RKolA 6527/2: 10, 'Denkschrift betreffend Ostafrika 1891/92', n.d. [1893], BAB RKolA 6527/21: 9, 'Denkschrift betreffend Deutsch-Ostafrika 1892/93', n.d. [1893], BAB RKolA 6528/2: 15–8, 'Bericht des Herrn Dr Stuhlmann' in 'Denkschrift betreffend das ostafrikanische Schutzgebiet 1893/94', n.d. [1894], BAB RKolA 7382/27: 65, 'Berichte der einzelnen Verwaltungsstellen in Deutsch-Ostafrika über Sklaverei', Bezirksamt Kilwa, Berichterstatter: Bezirksamtmann von Rode n.d. [1900] and BAB RKolA 6532/2: 16, 'Denkschrift über die Entwicklung der deutschen Schutzgebiete in Afrika und Übersee 1901/02', n.d. [1902]. For a detailed description of slave trading on the Rovuma River, see BAB RKolA 1003: 194, 'Bericht des Vorstehers des Bezirksnebenstelle Mikindani, Herrn Zollamts-Assistent Kärger', 28 November 1893.

36 See BAB RKolA 6527/2: 10, 'Denkschrift betreffend Ostafrika 1891/92', n.d. [1892], Mackenzie 1895: 76, BAB RKolA 7382/27: 57, 'Berichte der einzelnen Verwaltungsstellen in Deutsch-Ostafrika über die Sklaverei', Bezirksamt Bagamoyo, Berichterstatter: Bezirksamtssekretär Sperling, n.d. [1898] and *Documents relatifs* 1900: 12–3, von Liebert to Foreign Office, 23 November 1899.

37 Karstedt 1912: 110ff. See the well-informed account in BAB RKolA 1006: 178, extract from *Frankfurter Zeitung*, 8 September 1912. See also Nolan 1977: 265 and Sunseri 2002: 29.

38 Karstedt 1912: 111.

39 BAB RKolA 1004: 194, 'Grundsätze, welche bei der Entscheidung von Sklavensachen zu befolgen sind' by von Liebert, 3 March 1899.

40 BAB RKolA 1004: 213, 'Runderlass', 8 May 1899 and BAB RKolA 1004: 216, 'Runderlass', 30 December 1899.

41 BAB RKolA 4997: 497, 'Fragebogen über die Rechte der Eingeborenen in den deutschen Kolonien (Wakitu)', Bezirksamt Kilwa, 23 October 1910. For a similar report from Mafia Island, see RHO Afr Micr R.8/MF 19, Mafia District Book, 'Domestic Slavery in German East Africa' by N. King, Mafia, April 1915: 12. See also Sunseri 2002: 36 who claims that he has seen numerous archival records which includes 'many instances of children born after 1905 still ransomed or retained as slaves'.

42 BAB RKolA 4997: 497, 'Fragebogen über die Rechte der Eingeborenen in den deutschen Kolonien (Wakitu)', Bezirksamt Kilwa, 23 October 1910. See also BAB RKolA 1004/105: 10, 'Bericht des Bezirksamts Lindi', 14 September 1897 and Wright 1992: 141. Unfortunately, the evidence on the decline of pawning is exceedingly thin. Little is known beyond the fact that, as far as the colonial administration was concerned, the issue does not seem to have played a significant role.

43 *Die deutschen Schutzgebiete in Afrika und der Südsee 1912/13*, 1914: 7. See also Sunseri (2002: 29) who writes that people were sold into slavery in the period of famine following the devastation brought about by the suppression of the Maji Maji uprising.

44 See BAB RKolA 7382/27: 65, 'Berichte der einzelnen Verwaltungsstellen in Deutsch-Ostafrika über Sklaverei', Bezirksamt Kilwa, Berichterstatter: Bezirksamtmann von Rode n.d. [1900] and BAB RKolA 7367/20: 105, 'Anhang zu den Berichten der einzelnen Verwaltungsstellen', n.d. [1899–1900] and also BAB RKolA 1004/125: 2, 'Bericht des Bezirksamts Tanga', 10 September 1897. Monitoring the buying and selling of slaves sometimes included supervising 'transfers' of slaves' of a different kind, such as pawning, bequest or exchange. Such 'transfers' are, however, only rarely mentioned except in BAB RKolA 1004/120: 8, 'Bericht des Bezirksamts Kilwa', 10 September 1897, BAB RKolA 7382/27: 63, 'Berichte der einzelnen Verwaltungsstellen in Deutsch-Ostafrika über Sklaverei', Bezirksamt Kilwa, Berichterstatter: Bezirksamt-

mann von Rode n.d. [1900] and BAB RKolA 7382/27: 60, 'Berichte der einzelnen Verwaltungsstellen in Deutsch-Ostafrika über die Sklaverei', Bezirksamt Dar es Salaam, Berichterstatter: Bezirksamtssekretär Michels, n.d. [1899]. The available evidence on such 'transfers', especially through pawning, is inconclusive and does not allow for generalisation.

45 See BAB RKolA 7382/27: 56, 'Berichte der einzelnen Verwaltungsstellen in Deutsch-Ostafrika über die Sklaverei', Bezirksamt Pangani, Berichterstatter: Bezirksamtmann Sigl, n.d. [1898] and BAB RKolA 7367/20: 105, 'Anhang zu den Berichten der einzelnen Verwaltungsstellen', n.d. [1899–1900].

46 BAB RKolA 7411: 357, Bezirksamt Tanga to Gouvernement, 22 December 1896.

47 See Iliffe 1979: 123–5, Kjekshus 1996: 126–37 and Sunseri 2002: 29.

48 The rinderpest epidemic was followed by other plagues – smallpox in 1893 and locusts in 1894, 1895 and 1898 – all of which contributed to the sale of women and children into slavery in many parts of German East Africa during that period. There was also severe famine in the northern districts in 1898–9. See BAB RKolA 7367/20: 107, 'Anhang zu den Berichten der einzelnen Verwaltungsstellen', Bezirksamt Bagamoyo, n.d. [1899–1900]. See also *Documents relatifs* 1900: 12–13, von Liebert to Foreign Office, 23 November 1899. The selling of children in this period was still remembered some thirty years later. See RHO Micr Afr 397 vol. II, Rufiyi District Book, 'Notes on the Census' by McMillan, n.d. [1929]. For more detail on 'Massai' slaves, see Stuhlmann 1894: 812–14, Baumann 1894: 32ff., Hofmeister 1895: 27, Merker 1910: 348 and Stollowsky 1911: 516. For a discussion of the 'selling' of Mjikenda children on the Kenya coast in the 1890s, see Willis 1993: 47–59 and Morton 1994: 27–42.

49 In 1896, the Tanga district administration decided to ban further imports of 'Massai' slaves because the district officer realised that, by allowing slave imports into the district, he actually encouraged the sale of women and children in areas other than those thought to be occupied by 'Massai'. See BAB RKolA 7411: 357, Bezirksamt Tanga to Gouvernement, 22 December 1896.

50 BAB RKolA 7382/27: 56, 'Berichte der einzelnen Verwaltungsstellen in Deutsch-Ostafrika über die Sklaverei', Bezirksamt Pangani, Berichterstatter: Bezirksamtmann Sigl, n.d. [1898].

51 In 1900, the *majumbe* of Dar es Salaam district were told that all sales had to be registered in town in the presence of both the slave and the district officer. See *Deutsch-Ostafrikanische Zeitung*, 'Der Jumbentag in Daressalam', 28 July 1900. Previously, the district officer seems to have turned a blind eye to the 'transfer of slaves'. See BAB RKolA 1003: 103, 'Bericht des Bezirksamts Dar es Salaam', 14 October 1897. For a description of slave sales under government supervision, see BAB RKolA 1004/105: 5, 'Bericht des Bezirksamts Lindi', 14 September 1897.

52 For a different approach by the Tanga district office, see BAB RKolA 1004/125: 3, 'Bericht des Bezirksamts Tanga', 10 September 1897. The officer in charge of this district refused to recognise claims to ownership of a person, if the enslavement of that person had taken place after the assumption of colonial rule. See also BAB RKolA 7382/27: 44, 'Berichte der einzelnen Verwaltungsstellen in Deutsch-Ostafrika über die Sklaverei', Bezirksamt Tanga, Berichterstatter: Bezirksamtssekretär Blank, n.d. [1899] and BAB RKolA 7382/27: 52, 'Berichte der einzelnen Verwaltungsstellen in Deutsch-Ostafrika über die Sklaverei', Bezirksamt Pangani, Berichterstatter: Bezirksamtmann Sigl, n.d. [1898]. For a summary, see Karstedt 1912: 100.

53 BAB RKolA 7382/27: 90, 'Berichte der einzelnen Verwaltungsstellen in Deutsch-Ostafrika über die Sklaverei', Station Tabora, Berichterstatter: Hauptmann Puder, n.d. [1900]. For a summary of these regulations see RHO Afr Micr R.8/MF 19, Mafia District Book, 'Domestic Slavery in German East Africa' by N. King, Mafia, April 1915: 11.

54 BAB RKolA 1006: 192, 'Runderlass' by Acting Governor Methner, 3 February 1912. See also RHO Afr Micr R.8/MF 19, Mafia District Book, 'Domestic Slavery in German East Africa' by N. King, Mafia, April 1915: 15.

55 TNA G38/7, 'Verzeichnis der Sklavenkäufe und Verkäufe, 1911–1914', n.d. [April 1914]. It appears that – contrary to regulations – in some districts these registers were not kept at all. The district officer in Bagamoyo, for instance, stated that although all slave sales were conducted by him in the '*baraza*' [sic], in order to minimise the involvement of the district office he would not register such transactions ('um die behördliche

Mitwirkung nicht allzu sehr hervortreten zu lassen'). BAB RKolA 7367/20: 107, 'Anhang zu den Berichten der einzelnen Verwaltungsstellen', Bezirksamt Bagamoyo, n.d. [1899–1900]. The total number of slave sales supervised by German officials is difficult to estimate. If one accepts that that the figure of about 900 slave sales per year for Kilwa district for the years 1911–14 represent an average, then it appears that up to 7,500 slaves were officially sold in that district alone in the period 1890–1914. According to government estimates, Kilwa district harboured less then 10 per cent of all slaves in German East Africa. Thus one can safely conclude that thousands, if not tens of thousands of slaves were bought and sold with the connivance of the German colonial authorities. Note that the German government as a signatory to the 1890 Brussels agreement was bound to suppress slave trading.

56   The data for 1911–12 allow for a more detailed analysis. Between April 1911 and March 1912, the Kilwa *Bezirksamt* registered the sale of 250 slaves, about 90 women and 160 men, yielding a tax to the authorities of Rs414 on a total turnover of about Rs27,600 at an average slave purchase price of just under Rs114. Female slaves consistently fetched higher prices, on average Rs127, while male slaves were sold on average at Rs108. However, these are just average numbers, masking a wide range of purchase prices within each of these groups, as women were sold for between Rs60 and Rs280, and men in the range Rs60–240. Of these 250 slaves, 33 were sold by female slave owners to male buyers, 38 slaves by male owners to female buyers, and 24 slaves by female owners to female buyers. The remaining slaves were sold and bought by men. Note that a substantial number of the sales recorded in the Kilwa register actually took place on the island of Mafia and might not be representative of sale prices elsewhere on the coast or in the interior at the time. In any case, the figures above are considerably higher than those provided by August Leue, who was the district officer of Dar es Salaam in the later 1890s and early 1900s. This seems to suggest that slave prices substantially increased between the early 1890s and the late 1910s, but, as has been pointed out above, the evidence is not conclusive. For Dar es Salaam slave prices, see Leue, 'Sklaverei', p. 618.

57   See, for instance, the case of Rashid bin Salim in BAB RKolA 7411: 22, 'Verzeichnis der im Jahre 1894 verhängten Strafen wegen Menschenraub im Bezirk Bagamoyo', n.d. [1895].

58   TNA G38/7, 'Verzeichnis der Sklavenkäufe und Verkäufe, 1911–1914', n.d. [April 1914].

59   RHO Afr Micr R.8/MF 19, Mafia District Book, 'Domestic Slavery in German East Africa' by N. King, Mafia, April 1915: 14. For different views, see BAB RKolA 1004/125: 4, 'Bericht des Bezirksamts Tanga', 10 September 1897 and BAB RKolA 7382/27: 60, 'Berichte der einzelnen Verwaltungsstellen in Deutsch-Ostafrika über die Sklaverei', Bezirksamt Dar es Salaam, Berichterstatter: Bezirksamtssekretär Michels, n.d. [1899].

60   According to other reports, children could not be sold as slaves until they were fourteen. See BAB RKolA 1004: 94, 'Bericht des Bezirksamts Pangani', 7 September 1897.

61   RHO Afr Micr R.8/MF 19, Mafia District Book, 'Domestic Slavery in German East Africa' by N. King, Mafia, April 1915: 15.

62   Leue 1900–1(c): 621. In this context, it should be noted that in some areas, like Bagamoyo district, the local missionaries were highly critical of the administrative policy in slave matters, especially when they suspected that the district office condoned the selling of slave children. This practice was seen as particularly abhorrent. See BAB RKolA 1004/97: 7, 'Bericht des Bezirksamts Bagamoyo', 14 September 1897.

63   BAB RKolA 1006/201: 11, 'Denkschrift über die Haussklaverei in Deutsch-Ostafrika' by Governor Schnee, 28 October 1913.

64   BAB RKolA 1004/125: 12, 'Bericht des Bezirksamts Tanga', 10 September 1897.

65   BAB RKolA 1006/201: 11, 'Denkschrift über die Haussklaverei in Deutsch-Ostafrika' by Governor Schnee, 28 October 1913. See also Karstedt 1912: 105.

66   Leue 1900–1(c): 618. See also RHO Afr Micr R.8/MF 19, Mafia District Book, 'Domestic Slavery in German East Africa' by N. King, Mafia, April 1915: 12.

67   See, for instance, ZNA G2/47/2: 218, Euan-Smith to Michahelles, 18 March 1891. Euan-Smith inquired about the purchase of a 'concubine' by a German government official for Rs60. See also BAB RKolA 7412: 124, 'Verzeichnis der im Jahre 1896 im Bezirk Langenburg erteilten Freibriefe', n.d. [1897]. According to the register, Boots-

Unteroffizier Hockel bought a seventeen-year-old female slave for Rs165. Further evidence can be found in *Afrika*, 1895: 119, Hofmeister 1895: 19, Nolan 1977: 265 and in BAB RKolA 1006: 178, extract from *Frankfurter Zeitung*, 8 September 1912. See also the illuminating discussion in the Kolonialrat about this issue in BAB RKolA 7365/209: 10ff., 'Verhandlungen des Kolonialrats', 20 April 1892.

68 See, for instance, BAB RKolA 4711: 124, 'Verzeichnis der im Jahre 1894 im Bezirk Lindi erteilten Freibriefe', n.d. [1895].

69 BAB RKolA 7367/20: 98, 'Anhang zu den Berichten der einzelnen Verwaltungsstellen', n.d. [1899–1900].

70 See BAB RKolA 6528/2: 15–8, 'Bericht des Dr Stuhlmann' in 'Denkschrift, betreffend das ostafrikanische Schutzgebiet 1893/1894', n.d. [1894]. See also BAB RKolA 6533/2: 15, 'Denkschrift über die Entwicklung der deutschen Schutzgebiete in Afrika und Übersee 1902/1903', n.d. [1903].

71 Karstedt, who worked as a circuit judge in German East Africa, claimed that in 1910 slaves bought on the shore of Lake Tanganyika for Rs30 were resold in Dar es Salaam for Rs60–70, despite regulations banning these sales. Karstedt 1913: 619.

72 BAB RKolA 4997: 497, 'Fragebogen über die Rechte der Eingeborenen in den deutschen Kolonien (Wakitu)', Bezirksamt Kilwa, 23 October 1910. See also BAB RKolA 1004/105: 16, 'Bericht des Bezirksamts Lindi', 14 September 1897. See also RHO Afr Micr R.8/MF 19, Mafia District Book, 'Domestic Slavery in German East Africa' by N. King, Mafia, April 1915: 15.

73 BAB RKolA 1004/105: 1, 'Bericht des Bezirksamts Lindi', 14 September 1897 and BAB RKolA 7382/27: 69, 'Berichte der einzelnen Verwaltungsstellen in Deutsch-Ostafrika über Sklaverei', Bezirksamt Lindi, Berichterstatter: Bezirksamtmann Zache n.d. [1900]. See also BAB RKolA 6527/2: 10, 'Denkschrift betreffend Ostafrika 1891/92', n.d. [1893] and BAB RKolA 7411/22: 124, Bezirksamt Lindi to Gouvernement, 13 February 1895. In the latter report the *Bezirksamtmann* stated that in 1894 many slave-carrying caravans had arrived in the district. He estimated that about 800–900 slaves were sold in the vicinity of Lindi alone. Most of these slaves seem to have come from northern Mozambique. See BAB RKolA 1003: 153, 'Bericht der Kaiserlichen Gesandtschaft in Portugal', 19 July 1893. For a description of a slave caravan with about 250 'captives' on its way to Lindi in 1900, see Adams n.d. [1903]: 58.

On slave trading in Bukoba district and the import of slaves from Rwanda, see BAB RKolA 7382/27: 86, 'Berichte der einzelnen Verwaltungsstellen in Deutsch-Ostafrika über Sklaverei', Bezirksamt Bukoba, Berichterstatter: Hauptmann von Beringe n.d. [1900] and BAB RKolA 1006: 138, 'Zuschrift vom 25. Juni [1909] von Kardinal Ledochowski nach Berichten des apostolischen Vikars von Süd-Kassanga Monsignore Hirth', 29 June 1909.

74 BAB RKolA 1004/105: 2, 'Bericht des Bezirksamts Lindi', 14 September 1897. Sunseri reports that according to oral historical sources some people pawned themselves onto Mafia Island plantations during the famines that followed the suppression of the Maji Maji uprising. See Sunseri 1993a: 106. For some more detail, see Becker 2002: 124. This seems to have been an established pattern as in the mid-1880s and again in the mid-1890s 'many' people were taken as slaves via Lindi to Mafia island following locust plagues in the Rufiyi area, which had caused widespread famine. See Baumann 1957[1886]: 9 and King 1917: 121. See also Becker 2001: 57.

75 RHO Afr Micr R.8/MF 19, Mafia District Book, 'Domestic Slavery in German East Africa' by N. King, Mafia, April 1915: 15, 18.

76 Leue 1900–1(c): 622. See also RHO Afr Micr R.8/MF 19, Mafia District Book, 'Domestic Slavery in German East Africa' by N. King, Mafia, April 1915: 15.

77 See BAB RKolA 1003: 194, 'Bericht des Vorstehers der Bezirksnebenstelle Mikindani, Herrn Zollamts-Assistent Kärger', 28 November 1893 and BAB RKolA 1004/120: 8, 'Bericht des Bezirksamts Kilwa', 10 September 1897. See also TNA G8/68: 194, 'Deutsch-Ostafrikanische Gesellschaft to von Liebert, 22 Dec. 1896 and RHO Afr Micr R.8/MF 19, Mafia District Book, 'Domestic Slavery in German East Africa' by N. King, Mafia, April 1915: 15.

78 TNA G38/7, 'Verzeichnis der Sklavenkäufe und Verkäufe, 1911–1914', n.d. [April 1914] and BAB RKolA 1006/173, 'Bericht betreffend Vermehrung der Hörigen in Deutsch-Ostafrika', [by von Rechenberg?] 14 April 1912. In this report from 1912 the author states that several hundred slaves were bought and sold annually in Tabora and

Ujiji districts. Karstedt claimed that in Ujiji district alone about 500–1,000 slaves were sold in the presence of German administrative officers each year. He also indicates that many of the sales were not recorded. See Karstedt 1913: 620.

79 See, for instance, BAB RKolA 1004/120: 1, 'Bericht des Bezirksamts Kilwa', 10 September 1897. See also BAB RKolA 4997: 497, 'Fragebogen über die Rechte der Eingeborenen in den deutschen Kolonien (Wakitu)', Bezirksamt Kilwa, 23 October 1910.

80 BAB RKolA 7367/20: 101, 'Anhang zu den Berichten der einzelnen Verwaltungs- stellen', n.d. [1899–1900].

81 BAB RKolA 7382/27: 49, 'Berichte der einzelnen Verwaltungsstellen in Deutsch- Ostafrika über die Sklaverei', Bezirksamt Pangani, Berichterstatter: Bezirksamtmann Sigl, n.d. [1898].

82 For a detailed description, see BAB RKolA 1004/97: 8, 'Bericht des Bezirksamts Bagamoyo', 14 September 1897. See also BAB RKolA 7382/18: 44, 'Eingereicht mit Bericht des Gouverneurs Freiherrn von Schele aus Dar es Salaam', 30 October 1893, BAB RKolA 7382/27: 65, 'Berichte der einzelnen Verwaltungsstellen in Deutsch- Ostafrika über die Sklaverei', Bezirksamt Kilwa, Berichterstatter: Bezirksamtmann von Rode n.d. [1900], BAB RKolA 7382/27: 42, 'Berichte der einzelnen Verwaltungs- stellen in Deutsch-Ostafrika über die Sklaverei', Bezirksamt Tanga, Berichterstatter: Bezirksamtssekretär Blank, n.d. [1899], BAB RKolA 7382/27: 49, 'Berichte der einzelnen Verwaltungsstellen in Deutsch-Ostafrika über die Sklaverei', Bezirksamt Pangani, Berichterstatter: Bezirksamtmann Sigl, n.d. [1898] and BAB RKolA 7367/20: 100, 'Anhang zu den Berichten der einzelnen Verwaltungsstellen', n.d. [1899–1900]. It is worth noting that information about German district officers inflicting corporal punishment on African slaves for their supposed insubordination (*Widerspenstigkeit*) to their African owners was already widely available in 1903, since Velten explicitly mentioned the fact in his book (Velten 1903: 312). For the punishment of runaway, negligent or disobedient slaves in Kilwa district in 1896–7, see Sunseri 2002: 31, 41–4. For a description of the punishment of slaves in Pangani in 1894, see Meinecke 1894: 155. In this connection it should be noted that the widespread punishment of slaves strongly contradicts the colonial stereotype of the 'docile' slave.

83 BAB RKolA 7367/20: 101, 'Anhang zu den Berichten der einzelnen Verwaltungs- stellen', n.d. [1899–1900].

84 *Ibid.* See also BAB RKolA 7382/27: 56, 'Berichte der einzelnen Verwaltungsstellen in Deutsch-Ostafrika über die Sklaverei', Bezirksamt Pangani, Berichterstatter: Bezirk- samtmann Sigl, n.d. [1898].

85 See, for instance, the report in *Afrika*, 1886: 148.

86 BAB RKolA 1004/97: 9, 'Bericht des Bezirksamts Bagamoyo', 14 September 1897. See also BAB RKolA 1004/125: 2, 'Bericht des Bezirksamts Tanga', 10 September 1897 and BAB RKolA 7382/27: 55, 'Berichte der einzelnen Verwaltungsstellen in Deutsch- Ostafrika über die Sklaverei', Bezirksamt Pangani, Berichterstatter: Bezirksamtmann Sigl, n.d. [1898] and BAB RKolA 7382/27: 57, 'Berichte der einzelnen Verwaltungsstellen in Deutsch-Ostafrika über die Sklaverei', Bezirksamt Bagamoyo, Berichterstatter: Bezirksamtssekretär Sperling, n.d. [1898]. See also Meinecke 1894: 155.

87 See, for example, the range of possibilities mentioned in a report by the administrative officer in charge of Lindi district. BAB RKolA 1004: 105, 'Bericht des Bezirksamts Lindi', 14 September 1897.

88 See RHO Afr Micr R.8/MF 19, Mafia District Book, 'Domestic Slavery in German East Africa' by N. King, Mafia, April 1915: 11.

89 BAB RKolA 1004/125: 1, 'Bericht des Bezirksamts Tanga', 10 September 1897.

90 See BAB RKolA 7382/18: 43, 'Eingereicht mit Bericht des Gouverneurs Freiherrn von Schele aus Dar es Salaam', 30 October 1893. See also RHO Afr Micr R.8/MF 19, Mafia District Book, 'Domestic Slavery in German East Africa' by N. King, Mafia, April 1915: 16.

91 BAB RKolA 7382/27: 90, 'Berichte der einzelnen Verwaltungsstellen in Deutsch- Ostafrika über die Sklaverei', Station Tabora, Berichterstatter: Hauptmann Puder, n.d. [1900].

92 *Ibid.*

93 BAB RKolA 7382/27: 60, 'Berichte der einzelnen Verwaltungsstellen in Deutsch-

Ostafrika über die Sklaverei', Bezirksamt Dar es Salaam, Berichterstatter: Bezirksamtssekretär Michels, n.d. [1899]. For somewhat higher figures for Dar es Salaam, see BAB RKolA 7382/19: 8, 'Äusserung des Superiors der Kongregation der Väter vom heiligen Geist und unbefleckten Herzen Mariä zu Knechtsteden', 18 August 1896.

94 BAB RKolA 1004/125: 1, 'Bericht des Bezirksamts Tanga', 10 September 1897. For Mafia, see RHO Afr Micr R.8/MF 19, Mafia District Book, 'Domestic Slavery in German East Africa' by N. King, Mafia, April 1915: 11. See also BAB RKolA 7382/27: 44, 'Berichte der einzelnen Verwaltungsstellen in Deutsch-Ostafrika über die Sklaverei', Bezirksamt Tanga, Berichterstatter: Bezirksamtssekretär Blank, n.d. [1899]. For an overview, see BAB RKolA 7382/18: 44, 'Eingereicht mit Bericht des Gouverneurs Freiherrn von Schele aus Dar es Salaam', 30 October 1893.

95 See Eberstein 1896: 179 and BAB RKolA 7382/27: 66, 'Berichte der einzelnen Verwaltungsstellen in Deutsch-Ostafrika über Sklaverei', Bezirksamt Kilwa, Berichterstatter: Bezirksamtmann von Rode n.d. [1900].

96 See, for instance, BAB RKolA 1004/105: 10, 'Bericht des Bezirksamts Lindi', 14 September 1897. See also BAB RKolA 1004/125: 4, 'Bericht des Bezirksamts Tanga', 10 September 1897. According to a report from Pangani, slaves were sometimes rented out in lieu of debt repayments. In such cases, the slave owner did not receive any part of the slave's wage. The employers were said to be mostly Indians. See BAB RKolA 7382/27: 52, 'Berichte der einzelnen Verwaltungsstellen in Deutsch-Ostafrika über die Sklaverei', Bezirksamt Pangani, Berichterstatter: Bezirksamtmann Sigl, n.d. [1898].

97 BAB RKolA 1004/125: 8, 'Bericht des Bezirksamts Tanga', 10 September 1897.

98 See RHO Afr Micr R.8/MF 19, Mafia District Book, 'Domestic Slavery in German East Africa' by N. King, Mafia, April 1915: 18.

99 Karstedt 1912: 102.

100 *Ibid.*

101 BAB RKolA 7382/27: 49, 'Berichte der einzelnen Verwaltungsstellen in Deutsch-Ostafrika über die Sklaverei', Bezirksamt Pangani, Berichterstatter: Bezirksamtmann Sigl, n.d. [1898]. For more detail, see Chapter 7.

102 BAB RKolA 1004/125: 4, 'Bericht des Bezirksamts Tanga', 10 September 1897. See also RHO Afr Micr R.8/MF 19, Mafia District Book, 'Domestic Slavery in German East Africa' by N. King, Mafia, April 1915: 14, 16.

103 BAB RKolA 1002: 78, 'Erlass des stellvertretenden Reichskommissars Schmidt', 10 August 1890. For a similar statement, see ZNA G1/84, 'Aktennotiz', 23 June 1891.

104 BAB RKolA 1002: 78, 'Erlass des stellvertretenden Reichskommissars Schmidt', 10 August 1890. See also BAB RKolA 1002: 74, 'Bericht betreffend die Behandlung der Sklavenfrage in Ostafrika', 17 December 1890.

105 ZNA g2/47/1: 55, 'Enclosure' in Smith to Foreign Office, 13 September 1890.

106 Glassman 1994: 261. A similar development occurred in the south. When the *Wissmann-Truppe* reoccupied Kilwa in 1890, hundreds of slaves are said to have fled from plantations located at Kilwa, Lindi and Mikindani to set up independent villages. See Mann 2002: 86ff.

107 The *Times* articles can be found in BAB RKolA 1002: 58, 88. A further article entitled 'The Germans in East Africa', summarising the affair, was published on 23 October 1890. See BAB RKolA 1003: 48. The author of the first article believed that the Bagamoyo proclamation was a response to the anti-slavery declaration of the Sultan of Zanzibar, which the Sultan had issued on 1 August 1890. In this declaration the Sultan of Zanzibar had outlawed 'the exchange, sale, or purchase of slaves, domestic or otherwise' from that date. ZNA G2/47/1: 143, 'Decree by Sultan Ali bin Said', 1 August 1890. For more detail on this decree, see Coupland 1939: 247–52.

108 For German newspaper articles, see BAB RKolA 1002: 62–73 and *passim*. For letters from the British Ambassador, see BAB RKolA 1002: 121, Trenck to Marshall, 18 September 1890. For the letters from the British Consul, see BAB RKolA 1003: 23, Euan-Smith to Michahelles, 13 September 1890 and BAB RKolA 1003: 28, Euan-Smith to Michahelles, 19 September 1890. See also the report in *Deutsche Kolonialzeitung*, 3 (1890), 91, 168.

109 See the exchange of letters between the Foreign Office and the Reichskommissariat in Zanzibar in this matter in BAB RKolA 1003: 16–40.

110 See ZNA G2/47/1: 155, Schmidt to Michahelles, 18 September 1890 and BAB RKolA 1002: 110, Schmidt to Caprivi (copy), 18 September 1890. See also BAB RKolA 1003:

16, Michahelles to Caprivi, 1 October 1890 and BAB RKolA 1003: 33, Schmidt to Caprivi, 30 September 1890.

111 For the statement, see ZNA G2/47/2: 181, 'Statement' by 'Soliman bin Nassor' [sic], 1 October 1890. On Suleiman bin Nasr al-Lemki, see also Iliffe 1979: 94 and Glassman 1995: 7.

112 BAB RKolA 1003: 33, Schmidt to Caprivi, 30 September 1890.

113 BAB RKolA 1003: 77, von Soden to Foreign Office, 30 August 1891.

114 See below.

115 See, for instance, BAB RKolA 7382/27: 42, 'Berichte der einzelnen Verwaltungsstellen in Deutsch-Ostafrika über die Sklaverei', Bezirksamt Tanga, Berichterstatter: Bezirksamtssekretär Blank, n.d. [1899], BAB RKolA 7382/27: 65, 'Berichte der einzelnen Verwaltungsstellen in Deutsch-Ostafrika über die Sklaverei', Bezirksamt Kilwa, Berichterstatter: Bezirksamtmann von Rode n.d. [1900] and RHO Afr Micr R.8/MF 19, Mafia District Book, 'Domestic Slavery in German East Africa' by N. King, Mafia, April 1915: 11. See also Leue 1900–1(c): 621 and Leue 1903: 162. Leue (1903: 162) wrote that a district officer, presumably himself, told a female slave that she could not leave the town of Dar es Salaam without her owner's consent.

116 Leue 1903: 162 and RHO Micr Afr 446, 'Memoirs' by T. Gunzert, n.d. [1933].

117 *Ibid.*

118 BAB RKolA 1004/97: 9, 'Bericht des Bezirksamts Bagamoyo', 14 September 1897 and Nolan 1977: 266.

119 *Ibid.*

120 BAB RKolA 7382/27: 45, 'Berichte der einzelnen Verwaltungsstellen in Deutsch-Ostafrika über die Sklaverei', Bezirksamt Tanga, Berichterstatter: Bezirksamtssekretär Blank, n.d. [1899].

121 Leue 1900–1(c): 621.

122 Leue 1900–1(c): 623. See also BAB RKolA 7382/27: 45, 'Berichte der einzelnen Verwaltungsstellen in Deutsch-Ostafrika über die Sklaverei', Bezirksamt Tanga, Berichterstatter: Bezirksamtssekretär Blank, n.d. [1899].

123 Compare, for instance, the reports in BAB RKolA 1004/125: 2, 'Bericht des Bezirksamts Tanga', 10 September 1897 and BAB RKolA 7382/27: 42, 'Berichte der einzelnen Verwaltungsstellen in Deutsch-Ostafrika über die Sklaverei', Bezirksamt Tanga, Berichterstatter: Bezirksamtssekretär Blank, n.d. [1899].

124 For this quote, see Kaiserliches Gouvernement 1911: 198, 'Verordnung, betreffend die Gerichtsbarkeit und die Polizeibefugnisse der Bezirkshauptleute', 14 May 1891.

125 Leue 1900–1(c): 608 (translation by the author). For a similar view, see BAB RKolA 1004/97: 8, 'Bericht des Bezirksamts Bagamoyo', 14 September 1897.

126 Gann 1987: 1–17.

127 See Articles VII, XVII and LXIV of the Brussels Act, signed 2 July 1890. For a German translation of the Act, see Kaiserliches Gouvernement 1911: 39–66.

128 Note that some material in this section of the chapter has already been published in Deutsch 1999: 109–32. This chapter has greatly profited from the work by Sunseri 1993a: 481–511 and 1993b: 79–137.

129 For the text of the decree, see 'Verordnung, betreffend den Freikauf von Sklaven' by Governor von Soden, 1 September 1891 in *Documents relatifs* 1893: 62ff.

130 RHO Afr Micr R.8/MF 19, Mafia District Book, 'Domestic Slavery in German East Africa' by N. King, Mafia, April 1915: 16.

131 In one case, a certain Mustafa bin Mohammed from Istanbul had redeemed Ferusi bin Uledi from Unyanyembe for Rs80, of which Ferusi bin Uledi paid Rs26 and Mustafa bin Mohammed Rs54. The latter sum was to be worked off by Ferusi bin Uledi. According to the register, Ferusi bin Uledi worked in a bakery owned by Mustafa bin Mohammed. In the first four months, he was entitled to Rs15 per month, of which Rs11 was withheld by Mustafa bin Mohammed. In the fifth month Mustafa bin Mohammed was entitled to the remaining Rs10 of the total Rs54 owed. According to a handwritten note in the register, Ferusi bin Uledi, having worked off his debts within the five-month period, received his certificate of emancipation in December 1893. It should be noted that this was an exceptional case in so far as the slave in question was able to repay his debts quite quickly. BAB RKolA 7410: 338, 'Verzeichnis der im Jahre 1893 im Bezirk Dar es Salaam erteilten Freibriefe', n.d. [1894]. For similar agreements, see BAB RKolA 7410: 373, 'Verzeichnis der im Jahre 1893 im Bezirk Pangani erteilten

Freibriefe', n.d. [1894] and BAB RKolA 7411: 336, 'Verzeichnis der im Jahre 1896 im Bezirk erteilten Freibriefe', n.d. [1897].

132 For some striking examples involving cases of debt bondage, see RHO Afr Micr R.8/MF 19, Mafia District Book, 'Domestic Slavery in German East Africa' by N. King, Mafia, April 1915: 17.

133 *Ibid.*

134 For further detail, see Chapter 7.

135 See BAB RKolA 1004/105: 8, 'Bericht des Bezirksamts Lindi', 14 September 1897 and RHO Afr Micr R.8/MF 19, Mafia District Book, 'Domestic Slavery in German East Africa' by N. King, Mafia, April 1915: 1. For a comparison between Zanzibar and Malindi in this respect, see Cooper 1977: 177ff.

136 According to Sunseri 2002: 35, ransomed slaves sometimes received a *Dienstbuch* (service record) that documented the details of the ransoming contract.

137 BAB RKolA 7382/18: 44ff., 'Eingereicht mit Bericht des Gouverneurs Freiherrn von Schele aus Dar es Salaam', 30 October 1893.

138 See BAB RKolA 1003: 81, '*Runderlass*' by Governor von Soden, 4 September 1891.

139 For a detailed list of the reasons for issuing certificates of emancipation, see BAB RKolA 7382/27: 90, 'Berichte der einzelnen Verwaltungsstellen in Deutsch-Ostafrika über die Sklaverei', Station Tabora, Berichterstatter: Hauptmann Puder, n.d. [1900].

140 The information thus gathered was published annually in *Documents relatifs à la répression de la traite des esclaves publiés en exécution des articles LXXXI et suivants de l'acte général de Bruxelles*, Brussels 1892–1913.

141 BAB RKolA 1004/125: 3, 'Bericht des Bezirksamts Tanga', 10 September 1897. See also BAB RKolA 7382/27: 45, 'Berichte der einzelnen Verwaltungsstellen in Deutsch-Ostafrika über die Sklaverei', Bezirksamt Tanga, Berichterstatter: Bezirksamtssekretär Blank, n.d. [1899].

142 Some district officers seem to have enforced self-ransoming of slaves even before the enactment of the 1901 decree. See BAB RKolA 1004: 94, 'Bericht des Bezirksamts Pangani', 7 September 1897, BAB RKolA 1004/125: 4, 'Bericht des Bezirksamts Tanga', 10 September 1897 and BAB RKolA 7382/27: 69, 'Berichte der einzelnen Verwaltungsstellen in Deutsch-Ostafrika über Sklaverei', Bezirksamt Lindi, Berichterstatter: Bezirksamtmann Zache n.d. [1900]. Other district officers were more cautious in this regard. See, for instance, BAB RKolA 1004/97: 7, 'Bericht des Bezirksamts Bagamoyo', 14 September 1897.

143 See, for instance, the figures in BAB RKolA 1006/201: 11, 'Denkschrift über die Hausssklaverei in Deutsch-Ostafrika' by Governor Schnee, 28 October 1913. For a decidedly different interpretation, see Sunseri 1993b: 491.

144 Leue 1900–1(c): 621. See also BAB RKolA 1004/125: 3, 'Bericht des Bezirksamts Tanga', 10 September 1897.

145 BAB RKolA 1006/201: 11, 'Denkschrift über die Hausssklaverei in Deutsch-Ostafrika' by Governor Schnee, 28 October 1913.

146 For a detailed report on the emancipation of slaves during a 'punitive expedition', see BAB RKolA 1004: 88, 'Bericht des Premier-Lieutnants Engelhardt [Songea]', 2 August 1897.

147 See, for instance, Sunseri's analysis (1993b: 481–511).

148 *Ibid.* For slightly different percentages, see Iliffe 1979: 131.

149 In 1896, for instance, 226 of Abdallah bin Omari's slaves were issued with certificates of emancipation by the district officer von Eberstein. Abdallah bin Omari had been accused of having organised a local resistance movement. BAB RKolA 7412: 53, 'Nachweisungen der in Kilwa im Jahre 1896 erteilten Freibriefe', 31 December 1896.

150 Another reason for a decline in the issuing of *Freibriefe* might be that district officers took notice of a *Runderlass* by Governor von Liebert from 5 March 1899. It informed them that a new slavery decree was in the making (the 1901 decree) and until then nothing should be done to endanger or anticipate its implementation. See BAB RKolA 1004: 184, 'Runderlass' by Governor von Liebert, 5 March 1899. Finally, it should be noted that the number of slaves who received *Freibriefe* because their owners lived outside the territory of German East Africa (Pemba or Zanzibar) declined throughout the 1890s. See Leue 1900–1(c): 612.

151 See BAB RKolA 7382/27: 42–115, 'Berichte der einzelnen Verwaltungsstellen in Deutsch-Ostafrika über die Sklaverei' and 'Anhang zu den Berichten der einzelnen

Verwaltungsstellen in Deutsch-Ostafrika', 1 October 1901.

152 See Table 4.

153 See Chapter 7.

154 BAB RKolA 4997: 497, 'Fragebogen über die Rechte der Eingeborenen in den deutschen Kolonien (Wakitu)', Bezirksamt Kilwa, 23 October 1910.

155 For the various stipulations regarding the manumission of slaves in Islamic law, see Sachau 1897: 125–72. See also Velten 1903: 319 and Middleton 1992: 117. See also Cooper 1977: 227.

156 Again, it should be emphasised that these figures are only estimates, and they may not be very reliable. The direction and magnitude of the trend, however, is probably correct.

157 BAB RKolA 6527/2: 10, 'Denkschrift betreffend Ostafrika 1891/92', n.d. [1892]. Evidence on these flights is scattered throughout BAB RKolA 7410–12, 'Sammlung der zur Mitteilung an das Spezialbüro bestimmten Nachweisungen', October 1892–November 1901. For more detail, see BAB RKolA 7410: 355, 365, 373, BAB RKolA 7411: 45, 95, 111, 204, 298, 359, 515, BAB RKolA 7412: 30, 336.

158 BAB RKolA 7410: 385, von Schele to Foreign Office 31 May 1894.

159 See BAB RKolA 7382/27: 45, 'Berichte der einzelnen Verwaltungsstellen in Deutsch-Ostafrika über die Sklaverei', Bezirksamt Tanga, Berichterstatter: Bezirksamtssekretär Blank, n.d. [1899] and BAB RKolA 7410: 365, 'Verzeichnis der im Jahre 1893 im Bezirk Tanga erteilten Freibriefe', n.d. [1894], BAB RKolA 7411: 95, 'Verzeichnis der im Jahre 1894 im Bezirk Tanga erteilten Freibriefe', n.d. [1895], BAB RKolA 7411: 315, 'Verzeichnis der im Jahre 1895 im Bezirk Tanga erteilten Freibriefe', n.d. [1896] and BAB RKolA 7411: 359, 'Verzeichnis der im Jahre 1896 im Bezirk Tanga erteilten Freibriefe', n.d. [1897]. See also BAB RKolA 7382/27: 53, 'Berichte der einzelnen Verwaltungsstellen in Deutsch-Ostafrika über die Sklaverei', Bezirksamt Pangani, Berichterstatter: Bezirksamtmann Sigl, n.d. [1898]. The reason for the non-registration of fugitive slaves is not entirely clear, but one likely explanation is that as far as the district officers were concerned, the issuing of Brussels Act *Freibriefe* served no direct administrative purpose, since the export of slaves was explicitly forbidden. For a different view, see Karstedt 1912: 107.

160 The records can be found in BAB RKolA 7410–11, 'Sammlung der zur Mitteilung an das Spezialbüro in Brüssel bestimmten Nachweisungen', October 1892–January 1897.

161 This and the following three paragraphs are based on Deutsch 1999: 119–27.

162 BAB RKolA 7411: 27, 'Verzeichnis der im Jahre 1894 im Bezirk Kilwa erteilten Freibriefe', n.d. [1895].

163 BAP RKolA 7411: 258, 'Verzeichnis der im Jahre 1895 im Bezirk Dar es Salaam erteilten Freibriefe', n.d. [1896], no. 448. For another example, see BAB RKolA 7411: 43, 'Verzeichnis der im Jahre 1894 im Bezirk Bagamoyo erteilten Freibriefe', n.d. [1895]. According to the register, Kapitän Spring manumitted his female slave, Schausiku [in ki-Swahili *cha usiku* means '[born] at night'], a twenty-year-old woman who stated that she came from Unyanyembe.

164 BAB RKolA 7410: 385, von Schele to Foreign Office, 31 May 1894. According to Karstedt, many *askari* as well as members of the auxiliary troops owned female slaves whom they had 'acquired' from resisting groups in the conquest period (1890–8). See Karstedt 1912: 111. See also Wright 1993: 117.

165 On the social prestige of the various slave sub-groups, see Chapter 3. See also Glassman 1995: 29–54, 79–114. For some details on the development of plantation agriculture on the southern coast, see Becker 2002: 77–9, 82ff.

166 For a list of the different occupations of emancipated slaves, see, for instance, BAB RKolA 7412: 52, 'Verzeichnis der im Jahre 1896 im Bezirk Kilwa erteilten Freibriefe', n.d. [1897].

167 For more detail, see Chapter 3.

168 *Ibid.*

169 For more detail, see Chapter 3.

170 See, for instance, BAB RKolA 4711: 126, 'Verzeichnis der im Jahre 1894 im Bezirk Lindi erteilten Freibriefe', n.d. [1895]. Evidence on such redemptions is scattered throughout BAB RKolA 7410–12, 'Sammlung der zur Mitteilung an das Spezialbüro bestimmten Nachweisungen', October 1892–November 1901.

171 See, for instance, BAB RKolA 4711: 124, 'Verzeichnis der im Jahre 1894 im Bezirk

Lindi erteilten Freibriefe', n.d. [1895]. On this issue, see also Perras 1999: 265–84. Examples of these redemptions are scattered throughout BAB RKolA 7410–12, 'Sammlung der zur Mitteilung an das Spezialbüro bestimmten Nachweisungen', October 1892–November 1901.

172 Deutsch 1999: 121.

173 See, for instance, Weidner 1915: 16.

174 For a typical example of that view, see *RTA* 1912–14, no. 1395: 2885, 'Denkschrift über die Hausklaverei in Deutsch-Ostafrika' by Governor Schnee, 20 February 1914. The original *Denkschrift* was actually written in 1913. BAB RKolA 1006: 201, 'Denkschrift über die Hausklaverei in Deutsch-Ostafrika' by Governor Schnee, 28 October 1913.

175 BAB RKolA 7412: 53, 'Verzeichnis der im Jahre 1896 im Bezirk Kilwa erteilten Freibriefe', n.d. [1897]. See also BAB RKolA 7382/27: 66, 'Berichte der einzelnen Verwaltungsstellen in Deutsch-Ostafrika über Sklaverei', Bezirksamt Kilwa, Berichterstatter: Bezirksamtmann von Rode n.d. [1900]. Abdallah was the brother of Hassan bin Omari, who led the attack against the German Boma in Kilwa Kivinji in 1894. For more detail, see Becker 2002: 65ff. See also Mann 2002: 87, 211–3.

176 For sales prices, see Leue 1900–1(c): 618. For redemption prices, see RHO Afr Micr R.8/MF 19, Mafia District Book, 'Domestic Slavery in German East Africa' by N. King, Mafia, April 1915: 16, 18, BAB RKolA 1004/97: 4, 'Bericht des Bezirksamts Bagamoyo', 14 September 1897 and Sunseri 1993a: 93 note 40. For a different set of figures, see Karstedt 1912: 109 and BAB RKolA 1006/201: 11, 'Denkschrift über die Hausklaverei in Deutsch-Ostafrika' by Governor Schnee, 28 October 1913. Governor Schnee claimed that redemption prices averaged Rs30 to Rs40, probably with a view to minimising criticism. In this context it is worth noting that in the 1914 Reichstag debates (see Chapter 4) rising redemption prices in German East Africa played a major role. Erzberger, a leading member of the Zentrum party, claimed that between 1890 and 1913 the redemption prices for male slaves in the interior had risen from about Rs30 to Rs75. See *RT* 1912–14, 29 April 1912: 1530 and *RT* 1912–14, 7 March 1914: 7913. However, the source for this information has not yet been discovered and thus its value is difficult to assess. Since Erzberger was particularly well-informed about colonial affairs, it is unlikely that he merely invented these figures. In the debate on 10 March 1914, Noske, a member of the Social Democratic Party stated that redemption prices had risen to over Rs100. See *RT* 1912–14, 10 March 1914: 7985. As in the case of Erzberger, the source for this particular piece of information is unknown. However, his information seems to correspond with the actual sales prices recorded in TNA G38/7, 'Verzeichnis der Sklavenkäufe und Verkäufe, 1911–1914', n.d. [April 1914].

177 Redemption prices were sometimes limited to Rs100. See BAB RKolA 7382/27: 45, 'Berichte der einzelnen Verwaltungsstellen in Deutsch-Ostafrika über die Sklaverei', Bezirksamt Tanga, Berichterstatter: Bezirksamtssekretär Blank, n.d. [1899].

178 Thus these figures have to be taken with some caution. Most of the information regarding slave redemption prices comes from the urban coastal centres of East Africa and the adjacent islands. Little is known about the redemption prices in the vast coastal 'hinterland' or in the East African interior, except that they were on the whole much lower. Second, the composition of these groups drastically changed within age cohorts. There were, for instance, no *suria* in the childhood or old age group and few household slaves in the childhood and early adult group. Third, it appears from the names of the redeemed that comparatively few locally born slaves sought redemption. Finally, and perhaps most importantly, the social composition of the age groups reflected the relative attachment of female slaves to their owner's household. Those with the strongest ties were least likely to seek redemption.

179 Karstedt 1912: 109ff.

180 For this argument, see also Wright 1998: 43.

181 See Alpers 1983: 185–99.

182 Evidence of redemptions of this kind is scattered throughout BAB RKolA 7410–12, 'Sammlung der zur Mitteilung an das Spezialbüro bestimmten Nachweisungen', October 1892–November 1901.

183 BAB RKolA 4712: 10, 'Verzeichnis der im Jahre 1895 in Mikindani (Bezirksnebenstelle) erteilten Freibriefe', n.d. [1896].

184 BAB RKolA 4712: 108, 'Verzeichnis der im Jahre 1896 in Mikindani (Bezirksnebenstelle) erteilten Freibriefe', n.d. [1897].

185 BAB RKolA 7411: 126, 'Verzeichnis der im Jahre 1894 in Lindi erteilten Freibriefe', n.d. [1895]. There was probably a further case in 1898 involving the transfer of 21 slaves to the plantation owned by C. Perrot. See Sunseri 1993a: 101.

186 For the argument that slave ransoming was essential to the development of the colonial economy, see Sunseri 1993a: 81, 91, 97ff., 130, 136ff. and Sunseri 1993b: 482. Sunseri based his assertions almost entirely on evidence from Mafia Island, which is not representative of the whole of German East Africa. Moreover, except for the 1893–6 period, the *Freibrief* records do not reveal the identity of the redeemers.

187 King claims that he saw a German district report according to which there were about 5,500 slaves resident on Mafia Island in 1912. At that time, 'only' 208 ransomed slaves were said to have worked on European plantations. Their number, however, seems to have increased substantially, probably to as much as 700, in the following three years. RHO Afr Micr R.8/MF 19, Mafia District Book, 'Domestic Slavery in German East Africa' by N. King, Mafia, April 1915: 16. For slavery on Mafia Island, see RHO Mss Afr s274, 'Mafia History' by Page, 1924. See also Sunseri 1993a: 104–9, 131ff.

188 For a different view, see Sunseri 1993b: 481–511.

189 See, for instance, BAB RKolA 4712: 108, 'Verzeichnis der im Jahre 1896 in Mikindani (Bezirksnebenstelle) erteilten Freibriefe', n.d. [1897].

190 BAB RKolA 7411: 294, 'Verzeichnis der im Jahre 1895 im Bezirk Lindi erteilten Freibriefe', n.d. [1896].

191 BAB RKolA 7411/22: 124, Bezirksamt Lindi an Gouvernement, 13 February 1895. See also BAB RKolA 7411: 203, Bezirksamt Lindi to Gouvernement, 1 January 1896.

192 This is as best an informed estimate, based upon Kollman 2005: 45ff., note 3. See also references in Chapter 4, note 59, pp. 157ff. In this connection it might be worth noting that there is a peculiar mismatch between the considerable sums of money raised in Europe at the time specifically for the redemption of slaves in East Africa and the comparatively small amount the Catholic missions actually spent for that purpose. Further information on the redemption of slaves by the Catholic missions in East Africa can be found in their annual reports to the Congregazione de Propaganda Fide in Rome. These reports have not been used here in greater detail, because the Catholic missions contributed comparatively little to the decline of slavery in East Africa.

193 For this phrase, see Robertson and Klein 1983: 22.

194 BAB RKolA 7410: 365, 'Verzeichnis der im Jahre 1893 im Bezirk Tanga erteilten Freibriefe', n.d. [1894].

195 Wright 1968: 627.

Seven

Negotiating
Social Marginality

This chapter examines slave initiative during the German colonial period. The author's endeavour is greatly hampered by the lack of sources, as explained in the introduction. Still, it is possible to sketch some basic features of this initiative. The factors generating the decline of slavery in German East Africa are located above all in the multifaceted trans-formation of African societies and economies in the early colonial period. Yet, this transformation was by no means a single event but rather a slow, geographically highly uneven process affecting different groups of people at different points in time. Consequently, the decline of slavery in German East Africa was not a uniform experience. First, the sales records examined in the previous chapter suggest that the life worlds of *some* slaves had changed hardly at all, since they were still being bought and sold, exchanged or bequeathed. The fact that these transfers were conducted in the presence of district officers was probably of secondary importance to the slaves. Owners continued to treat them as their property and, in this respect, they experienced no substantive change.

Second, there were slaves who made a complete break with their past. As will be argued further on in this chapter, there is evidence to suggest that considerable numbers of slaves left their place of residence against their owner's will. The majority of them were probably young men whose emotive attachment to their owner's household was weak or non-existent. Those who achieved freedom through certificates of emancipation should be taken into account here,[1] as they too broke with their past, but not necessarily with their owners.

Finally, there were slaves who neither received a *Freibrief* nor took flight. They did not become free in the sense of breaking ties with their owners or their past, but, at the same time, they did not remain slaves in the sense that they could be freely sold by their owners. There is tentative evidence to show that these 'slaves in transition', the majority of whom were women, managed to renegotiate the character of their dependency and gain greater autonomy and control over their lives. Thus the experiences of slaves differed greatly in the German colonial period. This aspect of the decline of slavery in German East Africa should be kept in mind, although the lack of evidence can easily lead to false generalisations.

Several historical studies, including Iliffe's, have shown with great conviction that, for most East Africans, German colonial rule was an ordeal that brought great suffering and pain to those who were unfortunate enough to experience it.[2] Yet, it is sometimes overlooked that after the conquest some of the socially marginalised groups, such as slaves, encountered a new range of economic and social opportunities, notably a greater freedom of movement, that were previously unavailable to them.[3] It will be shown in the following how some – though certainly not all – slaves were able to use the colonial situation to their advantage. This chapter consist of two parts. The first part explores the role slaves played as wage earners and labourers in the emerging colonial economy,[4] demonstrating how certain groups of slaves were able to make a living independently of their former owners. The analysis will focus on two particular areas, the northern coastal districts and central Tanganyika. The second part looks at the social transformation of slavery under German colonial rule, that is, the subtle and gradual change of the relationship between owners and their slaves during the colonial period.

Colonial Capitalism and Slavery on the Northern Coast[5]

The linkage between European commercial expansion and slavery in East Africa actually predates the formal imposition of German colonial rule in 1890. In the 1880s, slaves had already constituted the main work force of the European companies based in Zanzibar, providing manual labour such as porterage and the loading of ships.[6] Some contemporary observers even believed that these firms were dependent on slave labour for their very existence.[7] Furthermore, most of the travellers who 'explored' the interior of East Africa from the 1860s onwards relied on slave labour as the principal means of transport. Even if they themselves walked – some were actually carried or rode donkeys – European travellers were usually accompanied by tens, sometimes hundreds of slave porters who carried their personal belongings and supplies.[8] These porters were usually rented out either in Zanzibar or in coastal towns such as Bagamoyo and Pangani for the length of the journey. The porters were supplied by labour agents like Sewa Hadji, who is said to have put together most of the European caravans that started out from the northern coast in the 1880s.[9] He received a fee for his services and part of the porters' wages. According to some sources, the majority of porters he rented out to European travellers were actually slaves.[10] It is not known how he managed to have access to such a large amount of slave labour. As a British Indian subject, Sewa Hadji himself was not allowed to own slaves. Presumably he obtained the slaves from his debtors in lieu of repayment, as many of the bigger slave owners were heavily indebted at the time. Renting slaves for fixed periods of time for specific tasks was thus a well-established practice before the first commercial plantation company – the Deutsch-Ostafrikanische Pflanzungs-gesellschaft (DOAPG), a subsidiary of the Deutsch-Ostafrikanische Gesellschaft (DOAG) – established its presence on the northern coast in 1886.[11]

From the very beginning of its activities, the DOAPG had great difficulty in recruiting labour for its various plantation projects in the coastal hinterland (Dunda, Kikogwe, Madimola, Usungula and Lewa). This was partly due to the general scarcity of 'free' wage labour.[12] The local population had little incentive to work for the DOAPG. The northern coastal hinterland had been involved in commercial relations with Zanzibar for almost half a century and there were numerous other opportunities to earn a living or produce the desired commodities for exchange.[13] Moreover, as mentioned in Chapter 3, many people on the coast disliked working in agriculture. It was considered a suitable activity for slaves but not for the free.[14] According to one source, when plantation companies approached village heads in the vicinity with a request for more labour, the latter often refused to comply with the words 'we are not your slaves'.[15]

The difficulties of the DOAPG also arose from the brutal treatment of workers meted out by plantation managers such as Schröder, who was in charge of a tobacco plantation known as Lewa in the Pangani hinterland.[16] He is reported to have greatly enjoyed whipping his labourers.[17] Many of the labourers who had voluntarily agreed to work for the DOAPG ran away after only a short period on the plantation, primarily because of their experience with company officials like Schröder. Most of the African workforce on the DOAPG Lewa plantation in late 1887 consisted of casual labourers who changed almost daily.[18] This greatly affected operations on the plantation, which had little to show for all the money it had spent in East Africa. With a view to further expansion, the company decided to employ slave labour. Since the buying of slaves was ruled out for political reasons,[19] renting slaves from local slave owners for specific periods of time and tasks was seen as a feasible alternative by the German plantation companies, especially since the renting of slaves was an already established pattern on the coast.[20] Thus, in early 1888, 500 slave workers were supplied to the Lewa plantation by the above mentioned Sewa Hadji, the well-known Bagamoyo merchant.[21] Most of these slaves were probably *vibarua* from Bagamoyo, slaves who had earned their living in the town as day labourers, builders, porters and stevedores.[22] Yet these slaves did not work for long on the plantation, either. Treated just as badly as the free labourers previously employed by the company, the slaves fled the plantation soon after their arrival.[23] Initially, slave owners were quite pleased with the commercial arrangements of slave renting to the DOAPG.[24] However, they soon changed their minds when they realised how badly their slaves were being treated on the Lewa plantation. Some even brought their slaves to the German consulate in Zanzibar in order to show the German Consul, Michahelles, the scars left after beatings received at the hands of DOAPG officials.[25]

The DOAPG's expansionist drive in the northern coastal hinterland had already come to an end by September 1888. Its parent company, the DOAG, had attempted to establish its administrative presence in coastal towns, sparking off a violent uprising that engulfed the entire coast.[26] The company's local representatives were forced to retreat hastily to Zanzibar, and the DOAPG's activities on the mainland came to a grinding halt. Lewa in the Pangani hinterland was actually destroyed during the uprising.[27] However, after the coast and its hinterland had been reoccupied by Reichskommissar von Wissmann and his army of Sudanese mercenaries in 1889,[28] the DOAG and its subsidiaries, now joined by other German companies and individual settlers, resumed its operations.

In this connection it might be worth noting that the conquest of the whole of what was to become German East Africa took much longer of course. Resistance to occupation continued until after the turn of the century.[29] But as far as the coast was concerned, colonial administration was soon in full military control, even though effective administrative rule at local level was still somewhat superficial, especially in the southern parts of the coast.[30]

The plantation companies concentrated their activities at first on Tanga, Pangani and Bagamoyo districts. They then moved into Wilhelmstal, a district in the northern hinterland quite far from the coast that encompassed the Usambara mountain range, the western slopes of which proved to be suitable for coffee growing. In the early 1890s, a number of German plantation companies and settlers invested heavily in the area, so that by the late 1890s Wilhelmstal had emerged as the centre of the German north-eastern plantation complex.[31]

However, the reoccupation of the coast by the *Schutztruppe* did not fundamentally change the labour situation on the plantations. Companies still found it difficult to attract sufficient quantities of 'free' wage labour for their operations and returned to utilising slave labour, this time on a massive scale.[32] Thus by 1895, they were employing large numbers of slaves, the majority of whom had been rented out from their African owners.[33] In addition, the companies received slaves from labour agents who were based in coastal towns such as Bagamoyo[34] and soon began to regulate the employment of these slaves officially. For this purpose, they used the same commercial contracts that European travellers had concluded with slave owners and their agents for the supply of servile porters back in the 1880s.[35] Now, in the 1890s, these contracts were regulating the supply of agricultural slaves.

The contracts specified the tasks slaves were expected to perform on the plantations, as well as the length of their service. They also stated the amount of money slaves were to be given for their work and what part of that sum was to be handed over to the owner.[36] In many instances, owners received their share of the slaves' wages several months in advance, a sum which sometimes equalled the market value of the slaves. This was because the companies needed an even greater flow of slaves to the plantations and hoped that the advance would provide an incentive in the right direction. The slaves' owners, on the other hand, required payments of this kind to protect themselves against possible losses, as many slaves did not return to them when their contracts had expired.[37] Owners received an advance on their slaves' wages on condition that they return or replace the slaves in the event that the latter ran away.[38] When this practice became more firmly established on the coast, large-scale slave owners, if in urgent need of cash, would approach the plantations on their own, offering their slaves for rent to whoever paid the highest advance.[39] On a number of occasions, slaves were even rented out with their overseers, an arrangement that, according to one source, was highly favoured by the plantation companies at the time.[40]

By the mid-1890s, the demand for rented slaves on the plantations had already reached such a scale that slave prices in the northern coastal districts increased.[41] Likewise, local wage rates rose.[42] Thus, taking the 1890–1900 period as a whole, the renting of slaves as well as 'free' wage labour employment became more and more attractive, drawing increasing numbers of free and unfree workers to the plantations.[43] According to administrative reports, agricultural slaves in Tanga in 1897 received between Rs4 and Rs5 per month from the plantation companies (plus a substantial daily food allowance called *posho*), while their owners received a similar amount.[44]

Yet the advance system had certain drawbacks, as some companies were to find out to their great financial loss.[45] The slaves they had hired through payment of an advance to the owners fled before their work contracts had actually expired. The slaves had disliked the arduous, brutally regimented work on the plantations as much as anybody else.[46] Attempts at forcing their owners to replace runaway slaves did not always succeed because many claimed that they were insolvent.[47] The district office could offer little help in the matter. As shown in the previous chapter, district officers were often unable to return fugitive slaves to their owners or to the plantations where they had worked. Administrative control of people's movements was not all-embracing, at least not in the early colonial period. If the place of residence of fugitive slaves was unknown, district officers were not in a position to do anything about what many of them considered to be the rightful claims of slave owners or plantation companies. Moreover, as far as the latter were concerned, the return of fugitive slaves or contract workers involved an enormous amount of administrative paper work; according to one source, the plantations simply gave up pursuing the matter through the district offices.[48]

Probably dissatisfied with the risks of the advance system rather than the renting of slaves, the plantation companies also tried to redeem slaves from their owners, especially if the latter had already worked for the company for some time and promised to be a good investment. As already mentioned in Chapter 6, ransoming involved the signing of two separate contracts, one with the slave and one with the owner. The owner was paid a lump sum by the companies for giving up his property rights. However, at the same time, slaves were required to sign a labour contract that specified the length of their employment and the amount of money to be deducted monthly from their wages to pay off the ransom. Thus the ransom payment became a freed slave's personal debt, disguised in the form of a corresponding labour contract. The great advantage of these contracts was that they were sanctioned by the local district officer, who then had to try to enforce their fulfilment. Some companies attempted to redeem slaves against their will, but they soon discovered that this strategy did not pay. Like the slaves who had been rented from their owners without their consent, slaves who had been involuntarily ransomed tended to run away shortly after they had been brought to the plantations.[49] Thus, a pattern emerged during the 1890s that was to remain almost unchanged throughout the rest of the German colonial period. Slaves on European plantations who wanted to be ransomed usually found an employer who was prepared to advance money for the ransom on condition that the slave signed an enforceable labour contract and agreed that the ransom was subsequently to be deducted from his or her wages.[50] It thus appears that slaves could choose to some extent whether to stay with their owners or have themselves ransomed by their European employers.[51] At the turn of the century, the going ransom rate for able-bodied male slaves amounted to about Rs50, although it should be noted that some slaves, especially if they were experienced workers or skilled artisans, were redeemed or ransomed themselves for much higher prices. Still, a slave could expect to work off his debt within a period of about two years.[52]

Alternatively, plantations employed slaves as 'free labourers' irrespective of their servile status.[53] Work contracts with fugitive slaves were similar to those signed by free labourers.[54] Some plantations even employed fugitive slave recruitment agents. They received Rs3 for each slave they brought to the plantation. This sum was subsequently deducted from the slave's wages.[55] Arrangements of this kind suited the plantation companies because whether the slaves shared their wages with their owners, or what proportion of the wage the latter were to receive, were issues of no concern to the companies.[56] As was shown in the previous chapter, it was left to the district officer to sort out the disputes over pay between slaves and their owners. Importantly, it should be noted that while owners sought to obtain their share of the slaves' wages, this does not mean that they actually succeeded in doing so.[57] It depended on the bargaining position of the slaves *vis-à-vis* their owners. There is some evidence to suggest that, throughout the 1890s, the owners' power over their slaves declined significantly.[58]

It is open to debate how widespread slave ransoming by the plantation companies actually was in the 1890s. The certificate of emancipation (*Freibrief*) records show that about 2,000 slaves were ransomed altogether in this period, of whom less than half were redeemed by German plantation companies (see Table 2). Yet the records do not reveal whether slaves were given money by their employers for self-redemption, on the tacit understanding that they would eventually repay their debts, or whether slaves had earned the required sum as 'free' labourers on the plantations. In the registers, cases of this kind would be listed under self-redemption. However, from more descriptive evidence, it is clear that the number of such cases was quite small during this period.[59]

In this connection it is worth noting that, at the turn of century, the total African workforce on German plantations in the northern coastal districts probably did not exceed 5,000 workers at any point in time.[60] This figure might appear small, both in absolute size and compared with the numbers of people who arrived a decade later to work for the plantation companies (about 92,000 in 1912–13).[61] Yet, it should be recognised that these labour force estimates frequently excluded short-term or casual labourers. The figure does not reveal how many people actually worked on German-owned plantations during the entire period from 1890 to 1900.[62] Given that the plantation workforce fluctuated considerably over time, the number of people drawn into the German plantation economy was very likely to have been much higher than the figure quoted above suggests. Moreover, up to about the turn of the century, long-distance labour migration into the northern coastal districts was quite small.[63] The impact of the growth of the plantation sector was thus most keenly felt in the surrounding areas. It appears, therefore, that while the overall impact of the activities of plantation companies on African agricultural production in German East Africa was rather weak for the period between 1890 and 1900, as Iliffe has argued,[64] Africans farming in the vicinity of those owned by German companies were nevertheless greatly affected.

In the early 1890s, African slave owners in the northern coastal districts profited substantially from the supply of slaves to German plantations, whether the latter were rented out, ransomed or 'only' temporarily contracted.[65] It is likely that many of these slaves had been acquired cheaply by their owners[66] in the years immediately preceding the establishment of colonial rule, and that the owners were now 'liquidating their capital assets at the current market rate' as economists would probably phrase it. However, renting out slaves proved to be a dead-end strategy. As already mentioned, slaves who had worked on German plantations frequently did not return to their owners after the expiry of their contract period.[67] Moreover, owners found it increasingly difficult to replenish their slave stocks, as gradual suppression of the commercial long-distance slave trade reduced the local supply of slaves. Thus, when owners actually began to transfer servile labourers from their own estates to the German plantations, the production of the former declined.[68]

Furthermore, African plantations faced strong competition from German companies in the immediate vicinity. This was also the case with government agencies located somewhat further away, such as the construction companies in Tanga that began building the northern railway in 1891 or the government porterage agencies (*Karawanserei*) in Bagamoyo and Dar es Salaam.[69] Finally, African plantation owners lost large numbers of slaves through flight during the 1890s. Taking all these factors together, it is hardly surprising that many African plantations in the northern coastal districts were abandoned by their owners around that time.[70] In 1894, 105 sugar estates in the Pangani valley produced 1,250 tons of crude sugar for export. Some 15 years later, sugar exports from this area had fallen to just over ten tons, as most of the estates had become defunct by the turn of the century.[71]

Slaves who worked for the German plantation companies did not form a permanent wage labour force. After their contracts had expired, they left their employers and became ordinary peasants, thus blurring the line between slaves who had escaped their owners and the free.[72] According to one report, slaves frequently settled near the plantation where they had previously worked, selling food crops to newcomers on the plantation.[73] Like free peasants in the coastal districts, they participated in the ongoing commercialisation of agricultural production in the region on their own terms, engaging primarily in more or less self-sufficient subsistence production while selling their agricultural surplus in local markets if they were in need of cash income. Sometimes these activities were combined with casual wage labour.[74] Like peasants everywhere, they did not wish to be proletarians or too dependent on market production.

Ex-slaves had little difficulty in gaining access to unused land on the coast or in the hinterland.[75] A number of them occupied the recently abandoned African plantations.[76] Some of these slaves were required to work for landowners for an agreed number of days per year, but this was an exception and very different from the kind of exploitation slaves had experienced previously.[77] Moreover, as there was no substantial difference between the free-born and the ex-slaves in this respect – both had to pay rent or fend off the demands of landowners – they became indistinguishable in the area concerned within a comparatively short period of time.[78]

Thus by the turn of the century European-owned plantation companies had three methods of acquiring slave labour. First, they rented slaves for specific tasks for very short periods of time, such as the planting season when the labour demand on the plantations reached its height. When labour was particularly scarce, plantations offered advances to slave owners. However, because of the inherent risks, they did this only as a last resort.[79] Second, they redeemed slaves from their owners, sometimes without actually getting involved in the required administrative process. Some plantation managers were prepared to lend the required sum of money to the slaves they trusted without a formal agreement.[80] The slaves then ransomed themselves from their owners. Third, plantations employed slaves as free labourers, 'if the slaves kept their status secret', as one administrative officer wrote.[81]

According to a number of administrative reports, flight to German-owned plantations was widespread.[82] The evidence is scattered, but it appears that by the late 1880s, the majority of the workers employed on the DOAPG plantations and trading stations were runaway slaves who had been hired as 'free' wage labour.[83] Flight increased further in the 1890s. According to one report, in the period 1888–98 some of the larger slave owners lost more than three-quarters of their slaves through flight, many of whom subsequently sought employment with plantation companies.[84] Consequently, in the 1890s, administrative officers in the northern coastal districts were inundated with requests by slave owners to return slaves who had fled to the plantations.[85]

As far as the plantation companies were concerned, flight was their preferred method of obtaining slaves, because it involved a minimum of paper work and administrative effort. They also avoided having to deal with the complaints or demands of slave owners.[86] Having concluded labour contracts with the slaves, the companies could expect their interests to be protected to some extent by the district officers, which was probably all they cared about. Whether plantation workers were free or unfree was immaterial to them, since this did not affect their balance sheets.[87]

The high incidence of flight to German plantations in the 1890s enabled colonial officials like Leue, the district officer of Dar es Salaam, to claim that as far as the slaves were concerned, slavery constituted a 'voluntary arrangement'.[88] Slave owners, he stated, could do little about slaves seeking employment on the plantations or in the towns.[89] If owners tried to impose their will on their slaves by demanding their share of the wages, for instance, the latter would simply take to flight. As already mentioned, district officers did not return fugitive slaves who worked on German plantations to their 'rightful' owners.

Leue's statement was published in 1901 and should be read as part of the propaganda effort to convince the German Reichstag and the public at large that administrative measures against slavery in the German colonies in Africa were not required, and that nothing should be done about abolition.[90] But still, given the high incidence of flight to the plantations, Leue's claim that slavery was already becoming an almost 'voluntary institution' in the 1890s arguably had a measure of truth in it.

In this connection, it should be remembered that, in the years immediately preceding the establishment of colonial rule, fugitive slaves faced the very real danger of becoming re-enslaved.[91] After 1890, this danger declined and eventually disappeared, as the German colonial government rigorously suppressed the kind of warlordism that had marked Tanganyika's late nineteenth century. When both slaves and the free-born became colonial subjects, they no longer needed to be afraid of kidnappers and slave raiders but rather of tax collectors, the *Schutztruppe* and imperial bureaucrats.[92] As Iliffe has pointed out, '[w]ith their brutal soldiers and police, German officials inspired great terror'.[93] Still, personal security did increase. By 1900, for instance, people in Dar es Salaam were no longer afraid to travel on their own in the coastal districts or in the hinterland, claiming that

> If somebody is walking on his or her own now, nothing terrible happens to that person, man or woman. People are no longer afraid on their way; even small children now go walking alone; they are not afraid; the troubles (insecurity) have come to an end.[94]

This quotation stems from a document composed for Velten, who was a government teacher in Tanga at the time. This fact may have influenced its content. Nevertheless, it is important to recognise that, with the imposition of colonial rule, one of the major obstacles preventing slaves from running away in the late nineteenth century had been removed.

The German plantations were not the only place to which fugitive slaves on the run could turn. The fluid, cosmopolitan coastal towns like Tanga and Dar es Salaam offered plenty of comparatively attractive income opportunities, particularly porterage.[95] Between 1890 and 1912, the wage rate for unskilled labourers in Dar es Salaam, for instance, rose from about Rs6 to Rs12 for 30 days of manual labour.[96] In the 1890s, an unknown number of fugitive slaves moved from the countryside into the growing towns in search of a better life. Those who could not find permanent employment joined the swelling urban informal sector.[97] Significantly, they were predominantly young men, since the very old and the very young, mostly women, remained on the plantations.[98] In the early 1890s, for instance, Dar es Salaam was known as a 'Manyema' town, because many of the people who settled there had originally been brought to the coast by force from Manyema region in the eastern Congo.[99] According to Iliffe, these Manyema settlers were 'freedmen', but it is not clear who freed them and why. It seems possible that these people merely claimed to be free men but were in fact slaves who had fled from their owners. This argument is supported by a report claiming that most slaves rented out by owners in the towns were 'Manyema' and not *wazalia* (locally born slaves).[100] These slaves had been forcefully transferred to German plantations from places like Dar es Salaam, and, when they fled, they stayed on the coast rather than returning to their places of origin. Similarly, missionaries based in Dar es Salaam believed that the town was full of freed slaves who were not born on the coast.[101] It is thus very likely that at least some of the 20,000 inhabitants of Dar es Salaam in 1901 were actually fugitive slaves who claimed that their owners had freed them.[102]

It could legitimately be asked how differently female and male slaves were affected by the growth of the northern plantation complex.[103] As far as the archival records are concerned, this question cannot be settled with certainty. One occasionally comes across the use of the possessive pronoun 'his', for instance in a phrase like 'the slave and his master',[104] but whether this was merely a manner of speaking or a description of reality is not easy to tell. There is some tentative evidence to show that the majority of those who took flight from African plantations were men.[105] It is also well known that plantation companies in the northern coastal districts generally preferred to employ male labourers.[106] However, as mentioned in the previous chapter, the *Freibrief* records show that plantation companies redeemed male and female slaves in almost equal numbers.[107] Moreover, wage rates were often quoted for both men and women, suggesting that plantations actively sought to employ female labourers.[108] It should also be remembered that in the 1880s the majority of agricultural slaves on the coast were women.[109] Finally, it should be recognised that even though it was mostly men who were employed on the plantations, free women and slave women found income opportunities in the vicinity: brewing beer, for instance, marketing foodstuffs or providing sexual services to plantation labourers.[110] According to the historian Wright, the 'divergence between male and female career lines persisted and widened when the commercial economy of the late nineteenth century merged into the colonial economy of the twentieth century'.[111] However, the great difficulty here is to determine how far male and female career lines diverged, and until such time as further local research has been carried out, this problem will remain unresolved.

In conclusion, it can be stated that slavery had already significantly declined in the 1890s in the northern coastal districts. Apart from the growth of colonial towns, one of the main factors that loosened owners' control over their slaves was the emergence of the colonial plantation economy. The latter drew slaves from African plantations, either by renting them from their owners – in which case the slaves did not return to their owners – or employing them after they had fled to the plantations.[112] This process began in the northern coastal district, but as time progressed it probably involved the whole coast.[113] This is not to say that German plantations were attractive places to work. According to many descriptions, quite the contrary was true.[114] Still, it appears that certain marginal groups such as agricultural slaves sought to improve their lives by becoming wage labourers – for a transitory period – before finally settling down as peasants. They were drawn to the plantations rather than forced to work there. It was clearly deemed to be the best choice among limited opportunities, as wage labour provided a path to freedom.[115]

So far, the narrative of the decline of slavery and the flight of slaves has concentrated exclusively on the developments in one particular area of German East Africa, the northern part of the coast. In the remainder of this chapter, the analysis will be extended to other parts of Tanganyika, mainly to Tabora district, which according to colonial sources harboured the largest number of slaves throughout the colonial period, and experienced the greatest impact from its decline. Before examining the evidence with regard to the flight of slaves in this area, it is necessary to briefly review the general development of wage labour employment in German East Africa.

The Growth of Wage Labour Employment

During the 1890s and again after 1904 German plantations experienced severe shortages of labour, a pattern which did not change until the outbreak of the First World War.[116] It resulted from the tremendous growth of the industry itself, especially of the sisal plantations in Tanga district in the late 1900s and early 1910s. The number of people employed on European plantations in German East Africa between 1900 and 1914 is an indication of this expansion. As with so many colonial statistics, these figures are fraught with problems. Plantations rarely reported the number of workers they employed on a casual basis, and some of the settlers were either unable or unwilling to fill out the required statistical returns.[117] Moreover, the number of people employed by the plantations fluctuated heavily during the year. Harvesting, for example, required vast amounts of casual labour.[118] Thus, these figures could be wrong by a considerable margin but they illustrate the general development of the plantation industry.

In 1902 plantation companies in the northern coastal districts employed about 5,000 people.[119] In the following two years, their numbers increased, exceeding 12,000 at the end of 1903.[120] No credible figures exist for the years 1904 and 1905, but it is certain that despite the Maji Maji uprising (1905–7), the plantation sector in the colony expanded to employ some 20,000 people in 1906.[121] Their numbers continued to rise, reaching 32,000 workers in 1908, most of whom (26,000) were employed in the north-eastern districts of the colony.[122] Their numbers almost tripled within the next five years. According to an official estimate, some 92,000 people were employed by German plantation companies in 1913.[123] The railway companies, particularly those involved in the construction of the central line to Lake Tanganyika, also employed masses of people, increasing from 6,000 in 1906 to a peak of about 25,000 in 1910–11.[124] Thereafter, railway employment seems to have dropped to about 20,000. All in all, some 172,000 people, or roughly 20 per cent of the African working population, were believed to be in paid employment in 1913, about 140,000 of whom were working for German and other European employers, mainly private plantation companies, the government, the railways and the missions.[125] In comparison, the number of people employed by Africans in the caravan trade in 1913 was estimated to have amounted to about 15,000.[126]

Again, it should be emphasised that these numbers represent only rough estimates. Nevertheless, given the difficulties German plantation companies experienced in the 1890s in finding sufficient labour for their estates when they operated at a much lower level, it is astounding that large-scale expansion was possible in such a short period of time. As has been shown by various authors, expansion was facilitated by the government response to labour shortages in the plantation industry.[127] The principal means applied by the colonial government were taxation and coercion.

Direct taxation was first introduced by Governor von Liebert in 1897. It consisted of a 'hut tax' (*Hüttensteuer*) of Rs3 per year and had to be paid by both men and women. This sum was exacted only in the rural areas, as taxes on stone buildings in towns were much higher.[128] The explicit purpose of this tax was to induce people to participate to a greater degree in the colonial economy, either by selling their surplus products or by seeking wage labour employment.[129] Contract labourers working on the plantations for more than six months were generally exempted from paying tax. In 1905, Governor von Götzen modified the hut tax system, allowing some districts in the interior to switch over to raising a poll tax (*Kopfsteuer*) of Rs3 per head. He also decreed that district officers should no longer accept tax payments in kind – a measure of grain for instance – but should insist that taxes be paid in cash.[130] Finally, Governor Schnee enacted a decree in 1912 that made the poll tax of Rs3 applicable in all districts of the colony. In 1912, economically 'independent women' were also expected to pay the poll tax, whereas the 1905 reform had largely exempted women from taxation.[131]

Africans who were unable or unwilling to pay the hut or the poll tax were forced to work for the local district office.[132] Instead of a wage, these so-called tax labourers merely received *posho*, a rudimentary food allowance. They had to work as long as it took to earn the required amount of money in that district. Thus the length of their 'employment' varied inversely with the wage rates paid in the district. In economically depressed regions tax work could therefore take months, whereas in the more 'developed' areas, such as the coast, tax labourers worked for shorter periods of time. The importance of the *Steuerarbeit* should not be underestimated, as road construction and maintenance and similar local 'development' projects were realised in many areas with unpaid tax labour.[133] Alternatively, tax defaulters were sent to the plantations, if there were any in the vicinity, to work off their taxes. Again, the labourers merely received a food allowance only. The difference between the allowance and the full wage was paid directly to the district office by the employers in lieu of the tax payment.[134] In the first few years after the introduction of the hut tax, according to Tetzlaff, tax defaulters made up a significant part of the 'free' casual labour force on the plantations.[135] Besides, the system was open to abuse by the plantation managers. However, it should be recognised that the importance of the imposition of taxation for mobilising labour varied greatly. As long as people had to make a living on the margins of the money economy and practise subsistence farming to provide for their needs, the payment of Rs3 hut tax could be a significant burden. Yet, for those who were in paid employment or sold part of their agricultural produce and cattle at local markets, Rs3 could be acquired comparatively easily, and in the case of wage earners in the 1900s may have involved less than ten days' work.[136]

Another strand of the government 'labour for the plantations' policy was more locally focused. From about the turn of the century, various administrative officers had introduced measures designed to force people more directly into wage labour employment, with the tacit approval of the colonial government. This was the infamous Wilhelmstal labour card system, pioneered in the Usambara Mountains in Wilhelmstal district and introduced later on a less rigorous basis in Morogoro, Dar es Salaam, Rufiyi and Lindi districts, as well as on Mafia Island.[137] Male residents of these districts were issued with labour cards for the purpose of registering the number of days on which they had taken up paid employment. Certain people were exempted from having to use these cards, such as the *majumbe* and the *akida*, who were regarded as government employees. But the great majority of the districts' male residents were instructed to work at least 30 days every four months for European employers, which basically meant working as casual labourers on European-owned plantations. If they failed to do so, they were recruited by the district officer to do unpaid work, especially road maintenance, for a similar length of time. One should probably add to this category of forced labour the establishment and maintenance of communal fields (*Kommunalschamben*) in Dar es Salaam, Kilwa, Lindi, Kilosa, Rufiyi and Songea districts. In the early 1900s *majumbe* and *akida* in the coastal districts were instructed by the local district offices to plant a certain acreage of export crops, especially cotton. However, this policy was abandoned after it was singled out as one of the major causes of the Maji Maji uprising.[138] In this connection, it should be noted that the colonial government made use of the lowest level of the administrative structure, the *majumbe*, the chiefs and local big men, to cajole their subjects into looking for work on the plantations.[139] This was a far more subtle approach than the Wilhelmstal labour card system. It is impossible to measure the exact overall effect of this kind of pressure on the chiefs, but as will be shown further down in this chapter, it was sometimes a highly effective policy, particularly in areas where most of the people were actually slaves.

Yet it should be recognised that taxation and forced labour were of limited significance as far as the vast districts in the interior were concerned. Local tax records reveal that, at least up to the late 1900s, district officers often refrained from collecting taxes.[140] This was in conformity with a stipulation in the relevant decrees according to which tax was to be collected only within the peaceful jurisdiction of the district offices (*im friedlichen Machtbereich der Stationen*).[141] District officers were free to decide whether to enforce payment of tax or not. In many districts, the officer in charge decided not to press too hard for payment because he was afraid that more rigorous collection would spark off local resistance. Thus, at least until after the Maji Maji uprising, taxes were only effectively raised in the coastal districts and their immediate hinterland, where civilian rule prevailed. Most of the districts in the interior, however, were still under military rule, which usually prohibited the wholesale introduction of direct taxation.[142] In these districts, tax collection was limited to the immediate vicinity of the district offices, but did not extend beyond the immediate reach of the *boma*, the fortified command post of the *Bezirksamtmann*. In 1905, about half the districts in German East Africa were ruled by military officers.[143] However, over time tax collection increased significantly, especially after 1905 when districts located in the interior became more closely connected to the commercial centres on the coast following the construction of the central railway line between Dar es Salaam and Kigoma on Lake Tanganyika.[144] As far as the labour card system is concerned, there is some evidence that the actual measures introduced under that policy were only fitfully and incompletely applied.[145] The labour card system was meant to be an emergency relief measure and not a permanent system, apart perhaps from the district of Wilhelmstal where the system was first introduced. This does not mean denying that administrative officers forced vast numbers of people to work on plantations, or claiming that these policies did not cause great suffering. It simply seems that neither the card system nor, indeed, forced labour was utilised in the areas in the interior from where so many workers came to work on the coastal plantations. In 1903, for instance, it was believed that over 4,000 Wanyamwezi labourers from central Tanganyika worked on the coast.[146] At that time, administrative presence in the area was largely restricted to the town of Tabora.[147] The district itself came under civilian rule in 1907 and only then did tax collection increase substantially.[148] It thus appears that other factors have to be found to explain why people moved from the interior to search for work on the coast.

Colonial Capitalism and Slavery in Central Tanganyika

In the early 1890s, the plantation companies had already tried to induce Wanyamwezi caravan porters to work on the plantations. Around this time they were still coming in their tens of thousands to the northern coast, particularly to Bagamoyo, which was then the centre of both the colonial administration and European commerce.[149] However, the independent 'workers of African trade' were not keen on becoming dependent wage labourers on the plantations, at least not at this early stage.[150] Consequently, in the mid-1890s the plantation companies sent out special labour recruiters to the interior, especially to Unyamwezi in central Tanganyika, to the southern coast, and even to northern Mozambique.[151] These early attempts at private labour recruitment were not a great success.[152] There was a series of scandals involving false declarations of advances, 'head hunting' by recruiters, deception of labourers and fraud.[153]

The Tanga district officer, Meyer, tried to help. He came up with the idea of a Wanyamwezi settlement scheme, whereby porters and labourers were recruited in the interior and then given plots near Tanga along the northern railway line to Korogwe.[154] In addition, they were to receive a start-up kit consisting of cotton seed and a machete. In return they were expected to work as casual labourers for the companies. According to Koponen, about 4,200 Wanyamwezi took part in the scheme.[155] Many of these were subsequently employed by construction companies involved in the rebuilding and extension of the northern railway line to Moshi and Arusha, but they were not prepared to work on the plantations. The district office thus decided to abandon the scheme.[156] By 1905, the experiment had manifestly failed when about half the Nyamwezi settlers fled across the border to Kenya as a result of conflicts with the district administration.[157]

Despite these inauspicious beginnings, however, more and more labourers came to the coast from Unyamwezi around the turn of the century, some of whom stayed there permanently.[158] They maintained contact with their areas of origin and induced others – neighbours, friends and followers – to migrate to the coast. This is why some plantations employed large numbers of workers from the same area in Unyamwezi.[159] In the 1900s, migrants from Unyamwezi dominated the coastal labour market. According to Iliffe, more than a quarter of Dar es Salaam's 23,000 inhabitants in 1905 were believed to be Wanyamwezi.[160] In this connection it is perhaps worth mentioning that in 1900 a fair share of the African contingent in the German colonial army consisted of Wanyamwezi soldiers – very likely former *ruga-ruga* bands – who found employment in the *Schutztruppe* when the Sudanese troops were replaced.[161]

In the early 1900s labour recruitment became more formalised.[162] It involved the signing of two contracts, one between the labour recruiters and the companies concerning the supply of labour, and one between the companies and the workers in question. The latter was the all-important labour contract, specifying wages, length of contract and the type of work labourers were expected to do. Sometimes these contracts were handed over to the labour recruiter in advance. The name of the prospective plantation worker was then to be filled in by the labour recruiter on the spot.

The contract between recruiters and companies was less standardised, but usually contained the number of labourers the recruiter was to bring to the plantation, the kind of work contract labourers were to sign on for, the advance payment recruiters were to receive for their services and the fee to be paid to the recruiter by the companies for each labourer delivered. The fee usually covered the labourers' transport costs from the interior to the plantation and varied greatly both between companies and over time. According to one source, these fees could be up to Rs60 per labourer delivered to the company, although Rs20 was more common.[163] Because there were so many recruiters – over a thousand in Tabora district alone in 1913[164] – competition among them was ferocious.[165] The competition between companies for contracted labourers was no less fierce. In some instances, workers were auctioned to the highest bidder – that is, to the company offering the largest fee for a labour contract already signed. The system was rife with abuse.[166] Both Governor von Rechenberg (1909) and Governor Schnee (1913) attempted to regulate and formalise labour recruitment by decree, but it is open to question whether their policies were effective.[167] In any case, with the expansion of the industry, especially after 1910, plantation companies experienced severe labour shortages and the old abuses reappeared.[168] However, migration patterns in Unyamwezi had already changed by that time. From about 1907 on, fewer and fewer migrant labourers left Unyamwezi to work on the coast.[169] Instead, Unyamwezi labourers went to work for construction companies that were building the central line between Lake Tanganyika and the coast.[170]

Construction on the central line began in 1905. In the first two years, the companies involved employed mainly migrant labourers, but also war captives (1,500) from the Maji Maji uprising and tax defaulters.[171] The Dar es Salaam to Morogoro section was completed in 1907. From there, it took five years to reach Tabora (1912) and another two years to arrive at

Kigoma on Lake Tanganyika.[172] From about 1908 on, growing numbers of Wanyamwezi labourers began to work on the railway line. In 1913, the construction companies employed over 16,000 people, the majority of whom were believed to have come from Tabora district.[173] The building of the railway line caused a dramatic decline in the caravan trade between Tabora and the coast. In 1912, less than a hundred porters arrived in Bagamoyo from the interior, whereas only ten years earlier tens of thousands had done so each year.[174]

The move of Unyamwezi migrant labourers into paid employment was accompanied by a massive decline in the resident population of some parts of Tabora district.[175] In the 1900s, labourers were often absent for years, especially men. Villages that had teemed with people in the 1890s were almost deserted, as only the aged and women and children remained in the settlements.[176] According to the missionary van der Burgt, who had been working in Unyamwezi since 1892, the population declined by over 50 per cent between 1890 and 1912 in some places.[177] An official report from Tabora claimed that in 1912–13 only ten out of a hundred taxpayers in the district were able-bodied men.[178] The issue raised enormous political interest and criticism, even in the Reichstag.[179]

Some historians are sceptical about this issue, arguing that depopulation statistics provided by contemporary observers[180] do not clarify how many people actually left Unyamwezi altogether and how many merely dispersed into smaller settlements of family units, a common occurrence at the time.[181] They have argued that the depopulation of villages in the late 1900s was primarily a means of avoiding tax payments to the colonial administration or tribute to the chiefs rather than a reaction to labour recruitment. In addition, they have claimed that the statistics provided do not show whether male absenteeism was a permanent or a temporary phenomenon.[182] One could add to this criticism that the depopulation hypothesis does not take the tremendous expansion of Tabora town fully into account, the population of which was estimated to be 30,000 in 1913, exceeding every other town in German East Africa at the time.[183]

However, the involvement of Wanyamwezi labourers in the plantation economy of the northern coastal districts and, subsequently, in the construction of the central railway line cannot be explained adequately by the trickery of labour recruiters, the application of forced labour policies or taxation. Though force was not completely absent, on the whole the colonial administration did not use coercive means – taxation or the labour card system – to induce Wanyamwezi labourers to take up work on the plantations or the railways.[184] Moreover, although labour recruiters often tried to lure people into wage labour employment with all kinds of false promises and material inducements, the actual work contract still had to be signed by the labourers themselves, in the case of railway employment in the presence of district officials. All the available evidence points to the fact that this was done voluntarily in the great majority of cases.[185] The question of what motivated people to seek wage labour employment in such large numbers thus still needs to be answered.[186]

One response to this question is to interpret the movement into wage labour as part of a wider restructuring process that took place in the caravan trade.[187] By 1912, many labourers who had previously worked as porters had to look for alternative means of employment.[188] The wages paid by construction companies were comparatively attractive. An unskilled labourer, for instance, received Rs8 to Rs13 per working month, that is 30 working days of employment.[189] Furthermore, as the railway line approached Unyamwezi, people spent less time travelling to the actual worksite, which in turn induced women to seek employment as day labourers.[190] Finally, it appears that work on the railways was less regimented than work on the plantations, which might also have influenced the decision to look for work with the construction companies.[191] But again, this only explains why people worked on the railways. Migration to the plantations had started much earlier, probably as early as 1895, in a period when porterage was still popular and remunerative. Moreover, the 'reconstruction of the caravan trade hypothesis' assumes a certain amount of continuity between those who worked as porters in the caravans and those who worked on the railway, and this is by no means certain.

Another set of answers revolves around the role of the chiefs in Unyamwezi during this period. The administration let it be known that they greatly favoured chiefs who were able to induce their subjects to seek employment on the plantations or the railways.[192] Further, recruiters were sometimes able to convince chiefs to pressure their subjects into seeking paid work.[193] In some instances, this even involved the signing of formal labour supply contracts between recruiters and some of the chiefs.[194] However, these 'abuses' did not occur on a large scale.[195]

Any analysis which exclusively focuses on external factors to explain the large-scale migration of Unyamwezi labourers to the coast and the railway construction sites fails to take into account the agency of those who were most directly concerned with this process, the labourers themselves.[196] Sunseri has pointed to the fact that labour migration in Unyamwezi was crucially affected by the gender division of labour.[197] The majority of men, he argued, migrated to the coast and elsewhere – sometimes with their wives – while the majority of women stayed in the villages until it was possible for them to combine agricultural production with day-labour employment on the railways. Yet it seems that the historians who examined the evidence concerning labour migration in Unyamwezi, including Sunseri, have overlooked the fact that a sizeable proportion of people living in Unyamwezi in 1900 were slaves and that their number declined sharply in the period under review.[198]

Admittedly, evidence on this issue is exceedingly scarce but it appears that in the early 1890s some chiefs 'sold' their subjects to labour recruiters and travelling traders for a fee, probably in order to recoup the losses sustained during the rinderpest epidemic of 1891.[199] Many labourers did not return to their former places of residence, preferring instead to remain on the coast or to move to Tabora town where income opportunities were more favourable.[200] Fearing the permanent loss of their subjects, which was after all the basis of their power and prestige, some chiefs introduced a new 'custom'. According to the most detailed contemporary document on this issue, these chiefs decreed that their 'serfs' (*Hörige*) were not allowed to leave the villages and hamlets without their explicit permission.[201] This permission could be acquired by the payment of a lump sum – an indemnity or 'ransom' – whereby the prospective migrant was relieved for all time of his or her supposed duty to pay tribute to the chief.[202]

In the previous chapter, it was suggested that the expression 'serf' used in contemporary reports was a phrase that actually meant 'slave'. Thus the document above arguably suggests that in the late 1890s and early 1900s some Nyamwezi chiefs allowed their slaves to travel to the coast, presumably after receiving an inducement from labour recruiters.[203] These agreements were the equivalent of the rent contracts coastal slave owners concluded with the plantation companies. However, having realised that slaves were not returning from the coast, the chiefs raised the fee to approximate the future tribute payments or labour service of the slave – that is, his or her commercial value.[204] This interpretation of the document above might seem far-fetched, but there is further archival evidence which points to widespread buying and selling of slaves in Unyamwezi. In 1900, the Tabora district officer informed the colonial government in Dar es Salaam that 'only the well-to-do owners would sell theirs slaves, as the poorer ones would fear losing their only labourers'.[205] Ten years later, the widely respected district judge, Karstedt, observed that 'hundreds' of slaves were sold in Tabora district each year.[206]

However, the power of the chiefs to sell slaves was limited. The Tabora district officer, Puder, reported in 1898 that 'owners treat their slaves well, for fear that they might run away'.[207] The reason for this development was that labour recruiters paid advances to anyone who wished to work on the coast, irrespective of the status of the person involved.[208] By the turn of the century, flight had become a matter of choice and, consequently, the authority of slave owners and chiefs declined.[209] According to Koponen, this development occurred in the first half of the 1900s. He relates that when the former district officer of Tanga, Meyer, visited Unyamwezi in 1906, he found that 'some 90 per cent of those who had gone to European farms had done so without the order of their chiefs and not seldom against it. The people sent by the chiefs were their slaves in most cases.'[210] Meyer also stated that Nyamwezi workers on the coast generally belonged to the 'lower classes'.[211] Thus, it appears that labour recruitment gave slaves an opportunity to flee from their owners. It also enabled the subjects of the chiefs to escape from their rapacious rulers.[212]

When the railway companies arrived in the area in 1907, the process was already advanced. According to one observer, by that time the chiefs and slave owners were no longer able to extract labour or tribute from their slaves and/or subjects.[213] Moreover, the latter were free to move, and this explains why they were able to set off in such large numbers to the construction sites or leave the concentrated villages for smaller, more autonomous settlements of family units. It also explains why slave ransoming prices in Unyamwezi rose in the late colonial period, since there were fewer slaves to be ransomed.[214] This argument is supported by circumstantial evidence. Seibt, a missionary who worked in Unyamwezi, reported in 1910 that slaves who had once been forced to live in the same village as their owner could now choose their place of residence freely.[215] Löbner, another missionary, observed that by 1910 a significant part of the slave population had been absorbed into the general population.[216]

The available evidence does not allow one to make a distinction between the actions of those who were regarded as slaves and those who were assumed to be free but were subjected to the whims of Unyamwezi chiefs. The sources are also silent about who was actually regarded as a 'chief' – whether these were 'sultans' appointed by the government as administrative agents and tax collectors, village heads who ruled over only a limited number of people, or merely 'commercial' slave owners who had acquired slaves in the 1880s to relieve labour shortages in their extended households.[217] Still, it is reasonable to assume that a significant number, probably even the majority, of the estimated 100,000 to 200,000 Wanyamwezi who left their villages to seek paid work in the emerging colonial economy between 1900 and 1914 were slaves who tried to better their lives through migration.[218] Clearly, new kinds of employment opportunities opened up for both the free and the slaves. However, as constraints on them diminished, the unfree probably responded more quickly than the free to these opportunities, since on the whole they had less to lose.[219]

In any case, the account above suggests that in the early colonial period the slaves and the free began to merge imperceptibly, as both groups applied the same strategies to make use of the wider opportunities offered to them by the imposition of colonial rule and the development of the colonial economy. From a certain point in time it was impossible for many observers – both local and 'foreign' – to tell the two groups apart.[220] The experiences of coastal slaves and those who lived in the interior in central Tanganyika were thus very similar. According to Iliffe, the 'first decade of German rule destroyed the wealth and influence of the slave owners'.[221] On the basis of the evidence from the northern coastal districts and central Tanganyika, it could be argued that while German colonial rule provided the means to destroy the power of the slave owner, namely wage labour employment and a minimum degree of personal security, it was left to the slaves to commit the deed themselves.

Yet, it should be recognised that flight was only one of the strategies slaves used to better their lives under German colonial rule, since many slaves retained strong social ties to their owners. Their relationships, however, also changed irreversibly. In the last section of this chapter some characteristics of this transformation will be outlined.

'The Slave No Longer Fears the *Mwungwana...*'[222]

As much as one would like to have detailed information on the negotiation of dependency and social marginality on the coast or in central Tanganyika, the scarcity of sources does not permit a comprehensive historical reconstruction of this process. Yet there is some scattered evidence that allows insights into how social relationships changed. This evidence largely concerns the fields of conflict between slaves and their owners, and will be reviewed further on in this chapter.

At this point it should be emphasised that the available evidence creates its own problems of interpretation. The sources sometimes suggest a 'heroic' struggle for honour and autonomy, which is arguably not representative of the actions and experiences of slaves.[223] There are indeed several accounts that highlight their 'apathy' and 'ignorance'.[224] Not all of these reports can simply be dismissed as racist diatribes by European officials. As one of the most acute observers remarked, slaves lived in a state of 'habitual subjection'.[225] Another eyewitness argued that the main factor protecting the interests of the slave owners was 'the power of custom and habits'.[226] As was shown in Chapter 3, slavery was deeply ingrained in the fabric of social life, both on the coast and in central Tanganyika. Thus, while many slaves were able and willing to seek a better life through their own initiative in the early colonial period, others clearly were not. After all, when the British took over Tanganyika after the First World War, they found several thousand slaves who could have walked away from their owners with impunity years before.[227] Flight involved taking risks, sacrificing a degree of social security for a greater amount of autonomy, and not all slaves, especially the older ones, were prepared to do that.[228] This feature of the decline of slavery should be kept in mind, even if the available evidence sometimes seems to point in a different direction.

Conflicts between slaves and their owners revolved essentially around the reappropriation of labour, honour and autonomy by slaves. A few examples illustrate this argument. One of the most important fields of conflict involved negotiating the actual amount of work that was due to the owner. Thus, for instance, agricultural slaves argued with their owners about the length of the working day, when they were required to start work in the fields and when they were free to leave, how many days they had to work for their owners during the week and how much time they had for themselves.[229] According to one source, some owners gladly accepted offers to have their slaves ransomed because they were tired of the endless disputes over the amount and the kind of work the latter were required to do.[230]

There were disputes about the amount owners were to receive from their slaves' wages. In 1898, for instance, slave owners in Dar es Salaam and Tanga frequently complained that the slaves they had rented out to European employers were not handing over the customary half of their earnings.[231] Equally contested was the amount of money slave owners demanded as a ransom.[232]

Moreover, there were disagreements between owners and slaves about the latter seeking wage labour employment.[233] Slaves often promised to surrender part of their future earnings, but after a while stopped these payments altogether. According to one source, this is why owners sometimes refused to comply with the request of their slaves to be allowed to take up paid employment.[234] Arguably, for many slaves, wage employment was preferable to working as a slave. The disputes between owners and slaves over the right to seek wage employment were in fact conflicts about the right to work for one's own benefit. This is also reflected in the life histories of slaves. Thus, for instance, Msatulwa Mwachitete, who worked as a trading slave in the 1890s, claimed to have said to her brother when she contemplated leaving her mistress: 'I long to go home. If I cannot do this I will go to the white men and find work, for the white men are not like our masters; they reward their people with clothing.'[235] European observers made similar observations. King, the British officer in charge of Mafia Island during the First World War, stated that

> it would be difficult to find a slave who when offered the alternative of slavery or freedom, would choose slavery nowadays. This I should attribute largely to the growth of European labour employing undertakings. The slave sees that the freeman can work more or less when he wants to.... [The freeman] can keep all his wages, whereas he, the slave, must either work four days every week for his owner for nothing or he must give him half of his wages he may earn.... [236]

As was shown in Chapter 3, slaves rarely received more from their owners than was necessary for bare survival.[237] In contrast, wage labour employment offered tangible rewards.

Pawns constituted a further point of contention since they were afraid that their owners would sell them as debt repayment and thus authenticate and perpetuate their servile status. They claimed that their masters had no right to sell them.[238] Conflict over the status of pawns was particularly pronounced in the southern coastal hinterland.[239] The Lindi district officer reported that he was frequently asked to sort out contradicting claims and counter-claims of ownership between neighbouring villages whose headmen and chiefs based their arguments on events that had sometimes happened several generations back. According to this report, government-appointed *majumbe* usually had the best chance of having their claims vindicated, since they enjoyed the support of the district office.[240]

The secondary literature suggests that in the late nineteenth century there were frequent conflicts between owners and their slaves regarding matters of inheritance, marriage and the status of slave children, as well as struggles for inclusion in the institutions of the community and society at large.[241] However, except for some published anecdotal evidence,[242] German colonial records are virtually silent on these topics. This does not mean that these disputes did not exist, but, unfortunately, the available evidence does not even permit speculation about their prevalence, direction or outcome. It appears that, as long as colonial order was not directly threatened, social conflicts within African societies were by and large of no concern to the German administration, and therefore no records of such conflicts were kept. Much more locally focused research involving sustained examination of oral historical sources is needed to achieve a better understanding of these processes and issues.

However, while there is an absence of more detailed evidence on conflicts between owners and slaves, there can be little doubt about their transformation. Importantly, over time, slave owners gradually lost out in these conflicts.[243] While slave owners in Dar es Salaam and Tanga were supposed to receive half their slaves' earnings by 'law and custom', by the turn of the century they had to be content with getting much less that that, if they received anything at all.[244] At about the same time, slave owners in Lindi and on Mafia Island tried to seize their slaves' property in lieu of these payments, and chiefs in Unyamwezi implored the district office to resolve the matter by government decree.[245] In the long run, however, these strategies failed. The slaves simply ran away if they felt the demands of their owners had become too great a burden.[246] In others words, as opportunities for flight increased, owners' control over their slaves slackened and there was little they could do about it without provoking further flight.[247] In the last decade of German rule, especially in the south-east, groups of slaves seem simply to have left their owners to establish their own independent 'runaway' villages, sometimes not far away from the plantation where they previously had been made to live and work.[248]

This loss of owner authority over slaves is reflected in a number of descriptions regarding changes in attitude and everyday behaviour of slaves on the coast.[249] Several observers noticed that, after colonial conquest, slaves no longer displayed the kind of respect or obedience they had previously shown to their owners.[250] Thus, for instance, slaves gradually appropriated the outward signs of authority and status. They began to wear clothing previously reserved for the 'better' classes. Writing about Dar es Salaam, Leue noted that slave women began to proudly wear the *ukaya* – a kind of headscarf made of blue cotton cloth – which according to him was the sign of free women.[251] Velten, another source, describes how male slaves were no longer afraid to carry an umbrella or wear a turban, or sandals, something which was unheard of previously and regarded as scandalous by his informants, Mtoro bin Mwenyi Bakari, Baraka bin Shomari, Mwenyi Hija bin Shomari and Muhamedi bin Madigani.[252] They also reported that around the turn of the century

> The slave no longer listens to his owner; he considers himself equal to his master. If he is asked to do some work, he must want to do it, and if the master admonishes his work with harsh words, he runs away and complains to the Bezirksamtmann ... saying 'I am not his slave, my brothers and sisters, my parents and their ancestors were stolen by him.' He only says this because he does not like slavery....[253]

In another context, they further explained that:

> Today, only a few remove their caps if a *jumbe* dies. It is no longer necessary. It is the same with manual work; the slaves did it in the old days; today, they do nothing

or only what they want to do. They refuse to do what they don't want to do.[254]

These quotes suggest that owner control over the remaining slaves had already experienced a sharp decline in the early colonial period. Unfortunately, such vivid descriptions are not available for Unyamwezi in central Tanganyika, but a similar development was noted there too.[255]

The decline of owner authority was also expressed in assertions of equality by ex-slaves as they tried to claim new identities for themselves. Both on the coast and in Unyamwezi,[256] ex-slaves who had gained their freedom one way or another claimed to be 'coastal gentlemen' or *waungwana*.[257] In Chapter 3 it was shown that the term was used by members of the coastal elite in self-reference in the late nineteenth century. This was in order to set themselves apart from those at the other end of the social scale, whom they despised as *washenzi* (sing. *mshenzi*) or 'barbarians'.[258] The term *washenzi* covered anyone who did not live on the coast or share its cultural traits, particularly the manner of dress and speech, and perhaps a nominal adherence to Islam. Further, it was applied to people who had only recently arrived on the coast, particularly up-country slaves. Yet, skilled artisans, second-generation slaves and freed slaves sometimes used this term to obscure their own or their parents' *washenzi* origins or to accentuate their claim to more equal participation in coastal society, irrespective of whether their descent, wealth, command of ki-Swahili or knowledge of the *Qur'an* warranted such a claim in the eyes of the coastal elite.[259]

Asserting a prestigious identity while being regarded by others as having no 'honour' was thus already a well-established pattern on the coast and elsewhere when, in the early colonial period, the number of those calling themselves *waungwana* greatly increased.[260] Consequently, the meaning of the term changed, losing much of its sharpness and ostensible precision. Like the use of the self-appellation *mswahili* (pl. *waswahili*), this term was the label most readily available for those who wanted to hide their slave origins and could not lay a convincing claim to other identities.[261] According to one source, the terms *mwungwana* and *mswahili* were used interchangeably in the early 1890s, depending solely on whether the speaker wanted to impress up-country people or reaffirm her or his claims to status within coastal society.[262] Conversely, calling someone *mswahili* became a way of referring to this person's slave descent.[263] In the late nineteenth century, servility had defined social relationships and inter-action on the coast. Importantly, as slavery declined, the former oppositional distinction between the *waungwana* and the *washenzi* became less pronounced, and in certain respects even vanished, between coastal people and those living in the interior as well as between the different social strata within coastal society.[264] Again, the subject needs more research, but it is tempting to speculate on how much the cosmopolitan appearance of coastal society in the latter half of the twentieth century owes to the decline of slavery.[265]

In this context, it should be mentioned that Islam became increasingly accepted in the coastal hinterland during the 1890s and 1910s.[266] It appears that the groups most actively seeking adherents at the time – notably the Qadiriyya brotherhood in Bagamoyo, which was led by a former slave, Sheikh Ramiya – offered lower status groups such as ex-slaves a more significant role in ritual practices than the established Islamic leadership did.[267] Joining Islamic groups was probably an attempt to 'shed the despised status of the *mshenzi* and to be admitted into the *waungwana* caste' as Iliffe has pointed out.[268] The connection between Islamisation and the decline of slavery in Tanganyika is not entirely clear. However, having cast off their servile social status, people searched for ways of improving their role within the community and society at large. One way of doing so was by conversion to new religions, including Islam.

In this chapter, an attempt was made to reconstruct the decline of slavery under German colonial rule. Velten's account of coastal culture gives a glimpse of the slaves' own perception of this process. According to his informants, slaves in Dar es Salaam began in the late 1890s to assert 'that they and the *waungwana* are equal to each other',[269] insisting that 'the slave no longer fears the *mwungwana*'.[270] In many ways, these statements reflect the very moment slavery was finally set to disappear in Tanganyika.

Notes

1 See Chapter 6.
2 Iliffe 1979: 4. See also Lonsdale 1985: 680–766 and Kjekshus 1996: 143–51, 186–90.
3 For this argument, see Willis and Miers 1997: 490. For an example with an emphasis on the totalitarian character of colonial rule, see Koponen 1995.
4 This part of the chapter draws heavily on Iliffe 1979: 123–67.
5 The sub-chapter title *Capitalism and Slavery* refers to the pioneering work by E. Williams on the end of colonial slavery in the Caribbean islands and capitalist expansion in Britain. See Williams 1944.
6 Fischer 1885: 65.
7 Fischer 1885: 74.
8 Fischer 1885: 85. See also Höhnel 1892: 16, 25. For a summary, see Beidelman 1982: 610–16.
9 Leue 1900–1(a): 15.
10 Schweinitz 1894a: 19 and Toeppen 1885–6: 230. For a biography of Sewa Hadji, see Matson 1966: 91–4 and Brown 1971: 185–99.
11 For an excellent summary of the activities of Peters and the DOAG/DOAPG, see Iliffe 1979: 88–91.
12 Baumann 1890: 215.
13 Iliffe 1979: 71.
14 Fischer 1885: 70. See also Pfrank 1919: 6.
15 Pfrank 1919: 27.
16 For more detail on Lewa, see Müller 1959: 243ff.
17 *Ibid.* See also Stollowsky 1911: 515ff. and Glassman 1995: 188ff.
18 Baumann 1890: 215.
19 Peters 1895: 402ff.
20 Stollowsky 1911: 533.
21 Müller 1959: 243. See also Tetzlaff 1970: 31 and Sunseri 2002: 32.
22 Glassman 1995: 189.
23 Müller 1959: 243.
24 Pfrank 1919: 111.
25 Glassman 1995: 189.
26 The origins of this uprising were far more complex. However, it appears that the

uprising itself was not related to slave employment on the DOAPG plantations and thus its history can be disregarded at this point of the narrative. For more detail on the uprising, see the excellent study by Glassman (1995).

27 For more detail, see Müller 1959: 376–91.
28 For a brief account of the conquest of the coast, see Iliffe 1979: 95–8.
29 Iliffe 1979: 98–107, 116–22.
30 See Chapter 6.
31 Iliffe 1979: 126.
32 Pfrank 1919: 25.
33 Schweinitz 1894b: 48.
34 BAB RKolA 1004/125: 8, 'Bericht des Bezirksamts Tanga', 10 September 1897.
35 For an example of this type of agreement, see Fischer 1882: 72.
36 Hofmeister 1895: 27.
37 Pfrank 1919: 112.
38 ZNA G2/59/1: 109, Deutsch Ostafrikanische Gesellschaft to Foreign Office, 16 May 1888.
39 BAB RKolA 7382/27: 51, 'Berichte der einzelnen Verwaltungsstellen in Deutsch-Ostafrika über Sklaverei', Bezirksamt Pangani, Berichterstatter: Bezirksamtmann Sigl n.d. [1899] and BAB RKolA 1004/125: 8, 'Bericht des Bezirksamts Tanga', 10 September 1897.
40 BAB RKolA 1004/125: 8, 'Bericht des Bezirksamts Tanga', 10 September 1897.
41 *Ibid.*
42 BAB RKolA 6475/13: 62–5, 'Denkschrift über die Entwicklung der deutschen Schutzgebiete in Afrika und der Südsee 1901/1902. Anlage VII. Nachweis über die in Deutsch-Ostafrika vorhandenen Plantagen und deren Stand am 1. Januar 1902', n.d. [1902].
43 Iliffe 1979: 157.
44 BAB RKolA 1004/125: 3, 'Bericht des Bezirksamts Tanga', 10 September 1897.
45 ZNA G2/59/1: 109, Deutsch Ostafrikanische Gesellschaft to Foreign Office, 16 May 1888.
46 Krenzler 1888: 39. See also BAB RKolA 7382/27: 51, 'Berichte der einzelnen Verwaltungsstellen in Deutsch-Ostafrika über Sklaverei', Bezirksamt Pangani, Berichterstatter: Bezirksamtmann Sigl n.d. [1899].
47 *Ibid.*
48 *Ibid.*
49 BAB RKolA 7382/27: 45, 'Berichte der einzelnen Verwaltungsstellen in Deutsch-Ostafrika über die Sklaverei', Bezirksamt Tanga, Berichterstatter: Bezirksamtssekretär Blank, n.d. [1899].
50 BAB RKolA 7382/27: 51, 'Berichte der einzelnen Verwaltungsstellen in Deutsch-Ostafrika über Sklaverei', Bezirksamt Pangani, Berichterstatter: Bezirksamtmann Sigl n.d. [1899].
51 For this argument, see also Sunseri 1993(a): 120.
52 BAB RKolA 1004/97: 4, 'Bericht des Bezirksamts Bagamoyo', 14 September 1897.
53 BAB RKolA 1004/125: 8, 'Bericht des Bezirksamts Tanga', 10 September 1897. See also BAB RKolA 7382/27: 44ff., 'Berichte der einzelnen Verwaltungsstellen in Deutsch-Ostafrika über die Sklaverei', Bezirksamt Tanga, Berichterstatter: Bezirksamtssekretär Blank, n.d. [1899].
54 For more details on labour contracts, see Iliffe 1979: 159.
55 BAB RKolA 7382/27: 51, 'Berichte der einzelnen Verwaltungsstellen in Deutsch-Ostafrika über Sklaverei', Bezirksamt Pangani, Berichterstatter: Bezirksamtmann Sigl n.d. [1899]. According to the *Bericht*, the Pangani district officer tried to curb such practices, insisting that contracts should be made with both the owner and the slave, but this policy met with little success. It is worth noting that recruitment was not restricted to the northern coastal districts since some slaves were actually recruited in Lindi district in the south. See BAB RKolA 1004/105: 10, 'Bericht des Bezirksamts Lindi', 14 September 1897. The document gives the impression that the practice was discouraged.
56 BAB RKolA 7382/27: 44ff., 'Berichte der einzelnen Verwaltungsstellen in Deutsch-Ostafrika über die Sklaverei', Bezirksamt Tanga, Berichterstatter: Bezirksamtssekretär Blank, n.d. [1899].
57 This is why owners tried to get an advance on payments of this kind from the plantation

whenever possible.

58 BAB RKolA 7382/27: 51, 'Berichte der einzelnen Verwaltungsstellen in Deutsch-Ostafrika über Sklaverei', Bezirksamt Pangani, Berichterstatter: Bezirksamtmann Sigl n.d. [1899]. See also Iliffe 1979: 126.

59 Leue 1900–1(c): 621.

60 BAB RKolA 6475/13: 62–5, 'Denkschrift über die Entwicklung der deutschen Schutzgebiete in Afrika und der Südsee 1901/1902. Anlage VII. Nachweis über die in Deutsch-Ostafrika vorhandenen Plantagen und deren Stand am 1. Januar 1902', n.d. [1902].

61 *Die deutschen Schutzgebiete in Afrika und der Südsee 1912/13*, 1914: 20 and Pfrank 1919: 31.

62 *Ibid.*

63 *Ibid.*

64 For this phrase, see Iliffe 1979: 123.

65 BAB RKolA 1004/125: 3, 'Bericht des Bezirksamts Tanga', 10 September 1897.

66 See Chapter 3.

67 Pfrank 1919: 112.

68 BAB RKolA 7382/27: 59, 'Berichte der einzelnen Verwaltungsstellen in Deutsch-Ostafrika über Sklaverei', Bezirksamt Bagamoyo, Berichterstatter: Bezirksamtssekretär Sperling n.d. [1898]. See also Pfrank 1919: 112.

69 BAB RKolA 7382/27: 59, 'Berichte der einzelnen Verwaltungsstellen in Deutsch-Ostafrika über Sklaverei', Bezirksamt Bagamoyo, Berichterstatter: Bezirksamtssekretär Sperling n.d. [1898]. See also Tetzlaff 1970: 64. The construction of the northern railway line was not completed until 1905.

70 BAB RKolA 7382/27: 59, 'Berichte der einzelnen Verwaltungsstellen in Deutsch-Ostafrika über Sklaverei', Bezirksamt Bagamoyo, Berichterstatter: Bezirksamtssekretär Sperling n.d. [1898]. See also Pfrank 1919: 112.

71 BAB RKolA 1004/97: 9, 'Bericht des Bezirksamts Bagamoyo', 14 September 1897 and BAB RKolA 7382/27: 51, 'Berichte der einzelnen Verwaltungsstellen in Deutsch-Ostafrika über Sklaverei', Bezirksamt Pangani, Berichterstatter: Bezirksamtmann Sigl n.d. [1899]. See also Tetzlaff 1970: 174. In this connection it is worth noting that German plantations showed no profits until well into the new century. However, they enjoyed the support of both the colonial and imperial governments, and their resources were much greater than those available to African plantation owners. For more detail, see Tetzlaff 1970: 72 and Iliffe 1979: 132.

72 RHO Micr Afr 297 vol. II, Pangani District Book, 'Ethnological and Anthropological Notes', n.d. [1929]. A similar development seems to have occurred in coastal Kenya. See Cooper 1980: 46–61.

73 Pfrank 1919: 6ff.

74 Iliffe 1979: 151ff. A similar process seems to have occurred in the southern part of the coast. See Cooper 1980: 5 and Becker 2002: 130. For a West African perspective, see Lovejoy and Hogendorn 1993: 229–33, 286.

75 Eberstein 1896: 171 and Pfrank 1919: 5. It is noteworthy that, unlike in coastal Kenya and Zanzibar where the British authorities had introduced a variant of British land law, (Cooper 1980: 192), the German authorities vested the ownership of land in the state. For more detail, Sippel 1996a: 3–38.

76 For the occupation of coastal plantations on the Kenyan coast by squatters, see Cooper 1980: 46–61. For a sharply different view, see Morton 1990: 172ff., especially 173 note 18 and Herlehy and Morton 1998: 256. In this respect it might be noted that Cooper's 'slave to squatter' paradigm seems not applicable to German East Africa. This does not mean that squatting by slaves did not happen, but no archival evidence has yet been found that would indicate that this was an important issue.

77 Middleton 1992: 26. For a comparative perspective with regard to coastal Kenya and Zanzibar, see Cooper 1980: 15, 90.

78 Leue 1900–1(c): 621.

79 BAB RKolA 7382/27: 44ff., 'Berichte der einzelnen Verwaltungsstellen in Deutsch-Ostafrika über die Sklaverei', Bezirksamt Tanga, Berichterstatter: Bezirksamtssekretär Blank, n.d. [1899].

80 *Ibid.*

81 *Ibid.* See also BAB RKolA 1004/125: 8, 'Bericht des Bezirksamts Tanga', 10 September 1897 and BAB RKolA 7382/18: 43ff., 'Eingereicht mit Bericht des Gouverneurs

Freiherrn von Schele aus Dar es Salaam', 30 October 1893.

82 Leue 1900–1(c): 621 and Karstedt 1913: 619ff.

83 Krenzler 1888: 39.

84 BAB RKolA 1004/97: 9, 'Bericht des Bezirksamts Bagamoyo', 14 September 1897 and BAB RKolA 1004/125: 8, 'Bericht des Bezirksamts Tanga', 10 September 1897.

85 BAB RKolA 1004/125: 8, 'Bericht des Bezirksamts Tanga', 10 September 1897. Significantly, according to Sunseri (2002: 41), 29 'Arabs' wrote a petition to the Pangani district office in 1895, stating that 'Our slaves don't listen to our orders and won't work for us as in times past, they just do what they want.'

86 *Ibid.*

87 BAB RKolA 1004/125: 8, 'Bericht des Bezirksamts Tanga', 10 September 1897.

88 Leue 1900–1(c): 621. For a similar argument with regard to the situation in coastal Kenya before the abolition of slavery in 1907, see Morton 1990: 203.

89 Leue 1900–1(c): 607.

90 Leue's article appeared at a crucial point in the 1901 debate in the Reichstag. Whether the article had any direct influence on the debate cannot be stated with certainty. In any case, the factual claims made by Leue in the article should be evaluated with great caution.

91 See Chapter 3.

92 For this argument, see Charisius 1907: 460. See also Seibt 1910, cited in Gottberg 1971: 177 and Abrahams 1967b: 12–15.

93 Iliffe 1979: 189.

94 The original text reads 'mtu ajapokwenda sasa nija pekeyake hana dara akiwa mwanamume ao wanawake hana dara; hatta hapana oga ijapokuwa mtoto mdogo nijani huenenda pekeyake sasa; hapana khofu kama ya kwanza, matata ya kwanza yamekwisha sasa.' ['Wenn jetzt jemand seines Weges alleine geht, dem wiederfährt nichts Böses, sei es Mann oder Frau; man kennt keine Furcht mehr unterwegs; selbst wenn es ein kleines Kind ist, geht es jetzt allein; es hat keine Angst mehr wie früher; die Unannehmlichkeiten (Unsicherheit) von früher sind jetzt zu Ende.'] [Translation by the author from Velten's German version of the text]. See Velten 1898: 77.

95 Thus, for instance, servants in European employment (of which there were many in the coastal towns) received wages of Rs12 to Rs15 per calendar month. See RHO Mss Afr s1175, 'Tanganyika Diary 1905–1943' by C. Gillman, entry '21 October 1905'. See also Tetzlaff 1970: 267 and Iliffe 1979: 157. For the number of domestic workers in European employment in 1912, see *Die deutschen Schutzgebiete in Afrika und der Südsee 1912/13*, 1914: 20. According to that report, 5,336 'Europeans' employed about 9,000 (!) 'servants'. It should also be remembered that, until the railway was built, an estimated 100,000 porters left the coast for the interior every year, many of whom were very likely to be runaway slaves. For more details on transport labour, see Sunseri (2002: 56). For more detail on the growth of Dar es Salaam and Tanga, see Tetzlaff 1970: 267. A similar development seems to have happened in coastal Kenya. See Cooper 1980: 46–61, Romero 1986: 504ff. and Morton 1990: 170–3.

96 Iliffe 1979: 157.

97 In this connection it might be noted that this pattern was well established before the advent of colonial rule.

98 Leue 1900–1(c): 607. See also Raum 1965: 186.

99 Iliffe 1979: 385. In this connection it might be mentioned that in the 1930s British officials believed that a substantial portion of the population of Tabora consisted of Manyema ex-slaves. See Unomah 1972: 113.

100 BAB RKolA 1003: 103, 'Bericht des Bezirksamts Dar es Salaam', 14 October 1897. See also RHO Afr Micr R.8/MF 19, Mafia District Book, 'Domestic Slavery in German East Africa' by N. King, Mafia, April 1915: 7.

101 Berliner Missionsarchiv, Berliner Missions-Gesellschaft, IV 2.1.1 (Dar es Salaam), vol. I: 129, 'Visitationsbericht Axenfeld', 16 June 1912. I owe this reference to Frank Raimbault who is currently preparing a thesis on the history of Dar es Salaam in the colonial period. For a similar view, see Raum 1965: 186.

102 For these figures, see Koponen 1995: 621. See also *Die deutschen Schutzgebiete in Afrika und der Südsee 1912/13*, 1914: 9.

103 See, for instance, the summary in Roberts and Miers 1988: 38–40. See also Robertson and Klein 1997 [1983]: 17.

104 See, for instance, BAB RKolA 7382/27: 66, 'Berichte der einzelnen Verwaltungsstellen in Deutsch-Ostafrika über Sklaverei', Bezirksamt Kilwa, Berichterstatter: Bezirksamtmann von Rode n.d. [1900].

105 BAB RKolA 7382/27: 44ff, 'Berichte der einzelnen Verwaltungsstellen in Deutsch-Ostafrika über die Sklaverei', Bezirksamt Tanga, Berichterstatter: Bezirksamtssekretär Blank, n.d. [1899]. See also Leue 1900–1(c): 607.

106 Stollowsky 1911: 515.

107 BAB RKolA 4712: 10, 'Verzeichnis der im Jahre 1895 in Mikindani (Bezirksnebenstelle) erteilten Freibriefe', n.d. [1896].

108 BAB RKolA 7382/27: 59, 'Berichte der einzelnen Verwaltungsstellen in Deutsch-Ostafrika über Sklaverei', Bezirksamt Bagamoyo, Berichterstatter: Bezirksamtssekretär Sperling n.d. [1898].

109 See Chapter 3. See also Deutsch 1999: 121.

110 Velten 1903: 308. See also Tetzlaff 1970: 258.

111 Wright 1993: 2.

112 For a similar conclusion, see Cooper 1977: 209, note 248.

113 There is almost no evidence on what actually happened in the northern coastal districts (or for that matter in the southern districts) after the turn of the century, as the relevant district records were destroyed by the colonial government during the First World War. One has to rely here on reports by British administrative officers, especially RHO Afr Micr R.8/MF 19, Mafia District Book, 'Domestic Slavery in German East Africa' by N. King, Mafia, April 1915: 7.

114 See, for instance, Iliffe 1979: 159 and Koponen 1995: 359–66.

115 A great deal more research is required here, but it is tempting to speculate that the emergence of semi-independent subsistence farming in some areas in north-eastern Tanganyika was a much more recent phenomenon than hitherto assumed, since many parents of these peasants were slaves who had managed to 'break their chains' not long before. For this argument, see also Sunseri 1993(a): 119ff. The phrase 'breaking the chains' refers to an important collection of articles on the end of slavery and emancipation, edited by Martin Klein (1993).

116 Pfrank 1919: 25.

117 See *Die deutschen Schutzgebiete in Afrika und der Südsee 1912/13*, 1914: 20.

118 Tetzlaff 1970: 194.

119 BAB RKolA 6475/13: 62–5, 'Denkschrift über die Entwicklung der deutschen Schutzgebiete in Afrika und der Südsee 1901/1902. Anlage VII. Nachweis über die in Deutsch-Ostafrika vorhandenen Plantagen und deren Stand am 1. Januar 1902', n.d. [1902]. For different figures, see Koponen 1995: 609.

120 BAB RKolA 6286: 156: Reichskolonialamt to Kolonialwirtschaftliches Komittee, 12 March 1910.

121 Iliffe 1979: 156.

122 *Die deutschen Schutzgebiete in Afrika und der Südsee 1912/13*, 1914: 20.

123 *Ibid.*

124 Koponen 1995: 609. See also Tetzlaff 1970: 194 and Iliffe 1979: 156f. It is noteworthy, that this number barely exceeded the number of slaves believed to be still resident in the colony at the time (165,000).

125 Iliffe 1979: 157. Most of the African labourers resided in the northern and central parts of the colony. According to Becker (2002: 128) in 1911–12 European plantation owners in the south employed only some 5,300 workers. For some details on the plantation companies involved, see Aas 1989: 101–5 and Sunseri 2002.

126 *Die deutschen Schutzgebiete in Afrika und der Südsee 1912/13*, 1914: 20 and Pfrank 1919: 31.

127 See, for instance, Koponen 1995, Sunseri 2002.

128 For a brief treatment of the tax legislation, see Tetzlaff 1970: 50ff., 209–11. According to Gillman, in 1905 Rs3 bought 1 lb of tobacco or 30 candles. See RHO Mss Afr s1175, 'Tanganyika Diary 1905–1943' by C. Gillman, entry '21 October 1905'.

129 Stollowsky 1911: 516. See also Iliffe 1979: 135.

130 Koponen 1995: 383. See also Tetzlaff 1970: 209.

131 Koponen 1995: 387.

132 *Ibid.*

133 For a detailed description, see Iliffe 1979: 134. See also Arnold 1994: 217–22.

134 *Ibid.*

135 Tetzlaff 1970: 51.
136 Sunseri 2002: 67. On the theme of regional economic differentiation, see Iliffe 1971.
137 For more detail, see Pfrank 1919: 144. See also Iliffe 1979: 153ff., Koponen 1995: 400–4 and Sippel 1996b: 326.
138 For more detail, see Tetzlaff 1970: 212.
139 For examples, see Koponen 1995: 404–10.
140 See the lists in Bald 1970: 55–7 and Koponen 1995: 386, 390.
141 Koponen 1995: 388.
142 See Tetzlaff 1970: 50.
143 Tetzlaff 1970: 40, note 13.
144 Tetzlaff 1970: 88.
145 Koponen 1995: 398.
146 Iliffe 1979: 160ff.
147 'Jahresbericht der Station Tabora 1900/1901' by Gansser, 20 June 1901, cited in Dauber 1991: 255. See also Fonck 1901, cited in Gottberg 1971: 385.
148 Koponen 1995: 386. Slaves in Tabora district were exempted from paying taxes as long as they worked for their owners. See Blohm 1931 vol. I: 73.
149 For the development of the caravan trade in the German period, see Iliffe 1979: 129. For some detailed figures for the year 1899 and 1890, see 'Jahresbericht der Station Tabora 1900/1901' by Gansser, 20 June 1901, cited in Dauber 1991: 255, Leue 1900–1(a): 31 and *Die deutschen Schutzgebiete in Afrika und der Südsee 1912/13*, 1914: 48.
150 Pfrank 1919: 25ff. The phrase 'workers of African trade' refers to the title of the ground-breaking volume on porterage in West Africa by Coquery-Vidrovitch and Lovejoy (1985).
151 Iliffe 1979: 160. See also Pfrank 1919: 11.
152 Pfrank 1919: 112.
153 Pfrank 1919: 25ff. See also Nolan 1977: 217. For a more general analysis, see 2002: 138–42.
154 BAB RKolA 6475/13: 66–9, 'Denkschrift über die Entwicklung der deutschen Schutzgebiete in Afrika und der Südsee 1901/1902. Anlage VIII. Bericht des Bezirksamts Tanga über die Bestrebungen des Kommunalverbandes Tanga auf Ansiedlung farbiger Arbeiter', n.d. [1902]. See also Sunseri 2002: 60.
155 Koponen 1995: 354.
156 BAB RKolA 6532/2: 15, 23 'Denkschrift über die Entwicklung der deutschen Schutzgebiete in Afrika und der Südsee 1901/1902', n.d. [1902].
157 Koponen 1995: 254.
158 The following paragraphs are largely based on Pfrank 1919: 113ff., Iliffe 1979: 151–63 and Koponen 1995: 348–53.
159 Charisius 1907: 461.
160 Iliffe 1979: 161.
161 Leue 1905: 135. See also Mann 2002: 222, 227ff. The wages received by African privates in the *Schutztruppe* were quite attractive, reaching Rs21 per month in 1900. However, it should be noted that the numerical strength of all African soldiers employed by the *Schutztruppe* never exceeded 2,500, only some of whom were Wanyamwezi. For more detail, see Mann 2002: 238 note 108, 257.
162 Sunseri 1998: 564. In this connection it should be noted that colonial subjects in German East Africa were not restricted in their freedom of movement. In effect, people could leave their villages and migrate to any place they wished. According to Sunseri (2002: 148) this was one of the fundamental principles underlying the government's labour policy. This was remarkably different from the policies pursued by the British authorities in neighbouring Kenya and Zanzibar. For further detail on Kenya and Zanzibar, see Cooper 1980: 2, 86, 111–21.
163 *Die deutschen Schutzgebiete in Afrika und der Südsee 1912/13*, 1914: 22. See also Tetzlaff 1970: 244.
164 Iliffe 1979: 160. For different figures, see Nolan 1977: 135.
165 For more detail on actual recruitment practices, see Sunseri 1998: 564.
166 *Ibid.*
167 Tetzlaff 1970: 260. See also Sippel 1996b: 322–4.
168 Pfrank 1919: 113–7. See also Tetzlaff 1970: 237–40
169 Iliffe 1979: 159. Some, however, seemed to have moved further afield. Cooper reports

that from about 1905 increasing if unknown numbers of Wanyamwezi labourers ('weeders') were employed on the Zanzibar clove plantations. They came 'without official recruitment – thanks no doubt to a Nyamwezi network that officials knew nothing about'. See Cooper 1980: 106. Their numbers increased further after the First World War.

170 According to Sunseri (2002: 168), after 1895 some 15,000 Nyamwezi labourers migrated to British East Africa to work on the Uganda railway line. It is tempting to speculate to what extent their migration set a precedent for the later migration movement to the Tanga and Central railway line.

171 Tetzlaff 1970: 88

172 For more detailed information on the construction of the central railway, see Tetzlaff 1970: 81–100, Iliffe 1979: 135–8 and Koponen 1995: 297–314.

173 *Die deutschen Schutzgebiete in Afrika und der Südsee 1912/13*, 1914: 60.

174 Iliffe 1979: 137. Sunseri (2002: 56) states that in 1907 an estimated 100,000 porters left the coast for the interior, which would have made transport the greatest employer at the time. For an even higher estimate ('20,000 … every month'), see Beidelman 1982: 613.

175 Seibt 1910, cited in Gottberg 1971: 176. On the aspect of labour migration in Unyamwezi, see also the illuminating report by Bishop F. Gerboin (White Fathers) in the Archivio Storico, Congregazione per L'Evangelizzione dei Popoli [Propaganda Fide], NS vol. 238: 396, 'Rapport Vicariat Apostolique L'Ounyanyembe', 2 August 1905. He also mentions in passing that slavery in the area was in rapid decline. There is an abundance of secondary literature on migrant labour in Africa. For a comprehensive introduction, see Stichter 1985.

176 *Ibid.*

177 Van der Burgt 1913: 706. See also BAB RKolA 278: 97–9, 'Abschrift: Bericht über eine Reise von Tabora nach Dar es Salaam', n.d. [1905?]. The author stated that many of the former Unyamwezi *ruga-ruga* 'warriors' had now become peasants. Others had moved away to work on plantations in the Usambara region or were employed by the railway construction companies, so that the villages in the region had now become almost empty. He estimated that 95 out of 100 able-bodied men had gone away to work on the coast.

178 This report was cited by Noske, a member of the Social Democratic Party in a Reichstag debate in 1913. See *RT* 1912–14, 7 March 1913: 4349.

179 *RT* 1912–14, 7 March 1913: 4344–50.

180 See van der Burgt 1913: 705–28 and van der Burgt 1914: 24–7. See also Löbner 1914: 267–70. For a detailed description of the dispersal of villages in Unyamwezi, see Nolan 1977: 136–40.

181 Iliffe 1979: 165, Koponen 1995: 641 and Sunseri 1998: 569. For a different view, see Tetzlaff 1970: 252.

182 Sunseri 1998: 570.

183 *Die deutschen Schutzgebiete in Afrika und der Südsee 1912/13*, 1914: 9. On the history of Tabora town, see Becher 1997, 42–71.

184 Koponen 1995: 352.

185 Sunseri 1998: 563. See also Koponen 1995: 352.

186 Sunseri 1998: 565.

187 Iliffe 1979: 137.

188 *Ibid.*

189 *Die deutschen Schutzgebiete in Afrika und der Südsee 1912/13*, 1914: 21.

190 This and the following three paragraphs draw heavily on Sunseri 1998: 558–83.

191 Sunseri 1998: 562.

192 For more detail, see Pfrank 1919: 148 and Sunseri 1998: 563.

193 Pfrank 1919: 113.

194 Sunseri 1998: 563.

195 *Ibid.*

196 For this argument, see Sunseri 1998: 574. On the issue of agency, see Ranger 1969.

197 Sunseri 1998: 576. See also Sunseri 2002: 165–78.

198 Sunseri 1998: 573. See also Sunseri 2002: 169. It is curious that Koponen and Iliffe cite the relevant archival files concerning slavery in Unyamwezi. However, both dismiss these files as irrelevant. See Iliffe 1979: 131 and Koponen 1994: 332.

199 Nolan 1977: 148, 170.

200 Charisius 1907: 459.
201 RKolA 1007: 65, 'Aufzeichnung des Bezirksamtmann Löhr', 31 May 1916. Löhr, who had spent many years in the interior of East Africa, particularly Langenburg and Mahenge, wrote: 'Etwas anderes als [das] Sklavenverhältnis an der Küste ist das Sklaven- oder Hörigenverhältnis zu beurteilen, das im Inneren besteht und zumeist lediglich aus den Hoheitsrechten der Stammeshäuptlinge fließt. Zu diesen Hoheitsrechten gehören hauptsächlich Ansprüche auf Arbeitsleistung bestimmter Art, wie die Feldbestellung, Lieferung von Lebensmitteln usw. Diese Hoheitsrechte bröckelten immer mehr dadurch ab, daß viele Arbeiter freiwillig oder angeworben zur Küste zur Arbeit auf den europäischen Pflanzungen gingen. Damit sahen sich die Stammeshäuptlinge in steigendem Maße ihres Reichtums und ihrer Macht, die hauptsächlich in der Arbeitsleistung ihrer Untertanen lagen, beraubt. Sie legten deshalb großen Wert darauf, daß ihre Stammesangehörigen nicht ohne ihre ausdrückliche Genehmigung auf Pflanzungsarbeit gingen oder verlangten, wenn sie diese auf Jahre ausdehnten, eine Art Ablösung der bestehenden Untertanenpflichten. Infolgedessen ist es auch in diesen Fällen in einzelnen Teilen üblich geworden, daß derartige Hörige, um sich ihren Verpflichtungen dauernd zu entziehen nach den für die Sklaverei geltenden gesetzlichen Bestimmungen ihren Häuptlingen eine einmalige Abfindungssumme zahlen'.
This kind of stylised German is exceedingly difficult to render into English, but as an approximation the text could be translated as: 'The servile relationship in the interior – based often merely on customary rights of the chiefs – has to be seen in a different light to the slave relationships on the coast. These customary rights mostly consisted of laying claim to certain kinds of agricultural labour, such as cultivating the fields, supplying foodstuff, etcetera. When the labourers went away – voluntary or recruited – to work on European plantations on the coast, these rights increasingly fell apart. Because of this development, the chiefs saw themselves increasingly deprived of their power and their wealth, which had mainly rested on the labour of their subjects. Therefore, they insisted that the members of their tribes should not set off for work on the plantations without their explicit permission and demanded from them, if they planned to stay away for an extended period of time, a kind of reimbursement for their customary dues as chiefly subjects. In certain parts of the country, it thus became customary for chiefly subjects – in line with the legal principles applied in slave cases – to pay their chiefs an indemnity in order to get rid of their customary dues once and forever.'
202 *Ibid.* For a similar description, see Nolan 1977: 148.
203 Sunseri 1998: 563. Sunseri suggests that some chiefs 'coerced' their subjects into labour migration, leading to popular resistance against chiefly authority and local rebellion as the workload of those who stayed behind steadily increased. For this argument, Sunseri 2002: 173.
204 For a similar view, see Nolan 1977: 222.
205 BAB RKolA 7382/27: 89, 'Berichte der einzelnen Verwaltungsstellen in Deutsch-Ostafrika über die Sklaverei', Station Tabora, Berichterstatter: Hauptmann Puder, n.d. [1900] [translation by the author].
206 Karstedt 1913: 619ff. See also *RT* 1912–14, 7 March 1914: 7906.
207 BAB RKolA 7382/27: 89, 'Berichte der einzelnen Verwaltungsstellen in Deutsch-Ostafrika über die Sklaverei', Station Tabora, Berichterstatter: Hauptmann Puder, n.d. [1900] [translation by the author].
208 Charisius 1907: 459. The cash advances, sometimes amounting to as much as Rs20, were subsequently recovered from the plantation companies or deducted from the labourers' future earnings. According to Nolan, cloth was also used to induce labourers to sign contracts. See Nolan 1977: 135.
209 RKolA 1007: 65, 'Aufzeichnung des Bezirksamtmann Löhr', 31 May 1916.
210 Koponen 1995: 352. I am quoting here from Koponen, as I was unable to locate the relevant file in the National Archives in Dar es Salaam.
211 *Ibid.*
212 For a similar view, see Nolan 1977: 154.
213 Seibt 1910, cited in Gottberg 1971: 206
214 Nolan 1977: 267. According to Nolan, ransoming prices increased from Rs7 just after the turn of the century to Rs20 in 1907, and climbed to as much as Rs40 just before the outbreak of the First World War.

215 Seibt 1910, cited in Gottberg 1971: 187.
216 Löbner 1910, cited in Gottberg 1971: 129.
217 Abrahams 1967: 45ff.
218 For these estimates, see Tetzlaff 1970: 252, 287.
219 For this argument, see Wright 1993: 42.
220 Nolan 1977: 154.
221 Iliffe 1979: 131.
222 Velten 1898: 76. For the original text, see below.
223 For a somewhat different view, see Glassman 1995: 8–12.
224 See, for instance, RHO Afr Micr R.8/MF 19, Mafia District Book, 'Domestic Slavery in German East Africa' by N. King, Mafia, April 1915: 10.
225 *Ibid.* The form of this subjection varied between localities. The most detailed description with regard to the Kenya coast can be found in Romero Curtin 1983 and Romero 1986.
226 Leue 1900–1(c): 623.
227 See PRO CO 691/45: 414, Governor Byatt to Secretary of State for the Colonies, 19 July 1921.
228 Moravian Archives Herrnhut, 'Nachlass T. Bachmann' vol. II: 11.
229 RHO Afr Micr R.8/MF 19, Mafia District Book, 'Domestic Slavery in German East Africa' by N. King, Mafia, April 1915: 11, 16.
230 RHO Afr Micr R.8/MF 19, Mafia District Book, 'Domestic Slavery in German East Africa' by N. King, Mafia, April 1915: 7.
231 BAB RKolA 1003: 103, 'Bericht des Bezirksamts Dar es Salaam', 14 October 1897 and BAB RKolA 7382/27: 43, 'Berichte der einzelnen Verwaltungsstellen in Deutsch-Ostafrika über die Sklaverei', Bezirksamt Tanga, Berichterstatter: Bezirksamtssekretär Blank, n.d. [1899]. See also Leue 1900–1(c): 607.
232 BAB RKolA 1004/125: 3, 'Bericht des Bezirksamts Tanga', 10 September 1897.
233 BAB RKolA 1004/97: 9, 'Bericht des Bezirksamts Bagamoyo', 14 September 1897.
234 *Ibid.*
235 See Msatulwa Mwachitete's life story in Wright 1993: 70.
236 RHO Afr Micr R.8/MF 19, Mafia District Book, 'Domestic Slavery in German East Africa' by N. King, Mafia, April 1915: 7ff.
237 BAB RKolA 7382/27: 67, 'Berichte der einzelnen Verwaltungsstellen in Deutsch-Ostafrika über die Sklaverei', Bezirksamt Kilwa, Berichterstatter: Bezirksamtmann von Rode n.d. [1900]
238 BAB RKolA 1004/97: 9, 'Bericht des Bezirksamts Bagamoyo', 14 September 1897.
239 BAB RKolA 1004/105: 8, 'Bericht des Bezirksamts Lindi', 14 September 1897.
240 *Ibid.*
241 See, for instance, Roberts and Miers 1988: 30, Wright 1993: 42ff., Glassman 1995: 267, Miers and Klein 1999: 8.
242 Leue 1900–1(c): 606–8, 617–25 and Eberstein 1896: 170–83.
243 See, for instance, BAB RKolA 7382/27: 89, 'Berichte der einzelnen Verwaltungsstellen in Deutsch-Ostafrika über die Sklaverei', Station Tabora, Berichterstatter: Hauptmann Puder, n.d. [1900] and BAB RKolA 1004/105: 8, 'Bericht des Bezirksamts Lindi', 14 September 1897. See also Leue 1900–1(c): 607 and Karstedt 1913: 617.
244 BAB RKolA 1003: 103, 'Bericht des Bezirksamts Dar es Salaam', 14 October 1897 and BAB RKolA 7382/27: 43, 'Berichte der einzelnen Verwaltungsstellen in Deutsch-Ostafrika über die Sklaverei', Bezirksamt Tanga, Berichterstatter: Bezirksamtssekretär Blank, n.d. [1899]. See also Leue 1900–1(c): 607.
245 BAB RKolA 1004/105: 12, 'Bericht des Bezirksamts Lindi', 14 September 1897 and Charisius 1907: 459. See also RHO Afr Micr R.8/MF 19, Mafia District Book, 'Domestic Slavery in German East Africa' by N. King, Mafia, April 1915: 13.
246 BAB RKolA 1003: 103, 'Bericht des Bezirksamts Dar es Salaam', 14 October 1897; BAB RKolA 7382/27: 43, 'Berichte der einzelnen Verwaltungsstellen in Deutsch-Ostafrika über die Sklaverei', Bezirksamt Tanga, Berichterstatter: Bezirksamtssekretär Blank, n.d. [1899] and BAB RKolA 1004/105: 12, 'Bericht des Bezirksamts Lindi', 14 September 1897. See also Leue 1900–1(c): 607 and Karstedt [1912]: 102.
247 For a similar argument with regard to coastal Kenya, see Willis and Miers 1997: 490.
248 Becker 2002: 130. See also Mann 2002: 87. The archival sources do not show how these ex-slave communities achieved a measure of integration into local society. Perhaps

oral historical research will reveal to what extent they suffered from social discrimination in the post-emancipation period. For the integration of ex-slave communities on the Kenya coast, see Cooper 1980: 5, Romero Curtin 1986: 498, Herlehy and Morton 1988: 254–81, and Morton 1990: 170–203.

249 See, for instance, RHO Afr Micr R.8/MF 19, Mafia District Book, 'Domestic Slavery in German East Africa' by N. King, Mafia, April 1915: 14. Unfortunately, evidence of a similar kind is not available for Unyamwezi.

250 RHO Afr Micr R.8/MF 19, Mafia District Book, 'Domestic Slavery in German East Africa' by N. King, Mafia, April 1915: 14.

251 Leue 1900–1(c): 608. On this issue, see also Fair 1998: 63–94.

252 Velten 1898: 75.

253 The original text reads 'mtumwa hamsikilizi bana wake. hujiona sasa sawasawa yeye na bana wake. kutumika sharti apende mwenyewe, na akipata maneno juu ya bana wake mabaya kwa sababu ya kazi – hutoroka akenda kwa bana mkubwa shauri ... ao atanena "mimi si mtumwa wake, na ndugu zanga na baba zangu na asili yake tume kwibwa" naye anasema hivi hwa sababu hapendi utumwa' [translation by the author from Velten's German version of the text]. See Velten 1898: 75.

254 Velten 1903: 314 [translation by the author].

255 Seibt 1910, cited in Gottberg 1971: 206. See also RKolA 1007: 65, 'Aufzeichnung des Bezirksamtmann Löhr', 31 May 1916.

256 Arens 1975: 428.

257 See Meyer 1894: 84–8, von Götzen 1895: 207, Leue 1900–1(c): 608, 624, Charisius 1907: 460.

258 Pouwels 1987: 72. See also Chapter 2.

259 For more detail, see Glassman 1991: 296ff., Glassman 1995: 4ff. and Rockel 1997: 48.

260 Meyer 1894: 84, Leue 1905: 120. See also Arens 1975: 429ff.

261 Meyer 1894: 85. See also Deutsch 1994: 215–24.

262 Meyer 1894: 52. See also Glassman 1988: 97ff.

263 Glassman 1988: 172.

264 BAB RKolA 1004/105: 2, 12, 'Bericht des Bezirksamts Lindi', 14 September 1897. See also Meyer 1894: 84 and Leue 1900–1(c): 608. For the connection between patterns of social interaction and modes of identification, see Parkin 1989: 162. See also Glassman 1991: 296.

265 On the 'elusive', cosmopolitan character of later-twentieth-century coastal culture, see Arens 1975: 426, 428.

266 Iliffe 1979: 211, 368ff. For a similar development on the Kenya coast, see Morton 1990: 184.

267 For more detail, see Nimtz 1980: 120ff.

268 Iliffe 1979: 214. See also Axenfeld 1912: 39, Reusch 1930: 273ff., Raum 1965: 166–8 and Cooper 1977: 239.

269 The complete original text reads 'wao wananena hali ya waungwana na watumwa sawasawa; na bana zao wamenyamaza, hawawezi kusema neno kwa sababu wanaogopa fitina kwa bana mkubwa' ['they say that slaves and the *waungwana* are equal to each other; their masters are silent, they cannot say anything because they are afraid of false complaints [intriguing by slaves] that could be brought to the district officer'] [translation from Velten's German version of the text by the author]. See Velten 1898: 75ff.

270 The complete original text reads 'walla mtumwa hamwogopi mungwana ... atakwenda Benderessalaama kwa bana mkubwa, kwa sababu hapendi sasa mambo ya kazi ya watumwa' [the slave no longer fears the *mungwana* ... he goes to Dar es Salaam to the district officer because he no longer likes working as a slave] [translation by the author from Velten's German version of the text]. See Velten 1898: 76. Both this quotation and the one above from Velten's text refer to the colonial government as an institution that protects the interests of slaves. The role of the administration has already been discussed in detail in Chapter 6.

Conclusion
Slavery under German Rule in East Africa

The history of slavery in Tanganyika since about 1800 was influenced decisively by the incorporation of East Africa into the world economy and the imposition of German colonial rule. However, this is not a history of European knights in shining armour eradicating the evils of slavery in East Africa, as claimed at the time by both government and missionaries alike. Far from it! On the contrary, it was shown that the decline of slavery in Tanganyika came about as a result of the prolonged struggle between owners and slaves, in which slaves tried to make the best of the limited choices and opportunities available to them.

In order to situate the transformative processes that occurred in the colonial period, the first chapters outlined the development of slavery in East Africa in the nineteenth century, focusing on the two particularly well-documented areas of Unyamwezi and the coast. Part I showed that the increase of slave populations in Tanganyika was caused by the expansion of commerce and agricultural production. In Unyamwezi this process was related to a growth in the caravan trade, which provided the wealth to import large numbers of slaves into the area as well as the need to do so. The coast experienced a similar rise in local slave populations. Here, the increase was mainly due to the development of clove plantations on the islands of Zanzibar and Pemba, which necessitated the import of foodstuffs from the mainland. These were produced by small-scale farmers and a growing number of plantation slaves, particularly in areas located in the northern parts of the coast.

Commercial and agricultural expansion was made possible by considerable social and economic dislocation and violence in the areas adjacent to the growth nodes of nineteenth-century economic development. The majority of the people who worked as slaves on Unyamwezi food farms and coastal plantations had come to these regions involuntarily. They were kidnapped close to their home villages, were sold by relatives to passing traders, or became victims of local wars and famines.

Yet, both in Unyamwezi and on the coast, slavery was not merely a mode of production based on violence and coercion. It was also a social system in which slaves, for lack of alternatives, often became subaltern members of their host societies over time. The means of integration varied. On the coast and in Unyamwezi they encompassed a broad range of patronage and kinship relationships, which, because they were flexible and open to interpretation and negotiation, were able to accommodate the vast increase in the number of people brought into these societies by force. In both areas the majority of slaves were women. There are indications of a change in the terms of incorporation during the second half of the nineteenth century, although the kinship and patronage terminology to express it remained basically the same.

In Unyamwezi, the opportunities and choices for most slaves, particularly for women and children, were practically limited to becoming full members of the owners' household, which at times was in itself a precarious position. As second-rate affiliates, they were the first to be sold in a period of crisis such as famine, exchanged for favours with neighbours, or handed over to passing traders for a few pieces of cloth. To be free in Unyamwezi meant to be kin and thus possess a measure of protection against possible sale.

Some male slaves were able to rise in status and acquire a measure of wealth and honour, but the great majority of slaves in Unyamwezi lived in relative poverty and shame at the margins of society. Most of the fruits of their labour belonged to the owners, and they were usually denied the means of independent social reproduction. The control exercised by owners over slaves was strengthened a great deal by the fact that it was difficult to escape to freedom. There were few havens to which slaves could safely turn. The 1860s, 1870s and 1880s were times of incredible danger and insecurity in central Tanganyika, when people could easily fall prey to warlords, kidnappers or slave traders.

In the late nineteenth century, the social situation of slaves on the coast was similar in some respects to that in Unyamwezi. Slaves had little opportunity to flee, and thus slave owners exercised a large measure of control over their lives, including possession of their children. However, there were also marked differences. On the coast, the relationship between slaves and their owners was predominantly but not exclusively expressed in the language of patronage and clientelism. Slavery was defined here by what the local Muslim elite believed to be the proper hierarchical divisions concerning descent, gender, occupation, manners and religious beliefs, most of which were strongly influenced by the teachings of Islam. Even if slaves doubted the validity of these claims, there was little they could do about it.

In the second half of the nineteenth century, older notions of reciprocity between slaves and owners came under increasing pressure when growing numbers of slaves were forced to work as manual labourers on food crop plantations, or sold as chattel slaves to Zanzibar and Pemba. Yet, despite these pressures, slaves were able to defend what they perceived to be their rights as clients, which included a negotiable measure of personal autonomy. Becoming free on the coast meant becoming a more respected member of the community and acquiring the means of independent social reproduction. This they achieved as peasants, whereby part of the product of their labour was to be shared with their owner, or as town dwellers whose relationship to their owner was reduced to surrendering part of their earnings.

Slavery was held together on the coast and in Unyamwezi by flexible kinship and patronage relationships rather than by mere brute force or sustained coercion. Since severing the relationship to their owners by flight was not a viable option for most of the slaves, their quest for greater personal security and autonomy was realised within established forms and norms of social interaction. The other side of this bargain was the acceptance by slaves of their social marginality within society.

Part II and III then examined the history of slavery in Tanganyika in the German colonial period, disentangling the complex relationship between imperial politics in Germany, administrative practice in German East Africa, the development of the colonial economy and the initiatives of slaves. The political debate in the Reichstag was shown to be of an entirely different character to the administrative discussions held in the Kolonialrat. The arguments concerning German anti-abolition policy need not be restated in great detail here, except perhaps to highlight that the German colonial administration thought that abolition would undermine the authority and prosperity of the local slave-owning elites, whose effective collaboration was believed to be indispensable to the functioning of colonial rule in German East Africa. This, for obvious political reasons, they were not prepared to admit to the public, to the opposition in the Reichstag or to the other colonial powers in Africa. Ostensibly committed to the anti-slavery cause, the government thus allowed one of the cruellest features of slavery – the buying and selling of men, women and children – to persist under official supervision.

Rather than outlawing slavery, the colonial authorities embarked on a policy of obfuscation and legal subterfuge that left core issues deliberately undecided, such as whether district officers were officially required to return fugitive slaves to their 'rightful' owners. The consequence was that 'nobody knew what the score [was]' as it was put at the time, because administrative practices varied greatly between the districts and over time.[1] The colonial government gradually suppressed wholesale slave raiding and commercial slave trading in the areas under its control, particularly the kind of warlordism that had previously guaranteed owners a steady supply of cheap captives. It thus became increasingly difficult for owners to replace the numbers of slaves lost through flight or natural death. However, direct government intervention was limited in effect and, as far as the relationship between slaves and their owners was concerned, of only secondary importance.

The development of the colonial economy in German East Africa was of far greater significance in this respect, because it strengthened the bargaining position of slaves *vis-à-vis* their owners. By forcing open roads and markets,[2] the colonial administration – largely unintentionally – removed major obstacles that previously had kept slaves in their place. Consequently, flight became a viable alternative to negotiating slavery within kinship or patronage relationships. Significant numbers of slaves, especially younger men, took up paid work with European employers without their owners' consent, particularly after the turn of the century when wage employment increased tremendously. Moreover, German plantation companies ransomed a number of slaves against their owners' will. Yet, these ex-slaves did not form a permanent wage labour force. Like free labourers, they only stayed on the plantations or the railways for a time, acquiring the social and economic means to survive and establish themselves as peasants, artisans or urban workers, the latter exploiting opportunities offered by the informal sector in the growing urban economies. Occasionally, wage labour created new forms of dependency that were even more exploitative and brutal than slavery. However, it was a temporary phenomenon, a calculated risk which slaves – both men and women – took, because it ultimately offered them the long-term prospect of finding a niche in the local economy. Thus slaves did not avoid wage labour if by that means they could become ex-slaves.

At the same time, the position of slaves who decided to remain with their owners changed significantly, too. The majority of them were probably women. Over time, they renegotiated their terms of service. Flight was a very real threat to owner control, so that if they wanted to retain their servile labourers, 'wives', followers and retainers, owners had to offer their slaves a better bargain. Integrating slaves more fully into kinship and patronage relationships was one means to prevent them from running away. Thus, slaves became more fully acknowledged kin or clients, which at least to some extent explains how it was possible for large numbers of slaves to be absorbed relatively smoothly into the general free population. It is likely that many slaves decided to stay where they were once they realised slavery was on its way out.[3] It was shown in this study that the decline of slavery in German East Africa was a quiet social revolution, a multifaceted struggle that comprised both highly disruptive moments of wholesale flight and, depending on the possibility of escape and individual circumstances, more subtle changes in servile relationships.[4]

The German case is relevant for the analysis of the end of slavery elsewhere in Africa, since in German East Africa it was not *because* but *in spite of* government policy that vast numbers of slaves gained greater control over their lives and means of social reproduction. In the early colonial period flight movements occurred all over Africa, notably in West Africa.[5] But in all these cases the colonial state had, at least officially, withdrawn its active support from the institution. Instead, the British and French authorities tried to control the movement of people and their freedom to work for themselves through vagrancy laws, the use of Islamic courts, restrictions on access to land by ex-slaves, and master and servant ordinances. Where it could rely on strong locally grounded institutions, such as Islamic courts and powerful chiefs, this policy was sometimes highly effective.[6] Here, the German East Africa case offers a different perspective. Slavery was legally recognised and maintained by the German colonial state, but, because of the political weakness of its local system of governance – ruling through largely illegitimate employees such as the aforementioned *Akiden*, *Sultane* and *Jumben* – to effect this policy, the results were, to say the least, mixed. The sources do not reveal how many slaves remained with their owners because of government policy in German East Africa, but in all probability they were a tiny minority. This, perhaps more than anything else, highlights the crucial role played by the slaves in the process of emancipation. By resisting colonial policy and its local institutions, they freed themselves from their owners and thus brought slavery to its final conclusion.

Notes

1 Leue 1900–1(c): 608 (translation by the author).
2 I owe this phrase to Lonsdale 1985: 736.
3 Until more locally focused research is undertaken, this issue has to remain unresolved.
4 For a similar perspective, see Roberts and Miers 1988: 30.
5 See, for instance, Roberts and Klein 1980: 375–94, Lovejoy and Hogendorn 1993: 31–63, and Klein 1998: 159–77.
6 See, for instance Lovejoy and Hogendorn 1993.

Appendix

Decree by Chancellor von Bülow concerning Domestic Slavery in German East Africa, 29 November 1901 (English version)

... An official Decree, which has been published, contains the following regulations on the subject of domestic slavery in German East Africa:

1. Neither by sale of the man's self, nor by sale effected by relations, nor as payment for debt of fulfilment of other obligations nor as punishment for adultery shall a relationship of slavery be henceforward established.

2. Every domestic slave is empowered to terminate his state of slavery by payment of a sum of money for his redemption. The amount of this sum shall be decided by the competent administrative authorities. Every slave who has paid the ransom appointed shall receive a certificate of emancipation from the authorities.

3. Every domestic slave must be permitted to work for himself during two days of the week, or to use for his own purposes the corresponding proceeds of his labour. In so far as existing custom is in this respect more favourable to the slave, it shall continue in force. In this matter, as well as in all other differences between masters and slaves, the decision shall lie with the competent authorities.

4. The master of a domestic slave is under the obligation to maintain him and provide for him in old age and in sickness. This obligation is not cancelled by emancipation granted during the period of old age or sickness.

5. The transfer of the rights of ownership can be accomplished only with the consent of the slave and before the competent authorities, upon whose assent it shall be dependent. Before according such assent the authorities shall, besides deciding other points which may appear important, carefully test the legality of the ownership, and shall take heed that members of the same family be not separated from one another without their consent.

6. The rights of ownership shall be forfeited in the event of the owners committing any grave breach of his duty towards his slave. The competent authorities shall officially inquire into cases of violation of duty which come to their knowledge, and are in such cases entitled to effect the liberation of the slave by issuing a certificate of emancipation, and in such cases the former owner shall not have any claim to compensation.

7. Offences against the provisions of this edict shall be punished by a fine not exceeding 500 r. [sic], or by imprisonment for a period not exceeding three months, except in those cases where a heavier penalty is incurred by virtue of other law....

Source: Extract from No. 2760 Annual Series, Diplomatic and Consular Reports, Germany. 'Report for the Year Ending 30 June 1901 on the German Colonies', Cd. 786–94, May 1902: 8ff.
Note: This translation is not entirely correct, since the German term *Haussklave* is gender neutral, whereas in this translation slaves are addressed only as men.

Appendix

Verordnung des Reichskanzlers, betreffend die Haussklaverei in Deutsch-Ostafrika. Vom 29. November 1901 (original version)

Um die Abschaffung der Haussklaverei in Deutsch-Ostafrika vorzubereiten, wird für das gesamte Schutzgebiet auf Grund des § 15 des Schutzgebietsgesetzes (Reichs-Gesetzbl. 1900 S. 813) folgendes bestimmt:

§ 1. Durch Selbstverkauf, durch Verkauf seitens der Verwandten, durch Schulden oder sonstige Verpflichtungen sowie als Strafe für Ehebruch kann das Sklavereiverhältnis nicht neu begründet werden.

§ 2. Jeder Hausklave ist befugt, die Beendigung des Sklavereiverhältnisses durch Zahlung eine Ablösesumme herbeizuführen. Die Höhe der Ablösesumme wird von der zuständigen Verwaltungsbehörde festgesetzt. Jedem Hausklaven, welcher die festgesetzte Ablösesumme gezahlt hat, ist von der Verwaltungsbehörde ein Freibrief auszustellen.

§ 3. Jedem Hausklaven muß gestattet werden, an zwei Tagen der Woche für sich selbst zu arbeiten oder den entsprechenden Betrag seiner Arbeit für sich zu verwenden. Soweit das bisherige Gewohnheitsrecht in dieser Beziehung noch günstiger für den Hausklaven war, bleibt dasselbe in Kraft. Hierüber, sowie über sonstige Streitigkeiten zwischen Herrn und Hausklaven entscheidet die zuständige Verwaltungsbehörde.

§ 4. Der Herr eines Hausklaven ist verpflichtet, denselben auch im Alter und bei Krankheit zu unterhalten und zu pflegen. Die nach dem Eintritt von Altersschwäche oder Krankheit erfolgende Freilassung eines Hausklaven hebt diese Verpflichtung nicht auf.

§ 5. Die Übertragung des Herrenrechts darf nur mit Zustimmung des Hausklaven vor der zuständigen Verwaltungsbehörde erfolgen und ist von deren Genehmigung abhängig. Vor Erteilung der Genehmigung hat die Behörde außer sonstigen ihr wichtig erscheinenden Punkten die Rechtmäßigkeit des Sklavereiverhältnisses zu prüfen und darauf zu achten, daß Familienmitglieder ohne ihre Zustimmung nicht voneinander getrennt werden.

§ 6. Das Herrenrecht wird verwirkt, wenn der Herr seine Pflicht gegen den Hausklaven schwer verletzt. Die zuständige Verwaltungsbehörde hat Fälle von Pflichtverletzung dieser Art, die zu ihrer Kenntnis gelangen, von Amts wegen zu untersuchen und ist gegebenenfalls befugt, die Freilassung des betreffenden Hausklaven durch Ausstellung eines Freibriefes herbeizuführen, ohne daß dem bisherigen Herrn ein Anspruch auf Entschädigung zusteht.

§ 7. Zuwiderhandlungen gegen die Vorschriften dieser Verordnung werden mit Geldstrafe bis zu 500 Rupie oder Freiheitsstrafe bis zu drei Monaten bestraft, soweit nicht durch sonstige Strafgesetze eine höhere Bestrafung verwirkt ist.

§ 8. Diese Verordnung tritt mit dem Tage ihrer Verkündigung in Kraft.

Der Reichskanzler   GRAF VON BÜLOW

Source: Kaiserliches Gouvernement von Deutsch-Ostafrika, *Die Landes-Gesetzgebung des Deutsch-Ostafrikanischen Schutzgebiets*, Tanga/Daressalam 1911: 331–2. For a slightly different version, see *Die Deutsche Kolonialgesetzgebung*, vol. 6, Berlin 1903, 426–7.

Bibliography

Archival Sources

Archiv der Brüder-Unität, Herrnhut [Moravian Archives Herrnhut]
    Theodor Bachmann Papers, Annual Reports Kilimani-Urambo
Archiv der Erzabtei St. Ottilien, St. Ottilien
    Journals and Periodicals, Annual Reports (Peramiho)
Archives Générales du P. P. des St. Esprit, Paris
    Journals and Periodicals
Archivio Storico, Congregazione per L'Evangelizzione dei Popoli [Propaganda Fide]
Auswärtiges Amt (Politisches Archiv), Berlin
    Afrika Generalia
Berliner Missionsarchiv, Berlin [abbreviated as BMA]
    Journals and Periodicals, Annual Reports (Dar es Salaam)
Bundesarchiv Abteilungen Berlin, Reichskolonialamt [abbreviated as BAB RKolA]
    Reichskolonialamt (various files)
Bundesarchiv Abteilungen Koblenz
    Wilhelm Solf Papers, Bernhard Dernburg Papers
Cambridge University Library, Cambridge
    Royal Commonwealth Society Archives, John Gray Papers
Dar es Salaam University Library
    Hans Cory Papers, Periodicals
Geheimes Preußisches Staatsarchiv, Berlin
    Heinrich Schnee Papers
Hamburger Staatsarchiv, Hamburg
    Wm. O'Swald Company Papers
Public Record Office, London [abbreviated as PRO]
    Tanganyika Official Correspondence (1916–29)
Rhodes House Library, Oxford [abbreviated as RHO]
    British District and Provincial Records, Gillmann Papers, Gunzert Papers
    Anti-Slavery Society Papers, Periodicals
School of Oriental and African Studies Library, London
    London Missionary Society Archives
Staats- und Universitätsbibliothek Hamburg
    Paul Kayser Papers
Tanzania National Archives [abbreviated as TNA]
    German Records, British Secretariat Records, District Books
University of Birmingham Library, Birmingham
    Church Missionary Society Archives
Zanzibar National Archives [abbreviated as ZNA]
    German Consular Records

Newspapers and Periodicals

Afrika
Afrika-Bote. Nachrichten aus den Missionen der Weissen Väter in Deutsch-Ostafrika
Anti-Slavery Reporter
Beiträge zur Kolonialpolitik und Kolonialwirtschaft
Central Africa. A Monthly Record of the Work of the Universities' Mission
Chronique Trimestrielle de la Sociète des Missionaires d'Afrique
Church Missionary Intelligencer
Deutsch-Ostafrikanische Zeitung
Deutsche Kolonialzeitung
Deutsches Kolonialblatt
Die Deutsche Kolonialgesetzgebung. Sammlung der auf die deutschen Schutzgebiete
    bezüglichen Gesetze, Verordnungen, Erlasse und internationale Vereinbarungen.
Die Deutschen Kolonien
Documents relatifs à la répression de la traite des esclaves publiés en exécution des articles
    LXXXI et suivants de l'acte général de Bruxelles
Gott will es. Katholische Zeitschrift für die Anti-Sklaverei-Bewegung
Koloniale Rundschau
Koloniales Jahrbuch
Missions Catholiques
Missionsberichte der Gesellschaft zur Beförderung der evangelischen Missionen unter den
    Heiden
Missionsblätter. Illustrierte Zeitschrift für das katholische Volk. Organ der St. Benediktus-
    Genossenschaft zu St. Ottilien
Missionsblatt der (Herrnhuter) Brüdergemeine
Mitteilungen des Seminars für orientalische Sprachen
Mitteilungen von Forschungsreisenden aus den Deutschen Schutzgebieten
Nachrichten aus der ostafrikanischen Mission
Stenographische Berichte über die Verhandlungen des Reichtages [abbreviated as *RT*]
Stenographische Berichte des Reichstages: Anlagen [abbreviated as *RTA*]
Verhandlungen der Deutschen Kolonialkongresse 1902, 1905, 1910
Zeitschrift für Kolonialpolitik, Kolonialrecht und Kolonialwirtschaft

Annual Reports

Jahresbericht über die Entwickelung der deutschen Schutzgebiete in Afrika und der Südsee
    [1893/94–1907/08]
Denkschrift über die Entwickelung der.Schutzgebiete in Afrika und der Südsee
    [1908/09]
Die deutschen Schutzgebiete in Afrika und der Südsee. Amtliche Jahresberichte
    [1909/10–1912/13]

Primary Sources

Acker, P., 'Über einige Mittel zur allmählichen Abschaffung der Sklaverei', *Verhandlungen der
    Deutschen Kolonialkongresse*, 1902, 452–9.
Adams, A. M., *Lindi und sein Hinterland*, Berlin, n.d. [1903].
Ankermann, B., 'Ostafrika', in E. Schulz-Ewerth and L. Adam, *Das Eingeborenenrecht. Sitten und
    Gewohnheitsrechte der Eingeborenen der ehemaligen deutschen Schutzgebiete in Afrika und Übersee*,
    Stuttgart 1929, 1–380.
Anonymous, 'Lavigerie', *Deutsche Kolonialzeitung*, 1 (1888), 266–8, 275–6.
Anonymous, 'Der Sklavenhandel in Afrika', *Hamburgische Börsenhalle*, 17 December 1888, 2.
Anonymous, *Sklavenhandel in Afrika*, by 'Humanus', Münster 1888.
Anonymous, *Wider die Sklaverei*, Bericht über die Verhandlungen der Vollversammlung in

Gürzenich zu Köln am 27. Oktober 1888, Düsseldorf 1888.

Anonymous, 'Die Antisklaverei-Bewegung und Deutsch-Ostafrika', *Deutsche Kolonialzeitung*, 1 (1888), 349–55.

Anonymous, *Gott will es! Wer bleibt zurück im heiligen Kampf für Christentum und Menschenrechte*, Münster 1889.

Anonymous, 'Was soll mit den befreiten Sklaven geschehen?', *Deutsche Kolonialzeitung*, 2 (1889). 89–90, 121–3, 145–7.

Anonymous, 'Was tun wir Deutsche gegen den Sklavenhandel?', *Deutsche Kolonialzeitung*, 4 (1891), 91–2.

Anonymous, 'Die Expeditionen des Antisklaverei-Komites', *Koloniales Jahrbuch 1891*, Berlin 1892, 141–80.

Anonymous, 'Die Expeditionen des Antisklaverei-Komites', *Deutsche Kolonialtzeitung*, 5 (1892), 133–5, 153–7, 176–81.

Anonymous, 'Karte der Zollämter und Karawanenstraßen', *Deutsches Kolonialblatt*, 3 (1892), n.p. [annex].

Anonymous, 'Die Expeditionen des Antisklaverei-Komites', *Deutsche Kolonialtzeitung*, 6 (1893), 16–19, 33–5, 71–3, 121–4.

Anonymous, 'Die Angriffe gegen das Anti-Sklaverei-Komite', *Deutsche Kolonialzeitung*, 6 (1893), 115–7.

Anonymous, 'Die Bevölkerung von Deutsch-Ostafrika', *Deutsches Kolonialblatt*, 5 (1894), 106–9.

Anonymous, 'Der deutsche Reichstag und die afrikanische Sklaverei', *Afrika*, 2 (1895), 119–21.

Anonymous, 'Sklaverei und Sklavenlos in Ostafrika', *Mitteilungen der K. K. Geographischen Gesellschaft zu Wien*, 28 (1895), 472.

Anonymous, 'Die Behandlung eines Sklaven in Ostafrika', *Afrika*, 3 (1896), 147–9.

Anonymous, 'Der Jumbentag in Daressalam', *Deutsch-Ostafrikanische Zeitung*, 28 July 1900, 1.

Anonymous, 'Sklavenverkäufe in Dar es Salaam', *Vorwärts*, 25 August 1900, 47.

Anonymous, 'Slavery in East Africa', *Church Missionary Intelligencer*, 26 (1901), 620–2.

Anonymous, 'Loskauf von Sklaven und Heidenkindern', *Afrika-Bote*, 1901/2, 101–2, 210–12.

Anonymous, 'Die Zukunft Mafias', *Deutsch-Ostafrikanische Zeitung*, 5 September 1908, 8.

Anonymous, 'German East Africa', *Encyclopædia Britannica*, vol. 11, eleventh ed., Cambridge 1910, 771–4.

Anonymous, *Militärisches Orientierungsheft für Deutsch-Ostafrika*, Deutsch-Ostafrikanische Rundschau, Dar es Salaam 1911.

Anonymous, 'Die Hörigkeit in Deutsch-Ostafrika', *Deutsch-Ostafrikanische Rundschau*, 15 June 1912, 4.

Anonymous, 'Slavery in German East Africa', *The Moslem World*, 1917, 437.

Arning, W., *Deutsch-Ostafrika gestern und heute*, Berlin 1936.

Axenfeld, K., *Küste und Inland. Ein Überblick über die Aufgaben der Berliner Mission in Deutsch-Ostafrika*, Berlin 1912.

Back, F., 'Die Unterbringung befreiter Sklaven. Denkschrift der Kommision V der Deutschen Kolonialgesellschaft', *Deutsche Kolonialzeitung*, 3 (1890), 43–6, 57–9, 68–70.

Baumann, O., *In Deutsch-Ostafrika während des Aufstandes. Reise der Dr. Hans Meyer'schen Expedition in Usambara*, Wien 1890.

Baumann, O., *Usambara und seine Nachbargebiete. Allgemeine Darstellung des nord-östlichen Deutsch-Ostafrika und seiner Bewohner*, Berlin 1891.

Baumann, O., *Durch Massailand zur Nilquelle. Reisen und Forschungen der Massai-Expedition des deutschen Antisklaverei-Komites in den Jahren 1891–1893*, Berlin 1894.

Baumann, O., *Der Sansibar-Archipel. Erstes Heft: Die Insel Mafia und ihre kleineren Nachbarinseln*, Leipzig 1896 [tr.: O. Baumann, 'Mafia', *Tanganyika Notes and Records*, (1957) 46, 1–24.]

Baumann, O., 'Sultanat Zanzibar', *Jahresbericht der k.u.k österr.-ungar. Consulats-Behörden*, Wien 1898, 543–58.

Baur, E. and A. Le Roy, *À Travers le Zanguebar. Voyage Dans L'Oudoé, L'Ouzigoua, L'Oukwéré, L'Oukami et L'Ousagara*, Tours 1886.

Becker, A., *Aus Deutsch-Ostafrikas Sturm und Drangperiode. Erinnerungen eines alten Afrikaners*, Halle 1911.

Becker, C. H., 'Materialien zur Kenntnis des Islams in Deutsch-Ostafrika', *Der Islam. Zeitschrift für Geschichte und Kultur des Islamischen Orients*, 2 (1911), 1–48

Becker, C. H., 'Islamisches und modernes Recht in der kolonialen Praxis', *Der Islam. Zeitschrift*

Bibliography

für Geschichte und Kultur des Islamischen Orients, 4 (1913), 169–72.

Becker, J., *La Vie en Afrique, ou Trois Ans dans l'Afrique Centrale*, 2 vols, second ed., Paris 1887.

Beech, M. W. H., 'Slavery on the Coast of Africa', *Journal of the African Society*, 15 (1916), 145–9.

Behr, H. F. von, *Kriegsbilder aus dem Araberaufstand in Deutsch-Ostafrika*, Leipzig 1891.

Behr, J. von, 'Lindi und die Handelsverhältnisse im Süden von Deutsch-Ostafrika', *Deutsches Kolonialblatt*, 3 (1892), 578–83.

Bigilimana, R. B. K. B., 'Historia ya Familia Kutokana na Utumwa', *Swahili*, 33 (1963) 2, 12–19.

Blohm, W., *Die Nyamwezi*, 2 vols, Hamburg 1931–3.

Bösch, F., *Les Banyamwezi. Peuple de l'Afrique Orientale*, Münster 1930.

Bokermann, A., 'Lutindi. Sklavenfreistätte, Waisen- und Irrenanstalt', *Die ärztliche Mission*, 6 (1911), 73–87.

Boshart, A., 'Die Zustände im deutschen Schutzgebiet von Ostafrika, deren Ursachen und Wirkungen', *Deutsche Rundschau für Geographie und Statistik*, 12 (1890), 390–400, 445–52.

Brose, M., 'Die deutsche Kolonialliteratur im Jahre 1898, 1899, 1900, 1901, 1902', *Beiträge zur Kolonialpolitik und Kolonialwirtschaft*, Berlin 1900–4.

Brose, M., 'Die deutsche Kolonialliteratur im Jahre 1903, 1904, 1905, 1906', *Zeitschrift für Kolonialpolitik, Kolonialrecht und Kolonialwirtschaft*, Berlin 1904–7.

Broyon-Mirambo, P., 'Description of Unyamwezi and the Best Routes Thither from the East Coast', *Proceedings of the Royal Geographical Society*, 22 (1877–8), 28–36.

Buchner, M., 'Zwei afrikanische Tagesfragen. Sklaverei und Schnaps', *Kölner Zeitung*, 28 August 1886, 7.

Büttner, C. G., *Swahili-Schriftstücke in arabischer Schrift, mit lateinischer Schrift umschrieben, übersetzt und erklärt*, Stuttgart/Berlin 1892.

Bursian, A., *Die Häuser- und Hüttensteuer in Deutsch-Ostafrika*, Jena 1910.

Burton, R. F., *The Lake Regions of Central Africa, a Picture of Exploration*, London 1860.

Burton, R. F., *Zanzibar. City, Island and Coast*, 2 vols, London 1872.

Burton, R. F. and J. H. Speke, 'A Coasting Voyage from Mombasa to the Pangani River (Parts I and II)', *Journal of the Royal Geographical Society*, 20 (1858), 188–226.

Busse, J., 'Die Sklaverei und die Frage ihrer Aufhebung in Deutsch-Ostafrika', *Afrika*, 7 (1900), 32–40, 60–70, 87–99.

Busse, J., 'Zur Frage der Sklaverei in Deutsch-Ostafrika', *Afrika*, 8 (1901), 49–59.

Cameron, V. L., *Across Africa*, 2 vols, London 1877.

Charisius, Hauptmann, 'Aus dem Bezirk Tabora', *Deutsches Kolonialblatt*, 18 (1907), 459–62.

Christie, J., 'Slavery in Zanzibar as It Is', in E. Steere (ed.), *The East African Slave Trade, and the Measures Proposed for its Extinction, as Viewed by Residents in Zanzibar, by H. A. Fraser, Bishop Tozer, and J. Christie*, London 1871, 38–47.

Christie, J., *Cholera Epidemics in East Africa, from 1821 till 1872*, London 1876.

Claus, H., *Die Wagogo. Ethnographische Skizze eines ostafrikanischen Bantustammes*, Leipzig 1911.

Colomb, Captain, *Slave Catching in the Indian Ocean. A Record of Naval Experiences*, London 1873.

Coulbois, F., *Dix Années au Tanganyka*, Limoges 1901.

Dundas, C., 'Native Law of Some Bantu Tribes in East Africa', *The Journal of the Royal Anthropological Institute of Great Britain and Ireland*, 51 (1921), 217–78.

Decle, L., *Three Years in Savage Africa*, London 1898.

Dernburg, B., *Zielpunkte des Deutschen Kolonialwesens. Zwei Vorträge*, Berlin 1907.

Devereux, W. C., *A Cruise in the 'Gorgon'*, London 1869.

Dietert, M., 'Bagamoyo und Handel und Wandel in Deutsch Ostafrika', *Beiträge zur Kolonialpolitik und Kolonialwirtschaft*, 1900–1, 584–602.

Documents relatifs la répression de la traite des esclaves publiés en exécution des articles LXXXI et suivants de l'acte général de Bruxelles, Brussels 1892–1913.

Dundas, C. C. F., *A History of German East Africa*, Dar es Salaam 1923.

Eberstein, Freiherr von, 'Rechtsanschauungen der Eingeborenen von Kilwa', *Mitteilungen von Forschungsreisenden und Gelehrten aus den deutschen Schutzgebieten*, 9 (1896), 170–83.

Elton, J. F., 'On the Coast Country of East Africa, South of Zanzibar', *Royal Geographical Society Journal*, 44 (1874), 227–52.

Elton, J. F., *Travels and Researches among the Lakes and Mountains of Eastern & Central Africa*, ed. by H. B. Cotterill, London 1879.

Erzberger, M., *Die Zentrumspolitik im Reichstage mit besonderer Berücksichtigung der Kolonialpolitik*, Berlin 1907.

Bibliography

Evangelischer Afrikaverein, *Das Deutsche Reich und die Sklaverei in Afrika! Stenographischer Bericht der am 18. Januar 1895 in der Tonhalle zu Berlin auf Veranlassung des ev. Afrikavereins abgehaltenen Versammlung*, Leipzig 1895.

Farler, J. P., 'Native Routes in East Africa from Pangani to the Masai Country and the Victoria Nyanza', *Proceedings of the Royal Geographical Society*, (1882) 4, 730–42, 776.

Fischer, G. A., 'Einige Worte über den augenblicklichen Stand der Sklaverei in Ostafrika', *Zeitschrift der Gesellschaft für Erdkunde zu Berlin*, 17 (1882), 70–5.

Fischer, G. A., *Das Massailand. Bericht über die im Auftrage der Geographischen Gesellschaft in Hamburg ausgeführten Reise*, Hamburg 1885.

Fischer, G. A., *Mehr Licht in dunklen Weltteil. Betrachtungen über die Kolonisation des tropischen Afrika unter besonderer Berücksichtigung des Sansibar-Gebiets*, Hamburg 1885.

Fuchs, P., *Die wirtschaftliche Erkundung einer ostafrikanischen Südbahn*, Berlin 1905.

Fuchs, P., *Wirtschaftliche Eisenbahn-Erkundungen im mittleren und nördlichen Deutsch-Ostafrika*, Berlin 1907.

Fülleborn, F., *Das Deutsche Njassa- und Ruwuma-Gebiet, Land und Leute, nebst Bemerkungen über die Schire-Länder*, Berlin 1906.

Grant, J. A., *A Walk Across Africa, or Domestic Scenes from my Nile Journal*, London 1864.

Great Britain, *Parliamentary Papers. Correspondence Relating to Zanzibar*, C. 4776, London 1886.

Great Britain, *Parliamentary Papers. Further Correspondence Respecting Germany and Zanzibar*, C. 5603, London 1888.

Hermann, A., 'Ugogo – Das Land und seine Bewohner', *Mitteilungen aus den deutschen Schutzgebieten*, 5 (1892), 191–203.

Hermann, A., 'Über den Sklavenhandel am Viktoria-Nyansa', *Deutsches Kolonialblatt*, 4 (1893), 43–4.

Hermann, R., 'Statistik der farbigen Bevölkerung von Deutsch Afrika, III. Ostafrika', *Koloniale Monatsblätter*, 16 (1914) 4, 172–6.

Höhnel, L. von, *Zum Rudolfsee und Stephaniesee. Die Forschungsreise des Grafen S. Teleki in Ostäquatorial-Afrika 1887–1888*, Wien 1891.

Hoffmann, H. Edler von, *Verwaltungs- und Gerichtsverfassung der deutschen Schutzgebiete*, Leipzig 1908.

Hofmeister, R., *Kulturbilder aus Deutsch-Ostafrika*, Bamberg 1895.

Hore, E. C., *Tanganyika. Eleven Years in Central Africa*, London 1892.

Hore, E. C., *Missionary to Tanganyika, 1877–1888*, ed. by J. B. Wolf, London 1971.

Joachim, M., 'Sizia oder Schicksale einer Negersklavin. Von ihr selbst erzählt', *Afrika-Bote*, 1905–6, 109–15.

Johannes, Major, 'Bericht über die Tätigkeit des Major Johannes vom 18. November 1905 bis 10. März 1906', *Deutsches Kolonialblatt*, 17 (1906), 601–11.

Johannes, Major, 'Bericht über die Tätigkeit des Major Johannes vom 11. März bis 5. August 1906', *Deutsches Kolonialblatt*, 18 (1907), 335–46

Jones-Bateman, P. L. (ed.), *The Autobiography of an African Slave Boy (Martin Furahani)*, London 1891.

Kaiserliches Gouvernement von Deutsch-Ostafrika, *Die Landes-Gesetzgebung des Deutsch-Ostafrikanischen Schutzgebiets*, Tanga/Daressalam 1911.

Kandt, R., *Caput Nili. Eine empfindsame Reise zu den Quellen des Nils*, third ed., Berlin 1914.

Karlowa, H., *Die Strafgerichtsbarkeit über die Eingeborenen in den deutschen Kolonien*, Borna/Leipzig 1911.

Karstedt, F. O., *Beiträge zur Praxis der Eingeborenenrechtsprechung in Deutsch-Ostafrika*, Dar es Salaam n.d. [1912].

Karstedt, F. O., 'Zur Sklavenfrage in Deutsch-Ostafrika', *Koloniale Rundschau*, 1913, 616–21.

Kaundinya, R., *Erinnerungen aus meinen Pflanzerjahren in Deutsch-Ost-Afrika*, Leipzig 1918.

Kaysel, P., *Die Gesetzgebung der Kulturstaaten zur Unterdrückung des afrikanischen Sklavenhandels*, Breslau 1905.

Kersten, O. (ed.), *Baron Carl Claus von der Decken's Reisen in Ost-Afrika*, 4 vol., Leipzig, 1869–79.

King, N, 'Mafia', *The Geographical Journal*, 50 (1917) 2, 117–125.

Klamroth, M., *Ein Christ. Wie ein ostafrikanischer Negerknabe zum Sklaven wurde und wie er die rechte Freiheit gewann*, third edn, Berlin 1927.

Kootz-Kretschmer, E., *Die Safwa. Ein ostafrikanischer Volksstamm*, 3 vols, Berlin 1926–9.

Krapf, J. L., *Reisen in Ostafrika ausgeführt in den Jahren 1837 bis 1855*, 2 vols, Kornthal/Stuttgart 1964 [first published 1858].

Bibliography

Krelle, H., *Anton und seine Anna*, Berlin 1929.

Krenzler, E., 'Sklaverei und Sklavenhandel in Ostafrika', *Jahresberichte des Württembergischen Vereins für Handelsgeographie*, 5–6 (1886–8), 69–79.

Krenzler, E., *Ein Jahr in Ostafrika*, Ulm 1888.

Kuntze, F., 'Der Sklaven-Freikauf in Deutsch-Ostafrika', *Kolonie und Heimat*, 20 December 1908, 8.

Langheld, W., *Zwanzig Jahre in deutschen Kolonien*, Berlin 1909.

Le Roy, A., *Mehr Licht in die Zustände des dunklen Weltteils. Die Slaverei und ihre Bekämpfung*, Münster 1890.

Leue, A., 'Dar es Salaam', *Deutsche Kolonialzeitung*, 2 (1889), 197–8, 206–7, 210–13.

Leue, A., 'Bagamoyo', *Beiträge zur Kolonialpolitik und Kolonialwirtschaft*, 1900–1a, 11–31.

Leue, A., 'Udjidji', *Beiträge zur Kolonialpolitik und Kolonialwirtschaft*, 1900–1b, 321–8.

Leue, A., 'Die Sklaverei in Ostafrika', *Beiträge zur Kolonialpolitik und Kolonialwirtschaft*, 1900–1c, 606–8, 617–25.

Leue, A., *Dar-es-Salaam. Bilder aus dem Kolonialleben*, Berlin 1903.

Leue, A. (ed.), *Mit der Schutztruppe durch Deutsch-Ostafrika*, Minden 1905.

Lieder, G., 'Zur Kenntniss der Karawanenwege im südlichen Theile des ostafrikanischen Schutzgebietes', *Mitteilungen von Forschungsreisenden und Gelehrten aus den deutschen Schutzgebieten*, 1894, 277–82.

Livingstone, D., *The Last Journals of David Livingstone in Central Africa, from 1865 to His Death*, ed. by H. Waller, London 1874.

Livingstone, D., *David Livingstone and the Rovuma*, ed. by G. Shepperson, Edinburgh, 1965.

Löbner, M. H., 'Fragebogen-Beantwortung für ganz Wanyamwezi durch Missionar M. H. Löbner, stationiert bei Tabora [Usoke, March 1910]', in A. Gottberg, *Unyamwesi. Quellensammlung und Geschichte*, Berlin 1971, 126–75.

Löbner, M. H., 'Zur Entvölkerungsfrage Unyamwezis', *Koloniale Rundschau*, 1914, 267–70.

Lugard, F. D., *Rise of Our East African Empire. Early Efforts in Nyassaland and Uganda*, 2 vols, London 1968 [first published 1893].

Lugard, F. D., 'Slavery under the British Flag', *Nineteenth Century*, 1896, 228, 335–55.

Mackenzie, D., 'A Report on Slavery and the Slave Trade in Zanzibar, Pemba and the Mainland of the British Protectorate of East Africa', *Anti-Slavery Reporter*, 15 (1895) 2, 69–96, 131.

Magan, A. C., *Kiungani; or, Story and History from Central Africa, Written by Boys in the Schools of the Universities' Mission to Central Africa*, London 1887.

Martitz, F. von, 'Das internationale System zur Unterdrückung des afrikanischen Sklavenhandels', *Archiv für öffentliches Recht*, 1885, 1–107.

Mbotela, J. J., *Uhuru wa Watumwa*, London 1934.

Meinecke, G., 'Pangani', *Deutsche Kolonialzeitung*, 7 (1894), 154–5.

Meinecke, G., 'Wirtschaftliche Untersuchungen in Ostafrika'. *Deutsche Kolonialzeitung*, 8 (1895a), 129–32, 154–6, 162–5.

Meinecke, G., *Aus dem Lande der Suahili. Reisebriefe und Zuckeruntersuchungen am Pangani*, Berlin 1895b.

Meinecke, G., 'Die Anti-Sklavereifrage in Ostafrika', *Koloniales Jahrbuch 1899*, Berlin 1900, 1–17.

Meinecke, G., *Die deutschen Kolonien in Wort und Bild*, Leipzig n.d. [1899].

Merensky, A., 'Was soll aus unseren befreiten Sklaven werden', *Afrika*, 1 (1894), 68, 95.

Merker, M., *Die Masai. Ethnographische Monographie eines ostafrikanischen Semitenvolkes*, Berlin 1910.

Methner, W., *Unter drei Gouverneuren. 16 Jahre Dienst in deutschen Tropen*, Breslau 1938.

Meyer, H. *Ostafrikanische Gletscherfahrten. Forschungsreise im Kilimandscharo-Gebiet*, Leipzig 1890.

Meyer, L., 'Wangwana und Waschensi', *Afrika*, 1 (1894), 52–6, 84–8.

Müller, G., 'Verhandlungen des Kolonialrats über die Versorgung der befreiten Sklaven', *Afrika*, 1 (1894), 137–8.

New, C., *Life, Wanderings, and Labours in Eastern Africa. With an Account of the First Successful Ascent of the Equatorial Snow Mountain Kilima Njaro, and Remarks upon East African Slavery*, London 1971 [first published 1873].

Niese, R., *Das Personen- und Familienrecht der Suaheli*, Marburg 1902.

Nigmann, E., *Schwarze Schwänke. Fröhliche Geschichten aus unserem schönen alten Deutsch-Ostafrika*, Berlin 1922.

Noske, G., *Kolonialpolitik und Sozialdemokratie*, Stuttgart 1914.

Bibliography

O'Neill, H. E., *The Mozambique and Nyassa Slave Trade*, London 1895.

Otto, G., 'Aus dem Leben befreiter Sklavenkinder', *Afrika*, 10 (1903), 25–9.

Peters, C., 'Zur Sklavenfrage in Deutsch-Ostafrika', *Kolonial-Politische Korrespondenz*, 1885, 130–2.

Picarda, C., 'Autour de Mandera. Notes sur L'Ouzigua, L'Oukwere et Oudoe', *Missions Catholique* 18 (1886), 184-9, 197-201, 208-11, 225-8, 234-7, 246-9, 258-61, 269-74, 281-5, 294-7, 322-4, 342-6, 356-7, 365-9.

Prince, T. von, 'Bericht des Lieutenants Prince über die Niederwerfung und Vernichtung des Häuptlings Sike von Tabora', *Deutsche Kolonialblatt*, 4 (1993): 198–204.

Prince, T. von, *Gegen Araber and Wahehe. Erinnerungen aus meiner ostafrikanischen Leutnantszeit, 1890–1895*, second edn, Berlin 1914.

Pruen, S. T., 'Slavery in East Africa. Letter from Dr. Pruen, Mpwapwa', *Church Missionary Intelligencer*, 13 (1888), 661–5.

Pruen, S. T., *The Arab and the African. Experiences in Eastern Equatorial Africa during a Residence of Three Years*, London 1891.

Reichard, P., 'Einiges über Afrikanische Sklaverei und das Arabertum', *Deutsche Kolonialzeitung*, 1 (1888), 377–9.

Reichard, P., 'Was soll mit den befreiten Sklaven geschehen?', *Deutsche Kolonialzeitung*, 2 (1889), 281–5.

Reichard, P., 'Die Bedeutung von Tabora für Deutsch-Ostafrika', *Deutsche Kolonialzeitung*, 3 (1890), 67–8.

Reichard, P., 'Die Wanyamwezi', *Deutsche Kolonialzeitung*, 3 (1890), 228–30, 239–41, 263–5, 276–8.

Reichard, P., *Deutsch-Ostafrika. Das Land und seine Bewohner, seine politische und wirtschaftliche Entwicklung*, Leipzig 1892.

Ruete, E., *Leben im Sultanspalast. Memoiren aus dem 19. Jahrhundert*, Frankfurt/Main 1989 [first published 1886].

Saadi, Kadhi A. O., 'Mafia-History and Tradition Collected by Kadhi Amur Omari Saadi', *Tanganyika Notes and Records*, (1941) 12, 23–7.

Sachau, E., *Muhammedanisches Recht nach schaffeitischer Lehre*, Stuttgart 1897.

Saget, P., *Die Gräuel der Sklaverei in Afrika und ihre Bekämpfung*, Aachen 1889.

Sauer, H., 'Die Arbeiterverhältnisse beim Bau der Ostafrikanischen Mittelbahn', *Deutsches Kolonialblatt*, 22 (1911), 708–9.

Schack, F., *Das deutsche Kolonialrecht in seiner Entwicklung bis zum Weltkriege. Die allgemeinen Lehren. Eine berichtende Darstellung der Theorie und Praxis nebst kritischen Anmerkungen*, Hamburg 1923.

Scherling, E., *Die Bekämpfung von Sklavenraub und Sklavenhandel seit Anfang diesen Jahrhunderts*, Breslau 1897.

Schnee, A. H. H. (ed.), *Deutsches Kolonial-Lexikon*, 3 vols, Leipzig 1920.

Schrader, R., *Das Arbeiterrecht für Eingeborene in Deutsch- und British-Ostafrika*, Hamburg 1920.

Schweinfurth, G. A., *Im Herzen von Afrika. Reisen und Entdeckungen im centralen Äquatorial-Afrika während der Jahre 1868 bis 1871*, 2 vols, Leipzig 1874.

Schweinitz, Graf H. von, 'Das Trägerpersonal der Karawanen', *Deutsche Kolonialzeitung*, 7 (1894a), 18–20.

Schweinitz, Graf H. von, *Deutsch-Ostafrika in Krieg und Frieden*, Berlin 1894b.

Schweinitz, Graf H. von, 'Die Unternehmungen des Deutschen Antisklaverei-Komites (in den Jahren 1891 bis 1893)', *Afrika*, 4 (1897), 161–71.

Seibt, A., 'Fragebogen-Beantwortung für ganz Unyamwezi durch Missionar A. Seibt, in Urambo stationiert [January 1910]', in A. Gottberg, *Unyamwesi. Quellensammlung und Geschichte*, Berlin 1971, 176–208.

Seidel, A., 'Die afrikanische Sklaverei', *Deutsche Kolonialzeitung*, 1 (1888), 157–9.

Sigl, A., 'Bericht des Lieutnants Siegl über den Sklavenhandel', *Deutsches Kolonialblatt*, 2 (1891), 509–11.

Sigl, A., 'Bericht des Stationschefs von Tabora, Lieutenant Sigl, über den Handelsverkehr von Tabora', *Deutsches Kolonialblatt*, 3 (1892), 165–6.

Smith, C. S., *Explorations in the Zanzibar Dominions*, London 1887.

Soden, Frh. von, 'Über die Sklavenausfuhr und die Behandlung befreiter Sklaven', *Deutsches Kolonialblatt*, 3 (1892), 359–60.

Speke, J. H., *Journal of the Discovery of the Source of the Nile*, Edinburgh 1863.

Spellig, F., 'Die Wanjamwezi. Ein Beitrag zur Völkerkunde Ostafrikas', *Zeitschrift für Ethnologie*,

(1927–8), 201–41.

Spellmeyer, H., *Deutsche Kolonialpolitik im Reichstag,* Beiträge zur Geschichte der nachbismarckschen Zeit und des Weltkrieges, Heft 11, Stuttgart 1931.

Spring, C., *Selbsterlebtes in Ostafrika von Kapitaen Spring,* Dresden n.d. [1896].

St. Paul-Illaire, W. von, 'Über die Rechtsgewohnheiten der im Bezirk Tanga ansässigen Farbigen', *Mitteilungen von Forschungsreisenden und Gelehrten aus den deutschen Schutzgebieten,* 1895, 191–209.

Steere, E., *Collections for a Handbook of the Nyamwezi Language as Spoken in Unyanyembe,* London 1871.

Steere, E. (ed.), *The East African Slave Trade, and the Measures Proposed for its Extinction, as Viewed by Residents in Zanzibar, by H .A. Fraser, Bishop Tozer, and J. Christie,* London 1871.

Steudel, E., 'Die ansteckenden Krankheiten der Karawanen Deutsch-Ostafrikas, ihre Verbreitung unter der übrigen Bevölkerung und ihre Bekämpfung', *Koloniales Jahrbuch 1894,* Berlin 1895, 171–202.

Stollowsky, O., 'Die Arbeiterfrage in Deutsch-Ostafrika', *Koloniale Zeitschrift,* 12 (1911), 515–17, 532–5.

Storms, E. Capt., 'L'esclavage entre le Tanganyika et la côte est', *La traite des esclaves en Afrique. Renseignements et documents recueillis pour la Conférence de Bruxelles (1840–1890),* Brussels 1889, 110–11.

Stuhlmann, F., *Mit Emin Pascha ins Herz von Afrika. Ein Reisebericht,* Berlin 1894.

Stuhlmann, F., *Die wirtschaftliche Entwickelung Deutsch-Ost-Afrikas,* Berlin 1898.

Stuhlmann, F., *Handwerk und Industrie in Ostafrika,* Hamburg 1910.

Stuhlmann, F., *Die Tagebücher von Dr. Emin Pasha,* 5 vols, Hamburg 1916–27.

Swann, A. J., *Fighting the Slave Hunters in Central Africa. A Record of Twenty Six Years of Travel and Adventure round the Great Lakes and of the Overthrow of Tip-Pu-Tip, Rumaliza and Other Great Slave-Traders,* London 1969 [first published 1910].

Thompson, J., 'The Slave Trade in East Africa', *Anti-Slavery Reporter,* 2 (1882), 1–3.

Tippu Tip, 'Autobiographie des Arabers Schech Hamed bin Muhammed el Murjebi, genannt Tippu Tip', ed. and tr. by H. Brode, *Mitteilungen des Seminars für orientalische Sprachen,* 1902, 175–277; 1903, 1–55.

Toeppen, K., 'Handel und Handelsverbindungen in Ostafrika', *Mitteilungen der Geographischen Gesellschaft in Hamburg,* 1885–6, 222–35.

Traite des esclaves en Afrique: lieux d'origine, routes des caravanes d'esclaves, croisières, pays de destination: renseignements et documents recueillis pour la Conférence de Bruxelles (1840–1889), Brussels 1889.

Tucker, J., 'The Famine in Usagara. Letters from Bishop Tucker and Dr. Baxter', *Church Missionary Intelligencer,* 20 (1895), 275–7.

Van der Burgt, J. M. M., 'Zur Entvölkerungsfrage Unjamwesis und Usumbwas', *Koloniale Rundschau,* 1913, 705–28; 1914, 24–7.

Velten, C., 'Sitten und Gebräuche der Suaheli', *Mitteilungen des Seminars für orientalische Sprachen. Afrikanische Studien I,* Berlin 1898, 9–83.

Velten, C. (ed.), *Desturi za Wasuaheli na Khabari za Desturi za Sheri`a za Wasuaheli,* Göttingen, 1903.

Waller, H., *Paths into the Slave Preserves of East Africa,* London 1876.

Weidner, F., *Die Haussklaverei in Ostafrika,* Jena 1915.

Werner, A. und W. Hichens (eds.), *Utendi wa Mwana Kupona (Mwana Kupona. Advice upon the Wifely Duties),* Medstead 1934.

Weston, F., *The Black Slaves of Prussia,* London 1918.

Weule, K., *Negerleben in Ostafrika. Ergebnisse einer ethnologischen Forschungsreise,* Leipzig 1908.

Wissmann, H. von, 'Araberfrage und Sklavenhandel. Ein Vortrag', *Deutsche Kolonialzeitung,* 1 (1888), 352.

Wissmann, H. von, *Unter deutscher Flagge quer durch Afrika; von West nach Ost; von 1880 bis 1883; ausgeführt von Paul Pogge und Hermann Wissmann,* Berlin 1889.

Zimmermann, A., *Geschichte der deutschen Kolonialpolitik,* Berlin 1914.

Unpublished Secondary Sources

el-Zein, A. 'The Sacred Meadows: A Structural Analysis of Religious Symbolism in an East African Town' (University of Chicago PhD thesis, 1972).

Becker, F., 'A Social History of Southeast Tanzania, ca. 1890–1950' (University of Cambridge PhD thesis, 2001).

Bibliography

Berg, 'Mombasa under the Busaidi Sultanate. The City and its Hinterland in the Nineteenth Century' (University of Wisconsin PhD thesis, 1971).

Bromber, K. *'Mjakazi, Mpambe, Mjoli, Suria* − Female Slaves in Swahili Sources' (paper presented to the international workshop 'Women in Slavery', Avignon, October 2002).

Brown, W. T., 'A Pre-Colonial History of Bagamoyo. Aspects of the Growth of an East African Coastal Town' (University of Boston PhD thesis, 1971).

Deutsch, J. G., 'Remembering Slavery in Contemporary Tanzania' (paper presented to the biennial conference of the German African Studies Association, Leipzig, March 2000a).

Deutsch, J. G., 'Slavery under German Colonial Rule in East Africa, *c.* 1860−1914' (Humboldt-University at Berlin Habilitationsschrift 2000b).

East, J. W., 'The German Administration in East Africa. A Select Annotated Bibliography of the German Colonial Administration in Tanganyika, Rwanda and Burundi, from 1884 to 1918' (Thesis Submitted for the Fellowship of the Library Association London, 1987).

Geider, T., 'The Memory of East Africa. A Survey of Swahili Ethnographies and Historiographies, 1890−1990' (MS, Berlin 1997).

Giblin, J., 'Chieftainship and Slavery in a Lineage Mode of Production. The Zigua and Nguu in the Nineteenth Century' (MS, Dar es Salaam 1982).

Glassman, C., 'The Illegal East African Slave Trade' (MS, Cambridge 1977).

Glassman, J., 'Social Rebellion and Swahili Culture. The Response to German Conquest of the Northern Mrima, 1888−1890' (University of Wisconsin PhD thesis, 1988).

Henschel, Fr. J., 'Bagamoyo and Slavery in the 19th Century' (MS, Bagamoyo 1999).

Kieran, J. A. P., 'The Holy Ghost Fathers in East Africa, 1863−1914' (University of London PhD thesis, 1966).

Kollman, P. V., 'Making Catholics: Slave Evangelization and the Origins of the Catholic Church in Nineteenth-Century East Africa' (University of Chicago PhD thesis, 2001).

Lampe, A., 'Anteil der Eingeborenen an der Verwaltung und Rechtspflege in unseren Kolonien' (University of Greifswald PhD thesis, 1919)

Larson, L. E., 'A History of the Mahenge (Ulanga) district, ca. 1860−1957' (University of Dar es Salaam PhD thesis, 1973).

List, W., 'Die Beteiligung Deutschlands an der Bekämpfung des Sklavenhandels und Sklavenraubs' (University of Würzburg Jur. Diss thesis, 1907).

Nolan, F. P., 'Christianity in Unyamwezi, 1878−1928' (University of Cambridge PhD thesis, 1977).

Ovaert, V., 'Das Geschlecht der Sklaverei' (MS, Berlin 1999).

Perras, A., 'Carl Peters and German Imperialism, 1856−1918. A Political Biography' (University of Oxford D. Phil. thesis, 1999).

Pfrank, C., 'Die Landarbeiterfrage in Deutsch Ostafrika' (University of Berlin PhD thesis, 1919).

Pogge von Strandmann, H., 'The Kolonialrat. Its Significance on German Politics 1890−1906' (University of Oxford D. Phil. thesis, 1970).

Prein, P., 'Differenz und Identität in Rungwe (Tanzania) während der deutschen Kolonialzeit (1890−1914)' (University of Hamburg MA thesis, 1995).

Rockel, S. J., 'Caravan Porters of the *Nyika*. Labour, Culture, and Society in Nineteenth Century Tanzania' (University of Toronto PhD thesis, 1997).

Schmidt, H., 'Girl or Woman? Statutory Rape in German East Africa, *c.* 1890−1915' (MS, San Diego, 2004).

Sunseri, T., 'A Social History of Cotton Production in German East Africa, 1884−1915' (University of Minnesota PhD thesis, 1993a).

Unomah, A. C., 'Economic Expansion and Political Change in Unyanyembe (ca. 1840 to 1900)' (University of Ibadan PhD thesis, 1972).

Wege, A., 'Die rechtlichen Bestimmungen über die Sklaverei in den deutschen afrikanischen Schutzgebieten' (University of Greifswald Jur. Diss thesis, 1914).

Westphal, G., 'Der Kolonialrat 1890−1907. Ein Beitrag zur Geschichte der Herausbildung des deutschen imperialistischen Kolonialsystems' (Humboldt-University at Berlin PhD thesis, 1964).

257

Published Secondary Sources

Aas, N., *Koloniale Entwicklung im Bezirksamt Lindi (Deutsch-Ostafrika). Deutsche Erwartungen und regionale Wirklichkeit*, Bayreuth 1989.

Abrahams, R. G., *The Peoples of Greater Unyamwezi, Tanzania. Nyamwezi, Sukuma, Sumbwa, Kimbu, Konongo*, London 1967a.

Abrahams, R. G., *The Political Organization of Unyamwezi*, Cambridge 1967b.

Abrahams, R. G., *The Nyamwezi Today. A Tanzanian People in the 1970s*, Cambridge 1981.

Akinola, G. A., 'Slavery and Slave Revolts in the Sultanate of Zanzibar in the Nineteenth Century', *Journal of the Historical Society of Nigeria*, 6 (1972) 2, 215–28.

Allen, J. de V., *Swahili Origins. Swahili Culture & the Shungwaya Phenomenon*, Athens, OH and London 1993.

Allen, R. B., *Slaves, Freedmen and Indentured Laborers in Colonial Mauritius*, Cambridge 1999.

Allen, R. B., 'Licentious and Unbridled Proceedings: The Illegal Slave Trade to Mauritius and the Seychelles during the early Nineteenth Century', *Journal of African History*, 42 (2002), 91–116.

Allen, R. B., 'The Mascarene Slave Trade and Labour Migration in the Indian Ocean during the Eighteenth and Nineteenth Centuries', in G. Campbell (ed.), *The Structure of Slavery in Indian Ocean Africa and Asia*, London 2004, 33–50.

Alpers, E. A., *The East African Slave Trade*, Nairobi 1967.

Alpers, E. A., 'The Coast and the Development of the Caravan Trade', in I. N. Kimambo and A. J. Temu (eds.), *A History of Tanzania*, Nairobi 1969, 35–56.

Alpers, E. A., *Ivory and Slaves in East Central Africa. Changing Patterns of International Trade in the Later Nineteenth Century*, London 1975a.

Alpers, E. A., 'Eastern Africa', in R. Gray (ed.), *Cambridge History of Africa*, vol. 4, Cambridge 1975b, 476–536.

Alpers, E. A., 'The Story of Swema. Female Vulnerability in Nineteenth-Century East Africa', in C. C. Robertson and M. A. Klein (eds.), *Women and Slavery in Africa*, Madison, WI 1983, 185–219.

Alpers, E. A., 'The Ivory Trade in Africa. An Historical Overview', in D. H. Ross (ed.), *Elephant. The Animal and its Ivory in African Culture*, Los Angeles 1992, 349–63.

Alpers, E. A., 'Flight to Freedom: Escape from Slavery among Bonded Africans in the Indian Ocean World, *c.* 1750–1962', in G. Campbell (ed.), *The Structure of Slavery in Indian Ocean Africa and Asia*, London 2004, 51–68.

Alpers, E. A. (ed.), *Slavery and Resistance in Africa and Asia*, London 2005.

Anderson-Morshead, A. E. M., *The History of the Universities' Mission to Central Africa*, 3 vols, London 1955–62.

Appadurai, A., 'The Production of Locality', in R. Fardon (ed.), *Counterworks*, London 1995, 205–25.

Arens, W., 'The Waswahili. The Social History of an Ethnic Group', *Africa*, 45 (1975) 4, 426–38.

Arens, W., 'Changing Patterns of Ethnic Identity and Prestige in East Africa', in W. Arens (ed.), *A Century of Change in Eastern Africa*, The Hague 1976, 65–75.

Arnold, B., *Steuer und Lohnarbeit im Südwesten von Deutsch-Ostafrika, 1891–1916*, Münster 1994.

Austen, R. A., *Northwest Tanzania under German and British Rule. Colonial Policy and Tribal Politics, 1889–1939*, New Haven 1968.

Austen, R. A., 'The 19th Century Islamic Slave Trade from East Africa (Swahili and Red Sea Coast). A Tentative Census', in W. G. Clarence-Smith (ed.), *The Economics of the Indian Ocean Slave Trade in the Nineteenth Century*, London 1989, 21–44.

Bade, K. J., 'Antisklavereibewegung in Deutschland und Kolonialkrieg in Deutsch-Ostafrika 1888–1890. Bismarck und Friedrich Fabri', *Geschichte und Gesellschaft*, 3 (1977) 1, 31–58.

Bade, K. J., 'Zwischen Mission und Kolonialbewegung, Kolonialwirtschaft und Kolonial-politik in der Bismarckzeit. Der Fall Friedrich Fabri', in K. J. Bade (ed.), *Imperialismus und Kolonialmission. Kaiserliches Deutschland und Koloniales Imperium*, Wiesbaden 1982, 103–41.

Bald, D., *Deutsch-Ostafrika 1900–1914. Eine Studie über Verwaltung, Interessengruppen und wirtschaft-liche Erschließung*, München 1970.

Bibliography

Baumgart, W., *Deutschland im Zeitalter des Imperialismus, 1890–1914. Grundkräfte, Thesen, Strukturen*, 5th edn, Berlin 1986.

Beachey, R. W., 'The Arms Trade in East Africa in the late Nineteenth Century', *Journal of African History*, 3 (1962) 3, 451–67.

Beachey, R. W., 'The East African Ivory Trade in the Nineteenth Century', *Journal of African History*, 8 (1967) 2, 269–90.

Beachey, R. W., *The Slave Trade of Eastern Africa*, London 1976.

Becher, J., 'Tabora: Der Einfluß der kolonialen Expansion auf die Entwicklung eines afrikanischen Handelszentrums im 19./20. Jahrhundert', in P. Heine and U. van der Heyden (eds.), *Studien zur Geschichte des deutschen Kolonialismus in Afrika*, Pfaffenweiler 1995, 126–46.

Becher, J., *Dar es Salaam, Tanga und Tabora. Stadtentwicklung in Tansania unter deutscher Kolonial-herrschaft (1885–1914)*, Stuttgart 1997.

Beidelman, T. O., 'The Organization and Maintenance of Caravans by the Church Mission-ary Society in Tanzania in the Nineteenth Century', *International Journal of African Historical Studies*, 15 (1982) 4, 601–23.

Bennett, N. R., *Mirambo of Tanzania, 1840?–1884*, New York 1971.

Bennett, N. R., *A History of the Arab State of Zanzibar*, London 1978.

Bennett, N. R., *The Arab State of Zanzibar. A Bibliography*, Boston 1984.

Bennett, N. R., *Arab versus European. Diplomacy and War in Nineteenth Century East Central Africa*, New York 1986.

Berman, B. and J. M. Lonsdale, 'Coping with Contradictions. The Development of the Colonial State, 1895–1914', in B. Berman and J. M. Lonsdale, *Unhappy Valley. Conflict in Kenya and Africa*, vol. 1, London 1992, 77–100.

Biermann, W., *Wachuurizi na Halasa. Händler und Handelskapital in der wirtschaftlichen Entwicklung Ostafrikas (900–1890)*, Münster 1993.

Binsbergen, W. M. J. van, 'The Unit of Study and the Interpretation of Ethnicity. Studying the Nkoya of Western Zambia', *Journal of Southern African Studies*, 8 (1981–2) 1, 51–81.

Birmingham, D. B. and P. M. Martin (eds.), *History of Central Africa*, 2 vols, London 1983.

Bley, H. *et al.* (eds.), *Sklaverei in Afrika. Afrikanische Gesellschaften im Zusammenhang von europäischer und interner Sklaverei und Sklavenhandel*, Pfaffenweiler 1991.

Bontinck, F., *L'autobiographie de Hamed ben Mohammed el-Murjebi, Tippo Tip (ca. 1840–1905)*, Brussels 1974.

Brenner, L. (ed.), *Muslim Identity and Social Change in Sub-Saharan Africa*, London 1993.

Bridgman, J. and D. E. Clarke, *German Africa. A Select Annotated Bibliography*, Stanford 1965.

Brown, B., 'Muslim Influence in Trade and Politics in the Lake Tanganyika Region', *International Journal of African Historical Studies*, 4 (1971) 3, 617–29.

Brown, W. T., 'Bagamoyo. A Historical Introduction', *Tanzania Notes and Records* (1970) 71, 69–83.

Brunschvig, R., 'Abd', *The Encyclopedia of Islam*, second edn, vol. 1, Leiden 1960, 24–40.

Bückendorf, J., *"Schwarz-Weiß-Rot über Ostafrika!" Deutsche Kolonialpläne und afrikanische Realität*, Münster 1997.

Büttner, K., *Die Anfänge der deutschen Kolonialpolitik in Ostafrika. Eine kritische Untersuchung an Hand unveröffentlicher Quellen*, Berlin 1959.

Campbell, G., 'The East African Slave Trade, 1861–1895. The "Southern" Complex', *International Journal of African Historical Studies*, 22 (1989a) 1, 1–26.

Campbell, G., 'Madagascar and Mozambique in the Slave Trade of the Western Indian Ocean 1800–1861', in W. G. Clarence-Smith (ed.), *The Economics of the Indian Ocean Slave Trade in the Nineteenth Century*, London 1989b, 166–93.

Campbell, G. (ed.), *The Structure of Slavery in Indian Ocean Africa and Asia*, London 2004.

Campbell, G. (ed.), *Abolition and its Aftermath in the Indian Ocean, Africa and Asia*, London 2005.

Caplan, A. P., 'Perception of Gender Stratification', *Africa*, 59 (1989) 2, 196–208.

Cassanelli, L. V., 'The Ending of Slavery in Italian Somalia. Liberty and the Control of Labour, 1890–1935', in S. Miers and R. Roberts (eds.), *The End of Slavery in Africa*, Madison 1988, 308–31.

Chanock, M., *Law, Customs and Social Order. The Colonial Experience in Malawi and Zambia*, Cambridge 1985.

Chanock, M., 'A Peculiar Sharpness – An Essay on Property in the History of Customary Law in Colonial Africa', *Journal of African History*, 32 (1991) 1, 65–88.

Bibliography

Chittick, H. N., *Kilwa. An Islamic Trading City on the East African Coast*, 2 vols, Nairobi 1974.

Chretien, J.-P., 'Mirambo. L'unificateur des Banyamwezi (Tanzanie)', in C.-A. Julien et al., *Les Africains*, vol. 6, Paris 1977, 127–57.

Clarence-Smith, W. G. (ed.), *The Economics of the Indian Ocean Slave Trade in the Nineteenth Century*, London 1989.

Collingwood, R. G., *The Idea of History*, Oxford 1993 [1946].

Comaroff, J., 'Sui Generis. Feminism, Kinship Theory and "Structural" Domains', in J. F. Collier and S. J. Yanagisako (eds.), *Gender and Kinship. Essays towards a Unified Analysis*, Stanford 1987, 53–85.

Comaroff, J., 'Governmentality; Materiality; Legality; Modernity. On the Colonial State in Africa' in J.G. Deutsch, P. Probst and H. Schmidt (eds.), *African Modernities*, Oxford 2002, 107–34.

Constantin, F., 'Social Stratification on the Swahili Coast. From Race to Class?', *Africa*, 59 (1989) 2, 145–60.

Cooper, F. L., *Plantation Slavery on the East Coast of Africa*, New Haven 1977.

Cooper, F. L., 'The Problem of Slavery in African Studies', *Journal of African History*, 20 (1979) 1, 103–25.

Cooper, F. L., *From Slaves to Squatters. Plantation Labour and Agriculture in Zanzibar and Coastal Kenya, 1890–1925*, New Haven 1980.

Cooper, F. L., 'Islam and Cultural Hegemony. The Ideology of Slaveowners on the East African Coast', in P. E. Lovejoy (ed.), *The Ideology of Slavery in Africa*, Beverly Hills/London 1981, 271–307.

Cooper, F., 'Conditions Analogous to Slavery. Imperialism and Free Labor Ideology in Africa', in F. Cooper, T. C. Holt and R. J. Scott, *Beyond Slavery. Explorations of Race, Labor, and Citizenship in Postemancipation Societies*, Chapel Hill 2000, 107–88.

Coquery-Vidrovitch, C. and P. Lovejoy (eds.), *The Workers of African Trade*, Beverly Hills 1985.

Coupland, R., *East Africa and its Invaders. From the Earliest Times to the Death of Seyyid Said in 1856*, Oxford 1938.

Coupland, R., *The Exploitation of East Africa, 1856–1890. The Slave Trade and the Scramble*, London 1939.

Dauber, H. (ed.), *'Nicht als Abentheurer bin ich hierhergekommen...' 100 Jahre Entwicklungs-'Hilfe'. Tagebücher und Briefe aus Deutsch-Ostafrika 1896–1902*, Frankfurt/Main 1991.

Deutsch, J.-G., 'Slavery, Coastal Identity and the End of Slavery in German and British East Africa' in J. Heidrich (ed.), *Changing Identities. The Transformation of Asian and African Societies under Colonialism*, Berlin 1994, 215–24.

Deutsch, J.-G., 'Inventing an East African Empire. The Zanzibar Delimitation Commission of 1885/1886', in P. Heine and U. van der Heyden (eds.), *Studien zur Geschichte des deutschen Kolonialismus in Afrika*, Pfaffenweiler 1995, 210–19.

Deutsch, J.-G., 'Weidner's Slaves. A Misunderstanding in German Colonial Thought', *Working Papers*, Institute of Development Studies, University of Helsinki, Helsinki 1996.

Deutsch, J.-G., 'Das Problem der Sklaverei in Afrika', in J.-G. Deutsch and A. Wirz (eds.), *Geschichte in Afrika. Einführung in Probleme und Debatten*, Berlin 1997, 53–74.

Deutsch, J.-G., '"Freeing" Slaves in German East Africa. The Statistical Record, 1890–1914', in S. Miers and M. Klein (eds.), *Slavery in Colonial Africa*, London 1999, 109–32.

Deutsch, J.-G., 'Celebrating Power in Everyday Life. The Administration of Law in Colonial Tanzania, 1890–1914', *Journal of African Cultural Studies*, 15 (2002) 1, 93–104.

Deutsch, J. G., 'Absence of Evidence is no Proof? Slave Resistance under German Colonial Rule in East Africa', in K. van Walraven (ed.), *Rethinking Resistance. Revolt and Violence in African History*, Leiden 2003, 170–87.

Drescher, S. and S. L. Engerman (eds.), *A Historical Guide to World Slavery*, New York 1998.

Eastman, C. M., 'Who are the Waswahili?', *Africa*, 41 (1971) 3, 228–36.

Eastman, C. M., 'Women, Slaves and Foreigners: African Cultural Influences and Group Processes in the Formation of Northern Swahili Coastal Society', *International Journal of African Historical Studies*, 21 (1988) 1, 1–20.

Eckert, A., 'Slavery in Colonial Cameroon, 1880s to 1930s', in S. Miers and M. Klein (eds.), *Slavery in Colonial Africa*, London 1998, 133–48.

Engerman, S., 'Comparative Approaches to the Ending of Slavery', *Slavery and Abolition*, 21 (2000) 2, 281–300.

Bibliography

Ewald, J. J., 'East Africa', in S. Drescherand and S. L. Engerman (eds.), *A Historical Guide to World Slavery*, New York 1998, 41–6.

Fabian, J., *History from Below. The 'Vocabulary of Elisabethville' by André Yav*, Amsterdam/Philadelphia 1990.

Fair, L., 'Dressing Up. Clothing, Class and Gender in Post-Abolition Zanzibar', *Journal of African History*, 39 (1998) 1, 63–94.

Fair, L., *Pastimes and Politics. Culture, Community, and Identity in Post-Abolition Urban Zanzibar, 1890–1945*, Oxford 2001.

Falola, T. and P. E. Lovejoy, 'Pawnship in Historical Perspective', in T. Falola and P. E. Lovejoy (eds.), *Pawnship in Africa. Debt Bondage in Historical Perspective*, Boulder 1994, 1–26.

Feierman, S., *The Shambaa Kingdom. A History*, Madison 1974.

Feierman, S., *Peasant Intellectuals. Anthropology and History in Tanzania*, Madison 1990.

Feierman, S., 'A Century of Ironies in East Africa (*c*. 1780–1890)', in P. Curtin, S. Feierman, S. Thompson and J. Vansina (eds.), *African History. From Earliest Times to Independence*, second edn, London 1995, 352–76.

Ferrant, L., *Tippu Tip and the East African Slave Trade*, London 1975.

Finkelman, P. and J. C. Miller (eds.), *Macmillan Encyclopedia of World Slavery*, 2 vols, New York 1998.

Finley, M. I., 'Slavery', *International Encyclopedia of the Social Sciences*, ed. by D. Sills, New York 1968, 307–13.

Finley, M. I., *Ancient Slavery and Modern Ideology*, rev. and exp. edition, Princeton, NJ 1998.

Fisher, A. G. B. and H. J. Fisher, *Slavery and Muslim Society in Africa. The Institution in Saharan and Sudanic Africa and the Trans-Saharan Trade*, London 1970.

Fisher, H. J., *Slavery in the History of Muslim Black Africa*, London 2001.

Förster, S., W. J. Mommsen and R. Robinson (eds.), *Bismarck, Europe and Africa. The Berlin Africa Conference 1884–85 and the Onset of Partition*, London 1988.

Forte, D. F., 'Law: Islamic Law', in P. Finkelman and J. C. Miller (eds.), *Macmillan Encyclopedia of World Slavery*, vol. 1, New York 1998, 494–7.

Fosbrooke, K., 'The Defensive Measure of Certain Tribes in North-Eastern Tanganyika, Part 2', *Tanganyika Notes and Records* (1954) 36, 50–7.

Fröhlich, M., *Von Konfrontation zur Koexistenz. Die deutsch-englischen Kolonialbeziehungen zwischen 1884 und 1914*, Bochum 1990.

Gann, L. H., 'German Governors. An Overview', in L. H. Gann and P. Duignan (eds.), *African Proconsuls. European Governors in Africa*, New York 1978, 467–72.

Gann, L. H., 'Marginal Colonialism. The German Case', in A. J. Knoll and L. H. Gann (eds.), *Germans in the Tropics. Essays in German Colonial History*, New York 1987, 1–17.

Gann, L. H., 'The Berlin Conference and the Humanitarian Conscience', in S. Förster, W. J. Mommsen and R. Robinson (eds.), *Bismarck, Europe and Africa. The Berlin Africa Conference 1884–85 and the Onset of Partition*, London 1988, 321–31.

Gann, L. H. and P. Duignan (eds.), *Colonialism in Africa 1870–1960*, 5 vols, Cambridge 1969–75.

Gann, L. H. and P. Duignan (eds.), *The Rulers of German Africa, 1884–1914*, Stanford 1977.

Getz, T. R., *Slavery and Reform in West Africa*, Oxford 2004.

Giblin, J. L., 'Famine and Social Change during the Transition to Colonial Rule in Northeastern Tanzania, 1880–1896', *African Economic History* (1986) 15, 85–105.

Giblin, J. L., *The Politics of Environmental Control in North-Eastern Tanzania, 1840–1940*, Philadelphia 1992.

Giblin, J. L., 'Pawning, Politics and Matriliny in Northeastern Tanzania', in T. Falola and P. E. Lovejoy (eds.), *Pawnship in Africa. Debt Bondage in Historical Perspective*, Boulder 1994, 43–53.

Gifford, P. and W. M. Louis (eds.), *Britain and Germany in Africa. Imperial Rivalry and Colonial Rule*, New Haven 1967.

Gilbert, E., *Dhows and the Colonial Economy of Zanzibar, 1860–1970*, Oxford 2004.

Giles, L. L., 'Possession Cults on the Swahili Coast. A Re-Examination of Theories of Marginality', *Africa*, 57 (1987) 2, 234–57.

Giles, L., 'Spirit Possession and the Symbolic Construction of Swahili Society', in H. Behrend and U. Luig (eds.), *Spirit Possession, Modernity, and Power*, London 1999, 142–64.

Glassman, J., 'The Bondsman's New Clothes. The Contradictory Consciousness of Slave Resistance on the Swahili Coast', *Journal of African History*, 32 (1991) 2, 277–312.

Bibliography

Glassman, J., *Feasts and Riot. Revelry, Rebellion, and Popular Consciousness on the Swahili Coast, 1856–1888*, London 1995.

Glassman, J., 'Slower than a Massacre: The Multiple Sources of Racial Thought in Colonial Africa', *American Historical Review*, 109 (2004) 3, 720–55.

Godelier, M., T. R. Trautmann and F. E. Tjon Sie Fat, 'Introduction', in M. Godelier, T. R. Trautman and F. E. Tjon Sie Fat (eds.), *Transformations of Kinship*, Washington 1998, 1–18.

Gondorf, B., *Das Deutsche Anti-Sklaverei-Kommitee in Koblenz. Eine Episode in der deutschen Kolonialgeschichte*, Veröffentlichungen des Landesmuseums Koblenz, Sammlung Technische Kulturdenkmäler Nr. 39, Koblenz 1991.

Goody, J., 'Slavery in Time and Space', in J. L. Watson (ed.), *Asian and African Systems of Slavery*, Oxford/London 1980, 16–42.

Gottberg, A., *Unyamwesi. Quellensammlung und Geschichte*, Berlin 1971.

Grace, J., *Domestic Slavery in West Africa, with Particular Reference to the Sierra Leone Protectorate, 1896–1927*, London 1975.

Gründer, H., '"Gott will es". Eine Kreuzzugsbewegung am Ende des 19. Jahrhunderts', *Geschichte in Wissenschaft und Unterricht*, 28 (1977), 210–24.

Gründer, H., *Christliche Mission und deutsche Imperialismus. Eine politische Geschichte ihrer Beziehungen während der deutschen Kolonialzeit (1884–1914) unter besonderer Berücksichtigung Afrikas und Chinas*, Paderborn 1982.

Gründer, H., *Geschichte der deutschen Kolonien*, 3rd edn, Paderborn 1995.

Guyer, J. I., 'Household and Community in African Studies', *African Studies Review*, 24 (1981) 2/3, 87–137.

Haenger, P., *Sklaverei und Sklavenemanzipation an der Goldküste*, Basel 1997.

Hahner-Herzog, I., *Tippu Tip und der Elfenbeinhandel in Ost- und Zentralafrika im 19. Jahrhundert*, Munich 1990.

Harding, L., 'Die deutsche Diskussion um die Abschaffung der Sklaverei in Kamerun', in P. Heine and U. van der Heyden (eds.), *Studien zur Geschichte des deutschen Kolonialismus in Afrika*, Pfaffenweiler 1995, 280–308.

Hartwig, G. W., 'Changing Forms of Servitude among the Kerebe of Tanzania', in S. Miers and I. Kopytoff (eds.), *Slavery in Africa. Historical and Anthropological Perspectives*, Madison, WI 1977, 261–85.

Herlehy, T. and F. Morton, 'A Coastal Ex-slave Community in the Regional and Colonial Economy of Kenya: The WaMisheni of Rabai, 1880–1963', in S. Miers and R. Roberts (eds.), *The End of Slavery in Africa*, Madison 1988, 254–81.

Hogendorn, J. S., 'Abolition and Anti-Slavery: Africa', in S. Drescher and S. L. Engerman (eds.), *A Historical Guide to World Slavery*, New York 1998, 1–5.

Holmes, C. F., 'Zanzibari Influence at the Southern End of Lake Victoria. The Lake Route', *International Journal of African Historical Studies*, 4 (1971) 3, 477–503.

Hopkins, A. G., *An Economic History of West Africa*, London 1973.

Hubatsch, W. et al., 'Die Schutzgebiete des Deutschen Reiches, 1884–1920. Das Schutzgebiet Deutsch-Ostafrika', in W. Hubatsch (ed.), *Grundriß zur deutschen Verwaltungsgeschichte, 1885–1945*, vol. 22, Marburg 1984, 364–423.

Iliffe, J., *Tanganyika under German Rule 1905–1912*, Cambridge 1969a.

Iliffe, J., 'The Age of Improvement and Differentiation (1907–45)', in I. N. Kimambo and A. J. Temu (eds.), *A History of Tanzania*, Nairobi 1969b, 123–160.

Iliffe, J., *Agricultural Change in Modern Tanganyika. An Outline History*, Nairobi 1971.

Iliffe, J. (ed.), *Modern Tanzanians. A Volume of Biographies*, Nairobi 1973.

Iliffe, J., *A Modern History of Tanganyika*, Cambridge 1979.

Iliffe, J., *Africans. The History of a Continent*, Cambridge 1995.

Iliffe, J., *Honour in African History*, Cambridge 2005.

International Council on Archives, *Quellen zur Geschichte Afrikas südlich der Sahara in den Archiven der Bundesrepublik Deutschland*, Zug 1970.

Isaacman, A. F. and R. Roberts (eds.), *Cotton, Colonialism and Social History in Sub-Saharan Africa*, Portsmouth 1995.

Isaacman, A. F. and D. Peterson, 'Making the Chicaned: Military Slavery and Ethnicity in Southern Africa, 1750–1900', *International Journal of African Historical Studies*, 36 (2003) 2, 257–81.

Isaacman, A. F. and B. S. Isaacman, *The Making of Men and Ethnic Chicaned Identities in the Unstable World of South-Central Africa, 1750–1920*, Portsmouth 2004.

Jacob, E. G. (ed.), *Deutsche Kolonialpolitik in Documented, Gedanken und Gestalten aus den letzten 50 Jahren*, Leipzig 1938.

Kaniki, M. H. Y. (ed.), *Tanzania under Colonial Rule*, London 1980.

Kjekshus, H., *Ecology Control and Economic Development in East African History. The Case of Tanganyika 1850–1950*, 2nd edn, London 1996 [first published 1977].

Klein, M. (ed.), *Breaking the Chains. Slavery, Bondage, and Emancipation in Modern Africa and Asia*, Madison, WI 1993.

Klein, M., *Slavery and Colonial Rule in French West Africa*, Cambridge 1998.

Knoll, A. J. and L. H. Gann (eds.), *Germans in the Tropics. Essays in German Colonial History*, New York 1987.

Kollman, P.V., *The Evangelization of Slaves and Catholic Origins in Eastern Africa*, New York 2005.

Koponen, J., *People and Production in Late Precolonial Tanzania. History and Structures*, Jyväskylä/Helsinki 1988.

Koponen, J., *Development for Exploitation. German Colonial Policies in Mainland Tanzania, 1884–1914*, Helsinki/Hamburg 1995.

Kopytoff, I., 'The Cultural Context of African Abolition', in S. Miers and R. Roberts (eds.), *The End of Slavery in Africa*, Madison 1988, 485–503.

Kopytoff, I., 'Perspectives on Slavery: Definitions', in P. Finkelman and J. C. Miller (eds.), *Macmillan Encyclopedia of World Slavery*, vol. 2, New York 1998, 676–83.

Kopytoff, I. and S. Miers, 'Introduction. African "Slavery" as an Institution of Marginality', in S. Miers and I. Kopytoff (eds.), *Slavery in Africa. Historical and Anthropological Perspectives*, Madison 1977, 3–81.

Kusimba, C. M., 'Archaeology of Slavery in East Africa', *African Archaeological Review*, 21 (June 2004) 2, 59–88.

Kwamena-Poh, M. *et al.*, *African History in Maps*, fifth edn. Harlow 1992.

Lackner, H., *Koloniale Finanzpolitik im Reichstag (von 1880 bis 1919)*, Berlin 1939.

Lamden, S. C., 'Some Aspects of Porterage in East Africa', *Tanganyika Notes and Records*, 61 (1963), 155–64.

Lienhardt, P. (ed.), *The Medicine Man (Swifa ya Nguvumali)*, Oxford 1968.

Lloyd, P. C., 'Part One. Introduction', in P. C. Lloyd (ed.), *The New Elites of Tropical Africa*, Oxford 1966, 1–65.

Lodhi, A., *The Institution of Slavery in Zanzibar and Pemba*, Uppsala 1973.

Lonsdale, J. M., 'States and Social Processes in Africa. A Historiographical Survey', *African Studies Review*, 24 (1981) 2/3, 139–225.

Lonsdale, J. M., 'The European Scramble and Conquest in African History', in R. Oliver and G. N. Sanderson (eds.), *Cambridge History of Africa*, vol. 6, Cambridge 1985, 680–766.

Lonsdale, J. M., 'The Conquest State of Kenya, 1895–1905', in B. Berman and J. M. Lonsdale, *Unhappy Valley. Conflict in Kenya and Africa*, vol. 1, London 1992, 13–44.

Lovejoy, P. E. (ed.), *The Ideology of Slavery in Africa*, Beverly Hills/London 1981.

Lovejoy, P. E., *Transformations in Slavery. A History of Slavery in Africa*, Cambridge 1983, 2nd edn, Cambridge 2000.

Lovejoy, P. E. and J. S. Hogendorn, *Slow Death for Slavery. The Course of Abolition in Northern Nigeria, 1897–1936*, Cambridge 1993.

Lovejoy, P. E. and T. Falola (eds.), *Pawnship, Slavery, and Colonialism in Africa*, Trenton/NJ 2003.

Lüdtke, A., 'Einleitung. Herrschaft als soziale Praxis', in A. Lüdtke (ed.), *Herrschaft als soziale Praxis*, Göttingen 1991, 9–63.

Machado, P. 'A Forgotten Corner of the Indian Ocean: Gujerati Merchants, Portuguese India and the Mozambique Slave Trade, *c.* 1730–1830', in G. Campbell (ed.), *The Structure of Slavery in Indian Ocean Africa and Asia*, London 2004, 17–32.

Maier, D. J. E., 'Slave Labor and Wage Labor in German Togo, 1885–1914', in A. Knoll and L. H. Gann (eds.), *Germans in the Tropics. Essays in German Colonial History*, New York 1987, 73–92.

Mamdani, M., *Citizen and Subject. Decentralized Despotism and the Legacy of Late Colonialism*, Delhi 1997.

Mann, E., *Mikono ya Damu: Hands of Blood. African Mercenaries and the Politics of Conflict in German East Africa, 1888–1904*, Frankfurt/Main 2002.

Mann, K. and R. Roberts (eds.), *Law in Colonial Africa*, London 1991.

Manning, P., *Slavery and African Life. Occidental, Oriental and African Slave Trades*, Cambridge 1990.

Bibliography

Martin, E. B. and T. C. I. Ryan, 'A Quantitative Assessment of the Arab Slave Trade of East Africa, 1770–1896', *Kenya Historical Review*, 5 (1977) 1, 71–91.

Matson, A. T., 'Sewa Hadji. A Note', *Tanzania Notes and Records*, 65 (1966), 91–4.

Maw, J. and D. Parkin, 'Introduction', in J. Maw and D. Parkin (eds.), *Swahili Language and Society*, Vienna 1985, 1–13.

Mazrui, A. M. and I. N. Shariff, *The Swahili. Idiom and Identity of an African People*, Trenton 1994.

McDougall, E. A., 'Islam', in P. Finkelman and J. C. Miller (eds.), *Macmillan Encyclopedia of World Slavery*, vol. 1, New York 1998, 434–9.

Meillassoux, C., *The Anthropology of Slavery. The Womb of Iron and Gold*, Chicago/London 1991 (originally published in French as *Anthropologie de l'esclavage. Le ventre de ver et d'argent*, Paris 1986).

Meillassoux, C., 'Female Slavery', in C. C. Robertson and M. A. Klein (eds.), *Women and Slavery in Africa*, Portsmouth 1997 [first published 1983], 49–66.

Middleton, J., *The World of the Swahili. An African Mercantile Civilization*, New Haven 1992.

Miers, S., 'The Brussels Conference of 1889–1890. The Place of the Slave Trade in the Policies of Great Britain and Germany', in P. Gifford and W. M. Louis (eds.), *Britain and Germany in Africa. Imperial Rivalry and Colonial Rule*, New Haven, CT 1967, 83–118.

Miers, S., *Britain and the Ending of the Slave Trade*, London 1975.

Miers, S., 'Humanitarianism at Berlin: Myth or Reality', in S. Förster, W. J. Mommsen and R. Robinson (eds.), *Bismarck, Europe and Africa. The Berlin Africa Conference 1884–85 and the Onset of Partition*, London 1988, 333–45.

Miers, S., 'Slavery and the Slave Trade as International Issues, 1890–1939', in S. Miers and M. A. Klein (eds.), *Slavery and Colonial Rule in Africa*, London 1999, 16–37.

Miers, S., 'Slavery to Freedom in Sub-Saharan Africa. Expectations and Reality', in H. Temperley (ed.), *Emancipation and its Discontents*, London 2000, 237–64.

Miers, S., *Slavery in the Twentieth Century. The Evolution of a Global Problem*, Oxford 2003.

Miers, S., 'Slavery: A Question of Definition', in G. Campbell (ed.), *The Structure of Slavery in Indian Ocean Africa and Asia*, London 2004, 1–16.

Miers S., and I. Kopytoff (eds.), *Slavery in Africa. Historical and Anthropological Perspectives*, Madison 1977.

Miers, S. and R. Roberts (eds.), *The End of Slavery in Africa*, Madison 1988.

Miers, S. and M. A. Klein (eds.), *Slavery and Colonial Rule in Africa*, London 1999.

Miers, S. and M. A. Klein, 'Introduction', in S. Miers and M. A. Klein (eds.), *Slavery and Colonial Rule in Africa*, London 1999, 1–15.

Miller, J. C., 'Muslim Slavery and Slaving. A Bibliography', in E. Savage (ed.), *The Human Commodity. Perspectives on the Trans-Saharan Slave Trade*, London 1992, 249–71.

Miller, J. C., *Slavery. A Worldwide Bibliography, 1900–1991*, New York 1993.

Miller, J. C., *Slavery and Slaving in World History: A Bibliography*, 2 vols, Armonk 1999.

Miller, J. C., 'Breaking the Historiographical Chains: Martin Klein and Slavery', *Canadian Journal of African Studies*, 34 (2000) 3, 512–31.

Mirza, S. and M. Strobel (eds.), *Three Swahili Women. Life Histories from Mombasa, Kenya*, Bloomington 1989.

Mitchell, T., *Colonising Egypt*, Cambridge 1988, 34–62.

Mommsen, W. J., 'Die Verfassung des Deutschen Reiches von 1871 als dilatorischer Herrschaftskompromiß', in W. J. Mommsen, *Der autoritäre Nationalstaat. Verfassung, Gesellschaft und Kultur des deutschen Kaiserreiches*, Frankfurt/Main 1990 [first published 1983], 39–65.

Morton, F., 'New Evidence Regarding the Shungwaya Myth of Miji Kenda Origins', *International Journal of African Historical Studies*, 10 (1977) 4, 628–43.

Morton, F., *Children of Ham. Freed Slaves and Fugitive Slaves on the Kenya Coast, 1873–1907*, Boulder, CO 1990.

Morton, F., 'Pawnship and Slavery on the Kenya Coast. The Miji Kenda Case', in T. Falola and P. E. Lovejoy (eds.), *Pawnship in Africa. Debt Bondage in Historical Perspective*, Boulder, CO 1994, 27–42.

Morton, F., 'East Africa: Swahili Region', in P. Finkelman and J. C. Miller (eds.), *Macmillan Encyclopedia of World Slavery*, vol. 1, New York 1998, 265–6.

Müller, F. F., *Deutschland-Zanzibar-Ostafrika. Geschichte einer deutschen Kolonialeroberung, 1884–1890*, Berlin 1959.

Napachihi, S. W., *The Relationship between the German Missionaries of the Congregation of St Benedict from St Ottilien and the German Colonial Authorities in Tanzania, 1887–1907*, Ndanda 1998.

Nassor, M. H., *Guide to the Microfilms of Regional and District Books*, Dar es Salaam 1973.

National Archives of Tanzania, *Das Deutsch-Ostafrika-Archiv/Guide to the German Records* (ed. by E. G. Franz und P. Geissler), 2 vols, Dar es Salaam/Marburg 1973.

Naucke, W., 'Deutsches Kolonialstrafrecht 1886–1918', *Rechtshistorisches Journal*, 7 (1988), 297–315.

Niboer, H. J., *Slavery as an Industrial System. Ethnological Researches*, The Hague 1900, [rev. edn. The Hague 1910].

Nicholls, C. S., *The Swahili Coast. Politics, Diplomacy and Trade on the East African Littoral, 1798–1856*, London 1971.

Nimtz, A. H., 'Islam in Tanzania: An Annotated Bibliography', *Tanzania Notes and Records* (1973) 72, 51–74.

Nimtz, A. H., *Islam and Politics in East Africa. The Sufi Order in Tanzania*, Minneapolis 1980.

Nipperdey, T., *Deutsche Geschichte 1866–1918*, 2 vols, vol. 1: *Arbeitswelt und Bürgergeist*, vol. 2: *Machtstaat vor der Demokratie*, Munich 1990–2.

Northrup, D., 'The Ending of Slavery in Eastern Belgian Congo', in S. Miers and R. Roberts (eds.), *The End of Slavery in Africa*, Madison 1988a, 462–82.

Northrup, D., *Beyond the Bend in the River: African Labor in Eastern Zaire, 1865–1940*, Athens, OH 1988b.

Nurse, D. and T. Spear, *The Swahili: Reconstructing the History and Language of an African Society, 800–1500*, Philadelphia, PA 1985.

Nwulia, M. D. E., *The History of Slavery in Mauritius and the Seychelles, 1810–1875*, London 1981.

Ohly, R., 'Mshenzi. The Barbarian (A Study in Sociolinguistics)', *Kiswahili*, 45 (1975) 2, 29–35.

Ohly, R., 'Ustaarabu', *Kiswahili*, 1976, 77–9.

Oliver, R., *The Missionary Factor in East Africa*, London 1965 .

Palmié, S. (ed.), *Slave Cultures and the Cultures of Slavery*, Knoxville 1995.

Page, M. E., 'The Manyema Hordes of Tippu Tip. A Case Study in Social Stratification and the Slave Trade in Eastern Africa', *International Journal of African Historical Studies*, 7 (1974a) 1, 69–84.

Page, M. E., 'Tippu Tip and the Arab "Defence" of the East African Slave Trade', *Etudes d'histoire africaine*, 6 (1974b), 105–17.

Parkin, D., *Town and Country in East and Central Africa*, Oxford 1975.

Parkin, D., 'Being and Selfhood among Intermediary Swahili', in J. Maw and D. Parkin (eds.), *Swahili Language and Society*, Wien 1985, 247–60.

Parkin, D., 'Swahili Mijikenda. Facing Both Ways in Kenya', *Africa*, 59 (1989) 2, 161–75.

Patterson, O., *Slavery and Social Death. A Comparative Study*, Cambridge, MA 1982.

Pels, P., 'The Construction of Ethnographic Occasions in Late Colonial Uluguru', *History and Anthropology*, 8 (1994), 321–51.

Perham, M. (ed.), *Ten African*, London 1936.

Pierard, R. V., 'The German Colonial Society', in A. J. Knoll and L. H. Gann (eds.), *Germans in the Tropics. Essays in German Colonial History*, New York 1987, 19–34.

Pogge von Strandmann, H. and A. Smith, 'The German Empire in Africa and British Perspectives. A Historiographical Essay', in P. Gifford and W. M. Louis (eds.), *Britain and Germany in Africa. Imperial Rivalry and Colonial Rule*, New Haven, CT 1967, 709–96.

Pouwels, R. L., 'Oral Historiography and the Problem of the Shirazi on the East African Coast', *History in Africa*, 11 (1984), 237–67.

Pouwels, R. L., *Horn and Crescent. Cultural Change and Traditional Islam on the East African Coast, 800–1900*, Cambridge 1987.

Presley, C., *Kikuyu Women, the Mau Mau Rebellion and Social Change in Kenya*, Boulder, CO 1992.

Prins, A. H. J., *The Swahili-speaking Peoples of Zanzibar and the East African Coast: (Arabs, Shirazi and Swahili)*, London 1961.

Prins, A. H. J., 'Introduction to the Second Edition', in A. H. J. Prins, *The Swahili-speaking Peoples of Zanzibar and the East African Coast: (Arabs, Shirazi and Swahili)*, London 1967, ix–xvi.

Ranger, T. O., 'The Recovery of African Initiative in Tanzanian History', *Inaugural Lecture Series No. 2*, The University College, Dar es Salaam 1969.

Ranger, T. O., *Dance and Society in Eastern Africa 1890–1970. The Beni Ngoma*, London 1975.

Raum, O. F., 'German East Africa – Changes in African Tribal Life under German Administration, 1892–1914', in V. Harlow and E. M. Chilver (eds.), *History of East Africa*, vol. 2, Oxford 1965, 163–207.

Bibliography

Redmayne, A., 'Research on Customary Law in German East Africa', *Journal of African Law*, 27 (1983), 22–41

Reid, R., 'Mutesa and Mirambo: Thoughts on East African Warfare and Diplomacy in the Nineteenth Century', *International Journal of African Historical Studies*, 31 1998) 1, 73–89.

Renault, F., *Lavigerie, l'Esclavage Africain, et l'Europe, 1868–1892*, 2 vols, Paris 1971.

Renault, F., *Tippo-Tip. Un Potentat Arabe en Afrique Centrale au XIXème siècle*, Paris 1987.

Renault, F., 'The Structures of the Slave Trade in Central Africa in the 19th Century', in W. G. Clarence-Smith (ed.), *The Economics of the Indian Ocean Slave Trade in the Nineteenth Century*, London 1989, 146–65.

Reusch, R., *Der Islam in Ostafrika mit besonderer Berücksichtigung der muhammedanischen Geheim-Orden*, Leipzig n.d. [1930].

Reusch, R., 'How the Swahili People and Language came into Existence', *Tanganyika Notes and Records* (1953) 34, 20–7.

Roberts, A. D., 'The Nyamwezi', in A. D. Roberts (ed.), *Tanzania before 1900*, Nairobi 1968, 117–50.

Roberts, A. D., 'Nyamwezi Trade', in R. Gray and D. Birmingham (eds.), *Pre-Colonial African Trade in Central and Eastern Africa before 1900*, London 1970, 39–74.

Roberts, A. D., 'Firearms in North-Eastern Zambia before 1900', *Transafrican Journal of History*, 1 (1971) 2, 3–21.

Roberts, A. D., 'A Bibliography of Primary Sources for Tanzania, 1799–1899', *Tanzania Notes and Records* (1974) 73, 65–92.

Roberts, R., *Warriors, Merchants and Slaves. The State and the Economy in the Middle Niger Valley, 1700–1914*, Stanford, CA 1987.

Roberts, R., 'Africa: The End of Slavery', in P. Finkelman and J. C. Miller (eds.), *Macmillan Encyclopedia of World Slavery*, vol. 1, New York 1998, 40–2.

Roberts, R. and M. Klein, 'The Banamba Slave Exodus of 1905 and the Decline of Slavery in the Western Sudan', *Journal of African History*, 21 (1980) 3, 375–94.

Roberts, R. and K. Mann, 'Law in Colonial Africa', in K. Mann and R. Roberts, *Law in Colonial Africa*, London 1991, 3–58.

Roberts, R. and S. Miers, 'Introduction. The End of Slavery in Africa', in S. Miers and R. Roberts (eds.), *The End of Slavery in Africa*, Madison 1988, 3–70.

Robertson, C. C. and M. A. Klein (eds.), *Women and Slavery in Africa*, Portsmouth 1997 [first published 1983].

Robertson, C. C. and M. A. Klein, 'Women's Importance in African Slave Systems', in Robertson, C. C. and M. A. Klein (eds.), *Women and Slavery in Africa*, Portsmouth 1997 [first published 1983], 3–25.

Rockel, S. J., 'Relocating Labor. Sources from the Nineteenth Century', *History in Africa*, 22 (1995a), 447–54.

Rockel, S. J., 'Wage Labor and the Culture of Porterage in Nineteenth Century Tanzania. The Central Caravan Route', *Comparative Studies of South Asia, Africa and the Middle East*, 15 (1995b), 14–24.

Rockel, S. J., 'The Roots of a Nation. Integration in Nineteenth-Century Tanzania', *History and African Studies Series*, University of Natal, Pietermaritzburg 30 September 1998, 1–18.

Rockel, S. J., '"A Nation of Porters". The Nyamwezi and the Labour Market in Mid-Nineteenth Century Tanzania', *Journal of African History*, 41 (2000a) 2, 173–95.

Rockel, S. J., 'Enterprising Partners: Caravan Women in Nineteenth Century Tanzania', in *Canadian Journal of African Studies*, 34 (2000a) 3, 748–78.

Romero Curtin, P. W., 'Laboratory for the Oral History of Slavery: The Island of Lamu on the Kenya Coast', *American Historical Review*, 88 (1983) 4, 858–82.

Romero, P. W., 'Where Have All the Slaves Gone? Emancipation and Post-Emancipation in Lamu, Kenya', *Journal of African History*, 27 (1986) 3, 497–512.

Romero, P. W., 'Mama Khadija. A Life History as Example of Family History', in P. W. Romero (ed.), *Life Histories of African Women*, London 1988, 140–58.

Romero, P. W., *Lamu. History, Society, and Family in an East African Port City*, Princeton 1997.

Sakarai, L. J., 'Indian Merchants in East Africa. Part 1, The Triangular Trade and the Slave Economy', *Slavery and Abolition*, 1 (1980) 3, 292–338.

Sakarai, L. J., 'Indian Merchants in East Africa. Part 2, Transformation of the Slave Economy', *Slavery and Abolition*, 2 (1981) 1, 2–30.

Salim, A. I., *The Swahili Speaking Peoples of Kenya's Coast, 1895–1965*, Nairobi 1973.

Salim, A. I., 'The Elusive "Mswahili" – Some Reflections on his Identity and Culture', in J. Maw and D. Parkin (eds.), *Swahili Language and Society*, Vienna 1985, 215–28.

Schacht, J., 'Notes on Islam in East Africa', *Studia Islamica*, 23 (1964), 91–136.

Schacht, J., *An Introduction to Islamic Law*, Oxford 1964.

Schröder, H.-C., *Sozialismus und Imperialismus*, Hannover 1968.

Schröder, M., *Prügelstrafe und Züchtigungsrecht in den deutschen Schutzgebieten Schwarzafrikas*, Münster 1997.

Schwarz, M., *MDR. Biographisches Handbuch der deutschen Reichstage*, Hannover 1965.

Schwarz, M. T., *Je weniger Afrika, desto besser' – die deutsche Kolonialkritik am Ende des 19. Jahrhunderts. Eine Untersuchung zur kolonialen Haltung von Linksliberalismus und Sozialdemokratie*, Frankfurt/Main 1999.

Sebald, P., *Malam Musa – Gottlob Adolf Krause, 1850–1938. Forscher – Wissenschaftler – Humanist. Leben und Lebenswerk eines antikolonial gesinnten Afrika-Wissenschaftlers unter den Bedingungen des Kolonialismus*, Berlin 1972.

Sender, J. and S. Smith, *The Development of Capitalism in Africa*, London 1986.

Sheriff, A. H. M., 'Tanzanian Societies at the Time of Partition', in M. H. Y. Kaniki (ed.), *Tanzania under Colonial Rule*, London 1980, 11–50.

Sheriff, A. H. M., 'The Slave Mode of Production along the East African Coast, 1810–1873', in J. R. Willis (ed.), *Slaves and Slavery in Muslim Africa*, vol. 2, London 1985, 161–81.

Sheriff, A. M. H., *Slaves, Spices and Ivory in Zanzibar. Integration of an East African Commercial Empire into the World Economy, 1770–1873*, London 1987.

Sheriff, A. M. H., 'Localisation and Social Composition of the East African Slave Trade, 1858–1873', in W. G. Clarence-Smith (ed.), *The Economics of the Indian Ocean Slave Trade in the Nineteenth Century*, London 1989, 131–45.

Shorter, A., 'Nyungu ya Mawe and the Empire of the Ruga-Ruga', *Journal of African History*, 9 (1968) 12, 235–59.

Sicard, S. von, *The Lutheran Church on the Coast of Tanzania, 1887–1914*, Lund 1970.

Sikainga, A. A., 'Shari'a Courts and the Manumission of Female Slaves in the Sudan, 1898–1939', *International Journal of African Historical Studies*, 28 (1995) 1, 1–24.

Sikainga, A. A., *Slaves into Workers. Emancipation and Labour in Colonial Sudan*, Austin 1996.

Sippel, H., 'Recht und Herrschaft in kolonialer Frühzeit. Die Rechtsverhältnisse in den Schutzgebieten der Deutsch-Ostafrikanischen Gesellschaft (1885–1890)' in P. Heine and U. van der Heyden (eds.), *Studien zur Geschichte des deutschen Kolonialismus in Afrika*, Pfaffenweiler 1995, 466–94.

Sippel, H., 'Aspects of Colonial Land Law in German East Africa: German East Africa Company, Crown Land Ordinance, European Plantations and Reserved Areas for Africans', in R. Debusmann and S. Arnold (eds.), *Land Law and Land Ownership in Africa. Case Studies from Colonial and Modern Cameroon and Tanzania*, Bayreuth 1996a, 3–38.

Sippel, H., '"Wie erzieht man am besten den Neger zur Plantagen-Arbeit?" Die Ideologie der Arbeitserziehung und ihre rechtliche Umsetzung in der Kolonie Deutsch-Ostafrika', in K. Beck and G. Spittler (eds.), *Arbeit in Afrika*, Hamburg 1996b, 311–33.

Sippel, H., 'Der Deutsche Reichstag und das "Eingeborenenrecht". Die Erforschung der Rechtsverhältnisse der autochthonen Völker in den deutschen Kolonien', *Rabels Zeitschrift für ausländisches und internationales Privatrecht*, 61 (1997), 714–38.

Sippel, H., 'Quellen des deutschen Kolonialrechts', in A. Eckert and G. Krüger (eds.), *Lesarten eines globalen Prozesses. Quellen und Interpretationen zur Geschichte der europäischen Expansion*, Hamburg, 1998, 213–29.

Sippel, H., 'Koloniale Begegnung im rechtsfreien Raum? Die Jurisdiktion der "Eingeborenenrichter" in den afrikanischen Kolonien des Deutschen Reiches', in: M. Bechhaust-Gerst and R. Klein-Arendt (eds.), *Die (koloniale) Begegnung. AfrikanerInnen in Deutschland 1880–1945, Deutsche in Afrika 1880–1918*, Frankfurt/Main 2003, 297–311.

Smith, A., 'The Southern Section of the Interior, 1840–84', in R. Oliver and G. Mathew (eds.), *History of East Africa*, vol. 1, Oxford 1963, 253–96.

Soénius, U. S., *Koloniale Begeisterung im Rheinland während der Kolonialzeit*, Cologne 1992.

Spear, T., 'The Shirazi in Swahili Traditions, Culture, and History', *History in Africa*, 11 (1984), 291–305.

Spear, T., 'Swahili History and Society to 1900: A Classified Bibliography', *History in Africa*, 27 (2000), 339–73.

Spear, T., 'Early Swahili History Reconsidered', *International Journal of African Historical Studies*,

33 (2000), 257–90.

Stichter, S., *Migrant Laborers*, Cambridge 1985.

Stoecker, H., 'The Position of Africans in the German Colonies', in A. J. Knoll and L. H. Gann (eds.), *Germans in the Tropics. Essays in German Colonial History*, New York 1987, 119–29.

Strobel, M., *Muslim Women in Mombasa, 1890–1975*, New Haven, CT 1979.

Strobel, M., 'Slavery and Reproductive Labor in Mombasa', in C. C. Robertson and M. A. Klein (eds.), *Women and Slavery in Africa*, Madison 1983, 111–29.

Sunseri, T., 'Slave Ransoming in German East Africa, 1885–1922', *International Journal of African Historical Studies*, 26 (1993b) 3, 481–511.

Sunseri, T., 'Dispersing the Fields. Railway Labour and Rural Change in Early Colonial Tanzania', *Canadian Journal of African Studies*, 32 (1998) 3, 558–83.

Sunseri, T., *Vilimani. Labour Migration and Rural Change in Early Colonial Tanzania*, Portsmouth 2002.

Sutton, J. E. G. and A. D. Roberts, 'Uvinza and its Salt Industry', *Azania*, 3 (1968) 45–86.

Sutton, J. E. G., 'Dar es Salaam. A Sketch of a Hundred Years', *Tanzania Notes and Records* (1970) 71, 1–213.

Tawney, J. J., 'Ugabire. A Feudal Custom amongst the Waha', *Tanganyika Notes and Records* (1944) 17, 6–11.

Temperley, H. (ed.), *Emancipation and its Discontents*, London 2000.

Temu, A. J., 'Tanzanian Societies and Colonial Invasion, 1875–1907', in M. H. Y. Kaniki (ed.), *Tanzania under Colonial Rule*, London 1980, 86–127.

Tetzlaff, R., *Koloniale Entwicklung und Ausbeutung. Wirtschafts- und Sozialgeschichte Deutsch-Ostafrikas 1885–1914*, Berlin 1970.

Tippu Tip, *Maisha ya Hamed bin Muhammed el Murjebi Yaani Tippu Tip*, ed. and trans. by W. H. Whiteley, Nairobi 1966 [first published 1902].

Tolmacheva, M., 'The Origin of the Name "Swahili"', *Tanzania Notes and Records* (1976) 77/78, 27–37.

Tominaga, C., 'Indian Immigrants and the East African Slave Trade', *Seri Ethnological Studies Osaka* (1996) 43, 295–317.

Trimingham, J. S., *Islam in East Africa*, Oxford 1964.

Trotha, T. von, 'Zur Entstehung von Recht. Deutsche Kolonialherrschaft und Recht im Schutzgebiet Togo, 1884–1914', *Rechtshistorisches Journal*, 7 (1988), 317–46.

Turner, H. A., 'Bismarck's Imperial Ventures', in P. Gifford and W. R. Louis (eds.), *Britain and Germany in Africa. Imperial Rivalry and Colonial Rule*, New Haven, CT 1967, 47–82.

Twaddle, M., 'The Ending of Slavery in Buganda', in S. Miers and R. Roberts (eds.), *The End of Slavery in Africa*, Madison, WI 1988, 119–48.

Twaddle, M. (ed.), *The Wages of Slavery. From Chattel Slavery to Wage Labour in Africa, the Caribbean and England*, London 1993.

Unomah, A. C. and J. B. Webster, 'East Africa. The Expansion of Commerce', in J. E. Flint (ed), *Cambridge History of Africa*, vol. 5, Cambridge 1976, 270–318.

Van Gennep, A., *The Rites of Passage*, transl. by M. B. Vizecom and G. L. Caffee, Chicago 1960.

Versteijnen, F., *The Catholic Mission of Bagamoyo*, Bagamoyo n.d. [1968].

Washausen, H., *Hamburg und die Kolonialpolitik des Deutschen Reiches 1880–1890*, Hamburg 1968.

Weber, M., 'Class, Status, Party', in H. H. Gerth and C. W. Mills (eds.), *From Max Weber. Essays in Sociology*, London 1948 [first published 1921], 180–95.

Wehler, H. U., *Das Deutsche Kaiserreich, 1871–1918*, Göttingen 1983.

Wehler, H. U., *Deutsche Gesellschaftsgeschichte. Dritter Band. Von der deutschen 'Doppelrevolution' bis zum Beginn des Ersten Weltkrieges, 1849–1914*, München 1995.

Wilding, R., *Bibliography of the East African Coast*, Nairobi 1994.

Williams, E., *Capitalism and Slavery*, Chapel Hill 1944.

Willis, J., 'The Making of a Tribe. Bondei Identities and Histories', *Journal of African History*, 33 (1992) 2, 191–208.

Willis, J., *Mombasa, the Swahili and the Making of the Mijikenda*, Oxford 1993a.

Willis, J., 'The Administration of Bonde 1920–60. A Study of the Implementation of Indirect Rule in Tanganyika', *African Affairs*, 92 (1993b) 366, 53–67.

Willis, J., 'The Nature of a Mission Community – The Universities Mission to Central Africa in Bonde', *Past and Present* (1993c) 140, 127–54.

Willis, J., 'Plantations: Zanzibar and the Swahili Coast', in P. Finkelman and J. C. Miller (eds.), *Macmillan Encyclopedia of World Slavery*, vol. 2, New York 1998, 730–1.

Willis, J. and S. Miers, 'Becoming a Child of the House. Incorporation, Authority and Resistance in Giryama Society', *Journal of African History*, 38 (1997) 3, 479–95.

Willis, J. R. (ed.), *Slaves and Slavery in Muslim Africa*, 2 vols, London 1986.

Wirz, A., *Sklaverei und kapitalistisches Weltsystem*, Frankfurt/Main 1984.

Wirz, A., 'Die deutschen Kolonien in Afrika', in R. von Albertini (with A. Wirz), *Europäische Kolonialherrschaft 1880–1940*, Zürich 1985, 302–27.

Worden, N. and C. Crais (eds.), *Breaking the Chains. Slavery and its Legacy in the Nineteenth-Century Cape Colony*, Johannesburg 1994.

Wright, M., 'Local Roots of Policy in German East Africa', *Journal of African History*, 9 (1968) 4, 621–30.

Wright, M., *German Mission in Tanganyika. Lutherans and Moravians in the Southern Highlands, 1891–1941*, Oxford 1971b.

Wright, M., *Strategies of Slaves and Women. Life-Stories from East/Central Africa*, London, New York 1993.

Wright, M., 'Women as Slaves in Africa', in P. Finkelman and J. C. Miller (eds.), *Macmillan Encyclopedia of World Slavery*, vol. 1, New York 1998, 43–5.

Wright, M. and P. H. Lary, 'Swahili Settlements in Northern Zambia and Malawi', *International Journal of African Historical Studies*, 4 (1971a) 3, 547–73.

Wrigley, C. C., 'Historicism in Africa. Slavery and State Formation', *African Affairs*, 70 (1971) 279, 113–24.

Ylvisaker, M., *Lamu in the Nineteenth Century: Land, Trade, and Politics*, Boston, MA 1979.

Index

DATE DUE